The
Breckenridge Enneagram

A Guide to Personal
and Professional Growth

Mark Bodnarczuk

Text edited by Cliff Carle

Cover design by Martha Nichols
Text design by Martha Nichols

Published by Breckenridge Press
Boulder, Colorado

The author would like to thank the following for permission to reprint from copyrighted works: Quotation of Claudio Naranjo from CHARACTER AND NEUROSIS by Claudio Naranjo, copyright © 1994 by Claudio Naranjo, pp. 14-16. Used by permission of Gateways/IDHHB, Inc. Quotation of Abraham Maslow from TOWARD A PSYCHOLOGY OF BEING by Abraham Maslow, p. 60. Used by permission of John Wiley & Sons, Inc.

ISBN-13: 978-0-9755115-2-7

1. Personal Growth   2. Enneagram   3. Personality

Book Category: Psychology/Self-Help

First Edition—April 2009

Breckenridge Press
PO Box 7950
Boulder, Colorado 80306
Tel 1-800-303-2554 Fax 1-888-745-1886
www.breckenridgeinstitute.com

The Breckenridge Enneagram

A Guide to Personal and Professional Growth

"We read to know we're not alone."

C. S. Lewis
Shadowlands

TABLE OF CONTENTS

PREFACE

We live in the three-pound universe between our ears, but it's surprising how little most people know about themselves. How we see the world develops from our earliest years as our innate, inborn tendencies (our temperament) interact with our experiences and the environment to build underlying patterns of thinking, emotions, and other characteristics that become what is commonly called our personality.[1] The Breckenridge Enneagram™ has an interdependent focus on both innate-inborn and contextual factors. More specifically, the formation of personality is both: a) an inside-out process where the innate, inborn tendencies of our temperament predispose us to behaviors and emotional responses through which we try to influence others, and b) an outside-in process where people, organizations, social structures, and the culture we grow up in, teach us how to see ourselves, others, and the world through the See-Do-Get Process®. To use a metaphor, the innate, inborn tendencies of our temperament function like an Excel® file in our brain from which our Enneagram type emerges over time, where the rows and columns in this mental Excel file are filled-in with the empirical data of our life experiences, our interactions with people, our context, and the culture in which we are raised. While the socio-cultural context in which we are raised is necessary for the development of our Enneagram type, it is not sufficient to explain the complexities and ubiquitous nature of the nine types and the three Somatic Instincts. In other words, the origin of the nine Enneagram types and the three Somatic Instincts are not reducible to just a "personality defense system" that results from early child wounding as argued by some authors[2], nor is it a complete map of the human psyche as claimed by many traditional Enneagram teachers.

As Linda Berens points out in her article, A History of Psychological Type and Temperament, that there was an entire movement of psychologists who developed personality typologies during the 1920s based on schools of thought that were prevalent in Europe at the end of the 18th Century.[3] In addition, G.I. Gurdjieff's work during this time period was later shaped into the traditional model of the Enneagram by Oscar Ichazo in the 1950s and 1960s and Claudio Naranjo in the 1970s.[4] These parallel traditions were part of a larger intellectual context from which the modern discipline of personality type theories emerged as the six traditions listed below.[5]

Jungian models	Five-Factor models
Temperament models	Circumplex models
Primary emotions models	Traditional Enneagram models

But the tendency has been for each tradition to view their model as describing "the" human personality. My view is that the totality of the human personality is greater than the sum of all possible personality typologies. More specifically, each of the traditions listed above explores a "slice" of our personality, character, and the contents of the human heart. So personality typologies like the Breckenridge Enneagram, traditional Enneagram models, Jungian type, Keirsey's four temperaments, Berens' Interaction Styles™, the Five-Factor Model, and others are only subsets (slices) of the much broader psychic reality that constitutes the set of underlying patterns, processes, and structures of the human personality. The Breckenridge Enneagram and the Breckenridge Type Indicator™ (BTI™) instrument help us identify a "slice" of the complexity of our overall personality by identifying a "needle" of underlying patterns, processes, and structures within the "haystack" of our personal paradigm. This becomes increasingly clear when we begin the task of establishing where the knowledge, beliefs, cognitive processes, and emotions that constitute our personality "happen" in the human brain and the overall organism, because as I describe in this book, if they do not happen physically, then they do not happen at all – they're not real.

I have always been captivated by the empirical power of the Enneagram to describe and predict the underlying patterns of emotions, actions, and interactions of a person of a given Enneagram type. But at the same time I have been skeptical about the claim of most Enneagram teachers that the underlying origins, causes, and purpose of the Enneagram are metaphysical in nature. Most of my skepticism comes from my background in particle physics at Fermilab and my research on the history and philosophy of science at the University of Chicago which gave me a decidedly naturalistic-perspective on the world and the people in it.[6] But as I point out in chapter 2 on Building New Foundations, holding to a naturalistic-perspective about the causes of things in the world, does not require a person to reject the notion of God and the metaphysical, or the possibility of personally knowing God. For example, my naturalistic-perspective on the human personality lives side-by-side with a deep and abiding faith in a God who I know personally. But what holding a naturalistic-perspective does require is that when constructing a model of what causes events in our world, our relationships, our brain, and our personality, that we do not invoke metaphysical causes to explain phenomena that have a reliable naturalistic explanation. The rigorous psychometric research and statistical work that Mark Majors and I conducted in the development of the BTI instrument only reinforced my naturalistic-perspective about the human personality.

The method that I used to deconstruct the traditional view of the Enneagram comes from countless examples in the history of science. More specifically, just because the Enneagram has its roots in the metaphysical-perspectives of Gurdjieff, Ichazo, and Naranjo does not mean that it can't be viewed from a naturalistic-perspective. In fact, the literature describing the origins and history of the natural sciences shows that many of today's scientific models were originally described as having meta-physical causes, but these references to metaphysical causation were theoretical place-holders because natural philosophers lacked a quantitative, naturalistic frame-work within which to describe the actions and interactions of natural phenomena. When a naturalistic framework was finally developed, the metaphysical assumptions were "swapped-out" for a naturalistic explanation. An example of using empirical observations and replacing the underlying metaphysical theories with naturalistic ones is the modern astronomers' and cosmologists' use of the empirical observations of Babylonian astronomy. The precision with which the Babylonians plotted the positions and trajectories of the stars and planets is extremely high even by modern scientific standards, but this entire body of empirical knowledge was moti-vated by religious reasons; e.g., the ancient Babylonians viewed the stars and planets as divine.[7] The notion that they could tease apart the empirical observations from the underlying theory that describes them allowed natural philosophers such as Ptolemy, Copernicus, Galileo, and Newton to replace metaphysical (place-holder) explanations of the underlying causes, with naturalistic models and mathematical formalisms that described the actions and interactions of natural phenomena more precisely.

Much like the swapping-out of the metaphysical foundations of Babylonian astron-omy, the Breckenridge Enneagram swaps-out the underlying metaphysical theory and framework of Gurdjieff, Ichazo, Naranjo and most traditional Enneagram teachers and replaces it with a model that integrates the empirical-clinical insights of Claudio Naranjo; Maslow's Psychology and Hierarchy of Needs; the See-Do-Get Process®; and a rigorous approach to empirical research and psychometric analysis. The Breckenridge Enneagram is set apart from other approaches to the Enneagram by its focus on a naturalistic, scientific view of personality and psychological processes that are linked to modern advances in the neurosciences. So while there are many similarities between the empirical-clinical aspects of Naranjo's model and the Breckenridge Enneagram, the underlying foundations are radically different. My goal in writing this book is to provide an alternative to the metaphysical-perspective of the traditional Enneagram for the myriad people who see themselves, others, and the world from a naturalistic-perspective.

Finally, taking the naturalistic-perspective creates subtle but profound differences when trying to obtain deep, sustainable, personal change, especially in what one expects as the outcome of the personal transformation process. This book will teach you how to transcend the tacit, autopilot responses of your personality with the goal of living life more authentically. This includes building more effective relationships in your personal and professional lives, and transcending the inauthentic edicts, demands, and norms of your socio-cultural context. The Breckenridge Enneagram is not a path to personal enlightenment or personal salvation; rather it's a road to psychological health, more effective relationships, and making lasting contributions to your world and the people in it.

Mark Bodnarczuk
Boulder, Colorado
January, 2009

ACKNOWLEDGEMENTS

This book is the culmination of many years of research and working with the Enneagram both personally and professionally as part of organizational culture assessments; change initiatives; leadership development programs; and mentoring and coaching activities conducted by the Breckenridge Institute®. Over the years, there have been many people who have helped to bring this work to its culmination in the form of this book.

First, I would like to thank my Enneagram teachers Don Richard Riso and Russ Hudson who gave me my first extensive training in the Enneagram. Completing all three parts of the Riso-Hudson training program allowed me to probe the depths of their understanding of the Enneagram first-hand through countless hours of teaching, group discussion, exercises, and one-on-one dialogue with Don and Russ. I still count them as mentors in the Enneagram and as friends. I would also like to thank Claudio Naranjo, whose model and writings about the Enneagram have had a powerful affect on how I see myself, others, and the world. His work is complex, insightful, and brilliant. I met Naranjo only once as a participant in a three-day workshop that he conducted at the International Enneagram Association (IEA) conference in Arlington, Virginia in 2004. Even in this group setting, I was profoundly affected by his presence, perspective, and depth of insight.

Jonathan Babicz of the Breckenridge Institute® staff was a sounding-board for my ideas all throughout the writing process and read multiple drafts of the manuscript. Jon has a deep understanding of the principles, practices, and theoretical foundations outlined in this book. He is a coach, mentor, and teacher of the Enneagram who has woven the principles and practices described in this book into the fabric of his life.

xii   BRECKENRIDGE ENNEAGRAM

I would also like to thank David Henderson, John Anderson, Paul Dobies, Clarke Turner, and Mark and Lori Leyba for helpful comments on early drafts of the manuscript.

My six-year-old son, Thomas Larson Bodnarczuk, is a constant inspiration to me. His gentle spirit, innocence, keen mind, insight, and curiosity teach me what it's like to be a little boy again.

Finally, I'd like to thank my wife, Elin Larson. As a professional partner, she has been an integral part of building the Breckenridge Institute®, especially the computing infrastructure that supports on-line instruments like the BTI™. As a life-partner, she has been a constant source of support – encouraging me in the writing of this book and other aspects of the work.

FOREWORD

The Enneagram may well be the oldest systematic model of human personality that exists. It is rooted in observations of human behavior patterns that have been noted across cultures and centuries. Mark Bodnarczuk invites us to make an important distinction between metaphysical and naturalistic perspectives on the nature of human experience, and he unapologetically suggests that the Enneagram has importance independent of mystical, spiritual, or metaphysical interpretations. Indeed, Bodnarczuk carefully lays out an argument that we should approach the Enneagram in a new way using scientific methods. He gives credit to all who have contributed to the model and builds on their observations to move the framework forward for the contemporary thinker. In fact, you will be hard pressed to find another text that so efficiently summarizes the key trends in psychology, and why these trends matter.

In over thirty years of research and work in the field of personality and development, I have rarely come across a work that so exquisitely integrates the key models of psychology into as practical a tool as you will find in this text. Relying on the best of what has been thought and scientifically validated in the fields of organizational and individual psychology, the scope of this work brings you to the realization that there is a way to understand how we behave and how we change that is grounded in science and common sense.

The Breckenridge Enneagram: A Guide to Personal and Professional Growth provides you with a way to see the links between your beliefs, your behavior, and your deep ingrained psychological dynamics. From the outset of this book, you will find insights into the key psychological and philosophical frameworks that provide the principles on which your understanding of behavior rests.

Through a careful review of how your needs, childhood experience, and contextual reinforcements help create nine types, or positions, on the Enneagram, you will begin a journey that opens windows on the psychological world of those around you – both the becoming and striving aspects of yourself and those whom you love, and with whom you work.

The nine Enneagram positions are grouped into threes around the themes of head, heart, and action. The core nature of each position and how the individual moves from this position to a fuller, more authentic self are outlined in this extraordinary book. Each position is thoroughly described in terms of its healthy and its deficiency aspects with tips and suggestions for attending to one in service of the other.

A dramatic insight that Bodnarczuk brings to the exploration is the influence of somatic instincts. Somatic – meaning body systems that connect the individual with his or her environment – color the nine positions in profound ways. Gaining insights into these instincts and their power over the individual's personality is worth the price of the book. Exploring how these somatic energies for preservation, cultivation, and transmitting influence your choices, how you and others see the world, and engage in your relationships provides a level of understanding you will not find in other books on development.

The final section of the book challenges you to explore your deep inward calling and movement toward a use of your talents with integrity and authenticity. Importantly, this book identifies markers to attend to when growth is going awry and the darker sides of our dual natures emerge.

True to the opening words of this book, Bodnarczuk invites us to transform ourselves by identifying our natural talents and allowing our unique blend of experience, motive, needs, and character to become increasingly conscious. True to the words of Carl Jung who suggested that becoming conscious first requires bringing light to the darkness of our psyche – those deep aspects of ourselves which have not been attended to and need resurrection for the purposes of releasing abundant creative energy – this book will enlighten, engage, and enthrall you with its scope and personal meaning.

Roger R. Pearman, Ed.D.
President
Qualifying.org, Inc.
Winston-Salem
North Carolina

CHAPTER 1

THE BRECKENRIDGE ENNEAGRAM

When we are finally old enough to realize that we have a personality, it's too late to have a hand in fashioning it. The formation of personality is both: a) an *inside-out* process where innate, inborn tendencies (our temperament) predispose us to actions and interactions with others, and b) an *outside-in* process where people, social structures, and our culture teach us how to see ourselves, others, and the world. The Breckenridge Enneagram shows us how to use the powerful See-Do-Get Process® to turn back the learning-clock and discover our true selves. Here's how the See-Do-Get Process® works. We see the world a certain way and specific behaviors and emotions naturally flow from that world view because we believe that it is "reality." When we act, people read our body language and respond to the message they see in us. Their responses reinforce how we see them. We see, we do, we get.

The Enneagram is a model of nine personality types that has evolved significantly since the late 1960s. Pronounced "any-a-gram," the word refers to a nine-pointed diagram enclosed within a circle ("ennea" is Greek for "nine;" "gram" means "drawing"). Enneagram theory started to take shape in the early 1970s due to the influence and scholarship of Claudio Naranjo, a psychiatrist who began attributing psychological principles to the model. Most people writing about or teaching the Enneagram today trace their roots either directly or indirectly to the work of Naranjo. A number of popular authors, such as Don Richard Riso, Russ Hudson, Helen Palmer, and David Daniels have contributed to the evolution of Enneagram theory, but much of this work has been based on a theoretical foundation of spiritual and metaphysical principles. The Breckenridge Enneagram integrates the empirical-clinical insights of Claudio Naranjo; Maslow's Psychology and Hierarchy of Needs; the

See-Do-Get Process; and a rigorous approach to empirical research and psychometric analysis. The Breckenridge Enneagram is set apart from other approaches to the Enneagram by its focus on a naturalistic, scientific view of personality and psychological processes that are linked to modern advances in the neurosciences.

The Breckenridge Enneagram can help identify key elements of your personality using nine the Enneagram types shown in Figure 1.[8] In many ways, your personality is like your philosophy of life. While the nine types have very different characteristics, over time *one* of them tends to dominate the others as your primary way of seeing the world. This becomes your dominant Enneagram type. One way to determine your dominant Enneagram type is to take the Breckenridge Type Indicator™ (BTI™) that is available from the Breckenridge Institute® at *https://survey.breckenridgeinstitute.com/products.bi*. The BTI is a psychometrically validated assessment tool designed to help identify your Enneagram type. The BTI can be used for both personal and professional applications, but it is especially effective when used as the basis for coaching, leadership development, or teambuilding exercises. In your *professional* life, a better understanding of your personality using the BTI will help identify decision-making bias and predictable errors in judgment in both strategic and tactical issues. When used in your *personal* life, the BTI gives you information to help you to identify underlying patterns of behavior that frustrate and undermine healthy relationships with friends and family members.

Readers who are already familiar with the Enneagram and other personality typologies such as Jungian type, Keirsey's four temperaments, the DiSC, the Five-Factor model, Berens' Interaction Styles, and Circumplex models of personality, and who want a more detailed explanation of the theoretical underpinnings of the Breckenridge Enneagram should begin by reading Chapter 2 and then return here to learn about the details of the Breckenridge Enneagram. Readers who are not familiar with the personality typologies named above should continue reading in the sequence that the material is presented.

Let's begin by reviewing the nine Enneagram types shown in Figure 1. Remember that your personality is like your philosophy of life. While the nine types have very different characteristics, over time *one* of them tends to dominate the others as your primary way of seeing the world. This becomes your dominant Enneagram type.

The nine types are grouped into three groups of three, where types Two, Three, and Four are in the Heart Group, types Five, Six, and Seven are in the Head Group, and types Eight, Nine, and One make up the Action Group. The description below begins

Breckenridge Enneagram

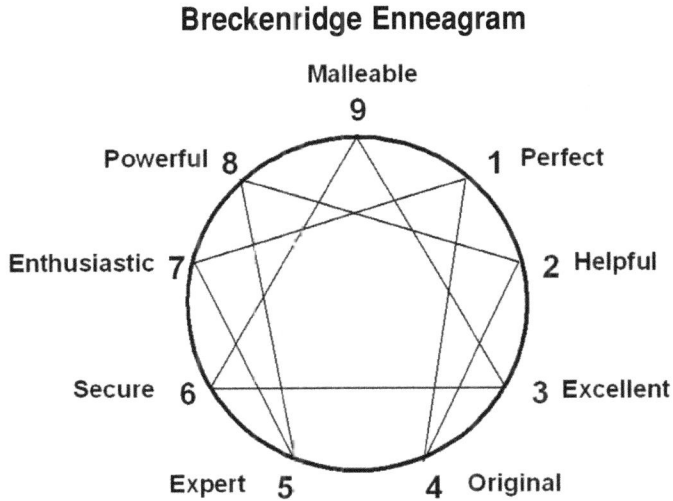

Figure 1

with the Heart Group, so the nine types are listed beginning with type Two. Each of the nine types lives by a Tacit Creed that shapes and defines how they see themselves, others, and the world around them. The nine Tacit Creeds are shown below:

Type Two: I must be helpful
Type Three: I must be excellent
Type Four: I must be original
Type Five: I must be an expert
Type Six: I must be secure
Type Seven: I must be enthusiastic
Type Eight: I must be powerful
Type Nine: I must be malleable
Type One: I must be perfect

Review the brief descriptions of the nine types below and reflect on the one that you most identify with. Remember that these descriptions are very brief summaries that do not describe the complete characteristics of any of the types. More detailed descriptions of the nine types are presented later in this chapter.

Type Two (I Must Be Helpful): When Twos are at their best, they are helpful, empathic, warm, supportive, compassionate, sensitive, and nurturing. They enjoy being close with (and connected to) people and focus on others' well-being by identifying and meeting their needs. When under pressure, they become overly intimate and intrusive, prone to build dependencies – they give to get and impose their will on others through flattery, guilt, and manipulation.

Type Three (I Must Be Excellent): When Threes are at their best, they are role models of achievement and success and establish and exemplify standards of excellence within their cultural context. They are ambitious, competitive, goal-oriented, and embody highly-valued competencies and talents. When under pressure, they become overly focused on self-promotion, creating an "idealized" self to be seen by others – they lose access to their depth feelings and true identity and mobilize their achievements as an "objective" validation of their value and worth.

Type Four (I Must Be Original): When Fours are at their best, they are original, creative, self-revealing, authentic, different from others, and express how they "see" the world *indirectly* by creating something; e.g., art, music, literature, technology, services, etc. When under pressure, they experience deep inner turmoil, moods of depression, melancholy, withdrawal and a poignant sense of "cosmic" suffering and compulsive longing.

Type Five (I Must Be an Expert): When Fives are at their best, they are reflective, analytical, curious, pioneering, open-minded, independent thinkers with deep insight into the connections between complex and seemingly unrelated concepts, bodies of knowledge, and human and natural phenomena. When under pressure, they detach from the arena of life's problems and become provocative, iconoclastic, and apathetic; stoically resigned to life's "cosmic" meaninglessness, and accumulate knowledge and understanding in the hope that it will alleviate their profound sense of neediness, inner-poverty, isolation, and alienation from themselves, others, and the world around them.

Type Six (I Must Be Secure): When Sixes are at their best, they are cautious, responsible, hard-working and vigilant about identifying potential problems in order to create a reliable and safe environment for themselves and others. When under pressure, they are hyper-alert, suspicious, chronically uncertain, looking for hidden meanings and underlying patterns of intention, and filled with anxiety in the absence of real threats.

Type Seven (I Must Be Enthusiastic): When Sevens are at their best, they are a limitless source of thoughts and ideas – they are spontaneous, curious, and adventurous, with quick, agile minds that focus on the positive aspects of life. When under pressure, they become restless, easily bored, overcommitted, stifled by stability and continuity in life, addicted to excitement, narcissistic with a subtle attitude of superiority and "entitlement" clothed beneath a calm, relaxed, confident exterior.

Type Eight (I Must Be Powerful): When Eights are at their best, they are strong, assertive, persistent, tenacious, seeking challenges, action-oriented with a take-charge attitude and enormous determination and will power to triumph over all obstacles and be influential in their world. When under pressure, they become hostile, vindictive, defiant, emotionally insensitive, desiring to control and dominate people and situations to get what they want, or exploiting people and situations by taking what they want by force and/or cunning.

Type Nine (I Must Be Malleable): When Nines are at their best, they are self-aware, seekers of self-actualization, engaged and connected to life, good-natured, friendly, easy-going, patient, tolerant, creative, imaginative, excellent mediators and communicators, emotionally stable, non-confrontational, and focused on life's simple pleasures. When under pressure, they become overly submissive and agreeable (peace at any price), distractible, mechanically going through the motions in life and desensitized to the point where their capacity for psychological insight is diminished substantially – they long not to long, to stay blind to their Blind Spots.

Type One (I Must Be Perfect): When Ones are at their best, they are conscientious, proper, correct, rational, self-disciplined, placing a high value on integrity, objectivity which gives them an extremely keen sense of what's right and wrong. When under pressure, they become overly critical, demanding, rigid, intolerant, overly detailed, methodical, afraid to make mistakes, and too focused on rule-keeping.

```

# BRECKENRIDGE ENNEAGRAM AND MASLOW'S PSYCHOLOGY

Take a moment to read and reflect on the emotions listed in Figure 2. Which ones do you relate to the most? Which ones do you relate to the least? Which ones do you experience most frequently in your day-to-day life? Which ones do you enjoy and even long for? Which ones do you avoid or even run from?

## Emotions Diagram

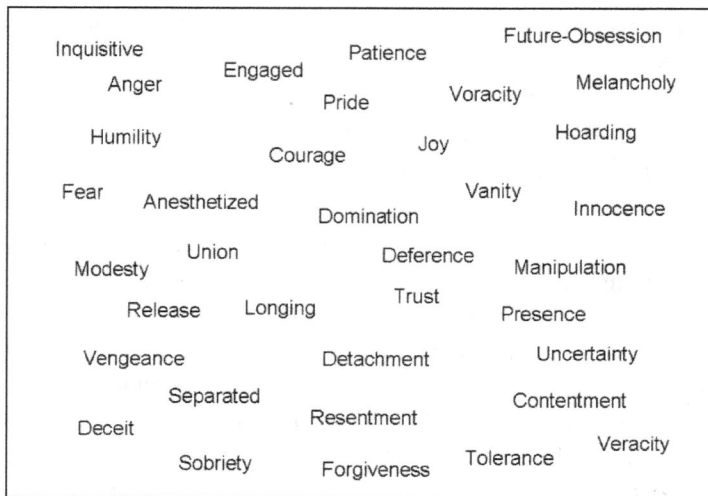

Figure 2

Now imagine that this seemingly random and unrelated set of positive and negative human emotions can be ordered in a circular configuration around the Enneagram in three groups of three. Figure 3 shows how the deficiency-driven emotions for the nine types are positioned around the Enneagram, with each pair of emotions bearing the *signature of dependency* on people, resources, and experiences outside of ourselves.

Figure 4 shows how the growth-motivated emotions for the nine types are positioned around the Enneagram, with each pair of emotions bearing the *signature of autonomy* from people, resources, and experiences outside of ourselves.
```

Breckenridge Enneagram
Deficiency-Driven Emotions (Dependency)

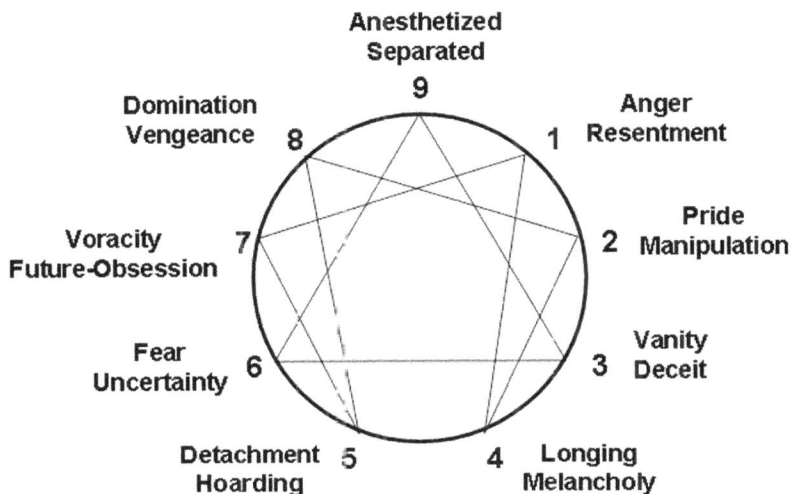

Anesthetized
Separated
9

Domination
Vengeance   **8**

Anger
1   Resentment

Voracity
Future-Obsession   **7**

Pride
2   Manipulation

Fear
Uncertainty   **6**

Vanity
3   Deceit

Detachment   **5**
Hoarding

4   Longing
Melancholy

Figure 3

Breckenridge Enneagram
Growth-Motivated Emotions (Autonomy)

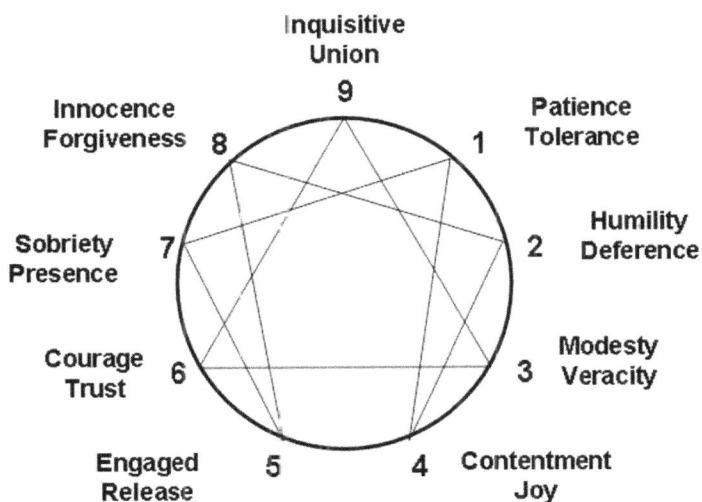

Inquisitive
Union
9

Innocence
Forgiveness   **8**

Patience
1   Tolerance

Sobriety
Presence   **7**

Humility
2   Deference

Courage
Trust   **6**

Modesty
3   Veracity

Engaged   **5**
Release

4   Contentment
Joy

Figure 4

The nine types are not simply a random collection of emotions and Enneagram styles. Rather, they are an organized and dynamic pattern of personality structures that have well-defined neighboring relationships where the further around the circular graph one moves the more *different* each type becomes until the ones positioned on the opposite side of the graph are actually polar opposites. Type Nine is the point to which the entire geometry of the Enneagram is anchored in terms of left-right and top-bottom symmetries. Figure 5 shows how these concepts can be *unified* into a single model for each of the nine types.

**Breckenridge Enneagram
Unified Model and 80-20 Rule**

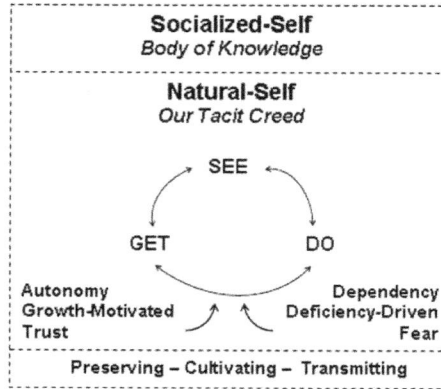

Socialized-Self
Body of Knowledge

Natural-Self
Our Tacit Creed

SEE

GET   DO

Autonomy   Dependency
Growth-Motivated   Deficiency-Driven
Trust   Fear

Preserving – Cultivating – Transmitting

Figure 5

The top of Figure 5 represents the Socialized-Self, which is the part of our personality that includes conscious, intentional behaviors and emotional responses that have been shaped by our environment. The bottom portion of Figure 5 represents the Natural-Self, which is the part of our personality that includes behaviors and cognitive or emotional responses that are on autopilot, *regardless* of whether they are innate or learned. Actions and interactions that come from the Socialized-Self are much more conscious and intentional, so we can morph our behaviors to "fit" a specific social setting, but the essential elements of our Natural-Self remain unchanged despite these on-the-surface alterations. A more extensive description of the Socialized-Self and the Natural-Self is given in Chapter 2. Notice that the top of Figure 5 also contains a person's body-of-knowledge, which includes their life experiences, professional training, disciplinary affiliations, and other key areas of knowledge. While the exact nature of the body-of-knowledge will vary from person to person, the underlying patterns associated with the Natural-Self will be more or less invariant given a person's dominant Enneagram type. As shown in Figure 5, the

Tacit Creed is produced by the See-Do-Get Process and can be either deficiency-driven or growth-motivated with deficiency being *driven* by dependency and fear, and growth being *motivated* by autonomy and trust. The same Tacit Creed has a much different look and feel when it's growth-motivated rather than deficiency-driven. For example, the Tacit Creed for type Ones (I must be perfect) is experienced much differently when it is driven by Anger and Resentment, rather than being motivated by Patience and Tolerance.

Notice that the three Somatic Instincts are shown at the bottom of Figure 5. The Somatic Instincts are formed prior to (and independent of) the Tacit Creeds, but are a key element of the interdependent reality that we call our personality type. The dominant Somatic Instinct powerfully shapes our Enneagram type and defines the overall direction of our lives, especially in regard to lifestyle issues. The 80-20 Rule is a pragmatic way to describe a person's level of psychological health. More specifically, if 80% of a person's actions and interactions are growth-motivated, rather than deficiency-driven, they are probably a fairly healthy individual as defined by the 80-20 Rule. This ratio is context and relationship dependent in the sense that our actions and interactions may follow the 80-20 Rule in some relationships where we get along with people, but then radically shift in the blink of an eye if people with whom we experience destructive conflict enter the situation. The characteristics of the 80-20 Rule will be discussed in more detail in Chapter 3.

Some of the key underlying theoretical principles of the Breckenridge Enneagram come from Abraham Maslow's Hierarchy of Needs and Psychology. Maslow's model is an integrated theory of human growth and human motivation that has a number of distinguishing characteristics; e.g., his work integrates a large body of research in the areas of biology, neuroscience, and psychology. Maslow's model synthesizes a biological perspective on human psychology, with a description of what energizes, directs, and sustains human behavior. His early work from the 1940s-1950s on instincts and human motivation is documented in *Motivation and Personality*[9] and his later work in *Toward a Psychology of Being* places his psychological model on an existentialist foundation.[10] Maslow's Hierarchy is one of the best known aspects of his psychological theory. Figure 6 shows how the hierarchy has been mapped to the Breckenridge Enneagram.

Maslow's Hierarchy and the Breckenridge Enneagram

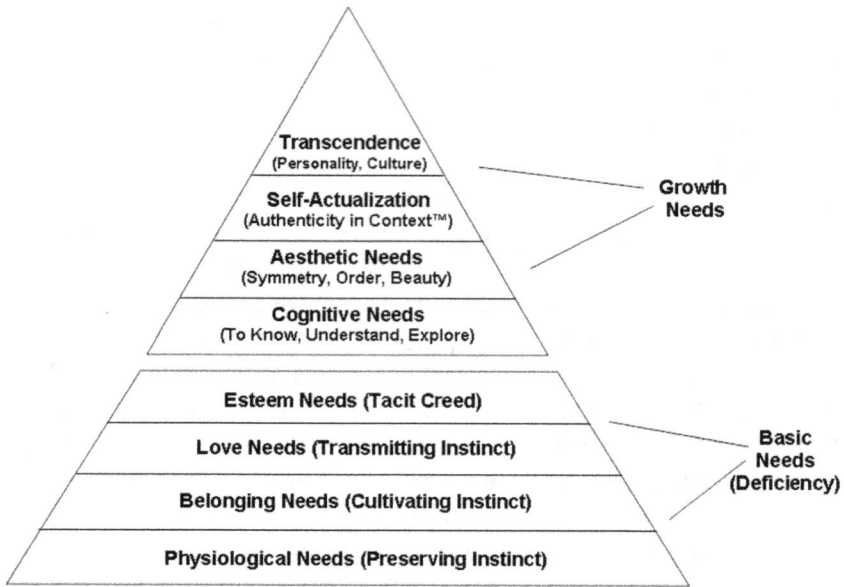

Figure 6

The bottom part of the pyramid contains four levels of Basic Needs that frequently are not *fully* gratified in childhood and are experienced later in life as deficiency needs. Notice how the Somatic Instincts and Tacit Creed have been mapped to the first four levels of the hierarchy. The *preserving* instinct is associated with the first level of physiological needs, while the *cultivating* instinct maps to the second level of belonging needs, and the *transmitting* instinct is associated with the third level of love needs. The Tacit Creed is mapped to the "esteem" needs and is related to how we "see" ourselves, others, and the world. While some interpreters of Maslow's work have broken safety needs out separately, this version of the hierarchy associates "safety" with all four levels of Basic Needs. The top part of the pyramid contains four levels of Growth Needs that are largely eclipsed from awareness in most people until the Basic Needs are gratified to a moderate-to-high level. Maslow's Hierarchy is one of the most wide-spread theories of human growth and human motivation anywhere. Linking the nine types and the Somatic Instincts to Maslow's Psychology provides a solid naturalistic foundation for the Breckenridge Enneagram. Using the framework shown in Figure 6 places the Breckenridge Enneagram within the larger context of a complete theory of personal growth that spans a lifetime.

Maslow described it as a strict hierarchy where the next higher need emerges sequentially only when the lower one is gratified. He argues that the gratification of a need in childhood decreases the intensity of that need later in life. For example, people who have had the belonging need gratified in childhood will be less deficiency-driven about that need as adults. Our own view is that while the overall structure of Maslow's Hierarchy is correct, it is not a strict hierarchy in the way he described it. Rather, the levels co-exist in need-clusters that are more or less gratified, balanced, and reach a state-of-equilibrium (homeostasis), so our lives are perfectly aligned to get the results we get. The nature of the dynamic interaction between the various levels of the hierarchy requires more empirical research with instruments like the BTI as well as more theoretical development.

The Somatic Instincts are formed in the first year of life and are the foundation of human emotions associated with the sense of being safe and secure in three areas: a) home-nurture (preserving), b) belonging (cultivating), and c) being loved (transmitting). Growth and gratification of these basic needs occur gradually as a child moves out to explore new experiences from a position of known safety and security. Maslow describes the level of deficiency in the area of love needs, belonging needs, etc., in terms of the depth and breadth of the emotional "holes" that need to be filled in the child. A sense of deficiency in the first four levels creates an inner sense that "something's missing" in the very fabric and foundation of life. A person's level of awareness of the "emptiness" varies based on the actual level of deficiency and their position on the Enneagram, with types on the top being less self-aware of their inner needs, and types on the bottom being more aware.

Let's discuss the nature of deficiency needs and growth needs in more detail. Deficiency needs are separate from (and prior to) human knowledge or experience and are the result of being a human organism. Like the body craves water or food and then stops craving it when these needs are gratified, humans also crave for the physiological, belonging, love, and esteem needs of the first four levels on the hierarchy. Here are some of the key characteristics of deficiency needs that are pointed out by Maslow:[11]

- Deficiency needs create the sense that "something's missing" in life with a desire or craving to eliminate (get rid of) the need; e.g., the empty hole that needs to be filled.
- They are an episodic, climactic, moment of consummation, goal-oriented, end-state; e.g., the problem with eating is that it kills my appetite.
- Deficiency needs are on autopilot and become unconscious patterns-of-interaction.

- They are compulsive, insatiable, fixated, and destructive.
- They create an instrumental view of living (striving to bring about desired gratification).
- Deficiency needs create a sense of being *inauthentic* because we try to fill an inner existential need with outer behavior, thus deficiency alienates us from ourselves, others, and the world.
- They make us dependent; outer-determined; and need-oriented, with an instrumental view of others.
- Deficiency needs tend to be past-oriented and based on life experience and our current state of actuality rather than potentiality.
- People who are driven by deficiency tend to be fear-based with a sense of scarcity and a deep belief that they won't survive biologically and psychologically.
- The first four levels of the hierarchy tend to reach a deficiency-driven state of equilibrium that is solidified through the See-Do-Get Process.
- We experience them as the underlying deficiency-driven emotions associated with the Tacit Creeds and with the overall life direction of the Downward Spiral of Striving.

It is important to note that the force-for-growth exists *at all times* in a person's life-history whether or not they are conscious of its existence or aware of its presence operating in their lives. We experience the growth needs like the quiet flow of a river – like a sense of calling, purpose, and destiny. Here are some of the key characteristics of growth needs that are pointed out by Maslow:[12]

- Growth needs create the sense of fulfillment, wholeness, joy with an endless desire that can never be attained or satisfied; e.g., the more one gets, the more one wants.
- We experience growth needs to be like a continuous, steady, upward path and forward movement toward the higher levels of the hierarchy; ultimately transcending the autopilot tendencies of personality, and the inauthentic edicts and demands of our cultural context.
- They are consciously chosen, deeply satisfying, constructive, and create a desire that continues at a higher level.
- The growth needs have an intrinsic view of living so that growth is an intrinsically rewarding and exciting process *in itself*.
- Growth creates a sense of being *authentic* where we are inwardly reunited with ourselves, others, and the world.
- Growth needs make us autonomous, inner-determined, abundance-oriented, and give us an intrinsic view of others.

- Growth needs tend to be future-oriented and impel us toward open exploration, seeking our potentiality, and toward what Maslow calls peak experiences.
- People who are motivated by growth tend to be trust-based, with a sense of abundance, and the tenacity to face the challenges of life with the deep belief that they will survive biologically and psychologically.
- The growth needs reach a state-of-equilibrium and a higher understanding that solidifies through the See-Do-Get Process.
- We experience them as the underlying growth-motivated emotions associated with the Tacit Creeds and with the overall life direction of the Upward Path of Becoming.

There are two forces at the foundation of our personality that powerfully shape our existence as humans. The strength and directionality of these two forces are defined by the extent to which a child is either deficiency-driven or growth-motivated. As Maslow states, "This basic dilemma or conflict between the defensive forces [of safety] and the growth trends I conceive to be existential, imbedded in the deepest nature of the human being, now and forever into the future."[13] The first force tends to focus on the *danger* involved in moving into new territory and draws us backward to cling to the *safety of our current-self* out of fear, defensiveness, embarrassment, or threat (see diagram below). Allowing the force-for-safety to direct the path of our lives makes us afraid to learn, explore, innovate, and take chances. It causes us to reject our independence and personal freedom, which ultimately leads to the rejection of our deepest and most authentic self.

Force-for-Safety (Deficiency) ←——→ **PERSON** ←——→ Force-for-Growth (Abundance)

The second force tends to focus on the *potential* of moving into new territory, and draws us forward toward *growth and our future-self* out of a deep and abiding longing for wholeness, openness, self-awareness, and self-control. Allowing the force-for-growth to direct our lives creates confidence when facing the future and the challenges that life brings; when dealing with the world around us; and this helps us become our most authentic selves within our context. For example, healthy infants are often intensely absorbed by exploring, manipulating, grasping, experimenting, and discovering new things. They have spontaneity and curiosity that make them want to taste, touch, feel, and experience the world around them. This is *their* unstated, unspoken, unconsciously motivated will that is designed to achieve *their* desired results. The force-for-growth draws infants forward to explore their world with little steps. Success builds self-esteem, self-determinism, and force of will.

The force-for-safety binds children to their past and to using previous strategies that may or may not be effective or appropriate for the challenges they face in the present. So before they are able to fully understand what their day-to-day, moment-by-moment experience of human existence means, infants live on the cusp of the *existential now*, where the past exists only in their emotional memory and the future does not yet exist because they have yet to create it. While the memories of the past and the vision of the future are "real" in the sense that they can (and do) direct and powerfully shape the actions and interactions of people living in the existential now, the foundation of our sense of personal responsibility and freedom is shaped by the outcome of the dialectic between the force-for-safety and the force-for-growth.

The active, tacit, and cultural teaching of parents and caretakers; the conscious and unconscious mirroring of their Tacit Creeds (both deficiency-driven and growth-motivated); and the confirming, rejecting, and disconfirming of the child's attempts to get *their* desired results are imprinted on unscripted and malleable hearts and minds that receive 93% of the communication through body language and tone of voice prior to being able to speak language. Even "good" parents can't lead children any further than they've been themselves, so the parent's personality, level of self-awareness and self-control, and the patterns-of-interaction that they are drawn into with the child create the contextual reality of "how the world is" for an infant or toddler. Over time, the patterns-of-interaction between the child, their parents or caretakers, and the edicts and demands of their contextual reality accumulate on a child's "emotional scoreboard" and begin to define their sense of whether the world can (or cannot) be trusted to meet their needs. The cumulative outcomes of the emotional scoreboard begin to form the child's basic beliefs and assumptions about themselves, others, and the world, and are stored in long-term emotional memory. The extent to which a child's basic needs are (or are not) met defines the degree to which they will be either deficiency-driven or growth-motivated as evidenced by the 80-20 Rule. It also defines the extent to which a child begins to "see" themselves as being either acceptable or unacceptable based on the degree to which they are allowed to exercise their own will and get *their* desired results, or they must comply with the will of their parents, caretakers, and the socio-cultural context.

Every relationship must be consciously or unconsciously defined (negotiated) by the participants as being either symmetric or complementary.[14] In symmetric interactions, people tend to mirror each other's behavior and emotional responses. Symmetric interactions are based on an assumption of *equality* that has been tacitly agreed to by the participants, and that tries to *minimize* the differences between the participants. In complementary interactions, one person's behavior and emotional responses complement (are different than) the other's behaviors and emotional responses. Complementary interactions are based on an assumption of difference that has been tacitly agreed to by the participants that tries to *maximize* the differences between the participants. Differences can include being assertive-submissive, superior-inferior, primary-secondary, or as being one-up or one-down. For example, a toddler who is an Enneagram type Eight is likely to have a complementary (one-up) relationship with a parent who is a type Nine. Over time, the actions and interactions of children, parents, and caretakers around the symmetric-complementary distinction solidify into autopilot, habitual patterns-of-interaction.

Eventually, children come to a fork-in-the-road and are faced with what Maslow calls the *Primal Choice*; e.g., whether to follow an overall path where they do what *others* want as a way of ensuring their safety, security, food, etc.; or to follow a path where they do what *they* want and risk losing the providers' love, belonging, and a sense of respect. Maslow argues that if the only way for a child to maintain their self-determinism (force-for-growth) is to risk losing others (force-for-safety), most children will give up themselves. Although the choice of an overall path for-self or for-others is unstated, unspoken, and unconscious in children, it is ultimately an existential choice for-or-against-self that is driven by a deep and profound fear of biological-psychological survival. Over time, the anesthetizing, deadening and cumulative effects of the choice-against-self solidify into patterns-of-interaction that create our beliefs about ourselves, others, and the world through the See-Do-Get Process. I will quote Maslow at length on this point, and highlight some of the key points that link his view to the Breckenridge Enneagram in bold letters:

> "How is it possible to lose a self? The treachery, unknown and unthinkable, begins with our secret death in childhood – if and when we are not loved and are cut off from our spontaneous wishes. But wait – it is not just this simple murder of the psyche. That might be written off, the tiny victim might even 'outgrow' it – but it is a perfect double crime in which he himself also gradually and unwittingly takes part. He has not been accepted for himself *as he is*. Oh, they 'love' him [Say], but they want him or force him or expect him to be different [Do]! Therefore he *must be unacceptable*. He himself learns to believe it and at last takes it for granted [Core Assumption]. He has truly given himself up. No matter now whether he obeys them, whether he clings, rebels or withdraws – his behavior, his performance is all that matters. His center of gravity is in 'them' not in himself – yet if he so much as noticed it he'd think it natural enough. And the whole thing is entirely plausible; all invisible, automatic, and anonymous! This is the perfect paradox. Everything looks normal; no crime was intended; there is no corpse, no guilt… But what has happened? He has been rejected, not only by them, but by himself… But alas, he is not dead. 'Life' goes on, and so must he. From the moment he gives himself up, and to the extent that he does so, all unknowingly he sets about to

create and maintain a pseudo-self [Tacit Creed]. But this is an expediency – a 'self' without wishes."[15]

As Maslow notes, the child deals with this decision-against-self by repression, ignoring it, controlling it with their will power, or letting it subside and ultimately die.[16] The frustration and undermining of the child's will toward desired results can create a deep sense of shame, anger, and fear that they are largely unaware of, or which they keep to themselves as an undiscussible secret about how they "see" themselves, others, and the world. Over time, the experiences associated with this loss of self become galvanized and are stored in long-term emotional memory. As adults, reconnecting to these key events in our psychological history requires us to overcome our deep fear of veridical self-knowledge; e.g., the psychological truth about our emotions, natural impulses, long-term emotional and cognitive memories, natural talents and abilities, and our calling and destiny in life.[17] Overcoming this fear is one of the key elements of Authenticity in Context.

THE EMERGENCE OF THE TACIT CREED AND THE SELF-SEALING PROCESS

As will be described in more detail in the section on *Empirical Existentialism* in Chapter 2, our experience of human existence begins at birth as our innate, inborn tendencies (our temperament) interact with our experiences and the environment to build underlying patterns of emotions that are stored in the long-term emotional memory of the Amygdala prior to the neocortex being formed and before our ability to use language. The universal nature of human emotions; the anatomical and operational similarities of the human organism; the biological purpose of the Somatic Instincts; the fact that life is an historical process of birth, infancy, adolescence, maturity, and death within space-and-time; and our concrete and symbolic experiences of these aspects of human existence *create* the deep and abiding sense that what is *most personal, is most universal.* In other words, when we identify an experience that goes to the core of our being – something that we would rather die than reveal to others – that experience is often most universal.

By the age of four or five, many children can frame penetrating questions about the nature of human existence regarding issues like: a) how they "see" themselves, being themselves, and finding an identity, b) how they should deal with (and face) the future, and c) how they should interact with the people and world around them.[18] Children aren't "taught" questions of human existence by parents, caretakers, and other adults. Rather, these questions emerge naturally, as do the self-evident conclusions that children come to about life, human existence, and their place in the universe.

Over time, answers to the existential questions about finding an identity, facing the future, and dealing with the environment form and begin to rise to the fringe of the child's consciousness. We experience these ways of "seeing" ourselves, others, and the world with an inner sense of *certainty* like self-evident, secret *truths* that cannot (and ought not) be questioned; objectively or publicly tested; or even verbalized, so we hide from ourselves, others, and the world. Most people would rather not ask or know, so they focus on the day-to-day realities of their lives and leave well enough alone. Given our fear of self-knowledge (good or bad) we tacitly decide that life goes on and so must we be about the task of building our day-to-day lives. *Accepting* this way of "seeing" as how we really "are" and believing it to be reality transforms it into a Core Assumption – a "fact" about ourselves, others, and the world that is "given" and reinforced through myriad cycles of the See-Do-Get Process. As children, we are not even capable of questioning or testing the Core Assumptions, and their acceptance as "true" begins a process of creating an *inauthentic-self* as we begin to live out this way of "seeing" like an inner "script." This reinforces our sense of being an inauthentic-self and exacerbates the experience that "something's missing" in life. The pattern by which the three existential questions and the beliefs associated with the Core Assumption *map* to the nine types is shown below:[19]

How Do I Find an Identity (Heart Group)?

- *Type Two:* If I died tomorrow, people would do fine without me.
- *Type Three:* I don't know who I am apart from the roles I play.
- *Type Four:* I'm lost in the collective ocean of people and life.

How Do I Face the Future (Head Group)?

- *Type Five:* I'll be engulfed by the collective demands of people and life.
- *Type Six:* I don't trust my ability to make decisions and cope with life.
- *Type Seven:* My inner world is a desolate, dry desert that's devoid of life.

How Do I Deal with the Environment (Action Group)?

- *Type Eight:* I'm weak and vulnerable when trying to get my needs met naturally by the world.
- *Type Nine:* My presence makes no tangible difference in life.
- *Type One:* I am fundamentally flawed and lack the ability to do what's correct, just, and moral.

Through countless cycles of the See-Do-Get Process, the fear, shame, anger, and beliefs that are connected with the nine Core Assumptions are buried in long-term emotional memory under myriad layers of day-to-day experience, but the patterns of emotions and belief associated with the nine Core Assumptions remain configured like a *signature pattern* that shapes and defines our Enneagram type.

As adults, we experience the key questions of human existence and Core Assumptions during *kairos* moments; e.g., facing life, death, new insights, suffering, and peak experiences. These moments quickly fade from consciousness and our resistance to experiencing the emotions of fear, shame, and anger associated with them snap back into place automatically. This allows most people to tune out the deep emotions associated with the Core Assumptions. They avoid them and deaden or anesthetize these aspects of their inner life by redirecting their focus onto the world around them through actions, interactions, and behaviors. In other words, people try to address their *inner* existential issues with *outer* behaviors and they succeed only in constructing an inauthentic "mask" between their deepest inner selves, and the world around them.

It's important to remember that the actions, interactions, and behaviors associated with our Tacit Creed can never truly address our deepest needs or fill the sense that "something's missing," because this is not the "lost key" to our true selves. But the emotions and beliefs associated with the Core Assumptions can be brought to the surface of awareness *purposely* by striking an inner emotional chord (tuning fork) that is tuned to that frequency (radio station), or by getting the "inner dog" barking. Identifying (putting a face on) the signature pattern of Core Assumptions means learning which ones resonate in us most deeply, and which one is the *dominant* Core Assumption, because the dominant assumption is the focus around which the Tacit Creed of our Enneagram type is formed. The list below shows the Core Assumption for each of the nine types, followed by the approach that each Enneagram type uses to redirect their attention *outwardly*, which over time becomes the Tacit Creed.

How Do I Find an Identity (Heart Group)?
- *Type Two:* I lack personal significance in life, so I will create personal significance by being helpful.
- *Type Three:* I lack personal identity in life, so I will create a personal identity by being excellent.
- *Type Four:* I lack an individual existence in life, so I will create an individual existence by being original.

How Do I Face the Future (Head Group)?

- *Type Five:* I lack the material existence to face the future, so I will create a material existence by being an expert.
- *Type Six:* I lack the discernment to face the future, so I will create a sense of discernment by being secure.
- *Type Seven:* I lack the inner-vitality to face the future, so I will create inner-vitality by being enthusiastic.

How Do I Deal with the Environment (Action Group)?

- *Type Eight:* I lack the ability to receive my needs from the environment naturally, so I will gratify my needs by being powerful.
- *Type Nine:* I lack the ability to act on the environment, so I will just go through the motions and be malleable.
- *Type One:* I lack the ability to do what's right in the environment, so I will bear down and be perfect.

Naranjo calls the mechanism that redirects our attention outwardly the Nasrudin Theory and illustrates its workings using a story about a Sufi master called the Mulla.

> "We are told that the Mulla was on all fours looking for something in one of the alleys at the market place. A friend joined him in the search for (as the Mulla explained to him) the key to his own house. Only after a long time had elapsed unsuccessfully did the friend think of asking Nasrudin, 'Are you sure that you lost it here?' To which he replied, 'No, I'm sure I lost it at home.' 'Then why are you looking for it here?' inquired the friend. 'There is much more light here!' explained the Mulla."[20]

As Maslow points out, it's the perfect double crime in which we ourselves take part by searching in all the wrong places. It's a kind of displacement where we search for the *inner* needs of finding: a) an identity, b) ways to face the future, and c) ways to deal with the environment *outwardly.*

Enneagram Type and the See-Do-Get Process

How we learn to "see" the world develops from our earliest years as our innate, inborn tendencies (our temperament) and our experiences and interactions with our environment build and accumulate underlying patterns of thinking, emotions, behavioral responses, biological needs and other characteristics through the See-Do-Get Process. By the time we are two or three years old, these underlying patterns shape and define how we see ourselves, others, and the world around us. They become a *philosophy of life* that powerfully defines the kinds of people, relationships, and experiences to which we are attracted or repulsed, and over time these preferences shape our relationships, families, careers, and lifestyles. The development process is self-referential in that our expectations for how the world *is* powerfully shape our perceptions, so in many ways we "see" exactly what we expect to see – in other words, what you see is what you get.

The See-Do-Get Process gives us enormous cognitive efficiency. But this cognitive efficiency is a double-edged sword, because while the underlying patterns free up the psychological energy we need to live our lives, they can become *too* automatic and ultimately self-defeating. They become the Tacit Creeds that we live by; e.g., unquestioned assumptions and autopilot responses to people and life. For example, one child slowly develops the Tacit Creed "I must be perfect" where he believes that it is not okay to make mistakes and errors, yet he feels helpless to change. Another child develops the Tacit Creed "I must be enthusiastic" believing that mistakes are the result of things that *can* be changed and that learning new approaches to problem-solving will help her succeed in areas where she has made mistakes the next time she tries them. Twenty years later she becomes his boss and they can't agree on how the day-to-day activities of the office should be accomplished or assessed.

Countless cycles through the See-Do-Get Process deepen the conviction that the view of the world that we have through the lens of our dominant Tacit Creed is actually reality. As Maslow said, "He who is good with a hammer thinks everything is a nail." When we unpack the autopilot operation of the See-Do-Get Process, we discover the four distinct, but related, steps that are shown on the right side of Figure 7.[21] Let's examine how this cognitive process works.

First, let's say that the interactions between us and others are recorded with a video camera. Video cameras don't have a personality and don't interpret or impose meaning on situations – they record events as they actually are. Second, when a person has the Tacit Creed (I must be perfect) they are hyper-sensitive to identifying mistakes in themselves and others, so they *unconsciously select* a small sub-set of data from the total events in the world that map on to the Tacit Creed of our Enneagram type. These data are selected again and again, regardless of how often others occur, or even how important other data are to the total picture. That's because they have special meaning and significance; e.g., they match the underlying patterns of this way of "seeing" ourselves, others, and the world and allow the person to feel more comfortable in a world of constant and frenetic change. Third, we impose meaning and intentionality on what others do; e.g., we automatically interpret the actions of

Figure 7

others through the autobiographical lens of *our* dominant Tacit Creed and the broader structures of our personal paradigm. Fourth, the imposition of meaning and intentionality produces behaviors and emotional responses that have been shaped by, and naturally flow from underlying patterns, often against our best intentions to act otherwise. With most people, all four steps happen on autopilot, without conscious thought or intention – *in the blink of an eye*. Each of the detailed descriptions of the nine types included below has a diagram like Figure 7 that is specific to its Tacit Creed.

The Self-Sealing Process of Personality in Context®

When we are finally old enough to realize that we *have* an Enneagram type, it's too late to have a hand in fashioning it because its formation and emergence is a self-sealing process that begins early in life. It is self-sealing in the sense that it *happens-to-us* and is not the result of conscious intent or conscious decision-making. In other words, we wake up one day and find ourselves with lives we have not chosen, in relationships we wish we weren't in pursuing professions that we tolerate (rather than enjoy), and not getting the results we want from our one-trip through life. We call this psycho-socio-cultural process of Personality in Context, which consists of the four-part self-sealing process described below.

Part 1: Blind Spots and Left-Hand Column

Part 2: Unintended Consequences

Part 3: Defense Routines

Part 4: State of Equilibrium

Part 1: Blind Spots and Left-Hand Column

Most people have Blind Spots in the sense that they tend to "see" themselves as being "at their best" and on the Upward Path of Becoming, while others tend to "see" their actions and interactions as being "under pressure" and on the Downward Spiral of Striving. This creates a Say-Do gap of duplicity where our deeds do not match what we say about ourselves. More specifically, given a choice between believing what we "say" and what we "do" other people will almost always believe what we do and this creates the Say-Do gap of duplicity. The gap between what we say and what we actually do builds in the Left-Hand Column of other people (and ours) and creates a differential pressure that powerfully shapes and defines our relationships. Because we sense the pressure build-up and duplicity in the Left-Hand Column, we redouble our efforts to get others to "see" us as we see ourselves – being at our best – and these efforts come from a sense of striving that is deficiency-driven. Our fear of self-knowledge causes us to by-pass and cover-up situations where our Blind Spots might surface out of a sense of embarrassment and threat, which only increases our level of inauthenticity with ourselves, others, and the world. A detailed description of the concepts of the Left-Hand Column and Blind Spots is given on page 273 and following.

Part 2: Unintended Consequences

Our intention is to have our actions-interactions (Do) align with how we "see" ourselves (being at our best), but these best intentions are often derailed; e.g., we intend to do X but get the unintended consequence of Y. As the frequency of unintended consequences increases, so does the risk of being embarrassed and threatened by others discovering our Say-Do gap and the extent of our inauthenticity. As such, we redouble our efforts to close the Say-Do gap out of the fear of being discovered by others. But these attempts emerge from striving and being deficiency-driven and consume enormous amounts of psychological energy which only widens the gap between what we say and what we actually do. A more detailed description of the concept of unintended consequences is given on page 278 and following.

Part 3: Defense Routines

Over time, through myriad cycles through the See-Do-Get Process, our actions and interactions go on autopilot, slip below the surface of conscious awareness, and become patterns-of-interaction (POI) that are triggered by both inner and outer stimuli. Defense routines emerge to protect people from real or perceived embarrassment and threat, and often follow the process defined by Chris Argyris; e.g., by-pass, cover-up (make undiscussible), cover-up the cover-up (make the undiscussibility undiscussible). Through repetition the defense routines themselves go on autopilot, slip below the surface of conscious awareness and become patterns-of-interaction with self, others, and the world. Not surprisingly, this only increases the Say-Do gap which makes it even more difficult to question or change, increases our sense of alienation from ourselves, others, and the world. A more detailed description of the concept of defense routines is given on page 278 and following.

Part 4: State of Equilibrium

As adults, the process by which our Enneagram type was created is sealed-off (hidden) from our conscious awareness in the flow and routine of day-to-day life. The four-part self-sealing process powerfully shapes and defines our attractions, repulsions, and preferences toward people, hobbies, knowledge areas, career and lifestyle choices. By the time we are young adults, much of the fabric of our life within context has been woven by myriad choices – most of which were made tacitly or without much conscious intention. The configuration of our emotional, cognitive, relational, lifestyle, and professional lives solidifies and reaches a state-of-equilibrium that is defined by the socio-cultural context within which we live, our patterns-of-interaction, the belief structure of our personal paradigm, and the results that we've gotten in our lives. In other words, the unique configuration of our inner and outer lives is perfectly aligned to get the results we get through the See-Do-Get Process. The interdependent actions of the four parts of the self-sealing process are the essence of the concept of Personality in Context.

ENNEAGRAM SYMMETRIES

Let's return to the geometric shape of the Enneagram. As mentioned previously, the nine types that are positioned around the Enneagram are not simply a random collection of personality styles. Rather, they are an organized and dynamic pattern of personality structures that have well-defined neighboring relationships where the further around the Enneagram one moves the more *different* each type becomes until the ones positioned on the opposite side of the graph are actually polar opposites. This section describes these inter-relationships and symmetries in more detail.

Breckenridge Enneagram
Tacit Creeds

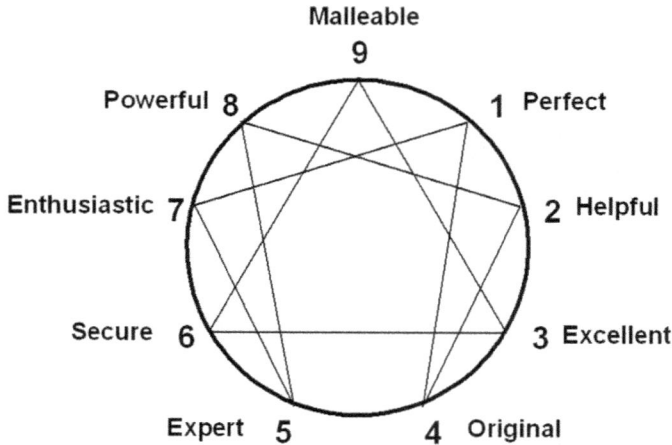

Malleable
9

Powerful 8   1 Perfect

Enthusiastic 7   2 Helpful

Secure 6   3 Excellent

Expert 5   4 Original

Figure 8

Type Nine is the cornerstone upon which the Enneagram is built because it repre-sents the natural tendency of all people (not just Nines) to succumb to the down-ward pull of unconsciousness whereby our awareness of ourselves, others, and the world is diminished. Part of this downward pull is the natural operation of the human brain where only a limited amount of data and information can be kept in conscious-awareness so this data and information are constantly being migrated to longer-term memory locations in our brains. A second part of the downward pull is our fear of self-knowledge and the mind's gate-keeping function that *blocks* unwanted thoughts, memories, and cognitive and emotional content from entering conscious-ness by redirecting our focus and attention outward toward actions and interactions in the world. Over time, things that are blocked from consciousness become less and less accessible to us as they are buried beneath myriad layers of experiences and cognitive and emotional data that we *prefer* to think about. Type Nine is also the point upon which the Enneagram symmetries are anchored in the sense that the configuration of the nine types can be divided into left-right, top-bottom, and tri-adic group symmetries. The left-right and top-bottom symmetries were originally described by Naranjo.[22]

Using type Nine as the cornerstone to which these symmetries are anchored, we see that the types positioned on the left side of the Enneagram are emotionally *dry* and can be thought of using the image of an arid, parched, resource-less desert.[23] Type Nine is the least emotionally dry, and Fives are the very most emotionally arid and dry, which often manifests itself as an apathetic (and even sardonic) attitude toward themselves, others, and the world.

Left-Right Symmetries

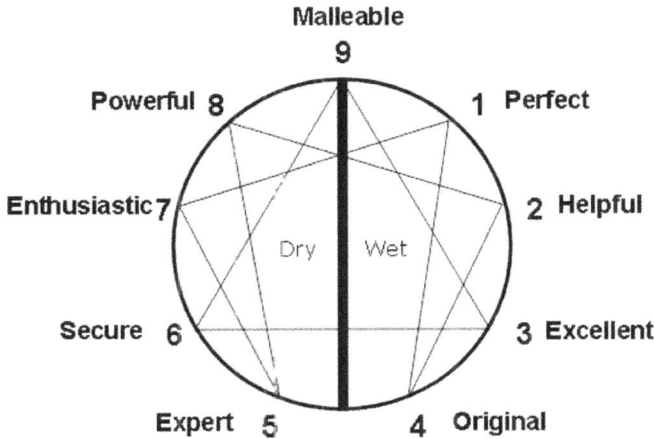

Figure 9

The types positioned on the right side of the Enneagram are emotionally *wet* and can be thought of using the image of the constant motion of water in the ocean, where waves are formed, rise, and then disappear into the collective body of water once again. Type Nine is the least emotionally wet and turbulent and Fours are the very most emotionally wet and turbulent. The types positioned on the left side of the Enneagram tend to be more anti-socially oriented and rebellious, with type Nine being the least rebellious and type Fives being the most rebellious. The types positioned on the right side of the Enneagram tend to be more socially oriented and seductive, with type Nine being the least seductive and type Fours being the most seductive.

Viewed from another perspective, the types on the top of the Enneagram have much different characteristics than the types on the bottom of the graph, and the nine types positioned around the Enneagram can be grouped into three groups of three that are sometimes called triads. Let's begin by discussing the top-bottom symmetries.[24]

Top-Bottom and Triadic Group Symmetries

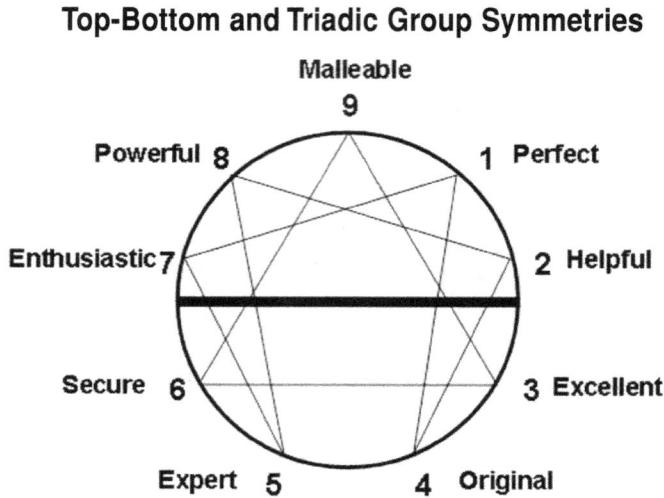

Figure 10

The types positioned at the top of the Enneagram tend to be viewed as more "normal" by the world because the characteristics of their personality tend to *mimic* psychological health by mapping more closely to socio-cultural norms. In addition, these types often seem to be more contented with themselves and their lot in life. The types positioned at the bottom of the Enneagram tend to be viewed as more "unusual" by the world because the characteristics of their personality tend to *mimic* psychological pathology because they tend to question (and oppose) socio-cultural norms. These types often seem to be more discontented with themselves and their lot in life.

The types at the top of the Enneagram are focused outward toward the world and have a psychological *resistance* to introspection and self-exploration – a non-inwardness that manifests itself as a lack of self-awareness and unconsciousness about underlying patterns, processes, and structures within themselves. They tend to turn a "deaf ear" and a "blind eye" to their pain, hurting, and the inner contents of their emotions and cognitive life. The types at the bottom of the Enneagram are focused inwardly toward the world within and have a profound and poignant awareness about the fact that "something's missing" in life. They tend to be acutely aware of their inner pain, despair, the inner contents of their emotions and mind and cannot help but notice underlying patterns, processes, and structures within themselves.

The nine types positioned around the Enneagram can also be viewed as three interrelated groups of three. Types Two, Three, and Four form the Heart Group and emerge from the Emotional Brain which resides in the Amygdala and related neurophysiologic and sensory structures. Heart types tend to be past-oriented because emotions are reactions to events, situations, and experiences that have already occurred. Types Five, Six, and Seven form the Head Group and emerge from the Cognitive Brain which resides in the Neocortex and related neurophysiologic and sensory structures. Head types tend to be future-oriented because their ideas and intellectual concepts are not bound to the realities of the past or present (space and time) and consequently they can travel far into the future. Types Eight, Nine, and One form the Action Group and emerge from the Sensory Brain which resides in the Brainstem and related neurophysiologic and sensory structures. Action types tend to be present-oriented because they are inextricably bound to the immediate context of what's going on in the world around them, including *where* things are happening and *who* is involved.

Figure 11 shows a final set of Enneagram symmetries and paradoxical relationships that was originally described by Naranjo.[25] Let's begin by discussing the notion of paradox. A paradox is a statement or proposition that *seems* self-contradictory or absurd, but in reality it reveals an underlying pattern, structure, process, reality, or truth. There are six paradoxical symmetries shown in Figure 11 by dotted lines where seemingly unrelated (or even oppositional) points around the Enneagram actually possess a paradoxical relationship with each other. In other words, Enneagram types that appear to be radically different in terms of surface traits, Tacit Creeds, and underlying motivations, are actually *paradoxical reflections* of each other in ways that are predicted by Naranjo's theory of the Enneagram.

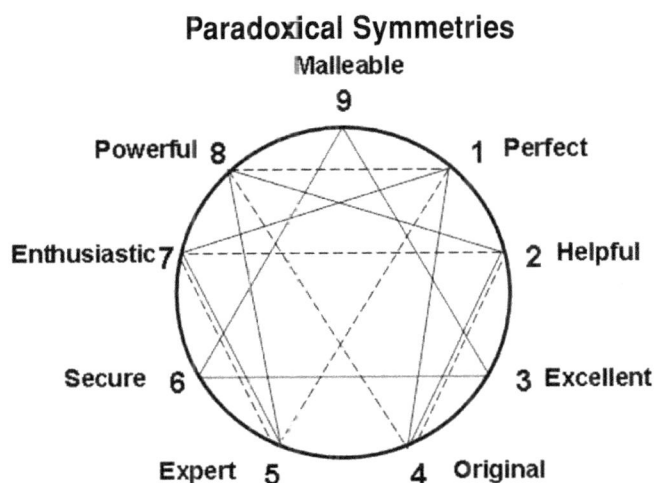

Figure 11

To begin with, what could be more different than the perfectionistic rule-keeping of type Ones and the intense desire for knowledge and expertise of the type Five personality? But on closer examination type Ones exhibit an externally focused perfectionism on people and the environment, while type Fives exhibit an internally focused perfectionism where they deepen and refine their knowledge in an endless search for intellectual perfectionism. In much the same way, type Fours and Eights exhibit very different surface traits, Tacit Creeds, and underlying motivations; but they are paradoxical opposites around the issue of *emotions* and *sensitivity*. Whereas type Fours tend to be the most emotionally sensitive of the Enneagram types and seek *intensity* through the deeper (and often darker) emotions of life rather than action, type Eights tend to be the least emotionally sensitive of the Enneagram types (turning their emotions off) and instead seek *intensity* through action and dominating their world. Type Twos and Sevens also exhibit very different surface traits, Tacit Creeds, and underlying motivations; but they too are paradoxical opposites around the issues of *manipulation* and *seduction*. Whereas type Twos manipulate and seduce people with warm, helpful, generosity with the goal of building dependencies, type Sevens manipulate and seduce people with their myriad ideas, smooth words, and intellectual breadth with the goal of impressing others with their renaissance perspective on life.

The three types that compose the Inner Triangle of the Enneagram have a slightly different form of paradoxical point. The Eight-One Paradox straddles type Nine, where Eights and Ones are isomorphic images of each other, with type Ones being too moral and type Eights being too anti-moral like laws un-to-themselves. Type Nines tend to be pulled along the axis of this paradox and can embody either set of characteristics if the environment forces them to. The Seven-Five Paradox straddles type Six, where Sevens and Fives are isomorphic images of each other, with type Sevens exhibiting too much doing and not enough thinking-through the consequences of their actions, and type Fives exhibiting too much thinking and not enough doing and acting in the world. Type Sixes tend to be pulled along the axis of this paradox and can embody either set of characteristics if their uncertainty in facing the future forces them to. The Four-Two Paradox straddles type Three, where Fours and Twos are isomorphic images of each other, with type Fours focusing too heavily on self-reflection and introspection and type Twos focusing too heavily on building and sustaining relationships. Type Threes tend to be pulled along the axis of this paradox and can embody either set of characteristics if issues with their identity force them to.

Finally, because of the neighboring relationships and related positions of the nine points on the Enneagram, each point is a hybrid of the two types on either side of it. For example, the type Four is a hybrid of the Five and the Three, and type Eights are actually a hybrid of types Seven and Nine. This hybrid relationship is the theoretical basis for what some Enneagram theorists call "wings."

CONFLICT PROCESSING STRATEGIES, GOTTMAN, ATTITUDES TOWARD SOCIO-CULTURAL CHANGE

This section discusses the Conflict Processing Strategies and how they relate to John Gottman's work. It also discusses the Attitudes toward Socio-Cultural Change for the nine types.

Conflict Processing Strategies

There are three conflict processing strategies used by the nine Enneagram types. These are the: a) *objective* strategy, b) *reactive* strategy, and the c) *reframing* strategy. These three strategies are distributed around the Enneagram and reveal a larger pattern of personality that I first learned from my teachers Don Riso and Russ Hudson. A more general discussion of this concept is presented here, and then we show how it applies to the nine types in the sections that follow.

Conflict Processing Strategies

Malleable
Reframing

9

Powerful 8
Reactive

1 Perfect
Objective

ACTION

Enthusiastic 7
Reframing

2 Helpful
Reframing

HEAD   HEART

Secure 6
Reactive

3 Excellent
Objective

Expert 5
Objective

4 Original
Reactive

Figure 12

People who exhibit the *objective* strategy tend to affirm and validate each other's right to have the feelings and views that they do with mutual respect, even if they don't agree with them. This problem-solving style is most typical of types One, Three, and Five who deal with conflict in relationships by putting their emotions and subjective feelings on the back burner, and resolving their differences by being objective, logical and effective. More specifically, type Ones want to work within the structures, systems and formal rules of the context or relationship, type Fives tend to reject the structures, systems and formal rules and work outside the established boundaries, and type Threes want to do both; e.g., they bend the structures, systems and formal rules to achieve their goals and needs.

People who exhibit the *reactive* strategy tend to exhibit strong reactions and explosive episodes that are a small part of an otherwise warm, supportive, loving relationship. They tend to argue through and openly share their thoughts and feelings with each other, which serve as a catalyst for both their positive and negative interactions. This problem-solving style is most typical of types Four, Six, and Eight who tend to react emotionally then look for an emotional response that mirrors their issues and concern. Initially, they have strong opinions and emotional reactions and want to vent their feelings *before* moving on in the relationships. More specifically, type Fours look for understanding and support, type Eights deny their need for understanding and support, and type Sixes look for understanding and support and often deny that they need it.

People who exhibit the *reframing* strategy tend to minimize conflict, make light of their differences rather than resolving them, and appeal to a basic philosophy that they share about their relationship or context. This problem-solving style is most typical of types Two, Seven, and Nine who deal with conflict and dissatisfaction in relationships by "reframing" them in some positive way that emphasizes a brighter, constructive, more uplifting way of "seeing" life – in other words, the glass is always half full. They have a difficult time seeing the destructive, painful, and negative aspects of themselves, others, and the world, and tend to have a problem balancing their own needs with the needs of others. More specifically, type Twos focus on the needs of others, type Sevens focus on their own needs, and type Nines focus on the needs of both others and themselves with neither getting filled adequately.

Links to Gottman's Research

Over the last 20 years, thousands of couples have participated in the research conducted by John Gottman.[26] He asks them to sit in a room and discuss any topic they want for 30 minutes while the research team video-tapes the couple's discussion.

Because 55% of communication is visual (body language), 38% is tone of voice, and only 7% is word choice, the researchers can analyze facial expressions, and shifts in tone (frequency) of voice in the video, along with other key indicators like increased heart rate. These extensive data confirm that people accurately read and respond to the emotional messages we send each other, *not* just the words we use. Once the couple's pattern of interaction in a video is fully analyzed, Gottman and his colleagues can predict with 94% accuracy whether or not the couple will still be married in 15 years.[27]

Gottman's research has identified three types of stable, happy relationships: a) validating, b) volatile, and c) conflict-avoiding, but all manifest a 5-1 ratio of constructive to destructive exchanges in their pattern of interaction – what we call the 80-20 Rule.[28] His data show that unhealthy relationships must *evolve* into some combination of these three because they are *universal* ways of maintaining the 80-20 balance. It is important to note that Gottman's research is not just his opinion about how to have a good marriage. These research findings are far more reliable than the intuitions and hunches of most popular self-help writers, marriage counselors, or therapists.

But while Gottman's body of research correctly identifies the empirical basis of the actions and interactions that frustrate and undermine relationships, it offers no systematic model for understanding and changing the underlying patterns of tacit beliefs, assumptions, and opinions that motivate these destructive behaviors and patterns-of-interaction. In other words, while Gottman's research powerfully describes the behaviors and the patterns-of-interaction that create problems in relationships, it does not address the underlying patterns of personality and belief structures that motivate these behaviors.[29] The Breckenridge Enneagram provides a "window" into the underlying mechanisms that cause problems in relationships. More specifically, the type of relationship that is most effective for two people is *directly linked* to the destructive and constructive forces of their respective personalities *and* the behaviors and patterns-of-interaction described by Gottman's research. The three Conflict Processing Strategies are listed below.

- *Objective Style (Type One, Three, Five)*
- *Reactive Style (Type Four, Six, Eight)*
- *Reframing Style (Type Two, Seven, Nine)*

Notice that each of the three effective Conflict Processing Strategies is composed of three of the nine types distributed across the three triads of the Breckenridge Enneagram. In other words, the *Objective Style* of relationships contains type One

(Action Group), type Three (Heart Group), and type Five (Head Group). The *Reactive Style* contains type Four (Heart Group), type Six (Head Group), and type Eight (Action Group). The *Reframing Style* contains type Two (Heart Group), type Seven (Head Group) and type Nine (Action Group). The three kinds of effective working relationships are alternative forms of problem-solving strategies that are linked to personality type.

Most people seem to have a primary, secondary, and tertiary hybrid of the three styles and often move from one style to another during a single discussion or argument. More specifically, each person has a preferred style based on their personality and they tend to *draw* the others into that form of problem-solving. A path forward to create more effective patterns-of-interaction in a relationship would be to consciously agree with others to embrace or use the third (non-preferred) problem-solving style to avoid the autopilot responses of personality and the destructive emotional messages that so often result. In other words, if your personality is characterized by type Four (Reactive Style) and the other person's personality is characterized by type Nine (Reframing Style), then the Objective Style will represent "neutral ground" upon which to process conflict that arises from these two very different ways of seeing themselves, each other, and the world.

Attitudes toward Socio-Cultural Change

In the section on Enneagram symmetries, we discussed the differing attitudes that the nine types have toward socio-cultural norms based on their position around the Enneagram. The types on the right side of the Enneagram tended to be more *socially* oriented and those on the left tend to be more *antisocially* oriented. In much the same way, the types on the top of the Enneagram tended to be viewed as more "normal" by the world and those on the bottom tended to be seen as more "unusual." Using a typology developed by Karen Horney where people tend to exhibit *compliant*, *aggressive*, and *withdrawn* attitudes toward other people, I will now present a more general discussion of the ways in which the differences between the nine types manifest themselves as differing attitudes toward socio-cultural *change* that occurs in families; social groups; and government, non-profit, and for-profit organizations (see Figure 13).

Attitudes toward Socio-Cultural Change

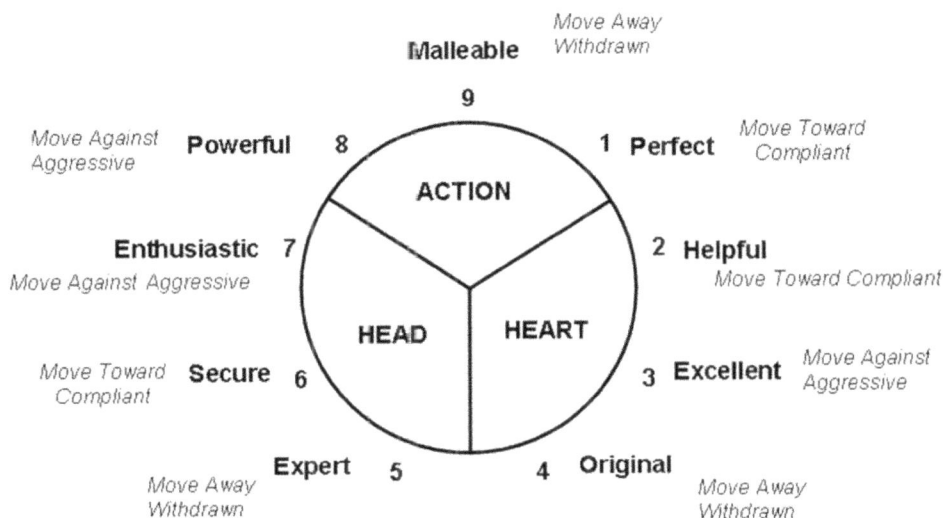

Move Away
Withdrawn

Malleable

9

Move Against   Powerful   8
Aggressive

1 Perfect   Move Toward
Compliant

ACTION

Enthusiastic   7

2 Helpful

Move Against Aggressive

Move Toward Compliant

HEAD   HEART

Move Toward   Secure   6
Compliant

3 Excellent   Move Against
Aggressive

Expert   5

4 Original

Move Away
Withdrawn

Move Away
Withdrawn

Figure 13

When a person of any given Enneagram type *agrees* with, *supports*, and *endorses* a set of socio-cultural changes; this is often because the resulting change in the configuration of their context will: a) give them the results they want, b) be in their best interest personally or professionally, and c) more closely map-to the cognitive and emotional configuration of their inner experience – how they have come to see themselves, others, and the world through the See-Do-Get Process. Consequently, their actions and interactions during the processes of change and transition will tend to be shaped and defined by: a) their Tacit Creed, b) the underlying deficiency-drivers and growth-motivators, c) the level of stress and potential for embarrassment and threat within the context of the change, and d) their level of psychological health, which is reflected in the extent to which their actions and interactions follow the 80-20 Rule.

But when people *do not agree* with, *support*, or *endorse* the socio-cultural change because: a) it *will not* give them the results they want, b) *is not* in their best interest personally or professionally, and c) the change *threatens* to disrupt the mapping (or state-of-equilibrium) between the configuration of their context and the cognitive and emotional configuration of their inner world; this creates *survival anxiety* and *learning* anxiety, especially during times of *transition* when the change has already occurred and people are going through the process of psychologically adjusting to that change.

So in the face of *survival* anxiety and *learning* anxiety, the actions and interactions of people who *don't* agree with, support, or endorse the change will tend to reflect the deficiency-driven form of their Tacit Creed because their level of stress is higher; *in addition* they will exhibit one of three types of attitudes toward socio-cultural change:

- A Compliant attitude
- An Aggressive attitude, or
- A Withdrawn attitude

As Horney points out, the attitudes of being *compliant*, *aggressive*, and *withdrawn* are an interdependent whole, where people ideally ought to be able to hold (and express) all three attitudes and use them at will in the appropriate situation. There is a time and place to *accept* socio-cultural changes, to overtly *fight* them, and to *disengage* from them. But for most people, *one* of the three attitudes tends to dominate their actions and interactions and this is related to their Enneagram type. Let's discuss each attitude in more detail.

Compliant types have a need to be *useful* and of *service* and tend to be more willing to comply, conform, cooperate, and assent to the requests and requirements of others, especially those in authority. When they do not *agree* with, *support*, or *endorse* a socio-cultural change, but are nonetheless *required* to conform to it, they often make an *external* commitment to the change and try to *support* those who are leading (and supporting) the change process. But Compliant types tend not to make an *internal* commitment to the change unless the "gap" between: a) the new configuration in their context, and b) the cognitive and emotional configuration of their inner experience is narrowed *and* they begin to "see" that the changes will: a) give them the results they want, and will b) be in their best interest personally and professionally. Type Ones, Twos, and Sixes are compliant types.

- Type Ones tend to be compliant with socio-cultural change that they don't agree with or support because their Tacit Creed "I must be perfect" drives them to comply with the structures, systems and formal rules defined by external contexts; and they tend to move toward people who support (or lead) the change process and try to improve and correct them.
- Type Twos tend to be compliant with socio-cultural change that they don't agree with or support because their Tacit Creed "I must be helpful" drives them to be useful and of service to others; and they tend to move toward people who support (or lead) the change process to avoid rupturing key relationships.

- Type Sixes tend to be compliant with socio-cultural change that they don't agree with or support because their Tacit Creed "I must be secure" drives them to minimize the risk and uncertainty of surviving in that context; and they tend to move toward people who support (or lead) the change process to identify hidden meanings and intentions.

Aggressive types need to have an *impact* and make an *impression* on their world and want to assert *their* will and desires to get the results they want, so they tend to be much less willing to comply, conform, cooperate, and assent to the requests and requirements of others, even those in authority. When they do not *agree* with, *support*, or *endorse* socio-cultural change, but are nonetheless *required* to conform to it, they tend to reject both external and internal commitment to the change, and oppose those who are leading (and supporting) the change process. Aggressive types will not make either an external or internal commitment to the change unless the "gap" between: a) the new configuration in their context, and b) the cognitive and emotional configuration of their inner experience is narrowed and they begin to "see" the changes as: a) giving them the results they want, and b) being in their best interest personally and professionally. Type Threes, Sevens, and Eights are Aggressive types.

- Type Threes tend to be aggressive toward socio-cultural change that they don't agree with or support because their Tacit Creed "I must be excellent" drives them to develop approaches that are more effective than those proposed; and they tend to move against people who support (or lead) the change process to compete with them.
- Type Sevens tend to be aggressive toward socio-cultural change that they don't agree with or support because their Tacit Creed "I must be enthusiastic" drives them to consider myriad alternatives to the proposed changes; and they tend to move against people who support (or lead) the change process because they believe their own needs are not being met.
- Type Eights tend to be aggressive toward socio-cultural change that they don't agree with or support because their Tacit Creed "I must be powerful" drives them to dominate their environment; and they tend to move against people who support (or lead) the change process to directly oppose their authority and leadership.

Withdrawn types have a need to *maintain a distance* and *be separate from* their world, so they tend to *disengage* from socio-cultural change, but not directly communicate this to those around them, especially those in authority. When they do not *agree* with, *support*, or *endorse* socio-cultural change but are nonetheless required to conform to it, they will tend to leave the issue of external commitment unstated, reject making an internal commitment, and *disengage* from those who are leading (and supporting) the change process. Withdrawn types will not make either *internal* or *external* commitment to the change unless the "gap" between: a) the new configuration in their context, and b) the cognitive and emotional configuration of their inner experience is narrowed and they begin to "see" the changes as: a) giving them the results they want, and b) being in their best interest personally and professionally. As a general rule, Withdrawn types are much less interested in fitting in and belonging than the other types and often maintain a distance even where they *agree* with, *support*, and *endorse* the socio-cultural norms of their context. Type Fours, Fives, and Nines are Withdrawn types.

- Type Nines tend to withdraw from socio-cultural change that they don't agree with or support because their Tacit Creed "I must be malleable" drives them to go through the motions, avoid conflict, and not "rock the boat." They *inwardly* disengage from people who support (or lead) the change process, but outwardly create the impression that they'll go along with the change process by not outwardly opposing *or* supporting it.

- Type Fives tend to withdraw and disengage from socio-cultural change that they don't agree with or support because their Tacit Creed "I must be an expert" drives them to analyze and evaluate the change model and process. They inwardly disengage from people who support (or lead) the change process and outwardly exhibit an iconoclastic attitude toward the change.

- Type Fours tend to withdraw from socio-cultural change that they don't agree with or support because their Tacit Creed "I must be original" drives them to be different and unique. They inwardly disengage from people who support (or lead) the change to develop alternative original approaches to the change process.

DOWNWARD SPIRAL OF STRIVING AND UPWARD PATH OF BECOMING

This section describes some of the key elements of the Downward Spiral of Striving. Notice the direction of the arrows within the Enneagram. For example, starting at type Four, the arrows proceed to type Two, then to type Eight, and then on to Five, Seven, One, and then back to type Four. Or starting at type Nine, the arrows go to Six, Three, and then back to type Nine.

**Downward Spiral of Striving
(Deficiency-Driven, Compulsive, Inauthentic,
Alienated, Dependent, Fear-Based)**

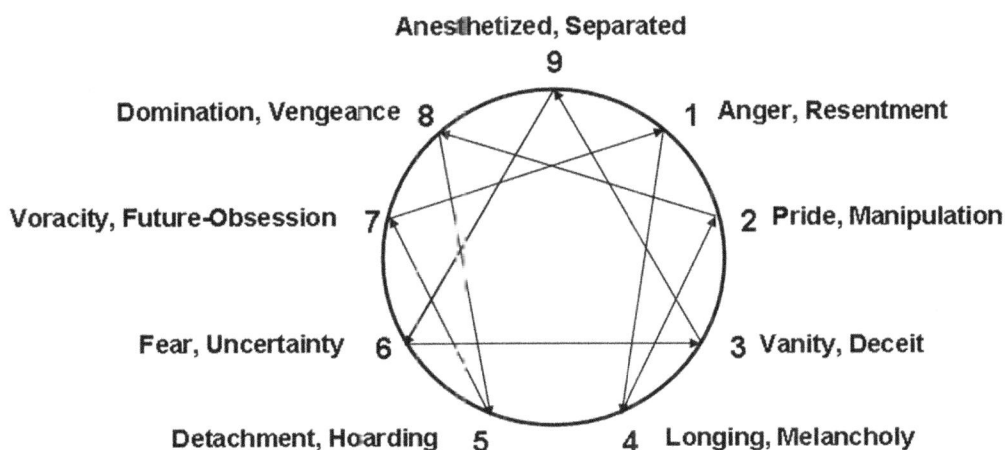

Anesthetized, Separated

Domination, Vengeance 8

Anger, Resentment 1

Voracity, Future-Obsession 7

Pride, Manipulation 2

Fear, Uncertainty 6

Vanity, Deceit 3

Detachment, Hoarding 5

Longing, Melancholy 4

Figure 14

As mentioned previously, the positioning of the nine types around the Enneagram graph is not a random collection of personality styles. Rather, it is an organized and dynamic pattern of personality structures that have well-defined neighboring relationships where the further around the Enneagram one moves the more different each type becomes, until those that appear on the *opposite* side of the graph are actually polar opposites. So the intra-psychic pattern established by the arrows for each of the nine types reveals deeper insights into the psychological processes and dynamic nature of the nine personality types. Let's discuss a few of the more important implications of this part of the Breckenridge Enneagram model.

First, when most people are faced with embarrassment or threat, their *natural*, autopilot response will often be in the direction of the arrows shown in the Downward Spiral of Striving. But while the nine patterns of arrows indicate *natural* tendencies and responses for the nine types, they are not fixed and determined, and rather, reveal probable ways that people will act given the positioning of the nine types around the Enneagram. It is important to note that the nine natural patterns indicated by the arrows can be powerfully shaped (and altered) by the See-Do-Get Process interacting with external forces in our context to form new patterns-of-interaction and directionality around the Enneagram.

Second, the Downward Spiral of Striving is (first and foremost) an indicator of the *overall direction* of our lives in terms of Maslow's two natural human forces and the never-ending series of choices between the force-for-safety and the force-for-growth. It is also an indicator of the extent to which our lives manifest the 80-20 Rule, where our interactions with others along the Downward-Spiral will tend to be deficiency-driven, compulsive, inauthentic, alienated, dependent, and fear-based. Over time, our behaviors and emotional responses to others *solidify* into robust patterns-of-interaction that go on autopilot, slip below the surface of conscious awareness, and powerfully shape the direction of our relationships and our lives. These patterns-of-interaction are an *objective* indicator of the extent to which the two human forces for growth or safety control our lives, *because* our behaviors and emotional responses to others can be observed and evaluated using the 80-20 Rule.

Third, it is important to remember that it's not just the number that an arrow points to along the Downward Spiral of Striving that's an indicator of the two human forces of safety or growth – it's whether or not the actions and interaction of a person *at that point* are deficiency-driven or growth-motivated. In other words, it's a *combination* of the behaviors and attitudes associated with that number; *and* the extent to which the person is either deficiency-driven or growth-motivated. So at a deeper level, the Downward Spiral of Striving and the Upward Path of Becoming are simply *surface-manifestations* of the more fundamental principle of Maslow's two human forces and the never-ending series of existential choices that we make for either safety or growth.

Let's discuss the Upward Path of Becoming as a counter point to the Downward Spiral of Striving. Notice that the direction of the arrows within the Enneagram is different from Figure 14. Now, starting at type Four, the arrows proceed to type One, then go to type Seven, and on to Five, Eight, Two, and then back to type Four. Or starting at type Nine, the arrows go to Three, Six, and then back to type Nine.

This represents a *different ordering* of the same set of personality structures positioned around the Enneagram. The Upward Path of Becoming changes the *sequence* in which the nine types emerge, but leaves the characteristics of the nine types and their underlying deficiency-drivers and growth-motivators unchanged. Moving in this direction over long periods of time creates new intra-psychic patterns-of-interaction that begin to reshape the autopilot responses of our personality, and this manifests itself *objectively* as growth-motivated patterns-of-interaction that positively change our relationships and our responses to life's circumstances. Let's discuss the most important implications of this part of the Breckenridge Enneagram model.

Upward Path of Becoming
(Growth-Motivated, Self-Determined, Authentic,
Reunited, Autonomous, Trust-Based)

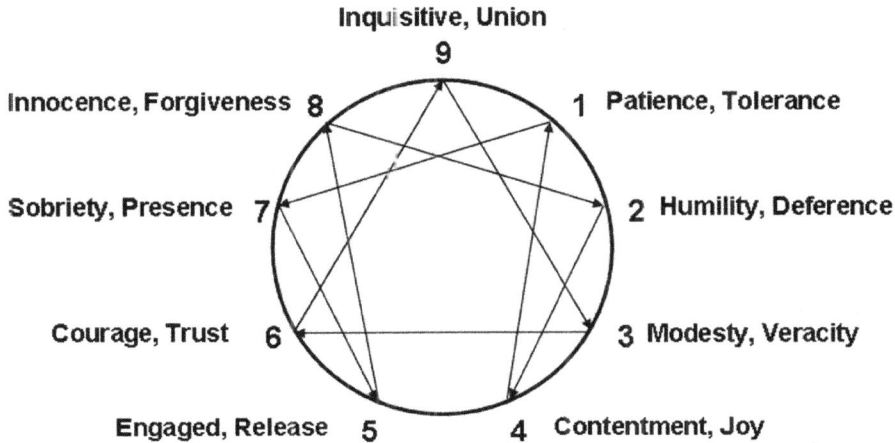

Inquisitive, Union
9

Innocence, Forgiveness 8

Patience, Tolerance 1

Sobriety, Presence 7

2 Humility, Deference

Courage, Trust 6

3 Modesty, Veracity

Engaged, Release 5

4 Contentment, Joy

Figure 15

First, when faced with embarrassment or threat, people who are on the Upward Path of Becoming do not respond out of the autopilot, deficiency-driven reactions of their personality. Rather, they *consciously choose* responses that are appropriate for the situations and challenges they face. By consciously shaping how they see themselves, others, and the world through the See-Do-Get Process, they can deconstruct (and ultimately transcend) the natural tendencies and autopilot responses of their personality. Remember that the nine natural autopilot patterns-of-interaction indicated by the arrows of the Downward Spiral of Striving can be *redirected* by the See-Do-Get Process *interacting with* external forces in our context to form new growth-motivated patterns-of-interaction.

Second, the Upward Path of Becoming is (first and foremost) an indicator of the overall direction of our lives in terms of Maslow's two natural human forces, and is an indicator of the extent to which our lives manifest the 80-20 Rule. In other words, it is a measure of the extent to which our actions and interactions tend to be growth-motivated, self-determined, authentic, reunited, autonomous, and trust-based. Over time, these healthy behaviors and emotional responses *solidify* into robust patterns-of-interaction that go on autopilot and slip below the surface of conscious awareness, so the new growth-motivated responses happen as naturally as the old ineffective responses once did. In fact, deep, sustainable, personal change *happens to us* in the sense that it emerges *indirectly* as a natural consequence of living out the Upward Path of Becoming. This becomes an *objective* indicator of the extent to which the 80-20 Rule is operating in our lives.

Third, it is important to remember that it's not just *the number* that an arrow points to along the Upward Path of Becoming; it's whether or not the actions and interactions of a person *at that point* are deficiency-driven or growth-motivated. In fact, one of the most difficult and pernicious problems to address when pursuing deep personal change is when the sequence of types along the Upward Path of Becoming are deficiency-driven, rather than growth-motivated. Some Enneagram theorists refer to this as the low side of the integrating point, but my own view is that facing and transforming the low side of *all points* along the direction of the Upward Path of Becoming is an enormous challenge that requires a deep commitment to self-awareness, self-control, and self-actualization.

Fourth, the sequence of types in the Upward Path of Becoming indicates areas in which we need to grow in order to "round out" *imbalances* in our personality. Consciously shaping how we see ourselves, others, and the world through the See-Do-Get Process and deconstructing the autopilot tendencies and responses of our personality enable us to build a more complete set of tools using the other eight types, all of which reside within us. Instead of just having our personality-hammer and treating every situation like it's a nail, we can develop a toolbox with different tools that we can more effectively apply to any situation in life.

THE NINE ENNEAGRAM TYPES (SUMMARY CHARTS)

Figure 16 shows the nine types and how they connect to each other on the Breckenridge Enneagram.[30] Each of the nine types lives by a Tacit Creed that can either be *deficiency-driven* by dependency and fear or *growth-motivated* by autonomy and trust. Figure 17 clusters the nine Enneagram types into three groups: Head, Heart, and Action; and lists the Tacit Creed for each of the types.

Figure 17 shows how a given Tacit Creed can either be: a) deficiency-driven by dependency and fear, or b) growth-motivated by autonomy and trust. The deficiency-drivers are viewed as being inappropriate in most cultures, with social sanctions against expressing them in personal and professional relationships, so they tend to be suppressed by the Socialized-Self. The growth-motivators are often coveted in a given culture, so people prefer to see their behavior in relationships as being motivated by these more noble characteristics. Figure 18 shows a summary of the Connecting Points.

Breckenridge Enneagram

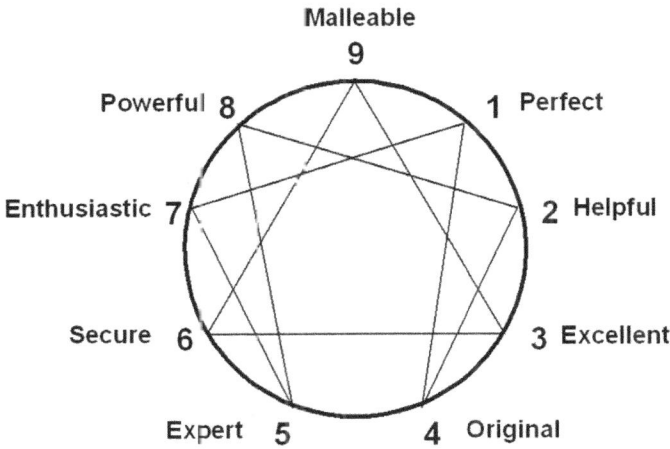

Figure 16

Summary Chart of Tacit Creeds[31]

Type	Group	Tacit Creed	Deficiency, Dependency (Fear)	Growth, Autonomy (Trust)
Two	Heart	I must be helpful	Pride-Manipulation	Humility-Deference
Three	Heart	I must be excellent	Vanity-Deceit	Modesty-Veracity
Four	Heart	I must be original	Longing-Melancholy	Contentment-Joy
Five	Head	I must be an expert	Detachment-Hoarding	Engaged-Release
Six	Head	I must be secure	Fear-Uncertainty	Courage-Trust
Seven	Head	I must be enthusiastic	Voracity-Future-Obsession	Sobriety-Presence
Eight	Action	I must be powerful	Domination-Vengeance	Innocence-Forgiveness
Nine	Action	I must be malleable	Anesthetized-Separated	Inquisitive-Union
One	Action	I must be perfect	Anger-Resentment	Patience-Tolerance

Figure 17

Summary Chart of Connecting Points

Type	Group	Tacit Creed	Striving	Becoming	Paradox	Paradox
Two	Heart	I must be helpful	Eight	Four	Seven	
Three	Heart	I must be excellent	Nine	Six		Two, Four
Four	Heart	I must be original	Two	One	Eight	
Five	Head	I must be an expert	Seven	Eight	One	
Six	Head	I must be secure	Three	Nine		Seven, Five
Seven	Head	I must be enthusiastic	One	Five	Two	
Eight	Action	I must be powerful	Five	Two	Four	
Nine	Action	I must be malleable	Six	Three		Eight, One
One	Action	I must be perfect	Four	Seven	Five	

Figure 18

Heart Group

This section describes the three types that form the Heart Group: Twos, Threes, and Fours. The types in the Heart Group emerge from the Emotional Brain which resides in the Amygdala and other related neurophysiologic and sensory structures. The heart types tend to "lead" with the emotional part of their being, with the neuropsychological functions of the Head and Action Groups playing key support roles. Heart types tend to be past-oriented because emotions are reactions to events, situations, and experiences that have already occurred.

The Tacit Creed for Two is, "I must be helpful" and can be either deficiency-driven by Pride and Manipulation or growth-motivated by Humility and Deference. The look and feel of this personality type, and our *experience* of it, are very different when it is growth-motivated by Humility and Deference, rather than deficiency-driven by Pride and Manipulation.

The Tacit Creed for Three is, "I must be excellent" and can be either deficiency-driven by Vanity and Deceit or growth-motivated by Modesty and Veracity. The look and feel of this personality type, and our *experience* of it, are very different when it is growth-motivated by Modesty and Veracity, rather than deficiency-driven by Vanity and Deceit.

Heart Group
(Emotional Brain, Amygdala, Past-Oriented)

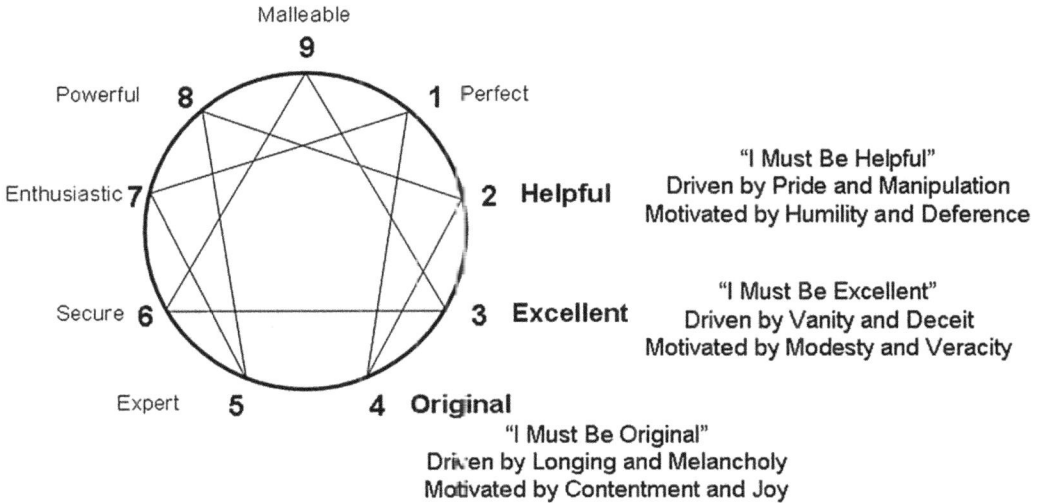

Malleable
9

Powerful **8**   **1** Perfect

Enthusiastic **7**   "I Must Be Helpful"
                            2 Helpful   Driven by Pride and Manipulation
                                            Motivated by Humility and Deference

Secure **6**   "I Must Be Excellent"
                            3 Excellent   Driven by Vanity and Deceit
                                            Motivated by Modesty and Veracity

Expert **5**   **4 Original**
                                "I Must Be Original"
                        Driven by Longing and Melancholy
                        Motivated by Contentment and Joy

Figure 19

The Tacit Creed for Four is, "I must be "original" and can be either deficiency-driven by Longing and Melancholy or growth-motivated by Contentment and Joy. The look and feel of this personality type, and our *experience* of it, are very different when it is growth-motivated by Contentment and Joy, rather than deficiency-driven by Longing and Melancholy.

The major center of the emotional brain (the Amygdala) is an almond shaped mass of nuclei located deep within the human brain that appraises situations from an emotional perspective and stores that information in long-term emotional memory. More specifically, long-term memories about key situations in life are not formed immediately, (rather) the Amygdala slowly and unconsciously summarizes and assimilates that information into long-term memory as a kind of emotional abstract (or lesson-learned) about that action, interaction, or situation. This emotional summary becomes a fairly fixed and permanent part of our recollections about key events in our lives.

Emotional memory also powerfully shapes our history and identity. In many ways, who we are emotionally reveals something very deep about who we are as human beings *regardless* of what our dominant Enneagram type is. Neurophysiologic research and studies on the nature of emotions have shown that human emotions are *universal* and can be identified by the facial expressions and body language that people display. Emotions from the emotional brain are experienced by all people, in all times, in all cultures; and the heart types are tuned-in to the constant ebb and flow of this part of the human experience. What changes from culture to culture are the rules for expressing and displaying those emotions. It is important to remember that the Heart space where types Two, Three, and Four live, is known to (and experienced by) all nine types, and powerfully shapes and defines how we see ourselves, others, and the world through the See-Do-Get Process.

Key Question

Twos, Threes, and Fours tend to be overly-preoccupied with the key question of human existence, "How do I find an identity?", although the three types tend to answer this same question in a very different way. It's not that the other types don't care about finding an identity it's just *not* the central concern of their lives and the focus of their values.

Twos tend to find their identity in relationships, where family, friends and working associates become defining elements of their lives. Threes tend to find their identity in defining and emulating standards of excellence which become an objective measurement of who they are and what they've achieved in life. Fours tend to find their identity by looking within – through deep introspection and self-exploration.

Heart Group
(Key Question: How Do I Find an Identity?)

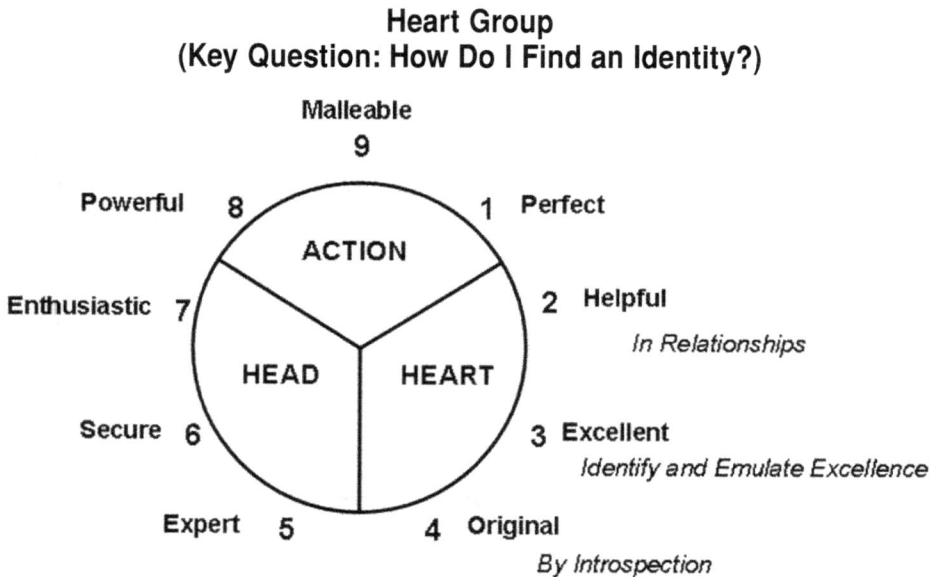

Figure 20

The heart types also ask the existential question that's common to all nine types, "How do I get the results that I want from my one-trip through life?" This key question forces types Twos, Threes, and Fours to see the *outcome* of their lives within the context of their past experiences and emotions.

Conflict Processing Strategies

Figure 21 shows the Conflict Processing Strategies for the Heart Group. Type Twos tend to use the *reframing* strategy where they deal with conflict and disappointment in relationships by "reframing" them in some positive way that emphasizes a brighter, more uplifting way of "seeing" life, and tend to have a problem balancing their own needs with the needs of others. More specifically, Twos tend to focus on identifying and meeting the needs of others, rather than their own needs.

Heart Group
(Conflict Processing Strategies)

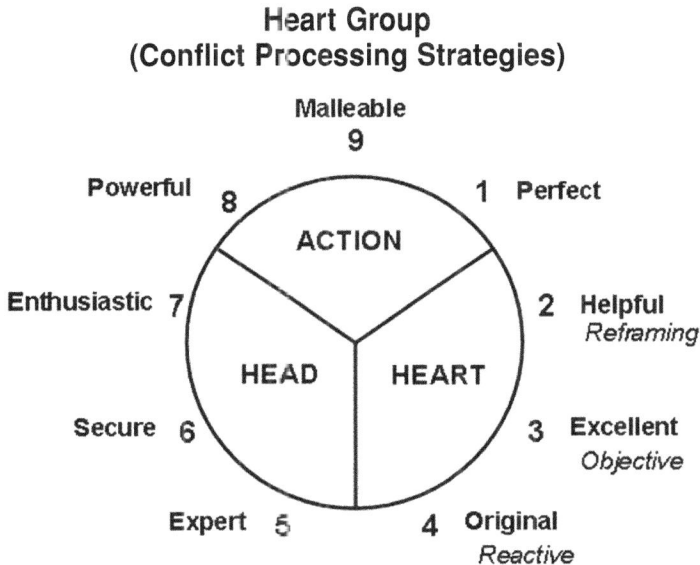

Figure 21

Type Threes use the *objective* strategy where they deal with conflict in relationships by putting their emotions and subjective feelings on the back burner, and resolving their differences by being objective, logical and effective. They will either work within the system and established rules of the relationship, reject them, or otherwise bend the rules and system to suit their needs. Type Fours tend to use the *reactive* strategy where they deal with conflict by reacting emotionally and then looking for an emotional response that mirrors their concern. They have strong opinions and emotional reactions and want to vent with their feelings and look for understanding and support *before* moving on in relationships.

Attitude toward Socio-Cultural Change

Let's review the attitudes toward socio-cultural change for the three types that make-up the Heart Group and see how they interact with each other. Note that type Two is a Compliant type, while Threes are an Aggressive type, and Fours are a With-drawn type.

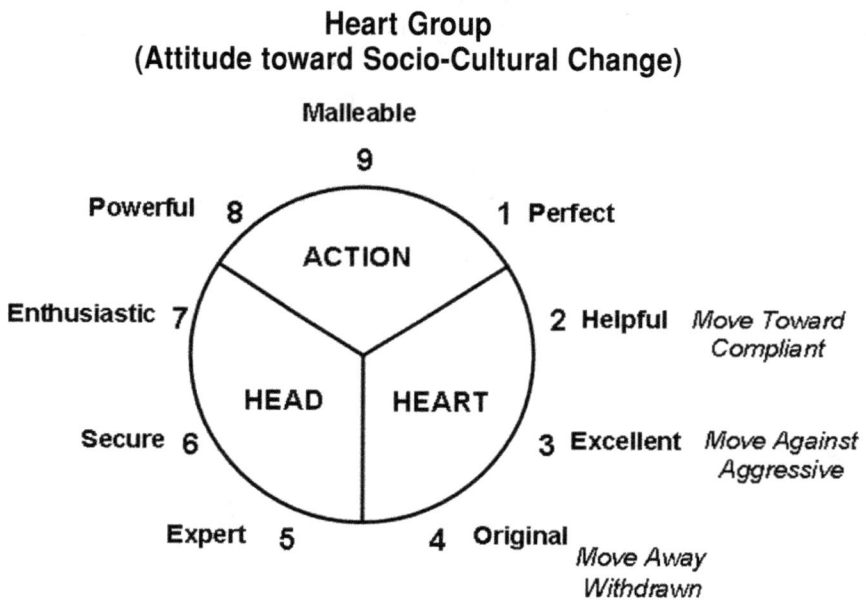

Heart Group
(Attitude toward Socio-Cultural Change)

Figure 22

Type Twos tend to be compliant with socio-cultural change that they don't agree with or support because their Tacit Creed "I must be helpful" drives them to be useful and of service to others; and they tend to move toward people who support (or lead) the change process to avoid rupturing key relationships. Type Threes tend to be aggressive toward socio-cultural change that they don't agree with or support because their Tacit Creed "I must be excellent" drives them to develop approaches that are more effective than those proposed; and they tend to move against people who support (or lead) the change process to compete with them. Type Fours tend to withdraw from socio-cultural change that they don't agree with or support because their Tacit Creed "I must be original" drives them to be different and unique. They inwardly disengage from people who support (or lead) the change to develop alternative original approaches to change.

Type Two (I Must Be Helpful)

When Twos are at their best, they are helpful, empathic, warm, supportive, compassionate, sensitive, and nurturing. They enjoy being close with (and connected to) people and focus on others' well-being by identifying and meeting their needs. When under pressure, they become overly intimate and intrusive, prone to building dependencies – they give to get and impose their will on others through flattery, guilt, and manipulation.

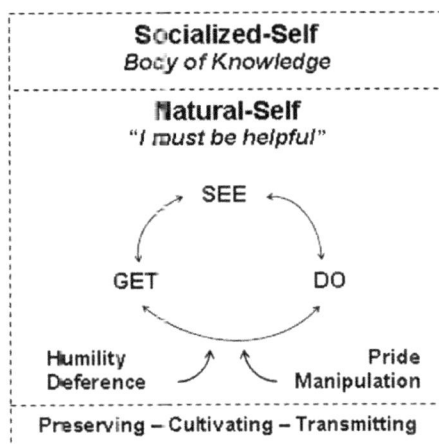

Figure 23

Take a few minutes to read (and reflect on) Figure 23. The very top of Figure 23 is made up of a person's Socialized-Self and body of knowledge, which form a major portion of the knowledge-base of their personal paradigm.

Tacit Creed

Twos live by the Tacit Creed "I must be helpful" – a belief that solidifies early in life through countless cycles through the See-Do-Get Process. When they are Deficiency Driven, they are hyper-sensitive to identifying others' needs, desires, interests, and preferences; they constantly evaluate their relationships and the environment for opportunities to "help" others (even when they don't want to be helped) and take pride in how important they are in others' lives. Pride and Manipulation are *inflamed* when under pressure or when they don't get the result they want; e.g., people either object to, or don't respond to, their *insatiable desire* to "help," seduce, and manipulate them with the goal of building dependencies. When under stress, they become "intoxicated" by the power of these emotions and have a *Blind Spot* about the extent to which Pride and Manipulation dominate their lives and create decision-making bias and predictable errors in judgment. While Sevens manipulate and seduce people through their myriad ideas, smooth words, and intellect, Twos manipulate and seduce others through warm, helpful, generosity designed to build dependencies.

When they are Growth Motivated, they are free to question their default way of seeing and their hyper-sensitivity *gives way* to Humility, Deference, and a deep desire to be loving, nurturing, and compassionate toward others for their own sake, rather than to meet their basic need to be needed. Twos begin to see that true (disinterested) compassion, caring, and nurture in relationships cannot exist when they are dependent on others and they experience this insight and new perspective as inner freedom and personal growth. For Twos, the key element of personal growth and building effective relationships is to follow the 80-20 Rule – where eight out of ten interactions with others are characterized by Humility and Deference, rather than Pride and Manipulation.

Lindsey's Story

Lindsey Barker's story is an example of what the Tacit Creed "I must be helpful" looks like when it's solidified in the life of a type Two. Relationships and helping others had always been the single most important thing in Lindsey's life. If you were to ask her, she would go on and on about how much she adores her mom and dad. But somehow even in childhood she felt that if she died tomorrow, people and life would go on, and do just fine without her. She came to believe that her life lacked personal significance, so she had to create a sense of personal significance by being helpful. *Service* was the road to being loved and feeling close to people both inside and outside her home.

Lindsey was the Human Resources (HR) Director at a Long Island company that does primarily defense-related work. During the Clinton years, the company went through numerous and devastating downsizing exercises as they lost one government contract after another. But after September 11, 2001, the tap of defense revenues had once again begun to flow from Washington to the island, and Lindsey had been under the gun to increase the company's staff by thirty percent almost overnight. Not only did she succeed at this superhuman task, but she was able to snatch up some of the most qualified people on Long Island because of her personal connections and how quickly she moved.

The president of the company, Mario, had come to view her as an indispensable part of the management team. Mario was primarily a technical person who had few if any interpersonal skills either in the office or at home. He relied heavily on Lindsey to balance him out and he had come to trust her to handle the human side of the equation for the company, as well as making suggestions on sending his wife flowers when he forgot their anniversary. Over the years, Lindsey had become the informal power behind the throne and everyone knew that going up against her in a meeting or on a major decision was like committing organizational suicide. While she always did it in private, she was the only person in the company who could put Mario in his place.

What the senior staff saw that Lindsey and Mario didn't was her thinly disguised inner conflict between wanting to be a loyal resource for Mario, and wanting to run the company from behind the scenes. Her incessant comments about how brilliant Mario was and what great insight he had in his handling of the *technical* side of the house, left them with an inference that she was running the *administrative* side of the house, including their departments. In meetings, her remarks gave other staff members the sickening feeling of out-and-out flattery, sometimes to the point of brown nosing. Mario didn't seem to object – he probably even enjoyed it.

Lindsey radiated a thinly veiled and inflated sense of pride in her own importance. She gave to get. Even her insistence that Mario allow her to organize the annual staff awards dinner to recognize high-performers in the company seemed to some to be simply a way for her to call attention to herself.

Her family and friends knew her to be compassionate and loving, a person who did not hold back her affection and was always ready to give people a big hug when they were down about something. Lindsey listened well if friends or family were hurting and she always seemed to know how to empathize and support them in a non-judgmental way. But those closest to her were as aware of some of the same Blind Spots as her colleagues were. Lindsey would constantly tell her friends and family how she really wanted to "be there" for them, but when push came to shove, she was noticeably absent when they needed her most.

She was overly aware of her positive and supportive feelings about them, but Lindsey had another, darker side that she seemed to have little or no consciousness of. What those closest to her found most destructive was that every *overt* thing that Lindsey did for them seemed to have a *covert* price of guilt and manipulation attached to it. When they backed away from this type of interaction, Lindsey would redouble her efforts to do more and try to get closer to them. Lindsey was a strange paradox of giving more than any person you knew, but at the same time coming across more emotionally needy than any person you knew. On the rare occasions when someone would confront her about her dark side, she would respond that she was just trying her best to care for them and be there for them. This left most people utterly confused about why her type of "caring" left them feeling like they had just been punched in the stomach.

In addition to the support she provided to Mario and managing the ten-person Human Resources Office, Lindsey taught workshops in coaching skills, personal effectiveness, time management, conflict resolution as well as actually facilitating meetings and situations where there was enormous interpersonal conflict. Lindsey was on the board of directors of the Society of Human Resource Managers, and had made numerous presentations on HR-related areas, in which she was considered a nationally recognized expert on conflict management and personal effectiveness. Lindsey had seen glimpses of her power-driven dark side in meetings and in interactions with family and friends. But she could not yet fully allow this hidden part of her personality into consciousness because it was so contradictory to everything she stood for. Lindsey honestly wanted to know her deeper self better, and to walk the road less traveled, but she didn't know where to find this inner road.

Lindsey's is only one of myriad possible stories that could be told to show what the Tacit Creed "I must be helpful" looks like in the life of an individual. While the surface traits; natural talents and abilities; life-experiences; relationships; socio-cultural setting; ethnicity; gender; and level of psychological health defined by the 80-20 Rule may vary dramatically from person-to-person, the underlying patterns, processes and structures of the stories of all type Twos will be similar.

Emergence of the Tacit Creed

The Two's Natural-Self occupies the bottom portion of Figure 23 where the Tacit Creed (I must be helpful) *emerges* from their innate, inborn temperament and the deep fear associated with the core assumption that they *lack personal significance in life.* The emphasis is on the word "personal" and the tacit conviction (and near certainty) that their lives will have little or no impact, significance, import, consequence or meaning in the lives of other people – the *human* dimension of life. Twos experience this core assumption emotionally as a deep and abiding sense that, "If I died tomorrow, people would do just fine without me, and the lives of the people that matter most to me would go on *unchanged* and without *disruption*."

They *experience* the core assumption with an inner sense of *certainty* as a *self-evident* truth that cannot (and ought not) be: a) questioned, b) objectively or publicly tested, or c) even verbalized. This belief that Twos hold about themselves is a *secret* truth that they hide from themselves, others, and the world. It's undiscussible and its un-discussibility is itself undiscussible. The fear of self-knowledge creates a sense of psychological survival in Twos that threatens their *existence* to the point where the gate-keeping function *blocks* these emotions from entering conscious awareness. But life goes on, and so must the Two. Over time, the emotional and cognitive memories associated with this core assumption are *buried* deeper and deeper within the psyche of type Twos to the point where they become largely inaccessible to conscious awareness and are only experienced at pivotal (*kairos*) moments in life. This *forces* a shift in the Two's focus in order to avoid the embarrassment and threat that the reality of the core assumption creates, so rather than face (or test) the *veracity* of not having personal significance in life, they *displace* the problem by creating personal significance by "being helpful." But trying to be "helpful" can never fill the deep inner need of type Twos because it tries to address an *inner* (existential) issue with *outer* behavior.

Notice how the Tacit Creed can either be *deficiency-driven* by Pride and Manipulation or *growth-motivated* by Humility and Deference and has a very different look and feel depending on whether it's driven or motivated – with the ratio of driven-to-motivated actions and interactions being defined as the 80-20 Rule. When Twos like Lindsey are at their best and are growth-motivated they are helpful, empathic, warm, supportive, compassionate, sensitive, nurturing and enjoy being close to (and connected with) the people in their lives. Their actions and interactions reflect an *intrinsic* (end-oriented) view that sees people as having inherent value, regardless of whether they can gratify the Two's needs. The relationships of healthy Twos reveal a creative way of exploring and discovering life that focuses on meeting *others'* needs and enhancing their well-being, regardless of the pragmatic value that they provide to the Two. In the words of the philosopher Martin Buber, the healthy Two's relationships have an I-Thou view of *people as people*, rather than a pragmatic I-It perspective of *people as interchangeable things* – tools and instruments for gratifying the Two's needs.

When they face embarrassment, threat or are deficiency-driven, Twos become overly intimate and intrusive and are prone to build dependencies. They tend to give-to-get and impose their will on others through flattery, guilt, and manipulation. Their actions and interactions reflect a pragmatic (means-oriented) view that sees people as a way to gratify their needs and get the results they want in life. Deficiency-driven Twos tend to have an I-It perspective of *people as interchangeable things* where others are used to gratify the Two's needs; rather than an I-Thou perspective that "sees" others as having *intrinsic* value and their own needs and perspective on life.

The three Somatic Instincts shown at the very bottom of Figure 23 are the first three levels of Maslow's Hierarchy and form the inner-core and foundation upon which the type Two's personality is built. The Somatic Instincts powerfully shape the overall direction of a Two's life in the sense that their deep inner yearnings and desires unconsciously draw them to people, experiences, careers, relationships, and life situations that will gratify these basic human needs. So the *autopilot needs* of deficiency-driven Preserving Twos can only be gratified by "helping" in areas associated with home, nurture and comfort while Cultivating Twos are unconsciously drawn to gratify their need to "help" in areas associated with belonging and affiliation with groups, and the autopilot needs of Transmitting Two's must be gratified by "helping" people in situations that revolve around love, affection, caring, and communicating their ideas.

Deficiency-Driven

As shown in Figure 23, when Twos are under pressure or are facing embarrassment or threat, Pride and Manipulation become the deficiency-drivers, and the Tacit Creed for people like Lindsey:

- Is like a hyper-sensitivity or allergic reaction to situations that fit the underlying pattern of having to be helpful, which for type Twos means identifying other people's needs, desires, interests, and preferences.

- Creates a narrowing of focus in their attention that is driven by a yearning and desire to gratify the fourth level of Maslow's Hierarchy – the esteem needs. So how Twos "esteem" themselves is powerfully shaped and defined by their need to "see" themselves as being helpful and by having other people *confirm* this self-perception by also "seeing" them as helpful.

- Becomes a cognitive and emotional angle or perspective on life that singles-out specific underlying patterns in relationships, interactions, and situations that will gratify the Two's basic need to be helpful.

- Causes them to constantly evaluate their relationships and the environment for opportunities to "help" others, even when other people don't want their help (or flatly refuse it), which indicates that their need to be "helpful" often satisfies *their own needs*, not the needs of other people.

Unconscious Appraisal and Selection

This section *links* the unconscious, autopilot cognitive and emotional appraisal and selection process for type Twos, to the See-Do-Get Process and the Downward Spiral of Striving described earlier in this section. Notice in Figure 24, that when the Tacit Creed "I must be helpful" is unpacked *as* the autopilot doing and learning process, Twos like Lindsey tend to be unconsciously drawn to specific people, relationships, situations, and events in the world that will gratify: a) their need to be helpful, and b) the basic needs of their dominant Somatic Instinct.

Unconscious Appraisal and Selection

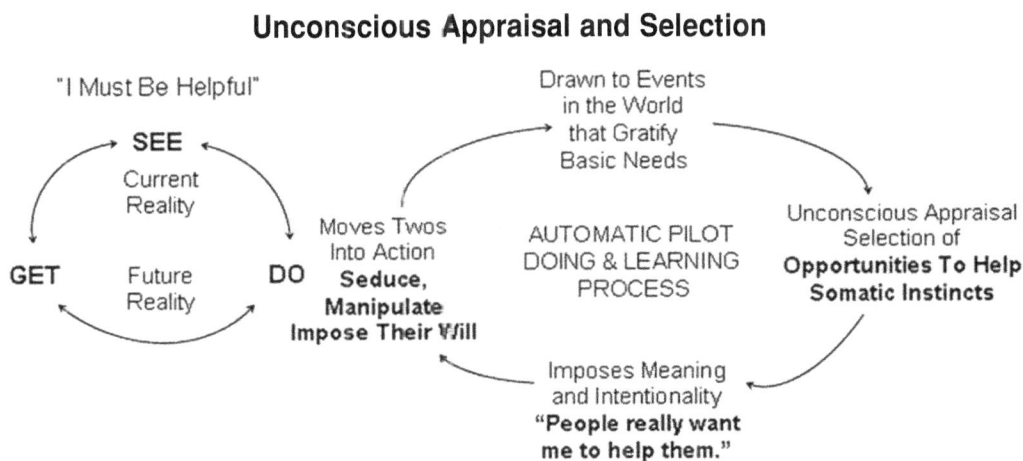

Figure 24

In the second step, Twos unconsciously *appraise* situations and *select* opportunities to get their basic needs met by "helping" others in ways that are shaped and defined by their dominant Somatic Instinct – whether preserving, cultivating, or transmitting. They unconsciously choose very specific cognitive and emotional data from the world because they "match" the underlying patterns and basic need to create a sense of personal significance by acting out the *inner mandate* to be helpful.

In the third step, the Two's Tacit Creed *imposes* meaning and intentionality on the actions and interactions of people and the situations they're involved in. A typical tacit belief that Twos might impose on a situation from their Left-Hand Column is, "People really want me to help them – they're just afraid to ask me for my help." This reveals the Two's tendency to *project* their own needs and beliefs onto the world around them.

In the final step, the momentum and psychological force of the first three steps move Twos *into action* and these actions will tend to follow the pattern just described, where they become overly intimate, intrusive, prone to build dependencies, give to get and impose their will on others through flattery, guilt, and manipulation – all with the unconscious goal of gratifying their own needs, but under the pretense of being "helpful" to others.

The entire process shown in Figure 24 happens beneath the surface of conscious awareness – in the blink of an eye. It's important to remember that the process can be growth-motivated where the four steps produce positive, constructive actions and interactions along the Upward Path of Becoming. Twos like Lindsey who want to move from being deficiency-driven to growth-motivated must consciously raise this autopilot process back into conscious awareness; deconstruct and reconfigure it by running the See-Do-Get Process backwards in the counter clockwise direction; and then migrate the new growth-motivated actions and interactions back to autopilot operation by embedding them through repetition. When Twos succeed in using this change process, the new growth-motivated actions and interactions begin to happen as naturally and automatically as the previous deficiency-driven ones once did. When eight out of ten behaviors are growth-motivated by Humility and Deference, rather than deficiency-driven by Pride and Manipulation, this is an indication that a Two is embodying the 80-20 Rule.

Blind Spots

When Twos are under pressure or facing embarrassment or threat, Pride and Manipulation become the deficiency-drivers for the Tacit Creed – "I must be helpful." Mounting evidence produced by countless cycles through the See-Do-Get Process gives Twos a *false sense* that being "helpful" has actually given them personal significance in life and this conviction breeds a deep sense of Pride about how important they are in the lives of others (see Figure 25).

As in the case of Lindsey, Twos tend to have "Blind Spots" about the *extent* to which Pride and Manipulation dominate their lives and create decision-making bias and predictable errors in judgment. Deficiency-driven Twos tend to "see" themselves as growth-motivated, while the people they interact with tend to "see" them as more deficiency-driven. The emotions of Pride and Manipulation are *inflamed* when Twos are under pressure or they don't get the results they want because people either object to (or don't respond to) their insatiable desire to "help" others by seducing and manipulating them with the goal of building dependencies. Twos become "intoxicated" by the emotional power of Pride and Manipulation, which makes it

```
┌ ─ ─ ─ ─ ─ ─ ─ ─ ─ ─ ─ ─ ─ ─ ─ ─ ─ ─ ┐
│            Socialized-Self            │
│          Body of Knowledge            │
├ ─ ─ ─ ─ ─ ─ ─ ─ ─ ─ ─ ─ ─ ─ ─ ─ ─ ─ ┤
│             Natural-Self              │
│          "I must be helpful"          │
│                                       │
│                 SEE                   │
│                                       │
│         GET             DO            │
│                                       │
│    Humility                  Pride    │
│    Deference             Manipulation │
├ ─ ─ ─ ─ ─ ─ ─ ─ ─ ─ ─ ─ ─ ─ ─ ─ ─ ─ ┤
│   Preserving – Cultivating – Transmitting │
└ ─ ─ ─ ─ ─ ─ ─ ─ ─ ─ ─ ─ ─ ─ ─ ─ ─ ─ ┘
```

Figure 25

more difficult for them to see their Blind Spots and unintended consequences for what they really are. Once the intoxicating energy of Pride and Manipulation subsides, Twos will settle back down to the normal state-of-equilibrium of their dominant type. But over time, this cycle of behaviors and emotional responses *solidifies* into a well-defined pattern of interaction that goes on autopilot and slips below the surface of conscious awareness. These patterns-of-interactions are commonly called "hot buttons" or defense routines.

The philosophy of *helping as the road to personal significance* powerfully shapes the day-to-day preferences of Twos about the people, relationships, careers, hobbies, and lifestyles they are attracted to (and repulsed by), and over time these myriad choices are woven into the fabric of their lives. By the time Twos are young adults, they have identified with the Tacit Creed of "being helpful" to the point where they are locked into a cognitive, emotional, social, and contextual configuration that solidifies, reaches a state-of-equilibrium, and *becomes* their day-to-day reality. The inner mandate to be "helpful" becomes externalized, objectified, and ultimately reified into a social mirror that seems to objectively affirm the belief that the Two's way of seeing themselves, others, and the world is *the* way that life should be lived. We described this earlier as the Self-Sealing Process of forming Personality in Context.

But the *false sense* of personal significance that comes from "helping," the *validation* that comes from the social mirror, and the *stability* of the day-to-day reality that Twos construct – *come* at an enormous price, because they deeply divide them at the very core of their being. *Secretly*, Twos know that they're not as helpful as they claim to be and the fear of this being discovered by others only *fuels* the autopilot, insatiable, destructive power of their Tacit Creed. Think about it – if the Tacit Creed of "being helpful" isn't true for Twos like Lindsey – then what is? If Twos are wrong about how they see themselves, others, and the world, then they may be wrong about almost everything in life.

Growth-Motivated

We've spent a significant amount of time discussing the Tacit Creed and underlying mechanisms of the deficiency-driver of type Twos like Lindsey because without a correct understanding of the process by which these underlying mechanisms bind and limit the choices, personal freedom, and self-determination of type Twos there is little or no hope of ever escaping the pernicious entanglements of Personality in Context. In this section, I'd like to focus on the *single point of leverage* that will address the question, "So what should type Twos *do* about the negative characteristics and effects of their personality?" I will also discuss the concrete changes that Twos can expect to see in their actions and interactions when they choose the Upward Path of Becoming. As shown in Figure 26, when Twos are at their best Humility and Deference become the growth-motivators for the Tacit Creed – "I must be helpful."

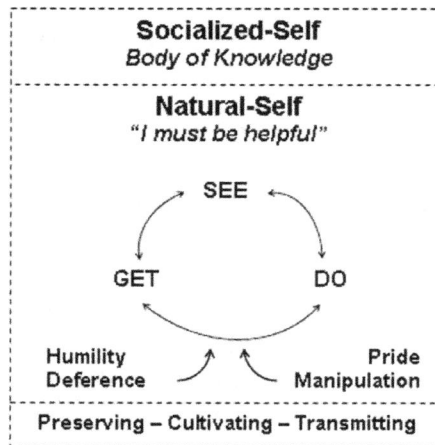

Figure 26

Growth-motivated Twos are helpful, empathic, warm, supportive, compassionate, sensitive, nurturing and enjoy being close to (and connected with) the people in their lives. Their actions and interactions reflect an *intrinsic* (end-oriented) view that sees people as having intrinsic value, regardless of whether they can gratify the Two's needs. The relationships of healthy Twos reveal a creative (end-oriented) way of exploring and discovering life that focuses on meeting *others'* needs and enhancing *their* well-being, regardless of the pragmatic value that they provide to the Two. In addition, their relationships have an I-Thou view of *people as people*, rather than a pragmatic I-It perspective of *people as interchangeable things* that gratify the Two's needs.

While the Two's Blind Spots, defense routines, and the inner mandate to be "helpful" *combine* with the social mirror and the edicts of their socio-cultural context to form deep barriers to deep change, they all rest on the foundation of the Two's core assumption that they lack a personal significance in life. Twos experience this "lack of personal significance in life" as a self-evident truth that cannot (and should not) be questioned or tested, *but this is precisely what Twos must do*: face their fear of self-knowledge by questioning, and publicly testing, the truth of this claim. They must come to "see" themselves as having the tools to unlearn these *biased*, *misguided*, and *erroneous* ways of seeing themselves, others, and the world. Like the story of the Mulla, looking for the key in the *right* place becomes the *single point of leverage* that will enable Twos to ignite deep personal change.

Focusing on the *single point of leverage* acts like a *solvent* that begins to dissolve the *hidden inauthentic layers* of cognitive, emotional, social, and contextual strata from which the Two's life has been built. Using the single point of leverage enables Twos to begin living more authentically in terms of their actions, interactions, and decision-making within the current context of their lives. It helps them to do the right things, for the right reasons. There are a number of very concrete indicators that emerge when Twos like Lindsey begin the journey on the Upward Path of Becoming:

- Twos are free to question their default way of seeing themselves as having to be "helpful" and others as being dependent on their help.
- Their hyper-sensitivity toward identifying people's needs and preferences gives way to an attitude of learning about people – for their own sake.
- They begin to experience a sense of Humility where they develop a more realistic estimate of their importance in people's lives, as well as understanding the intrinsic-value of other people – independent of others' ability to meet the Two's needs.
- They also begin to experience a sense of Deference where they respectfully submit and yield to the judgments, decisions, opinions, and will of others to decide what's best for *their* lives.
- They begin to see that true (disinterested) compassion, caring and nurture in relationships cannot exist when people are dependent on the Two, and this

inner insight and new way of "seeing" gives Twos a deep sense of inner freedom and personal growth.

• Over time, Twos gain new confidence in their ability to transcend the constraints of their personality and cultural context as they see the concrete evidence of change indicated by their ability to act-out the 80-20 Rule – where eight out of ten interactions are motivated by Humility and Deference, rather than being driven by Pride and Manipulation.

Connecting Points

As we saw in the case of Lindsey, Twos intentionally alter their actions and inter-actions to "fit" the requirements and norms of a specific social or cultural context because doing otherwise might be inappropriate and could have negative conse-quences on them personally and professionally. In a previous section, I referred to this as the Socialized-Self. But buried deep beneath the Two's Socialized-Self, family background, life experiences, and body of knowledge is a unique underlying *signature pattern* of connecting points that identifies what it means to be a type Two – their Natural-Self.

Connecting Points
(Conflicting Inner Mandates and Mixed Emotions)

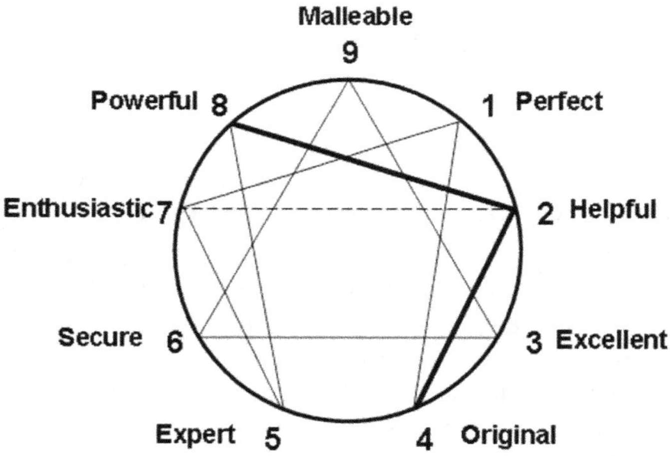

Figure 27

The underlying pattern and characteristics of the connecting points remain relatively constant over time and with changes in context. They are a well-defined intra-psychic pattern of interaction that shapes and defines Two's behaviors and responses in day-to-day discourse, especially in situations where they face *embarrassment* or *threat*. The patterns-of-interaction associated with the connecting points are also an indicator of whether or not the overall direction of the Two's life tends toward the Downward Spiral of Striving or the Upward Path of Becoming.

The Two's dominant type anchors them to the Enneagram and is a necessary element of verifying a person's Enneagram type. The signature pattern for type Two consists of four connecting points: types 2, 8, 4, and 7.

- Type Two is the Tacit Creed which we've already discussed in detail.

- Type Eight is the Striving Point which is referred to by some Enneagram theorists as the point that indicates the direction of disintegration.

- Type Four is the Becoming Point which is referred to by some Enneagram theorists as the point that indicates the direction of integration.

- Type Seven is the Paradox point. Originally identified by Naranjo – it reveals an underlying paradoxical relationship between Twos and Sevens around the issues of seduction and manipulation, where Sevens manipulate and seduce people through their myriad ideas, smooth words, and intellect, and Twos manipulate and seduce others through warm, helpful, generosity designed to build dependencies.

- While the connecting points for Twos represent the *natural* pattern, process, and structure of this Enneagram type, they should not be viewed as rigid and determined. Given sufficient pressure and influence from family or the social-cultural context, these natural tendencies can be powerfully shaped and defined in other ways, with the original signature pattern of the type Two being hidden (or buried) beneath other configurations of Enneagram points.

What is important to note is that the foundation of the type Two's personality is an *interdependent configuration* of conflicting inner mandates and mixed emotions that includes four types, their Tacit Creeds, and their destructive and constructive emotions. In other words, the type Two's personality is not a homogeneous set of beliefs; instead it is a portfolio of interdependent, complementary, competing, and conflicting ways of seeing themselves, others, and the world.

So when Twos like Lindsey are stressed and facing embarrassment and threat, the autopilot patterns-of-interaction between their tacit, Striving, Becoming, and Paradox points can (and often do) create inner conflict and mixed emotions. This is especially true when Twos are faced with a problem that requires a *single* solution. In other words, Lindsey would find herself wondering, "Should I do this, or should I do that? Should I be helpful or powerful?" This inner conflict is *intensified* when external pressures force Twos to act, interact, or make decisions *now*!

There are some key concepts that I'd like to review to define the psychological patterns, processes, and structure of the connecting points for type Twos in more detail.

- The actions and interactions of the other eight Enneagram types are done *in the service of* following the inner mandate to be "helpful" and maintaining the equilibrium of the cognitive, emotional, social, and contextual configuration that the Two builds as their life – their Personality in Context.

- When they are growth-motivated, the connections between type Two, Four, Eight and Seven can help to balance some of the symmetries by giving Twos at least one Enneagram point in each of the three triads, thus straddling the emotional, cognitive, and sensory parts of the human brain. The Two's connecting points also help to balance the left-right and top-bottom symmetries, where types Eight and Seven provide a left-side balance for Twos, and the type Four provides an Enneagram point that balances the top-bottom symmetry.

- Another key concept centers on the *combining* of the Tacit Creeds and underlying emotions into what is referred to as conflicting inner mandates and mixed emotions for type Twos. One of the key issues with how traditional theorists and practitioners of the Enneagram present their models is that they tend to pay lip service to the principle that an individual's personality is composed of *all nine types*, but then go on to talk almost exclusively in terms of that individual as being their dominant type. But in reality, people rarely act univocally. Rather, actions, interactions (and eventually patterns-of-interaction) come in complex, interdependent bundles, where the Tacit Creeds and underlying emotions of the Two's connecting points *combine* and *co-mingle* to form extremely complex packages of emotional messages that are communicated to others.

A solid understanding of the signature pattern is the key to *unbundling* the complex packages of emotional messages and patterns-of-interaction that type Twos often exhibit in day-to-day interactions.

Type Two Summary Profile

Figure 28 provides an overall summary of the key patterns, structures, and processes that were described in this section and that typify the Enneagram type Two.

Type Summary Profile - Type Two	
Core Assumption	I lack personal significance in life
Tacit Creed (Mulla)	I must be helpful
Unconscious Appraisal	Opportunities to help and Somatic Instincts
Impose Meaning	People really want me to help them
Move Into Action	Seduce, manipulate, impose their will
Deficiency Drivers	Pride, Manipulation
Growth Motivators	Humitility, Deference
Striving Point	Type Eight
Becoming Point	Type Four
Paradox Point	Type Seven
Group (Triad)	Heart, leads with the emotional part of the brain (Amygdala)
Existential Question	How do I find an identity?
Conflict Processing Strategy	Reframing
Attitude Towards Socio-Cultural Change	Move Toward/Compliant
Single Point of Leverage	Question and publicly test the core assumption

Figure 28

In keeping with the overall approach of the Breckenridge Enneagram, the characteristics and dynamics shown in Figure 28 are not surface-traits or behaviors. Rather, they describe the underlying patterns, structures, and processes that define what makes type Twos like Lindsey different from the other eight Enneagram types.

Examples and Movies

While Twos are found in every area of life and all professional fields, the list below shows some famous examples of people who are probably type Twos. How many names do you recognize? Which ones are you interested enough in to learn more about by reading a biography or autobiography?

- *Examples* – Famous examples who exhibit Two traits: Mother Teresa, Barry Manilow, Ann Landers, Sammy Davis, Eleanor Roosevelt, Desmond Tutu, Bill Cosby, Jerry Lewis, Stereotypic "Jewish Mother."

Another way to see Enneagram type in action is through the characters and story lines in movies. Select some of the movies listed below and take some time to watch Twos in action.

- *Movie Characters* – Roles in movies that exemplify Two traits: Frances Fisher as Rose's mother (Titanic), Barbra Streisand (The Way We Were), Glynis Johns and Isabella Rossellini (Zelly and Me), Mia Farrow as Hannah (Hannah and Her Sisters).

To deepen your understanding of this Enneagram type, identify people who you *know* that embody this personality type and become more observant about their behaviors, attitudes, and decision-making strategies. Ask them to share their thoughts, views, and perspectives on key issues and criteria for decision-making and see how closely the descriptions in this section describe and predict their responses. To further solidify and deepen your understanding, log your insights and observations about this personality type in a journal. You can use this exercise for the other eight types as well.

Type Three (I Must Be Excellent)

When Threes are at their best, they are role models of achievement and success and establish and exemplify standards of excellence within their cultural context. They are ambitious, competitive, goal-oriented, and embody highly-valued competencies and talents. When under pressure, they become overly focused on self-promotion, creating an "idealized" self to be seen by others – they lose access to their deep feelings and true identity and mobilize their achievements as an "objective" validation of their value and worth.

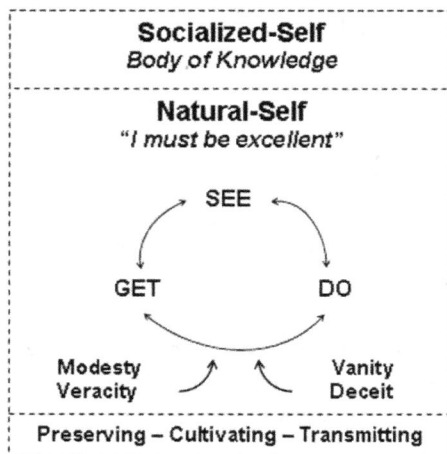

Figure 29

Take a few minutes to read (and reflect on) Figure 29. The very top of Figure 29 is made up of a person's Socialized-Self and body of knowledge, which form a major portion of the knowledge-base of their personal paradigm.

Tacit Creed

Threes live by the Tacit Creed "I must be excellent" where what counts as "excellence" is defined by their cultural context. This belief solidifies early in life through countless cycles through the See-Do-Get Process. When they are Deficiency Driven, they are hyper-sensitive to identifying differences between their own achievements and others', they constantly evaluate their relationships and the environment for opportunities to improve themselves and compete with others. Vanity and Deceit are *inflamed* when under pressure or when they don't get what they want; e.g., people either object to, or don't respond to, their *insatiable desire* to showcase their achievements as evidence of their worth and value; plus image morphing, pragmatism, and superficiality. When under stress, they become "intoxicated" by the power of these emotions and have a *Blind Spot* about the extent to which Vanity and Deceit dominate their lives and create decision-making bias and predictable errors in judgment.

When they are Growth Motivated, they are free to question their default way of seeing, and their hyper-sensitivity *gives way* to Modesty, Veracity, and a deep desire to live by inner standards of excellence, build true self-esteem, and be authentic in everything they do for their own sake; not just to be seen by others. They begin to see that they must accept themselves and their limitations as they are, and take personal responsibility for modeling social values that are authentic and embody integrity and truth. For Threes, the key element of personal growth and building effective relationships is to follow the 80-20 Rule – where eight out of ten interactions with others are characterized by Modesty and Veracity, rather than Vanity and Deceit.

Maggie's Story

Maggie Spinner's story is an example of what the Tacit Creed "I must be excellent" looks like when it's solidified in the life of a type Three. Maggie had always been the quintessential image of success who had pushed her way to the top of every challenge she'd taken on by the power of her raw, unmitigated competitive will. Maggie grew up on a farm in the Midwest and for as long as she could remember she didn't know who she was apart from the roles that she played in life. She didn't feel loved for who she was, independent of her achievements, successes, and super human victories. Maggie came to believe that her life lacked personal identity, so she had to create a personal identity by being excellent. In her mind, the ticket to "being someone" was to succeed at everything. Her life was a fast-moving tread-mill, and at forty she was really, really tired of running what felt like the race of life.

Maggie was the Vice President of Public Relations for a large chemical corpora-tion near Rocky Flats, Colorado. She lived in the cultural center of Boulder and had been doing graduate level studies in spirituality and world religions at CU Boulder part-time. Maggie's twenty-year-old daughter, Rena, was the only reminder of a long-gone marriage that she never talked about out of a deep sense of shame. Rena attended Colorado College, a small private liberal arts school in Colorado Springs, and on weekends and over school breaks the two women would spend time skiing, hiking, biking, and scuba diving, which Maggie had learned years earlier.

Maggie and Rena were riding up the chair lift to the bowl high above the Winter Park ski area and Maggie started chatting with Troy, one of the ski instructors. It was his day off and he offered to show them around the mountain, so Maggie and Rena got the royal tour of the best skiing that Winter Park had to offer, followed by cocktails in the hot tub at the townhome complex where Troy lived. Maggie was used to being treated like royalty. She was stunningly beautiful in a healthy, out-door looking way which almost always turned men's heads. Many of the guys who competed for the "privilege" of waiting on her hand and foot called her a queen, but only on his way out of the door of her life. More than anything, men and women alike have accused her of being vain, but since she seemed to have all the goods to back-up her image, she just dismissed this commentary as the envy of those who were less successful in life.

Troy had studied philosophy at CU Boulder, and since the only thing his degree enabled him to do was to go to graduate school, he decided to take a job as a ski instructor and see if any new direction came into his life. That was fifteen years ago, and Troy hadn't looked back since. He was a different sort of guy –introspec-tive, connected to the deeper things in life, sensitive to people, and intent on finding a sense of meaning and contribution in life. He was an incredibly good-looking guy who had done some modeling in ski magazines, but unlike Maggie, he wasn't pretentious about it – he just was what he was.

Over the next year, Maggie spent more time at Troy's place in Winter Park than she did at her house in Boulder and she found herself falling in love with Troy in a way that she had never experienced before. In the summer, they would go for hikes in the mountains and Maggie would feel an inner sense of freedom as she let her feet dangle in the crystal clear, cold water of a Colorado mountain stream. As winter came they would trek into the back-country on snow shoes and overnight in back country huts that overlooked the continental divide. Troy was not like the other men that she had been with and somehow he was waking up emotions and a vision for her life that she had never felt before. But what she found most interesting was that Troy was completely unimpressed with her image and the emphasis that she put on competing about almost everything and being the best at any price.

At the office, Maggie had been thrust into the middle of an enormous corporate crisis and she was at the focal point of the action. Local environmental groups had become more and more insistent and vocal that her company was secretly dumping chemicals into the ground upstream of their city's aquifer. As the Vice President of Public Relations, she was forced to face off with these people who hounded her night and day and had even begun calling her at home. Maggie was able to counteract every allegation with a masterful combination of factual information, spin, and when necessary smoke and mirrors. Every attack they mounted, she was able to disarm. She tried to give the impression that she really cared for them and their concerns, but under these thinly veiled lies she disdained this bunch of environmental do-gooders and whiners. The company president, J.R., and the Board of Directors were pleased and relieved that Maggie seemed to be winning this war of words, factoids, and emotions that played out daily on the front pages of the Denver Post.

But during her field research to refute one of the environmentalists' claims, Maggie discovered an underground discharge pipe from the plant that was not on any of the facility drawings. When she began to inquire about it, no one in the company seemed to know about it. Then she found herself summoned to J.R.'s office where she was emphatically instructed to stop asking questions about the discharge pipe and to just stick to the fine job she had been doing defeating those people's claims. But as she secretly did more field research, she became increasingly convinced that the company was indeed discharging poisonous chemicals underground and that the local environmental groups were right in their allegations.

Maggie had a tendency to put her psychological energy into being what people wanted to see, making a good impression, form over substance, and coming across well. Troy saw a different side of Maggie, deep below the surface of her charm, white lies, and cool-and-calculated image. Despite her singular focus on success, Troy saw in her the power to be inner-directed, to be motivated by the value of helping others, regardless of whether or not it led to success. Certainly she was ambitious, but her best-side was when she used this inner motivation to grow psychologically and improve herself. Troy wasn't sure that *Maggie* could see this deeper part of herself that was committed to integrity and truth, because she had locked it away in a compartment somewhere deep in her heart. On the occasions when it forced its way to freedom and escaped, she tended to rationalize and disown this part of her true self so she could keep up the show and go on performing.

Maggie had left the office for the weekend troubled in a way that she'd never been before. The drive into the snow-covered foothills to the west of Boulder, up over the eleven thousand-foot pass, and down into the secluded valley where Winter Park sits was a time of quiet reflection and soul searching for Maggie. One of the things she always looked forward to was to sit in the hot tub with Troy looking toward the runs of the ski area and just talk about their day, their week, and what they wanted from each other and life. That day, she poured her heart out to Troy about the discharge pipe she had discovered. He was really taken aback, but not totally surprised because he never really trusted J.R.

Troy said, "Why don't you just put the evidence you have in an envelope and send it to the reporter at the Denver Post who's been covering the story, then walk into J.R.'s office and just quit?"

"I can't do that," Maggie protested.

"Why not?" Troy pressed. "I'll bet you could make decent money tending bar here at night in the base lodge, ski all day, and not have to burden yourself with these corporate problems and the pressure to lie and cover up just to keep your job."

Monday morning, she was back on the job defending the company and defeating the arguments of the local environmentalists, but now she was doing her job knowing that they were right.

Maggie was trying to decide if she should take Troy's advice, and she had use-or-lose vacation time building up, so she took some time off, and put off the issue of confronting J.R. until after she got back. She knew she was good at what she did – in fact, she was probably the best in the business. But when she was really honest with herself, looked inside and asked who she was independent of her professional image, she had no idea. That scared her to the depths of her soul. Troy saw things in her that she didn't, and their relationship had mirrored them so powerfully that Maggie was finally starting to get a glimmer of them for herself. She was tiring of the image and persona she had worn all her life. Maggie hungered for integrity and truth. She had a hounding thirst for authenticity and wanted to be real for the first time in her life, but she didn't know how to go about satisfying these deep desires.

Maggie's story is only one of many that could be told to show what the Tacit Creed "I must be excellent" looks like in the life of an individual. While the surface traits; natural talents and abilities; life-experiences; relationships; socio-cultural setting; ethnicity; gender; and level of psychological health defined by the 80-20 Rule may vary dramatically from person-to-person, the underlying patterns, processes and structures of the stories of all type Threes will be similar.

Emergence of the Tacit Creed

The Three's Natural-Self occupies the bottom portion of Figure 29 where the Tacit Creed (I must be excellent) *emerges* from their innate, inborn temperament and the deep fear associated with the core assumption that they *lack personal identity in life*. The emphasis is on the word "identity" and the tacit conviction (and near certainty) that they lack any inward experience of self that would provide a sense and experience of *sameness* and *continuity* of personality over time and in varied situations; e.g., an inner "fingerprint" that identifies them as who they are. Threes experience this core assumption emotionally as a deep and abiding sense that, "I don't know who I am, apart from the roles I play. When I do a job at the office, a project at home, or get involved with a hobby I am often the very best; but when I look inside and ask myself who I am apart from these things – I have no idea." They *experience* the core assumption with an inner sense of *certainty* as a *self-evident* truth that cannot (and ought not) be: a) questioned, b) objectively or publicly tested, or c) even verbalized. This belief that Threes hold about themselves is a *secret* truth that they hide from themselves, others, and the world. It's undiscussible and its un-discussibility cannot be discussed. Their fear of self-knowledge creates a sense of psychological survival in Threes that threatens their *existence* to the point where the gate-keeping function *blocks* these emotions from their conscious awareness. But life goes on, and so must the Three. Over time, the emotional and cognitive memories associated with this core assumption are *buried* deeper and deeper within the psyche of type Threes to the point where they become largely inaccessible to conscious awareness, and are only experienced at pivotal (*kairos*) moments in life. This *forces* a shift in the Three's focus in order to avoid the embarrassment and threat that the reality of the core assumption creates, so rather than face (or test) the *truth* of not having a personal identity in life, they *displace* the problem by creating a personal identity by "being excellent." But trying to be "excellent" can never fill the deep inner need of type Threes because it tries to address an *inner* (existential) issue with *outer* behavior.

Notice how the Tacit Creed can either be *deficiency-driven* by Vanity and Deceit or *growth-motivated* by Modesty and Veracity and has a very different look and feel depending on whether it's driven or motivated – with the ratio of driven-to-motivated actions and interactions being defined as the 80-20 Rule. When Threes like Maggie are at their best and are growth-motivated, they are role models of achievement and success, and establish and exemplify standards of excellence within their cultural context. They are ambitious, competitive, goal-oriented, and embody competencies and talents that are highly valued by others. When they face embarrassment, threat or are deficiency-driven, Threes become overly focused on self-promotion, creating an "idealized" self in order to be noticed and seen by others. Because they reject the parts of themselves that don't fit with the image of excellence, they lose access to their depth feelings and true identity and mobilize their achievements as an "objective" measure and validation of their value, work, and personal identity. They *become* their achievements.

The three Somatic Instincts shown at the very bottom of Figure 29 are the first three levels of Maslow's Hierarchy and form the inner core and foundation upon which the type Three's personality is built. The Somatic Instincts powerfully shape the overall direction of a Three's life in the sense that their deep inner yearnings and desires unconsciously draw them to people, experiences, careers, relationships, and life situations that will gratify these basic human needs. So the *autopilot needs* of deficiency-driven Preserving Threes can only be gratified by "being excellent" in areas associated with home, nurture, and comfort, while Cultivating Threes are unconsciously drawn to gratify their need to "be excellent" in areas associated with belonging and affiliation with groups, and the autopilot needs of Transmitting Threes must be gratified by "being excellent" in situations that revolve around love, affection, caring, and communicating their ideas.

Deficiency-Driven

As shown in Figure 29, when Threes are under pressure or are facing embarrassment or threat, Vanity and Deceit become the deficiency-drivers, and the Tacit Creed for people like Maggie:

- Is like a hyper-sensitivity or allergic reaction to situations that fit the underlying pattern of having to be excellent, which for type Threes means identifying differences between their own achievements and level of success, and the achievements and level of success of others.

- Creates a narrowing of focus in their attention that is driven by a yearning and desire to gratify the fourth level of Maslow's Hierarchy – the esteem needs. So how Threes "esteem" themselves is powerfully shaped and defined by their need to "see" themselves as being excellent and by having other people *confirm* this self-perception by also "seeing" them as excellent.

- Becomes a cognitive and emotional angle or perspective on life that singles-out specific underlying patterns in relationships, interactions, and situations that will gratify the Three's basic need to be excellent.

- Causes them to constantly evaluate their relationships and the environment for opportunities to be "excellent" even when it's not required by the context (and may even be considered inappropriate), which indicates that their need to be "excellent" often satisfies *their own needs*, not the needs of the situation.

Unconscious Appraisal and Selection

This section *links* the unconscious, autopilot cognitive and emotional appraisal and selection process for type Threes, to the See-Do-Get Process and the Downward Spiral of Striving. Notice in Figure 30, that when the Tacit Creed "I must be excellent" is unpacked *as* the autopilot doing and learning process, Threes like Maggie tend to be unconsciously drawn to specific people, relationships, situations, and events in the world that will gratify: a) their need to be excellent, and b) the basic needs of their dominant Somatic Instinct.

Unconscious Appraisal and Selection

Figure 30

In the second step, Threes unconsciously *appraise* situations and *select* opportunities to get their basic needs met by "being excellent" in ways that are shaped and defined by their dominant Somatic Instinct – whether preserving, cultivating, or transmitting. They unconsciously choose very specific cognitive and emotional data from the world because they "match" the underlying patterns and basic need to create a sense of personal identity by acting out the *inner mandate* to be excellent.

In the third step, the Three's Tacit Creed *imposes* meaning and intentionality on the actions and interactions of people *and* the situations they're involved in. A typical tacit belief that Threes might impose on a situation from their Left-Hand Column is, "People aren't really as good as they appear to be because everybody tries to fake it till they make it." This reveals the Three's tendency to *project* their own needs and beliefs onto the world around them.

In the final step, the momentum and psychological force of the first three steps move Threes *into action* and these actions will tend to follow the pattern just described, where they compete with people, become overly focused on self-promotion, and create an "idealized" image, and long to be being "seen" by others – all with the unconscious goal of gratifying their own needs, but under the pretense of being excellent.

The entire process shown in Figure 30 happens beneath the surface of conscious awareness – in the blink of an eye. It's important to remember that the process can be growth-motivated where the four steps produce positive, constructive actions and interactions along the Upward Path of Becoming. Threes like Maggie who want to move from being deficiency-driven to growth-motivated must consciously raise this autopilot process back into conscious awareness; deconstruct and reconfigure it by running the See-Do-Get Process backwards in the counter clockwise direction; and then migrate the new growth-motivated actions and interactions back to autopilot operation by embedding them through repetition. When Threes succeed in using this change process, the new growth-motivated actions and interactions begin to happen as naturally and automatically as the previous deficiency-driven ones once did. When eight out of ten behaviors are growth-motivated by Modesty and Veracity, rather than deficiency-driven by Vanity and Deceit, this is an indication that a Three is embodying the 80-20 Rule.

Blind Spots

When Threes are under pressure or facing embarrassment or threat, Vanity and Deceit become the deficiency-drivers for the Tacit Creed – "I must be excellent." Mounting evidence produced by countless cycles through the See-Do-Get Process gives Threes a *false sense* that being "excellent" has actually given them a personal identity in life, and this conviction breeds a deep sense of Vanity about their talents, competencies, and level of achievement (see Figure 31).

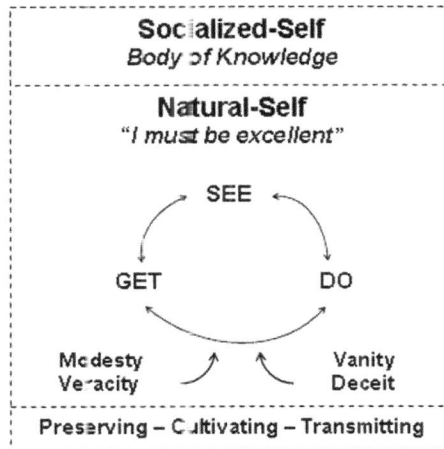

```
┌ ─ ─ ─ ─ ─ ─ ─ ─ ─ ─ ─ ─ ─ ─ ─ ─ ─ ─ ┐
        Socialized-Self
        Body of Knowledge
├ ─ ─ ─ ─ ─ ─ ─ ─ ─ ─ ─ ─ ─ ─ ─ ─ ─ ─ ┤
         Natural-Self
       "I must be excellent"

              SEE

      GET              DO

    Modesty            Vanity
    Veracity           Deceit
├ ─ ─ ─ ─ ─ ─ ─ ─ ─ ─ ─ ─ ─ ─ ─ ─ ─ ─ ┤
   Preserving – Cultivating – Transmitting
└ ─ ─ ─ ─ ─ ─ ─ ─ ─ ─ ─ ─ ─ ─ ─ ─ ─ ─ ┘
```

Figure 31

Much like Maggie, Threes tend to have "Blind Spots" about the *extent* to which Vanity and Deceit dominate their lives and create decision-making bias and predictable errors in judgment. Deficiency-driven Threes tend to "see" themselves as growth-motivated, while the people they interact with tend to "see" them as more deficiency-driven. The emotions of Vanity and Deceit are *inflamed* when Threes are under pressure or they don't get the results they want because people either object to (or don't respond to) their insatiable desire to showcase their achievements as evidence of their worth and value, and to morph their image to fit the context in a pragmatic and superficial way. Threes become "intoxicated" by the emotional power of Vanity and Deceit, which makes it more difficult for them to see their Blind Spots and unintended consequences for what they really are. Once the intoxicating energy of Vanity and Deceit subsides, Threes will settle back down to the normal state-of-equilibrium of their dominant type. But over time, this cycle of behaviors and emotional responses *solidifies* into a well-defined pattern of interaction that goes on autopilot and slips below the surface of conscious awareness. These patterns-of-interactions are commonly called "hot buttons" or defense routines.

The philosophy of *being excellent as the road to personal identity* powerfully shapes the day-to-day preferences of Threes about the people, relationships, careers, hobbies, and lifestyles they are attracted to (and repulsed by), and over time these myriad choices are woven into the fabric of their lives. By the time Threes are young adults, they have identified with the Tacit Creed of "being excellent" to the point where they are locked into a cognitive, emotional, social, and contextual configuration that solidifies, reaches a state-of-equilibrium, and *becomes* their day-to-day reality. The inner mandate to be "excellent" becomes externalized, objectified, and ultimately reified into a social mirror that seems to objectively affirm the belief that the Three's way of seeing themselves, others, and the world is *the* way that life should be lived. We described this earlier as the Self-Sealing Process of forming Personality in Context.

But the *false sense* of personal identity that comes from being "excellent," the *validation* that comes from the social mirror, and the *stability* of the day-to-day reality that Threes construct – *come* at an enormous price, because they deeply divide them at the very core of their being. *Secretly*, Threes know that they're not as excellent as they claim to be, and the fear of this being discovered by others only *fuels* the autopilot, insatiable, destructive power of their Tacit Creed. Think about it – if the Tacit Creed of "being excellent" isn't true for Threes like Maggie – then what is? If Threes are wrong about how they see themselves, others, and the world, then they may be wrong about almost everything in life.

Growth-Motivated

We've spent a significant amount of time discussing the Tacit Creed and underlying mechanisms of the deficiency-driver of type Threes like Maggie because without a correct understanding of the process by which these underlying mechanisms bind and limit the choices, personal freedom, and self-determination of type Threes, there is little or no hope of ever escaping the pernicious entanglements of Personality in Context. In this section, I'd like to focus on the *single point of leverage* that will address the question, "So what should type Threes like Maggie *do* about the negative characteristics and effects of their personality?" I will also discuss the concrete changes that Threes can expect to see in their actions and interactions when they choose the Upward Path of Becoming. As shown in Figure 32, when Threes are at their best Modesty and Veracity become the growth-motivators for the Tacit Creed – "I must be excellent."

Growth-motivated Threes are role models of achievement and success, and establish and exemplify standards of excellence within their cultural context. They are ambitious, competitive, goal-oriented, and embody competencies and talents that are highly valued by others.

While the Three's Blind Spots, defense routines, and the inner mandate to be "excellent" *combine* with the social mirror and the edicts of their socio-cultural context to form barriers to deep change, they all rest on the foundation of the Three's core assumption that they lack a personal identity in life. Threes experience this "lack of personal identity in life" as a self-evident truth that cannot (and ought not) be questioned or tested, *but this is precisely what Threes must do*: face their fear of self-knowledge by questioning, and publicly testing, the truth of this claim. They must come to "see" themselves as having the tools to unlearn these *biased, misguided*, and *erroneous* ways of seeing themselves, others, and the world. Like the story of the Mulla, looking for the key in the *right* place becomes the *single point of leverage* that will enable Threes to ignite deep personal change.

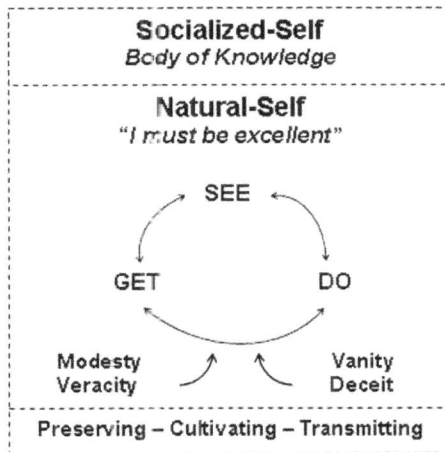

Figure 32

Focusing on the *single point of leverage* acts like a *solvent* that begins to dissolve the *hidden inauthentic layers* of cognitive, emotional, social, and contextual strata from which the Three's life has been built. Using the single point of leverage enables Threes to begin living more authentically in terms of their actions, interactions, and decision-making within the current context of their lives. It helps them to do the right things, for the right reasons. There are a number of very concrete indicators that emerge when Threes like Maggie begin the journey on the Upward Path of Becoming:

- Threes are free to question their default way of seeing themselves as having to be "excellent," and others as being impressed by their accomplishments.

- Their hyper-sensitivity toward identifying differences between their own achievements and level of success and the achievements and level of success of others gives way to an attitude of learning about people – for their own sake. They begin to experience a sense of Modesty where they become increasingly free from self-promotion and develop a desire to live by inner standards of excellence and to build genuine self-esteem.

- Threes also begin to experience a sense of Veracity where they become increasingly authentic and truthful in everything they do and say for their own sake, *not* as a strategy for being "seen" by others.

- They begin to see that they must accept themselves and their limitations for what they are, and take personal responsibility for modeling behaviors and social values that are authentic and embody integrity and truth.

- Over time, Threes gain new confidence in their ability to transcend the constraints of their personality and cultural context as they see the concrete evidence of change indicated by their ability to act-out the 80-20 Rule – where eight out of ten interactions are motivated by Modesty and Veracity, rather than being driven by Vanity and Deceit.

Connecting Points

Much like the story of Maggie, Threes intentionally alter their actions and interactions to "fit" the requirements and norms of a specific social or cultural context because doing otherwise might be inappropriate and could have negative consequences on them personally and professionally. In a previous section, I referred to this as the Socialized-Self. But buried deep beneath the Three's Socialized-Self, family background, life experiences, and body of knowledge is a unique underlying *signature pattern* of connecting points that identifies what it means to be a type Three – their Natural-Self.

Connecting Points
(Conflicting Inner Mandates and Mixed Emotions)

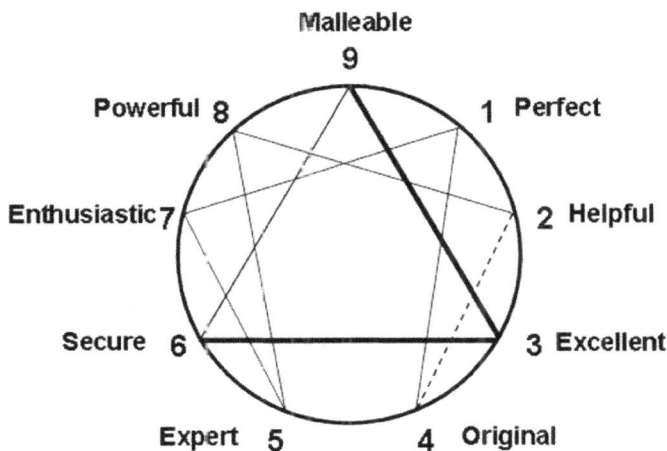

Figure 33

The underlying pattern and characteristics of the connecting points remain relatively constant over time and with changes in context. They are a well-defined intra-psychic pattern of interaction that shapes and defines Three's behaviors and responses in day-to-day discourse, especially in situations where they face *embarrassment* or *threat*. The patterns-of-interaction associated with the connecting points are also an indicator of whether or not the overall direction of the Three's life tends toward the Downward Spiral of Striving or the Upward Path of Becoming.

The Three's dominant type anchors them to the Enneagram and is a necessary element of verifying a person's Enneagram type. The signature pattern for type Three consists of five connecting points: types 3, 6, 9, 4, and 2.

- Type Three is the Tacit Creed which we've already discussed in detail.
- Type Nine is the Striving Point which is referred to by some Enneagram theorists as the point that indicates the direction of disintegration.
- Type Six is the Becoming Point which is referred to by some Enneagram theorists as the point that indicates the direction of integration.
- The Four-Two Paradox straddles type Three, where Fours and Twos are isomorphic images of each other, with type Fours focusing too heavily on self-reflection and introspection and type Twos focusing too heavily on building and sustaining relationships. Type Threes tend to be pulled along the axis of this paradox and can embody either set of characteristics if issues with their identity force them to.

- While the connecting points for Threes represent the *natural* pattern, process, and structure of this Enneagram type, they should not be viewed as rigid and determined. Given sufficient pressure and influence from family or the social-cultural context, these natural tendencies can be powerfully shaped and defined in other ways, with the original signature pattern of the type Three being hidden (or buried) beneath other configurations of Enneagram points.

What is most important to note is that the foundation of the type Three's personality is an *interdependent configuration* of conflicting inner mandates and mixed emotions that includes five types, their Tacit Creeds, and their destructive and constructive emotions. In other words, the type Three's personality is not a homogeneous set of beliefs; instead it is a portfolio of interdependent, complementary, competing, and conflicting ways of seeing themselves, others, and the world.

So when Threes like Maggie are stressed and facing embarrassment and threat, the autopilot patterns-of-interaction between their tacit, Striving, Becoming, and Paradox points can (and often do) create inner conflict and mixed emotions. This is especially true when Threes are faced with a problem that requires a *single* solution. In other words, Maggie would find herself wondering, "Should I do this, or should I do that? Should I be excellent or malleable?" This inner conflict is *intensified* when external pressure forces Threes to act, interact, or make decisions *now*!

There are some key concepts that I'd like to review to define the psychological patterns, processes, and structure of the connecting points for type Threes in more detail.

- The actions and interactions of the other eight Enneagram types are done *in the service of* following the inner mandate to be "excellent" and maintaining the equilibrium of the cognitive, emotional, social, and contextual configuration that the Three builds as their life – their Personality in Context.
- When they are growth-motivated, the connections between type Three, Six, Nine, Four and Two can help to balance some of the symmetries by giving Threes at least one Enneagram point in each of the three triads, thus straddling the emotional, cognitive, and sensory parts of the human brain. The Three's connecting points also help to balance the left-right and top-bottom symmetries, where type Six provides a left-side balance for Threes, and type Nine provides an Enneagram point that provides some balance for the top-bottom symmetry, although the majority of the connecting points for Threes are on the top and right side of the Enneagram.
- Another key concept centers on the *combining* of the Tacit Creeds and underlying emotions into what is referred to as conflicting inner mandates and mixed emotions for type Threes. People rarely act univocally. Rather, actions,

interactions (and eventually patterns-of-interaction) come in complex, interdependent bundles, where the Tacit Creeds and underlying emotions of the Three's connecting points *combine* and *co-mingle* to form extremely complex packages of emotional messages that are communicated to others.

A solid understanding of the signature pattern is the key to *unbundling* the complex packages of emotional messages and patterns-of-interaction that type Threes often exhibit in day-to-day interactions.

Type Three Summary Profile

Figure 34 provides an overall summary of the key patterns, structures, and processes that were described in this section and that typify the Enneagram type Three.

Type Summary Profile - Type Three	
Core Assumption	I lack personal identity in life
Tacit Creed (Mulla)	I must be excellent
Unconscious Appraisal	Opportunities to be excellent and Somatic Instincts
Impose Meaning	Most people fake it till they make it
Move Into Action	Compete, self-promotion, being "seen"
Deficiency Drivers	Vanity, Deceit
Growth Motivators	Modesty, Veracity
Striving Point	Type Nine
Becoming Point	Type Six
Paradox Point	Type Two, Type Four
Group (Triad)	Heart, leads with the emotional part of the brain (Amygdala)
Existential Question	How do I find an identity?
Conflict Processing Strategy	Objective
Attitude Towards Socio-Cultural Change	Move Against/Aggressive
Single Point of Leverage	Question and publicly test the core assumption

Figure 34

In keeping with the overall approach of the Breckenridge Enneagram, the characteristics and dynamics shown in Figure 34 are not surface-traits or behaviors. Rather, the content of Figure 34 describes the underlying patterns, structures, and processes that define what makes type Threes like Maggie different from the other eight Enneagram types.

Examples and Movie

While Threes are found in every area of life and all professional fields, the list below shows some famous examples of people who are probably type Threes. How many names do you recognize? Which ones are you interested enough in to learn more about by reading a biography or autobiography?

- *Examples* – Famous examples who exhibit Three traits: Dick Clarke, Bill Clinton, Tiger Woods, Paul McCartney, Oprah Winfrey, Tom Cruise, Elvis Presley, Arnold Schwarzenegger, William Shatner (Captain Kirk), Barack Obama.

Another way to see Enneagram type in action is through the characters and story lines in movies. Select some of the movies listed below and take some time to watch Threes in action.

- *Movie Characters* – Roles in movies that exemplify Three traits: Richard Gere (Pretty Woman), Billy Zane as Cal (Titanic), Oskar Schindler (Schindler's List), Mary Tyler Moore (Ordinary People).

To deepen your understanding of this Enneagram type, identify people who you *know* that embody this personality type and become more observant about their behaviors, attitudes, and decision-making strategies. Ask them to share their thoughts, views, and perspectives on key issues and criteria for decision-making and see how closely the descriptions in this section describe and predict their responses. To further solidify and deepen your understanding, log your insights and observations about this personality type in a journal. You can use this exercise for the other eight types as well.

Type Four (I Must Be Original)

When Fours are at their best, they are original, creative, self-revealing, authentic, different from others, and express their own way of "seeing" the world *indirectly* by creating something; e.g., art, music, literature, technology, architecture, services, etc. When under pressure, they experience deep inner turmoil, depression, compulsive longing for love, envy, a poignant sense of "cosmic" suffering, and they express the emotional intensity of this inner experience through creative and symbolic means as a way of "making sense" of their suffering, pain, neediness, inner-poverty, and alienation from themselves, others, and the world around them.

Take a few minutes and reflect on Figure 35. The very top of Figure 35 is made up of a person's Socialized-Self and body of knowledge, which form a major portion of the knowledge-base of their personal paradigm.

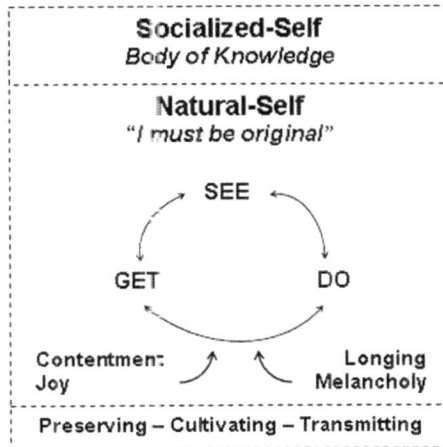

```
┌─────────────────────────────────────────────┐
│            Socialized-Self                    │
│            Body of Knowledge                  │
├ ─ ─ ─ ─ ─ ─ ─ ─ ─ ─ ─ ─ ─ ─ ─ ─ ─ ─ ─ ─ ─ ┤
│             Natural-Self                      │
│          "I must be original"                 │
│                                               │
│                  SEE                          │
│                                               │
│         GET              DO                    │
│                                               │
│   Contentment          Longing                │
│   Joy                  Melancholy             │
├ ─ ─ ─ ─ ─ ─ ─ ─ ─ ─ ─ ─ ─ ─ ─ ─ ─ ─ ─ ─ ─ ┤
│   Preserving – Cultivating – Transmitting     │
└─────────────────────────────────────────────┘
```

Figure 35

Tacit Creed

Fours live by the Tacit Creed "I must be original" – a belief that solidifies early in life through countless cycles through the See-Do-Get Process. When they are Deficiency Driven, they are hyper-sensitive to identifying ways to express their originality and individualism, they constantly evaluate their relationships and environment for ways to express their inner experience and depth of emotions in different and unique ways, even when doing so is unnecessary or inappropriate. Longing and Melancholy are *inflamed* when under pressure or when they don't get the result they want; e.g., people object to, or don't respond to, their *insatiable focus* on life's suffering, loneliness, compulsive longing for love and true contentment, poor self-image, envy, and emotional intensity, that are masked beneath a façade of appearing special, different, unique. When under stress, they become "intoxicated" by the power of these emotions and have a *Blind Spot* about the extent to which Longing and Melancholy dominate their lives and create decision-making bias and predictable errors in judgment. While Eights are the most *insensitive* of the nine types, thirsting for intensity through action, Fours are the most *sensitive* and thirst for intensity through their emotions.

Thomas' Story

Thomas Rose's story is an example of what the Tacit Creed "I must be original" looks like when it's solidified in the life of a type Four. Thomas was raised in upstate New York and the dark, cold winters were an outer expression of his dark, introspective moods. Even as a child, he felt like he was lost in the collective ocean of people and life – like a single drop of water merged with the deep blue sea. From his earliest days, he came to believe that he lacked an individual existence in life, so he was determined to create an individual existence by being original. Thomas was always drawn to the dark, painful side of life where he tried to find meaning in his suffering, but this only led him farther into a downward spiral of depression and despair.

What he did best was introspecting, analyzing, reflecting on, and describing his emotions and inner experience. In fact, the only thing that Thomas felt he could depend on was the understanding that he had about life through his own inner experience. He learned how to trust that experience and that he must always be true to himself when it revealed something to him. But how does one parlay that talent into a job that someone will pay you to do? He had no idea what the answer was to that question.

He put himself through a degree in philosophy at Columbia as a night club entertainer in New York City, and then was accepted to a graduate program in philosophy at Berkeley with the hopes of getting a teaching job in a small college or university. To support himself while in graduate school, he got a temporary job at Lawrence Berkeley Laboratory (LBL) as a technician. Given his work at LBL, his interest turned to philosophy of physics and this created a synergy for his graduate studies and his new job. After six months as a temporary worker, he accepted a full time entry-level position operating the particle accelerator at the laboratory.

Thomas always had a sense that he was "different" and had special gifts and a destiny in life, but he really didn't know what that destiny was. Thomas was always self-conscious and felt *unusual* in some unexplainable way, perhaps weird. As a way of dealing with these feelings, he externalized them in the way he dressed, talked, and the things he did and didn't do. His feelings were so deep and overwhelming that he learned to express himself indirectly, especially through music and writing. The only way people could actually know him would be to see his image indirectly in a song or a book he had written, a movie in which the characters expressed who he was, or some other indirect self-representation.

Thomas had been in and out of many different relationships, always searching for the ideal partner, but never finding her. When he looked at the relationships that other more "normal" people had he felt a deep sense of longing to the depths of his terminally lonely soul. He escaped the trap of these depressing feelings by reasoning that these were "surface" people who were an inch deep and a mile wide. Of course they would have relationships, but who wanted the prospect of skipping across the surface of life. He was better off being alone, he rationalized, rather than being latched to someone who was only interested in the mundane goings on of day-to-day life.

Thomas always had deep intuitions about people, life and things, as if he could see below the surface of the everyday events of life. He could peer into the bizarre, forbidden, unspeakable soft underbelly of human existence, the kind of things people would hardly acknowledge to themselves even in the quietness of their own soul. He learned the hard way that he should keep these insights, premonitions, and intuitions to himself. On the occasions that he didn't, he was humiliated when people looked at him like he had three heads. He needed time to sort out whether they came from others, or whether they were artifacts of his own complicated experience of himself.

One of his many relationships came to an end, and as he was devastated for the nth time, Thomas began to realize how tired he was of this type of personal history repeating itself. He longed to get it right and move on into a deeply satisfying relationship. The break up with this woman had been more devastating than the others largely because he was so psychologically tired of failure. He began seeing a Jungian analyst named Trina. At the age of twenty-eight, Thomas was sinking down into the black hell of the unconscious, and mapping out what he saw by recording his dreams in a journal. Sometimes he'd paint or draw the confusing or terrifying images that appeared to him nightly. Analysis was a long process of looking under every psychic rock, trekking down every beckoning emotional trail, exploring every archetypal cave that presented itself as an image in some dream regardless of how ridiculous or painful it was.

Five years into the analytic process with Trina, Thomas learned the hard lesson that all who travel the road of analysis learn. After you have analyzed every dream symbol; relived the emotions of every traumatic experience in life, turned things over and over in your mind: yes, long after your psychological life has been completely dismantled, the process of analysis leaves you standing there in pieces. After all, analysis is the process of taking apart, and the sad fact is, it comes without a manual on how to put yourself back together again. But by staying with it, Thomas learned that the secret of deep change is that it's something that happens to you, not something you do for yourself. In fact, the first and most important step in following the natural process that Jung called Individuation was to stop trying to change yourself and simply be open to the naturally occurring process of change that happens within you.

His job at the laboratory and his interest in the social structure of large physics collaborations got him interested in how science was managed. One of his dissertation topics that didn't work out was an analysis of large physics collaborations at Fermilab, another high-energy physics laboratory, about thirty miles outside of downtown Chicago. Thomas began writing and publishing papers on the management of government-funded science, and giving invited talks at nationally sponsored conferences, which gave him lots of visibility. With the threat of a 30 percent cut in the U.S. high-energy physics budget, Thomas was laid off. Although this was traumatic, he used the notoriety he had garnered and the connections he had made through his publications and talks, to build his own full-time consulting practice.

The consulting world put a different kind of pressure on Thomas than he had previously experienced, but after eighteen years of analysis with Trina, he had learned the final lesson of walking the path toward wholeness. The job of every analyst is to work themselves out of a job, in other words, to get you to the psychological place where you can carry on the process of discovering who you really are by yourself.

At forty-seven, when Thomas met and married his wife Grace, the analytic process had taught him that finding his identity lay not in more introspection, but in the simple, mundane realities of life. More than anything, the birth of Thomas' son Mark was the capstone on an inner healing process that had taken so many years from the time he started working with Trina. Ironically, Thomas learned that he could only find himself by connecting to and participating in the very things he used to disdain – the realities of life: cooking, changing diapers, chopping wood, and the relaxation that came from hobbies like scuba diving.

Thomas' is only one of many possible stories that could be told to show what the Tacit Creed "I must be original" looks like in the life of an individual. While the surface traits; natural talents and abilities; life-experiences; relationships; socio-cultural setting; ethnicity; gender; and level of psychological health defined by the 80-20 Rule may vary dramatically from person-to-person, the underlying patterns, processes and structures of the stories of all type Fours will be similar.

Emergence of the Tacit Creed

The Four's Natural-Self occupies the bottom portion of Figure 35 where the Tacit Creed (I must be original) *emerges* from their innate, inborn temperament and the deep fear associated with the core assumption that they *lack individual existence in life*. The emphasis is on the word "individual" and the tacit conviction (and near certainty) that they are not a *single* (distinct) human being, as distinguished from a group, socio-cultural context, or the collective masses of all humanity. Fours experience this core assumption emotionally as a deep and abiding sense that, "I'm lost in the collective ocean of people and life, and long to have an independent existence *apart from* things that are "common" to all. I want to be distinguished by special, singular, and markedly personal qualities that set me apart from the sea of humanity." They *experience* the core assumption with an inner sense of *certainty* as a *self-evident* truth that cannot (and ought not) be: a) questioned, b) objectively or publicly tested, or c) even verbalized. This belief that Fours hold about themselves is a *secret* truth that they hide from themselves, others, and the world. It's undiscussible and its un-discussibility is itself undiscussible. The fear of self-knowledge creates a sense of psychological survival in Fours that threatens their *existence* to the point where the gate-keeping function *blocks* these emotions from conscious awareness. But life goes on, and so must the Four. Over time, the emotional and cognitive memories associated with this core assumption are *buried* deeper and deeper within the psyche of type Fours to the point where they become largely inaccessible to conscious awareness and are only experienced at pivotal (*kairos*) moments in life. This *forces* a shift in the Four's focus in order to avoid the embarrassment and threat that the reality of the core assumption creates, so rather than face (or test) the *veracity* of not having an individual existence in life, they *displace* the problem by creating an individual existence by "being original." But trying to be "original" can never fill the deep inner need of type Fours because it tries to address an *inner* (existential) issue with *outer* behavior.

Notice how the Tacit Creed can either be *deficiency-driven* by Longing and Melancholy or *growth-motivated* by Contentment and Joy and has a very different look and feel depending on whether it's driven or motivated – with the ratio of driven-to-motivated actions and interactions being defined as the 80-20 Rule. When Fours like Thomas are at their best and are growth-motivated, they are original, creative, self-revealing, authentic (different from others) and express their own way of seeing the world "indirectly" by creating tangible representations like art, music, literature, technology, architecture, or innovative products and services. When they face embarrassment, threat, or are deficiency-driven, Fours experience deep inner turmoil, depression, compulsive longing for love, envy, and a poignant sense of "cosmic" suffering. They express the emotional intensity of this inner experience through creative and symbolic means as a way of "making sense" of their suffering, pain, neediness, inner poverty, and alienation from themselves, others, and the world around them.

The three Somatic Instincts shown at the very bottom of Figure 35 are the first three levels of Maslow's Hierarchy and form the inner core and foundation upon which the type Four's personality is built. The Somatic Instincts powerfully shape the overall direction of a Four's life in the sense that their deep inner yearnings and desires unconsciously draw them to people, experiences, careers, relationships, and life situations that will gratify these basic human needs. So the *autopilot needs* of deficiency-driven Preserving Fours can only be gratified by being "original" in areas associated with home, nurture and comfort, while Cultivating Fours are unconsciously drawn to gratify their need to be "original" in areas associated with belonging and affiliation with groups, and the autopilot needs of Transmitting Four's must be gratified by being "original" in situations that revolve around love, affection, caring, and communicating their ideas.

Deficiency-Driven

As shown in Figure 35, when Fours are under pressure or facing embarrassment or threat, Longing and Melancholy become the deficiency-drivers, and the Tacit Creed for people like Thomas:

- Is like a hyper-sensitivity or allergic reaction to situations that fit the underlying pattern of having to be original, which for type Four means identifying ways to express their uniqueness and individualism.

- Creates a narrowing of focus in their attention that is driven by a yearning and desire to gratify the fourth level of Maslow's Hierarchy – the esteem needs. So how Fours "esteem" themselves is powerfully shaped and defined by their need to "see" themselves as being original and by having other people *confirm* this self-perception by also "seeing" them as original and different from others.

- Becomes a cognitive and emotional angle or perspective on life that singles-out specific underlying patterns in relationships, interactions, and situations that will gratify the Four's basic need to be original.

- Causes them to constantly evaluate their relationships and the environment for opportunities to be "original," even when other people don't want new solutions (or flatly refuse them) indicates that their need to be "original" often satisfies *their own needs*, not the needs of other people.

Unconscious Appraisal and Selection

This section *links* the unconscious, autopilot cognitive and emotional appraisal and selection process for type Fours, to the See-Do-Get Process and the Downward Spiral of Striving. Notice in Figure 36, that when the Tacit Creed "I must be original" is unpacked *as* the autopilot doing and learning process, Fours like Thomas tend to be unconsciously drawn to specific people, relationships, situations, and events in the world that will gratify: a) their need to be original, and b) the basic needs of their dominant Somatic Instinct.

Unconscious Appraisal and Selection

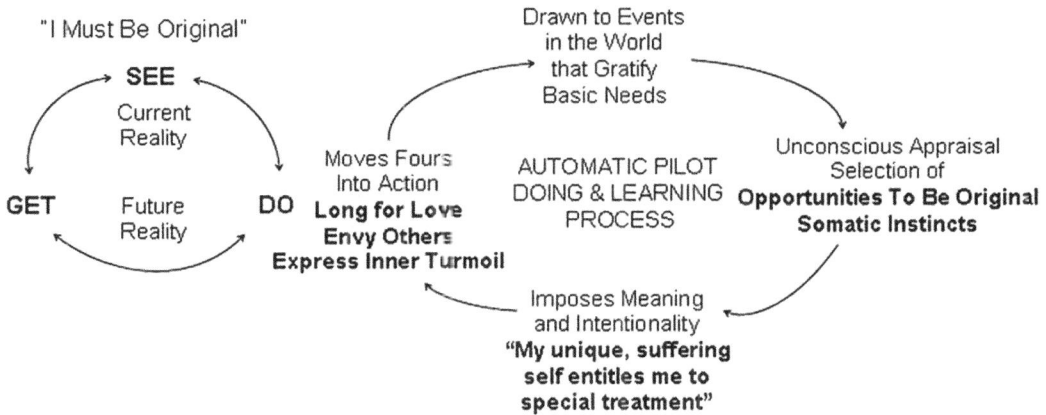

Figure 36

In the second step, Fours unconsciously *appraise* situations and *select* opportunities to get their basic needs met by being "original" in ways that are shaped and defined by their dominant Somatic Instinct – whether preserving, cultivating, or transmitting. They unconsciously choose very specific cognitive and emotional data from the world because they "match" the underlying patterns and basic need to create a sense of individual existence by acting out the *inner mandate* to be original.

In the third step, the Four's Tacit Creed *imposes* meaning and intentionality on the actions and interactions of people *and* the situations they're involved in. A typical tacit belief that Fours might impose on a situation from their Left-Hand Column is, "My uniqueness and the deep level of suffering that I've endured in my life entitles me to special treatment and to be loved." This reveals the Four's tendency to *project* their own needs and beliefs onto the world around them.

In the final step, the momentum and psychological force of the first three steps move Fours *into action* and these actions will tend to follow the pattern just described, where they deeply long for love, envy others' lives, and express the intensity of their inner turmoil, all with the unconscious goal of gratifying their own needs, but under the pretense of being original.

The entire process shown in Figure 36 happens beneath the surface of conscious awareness – in the blink of an eye. It's important to remember that the process can be growth-motivated where the four steps produce positive, constructive actions and interactions along the Upward Path of Becoming. Fours like Thomas who want to move from being deficiency-driven to growth-motivated must consciously raise this autopilot process back into conscious awareness; deconstruct and reconfigure it by running the See-Do-Get Process backwards in the counter clockwise direction; and then migrate the new growth-motivated actions and interactions back to autopilot operation by embedding them through repetition. When Fours succeed in using this change process, the new growth-motivated actions and interactions begin to happen as naturally and automatically as the previous deficiency-driven ones once did. When eight out of ten behaviors are growth-motivated by Contentment and Joy, rather than deficiency-driven by Longing and Melancholy, this is an indication that a Four is embodying the 80-20 Rule.

Blind Spots

When Fours are under pressure or facing embarrassment or threat, Longing and Melancholy become the deficiency-drivers for the Tacit Creed – "I must be original." Mounting evidence produced by countless cycles through the See-Do-Get Process gives Fours a *false sense* that being "original" has actually given them an individual existence in life, but this breeds an even deeper sense of Longing and Melancholy because of how alienated and isolated their special uniqueness makes them feel from other people (see Figure 37).

As in the case of Thomas, Fours tend to have "Blind Spots" about the *extent* to which Longing and Melancholy dominate their lives and create decision-making bias and predictable errors in judgment. Deficiency-driven Fours tend to "see" themselves as growth-motivated, while the people they interact with tend to "see" them as more deficiency-driven. The emotions of Longing and Manipulation are *inflamed* when Fours are under pressure or they don't get the results they want because people either object to (or don't respond to) their insatiable focus on suffering, loneliness, longing for love, and emotional intensity – masked beneath a façade of appearing special, different, and unique. Fours become "intoxicated" by the emotional power of Longing and Melancholy, which makes it more difficult for them to see their Blind Spots and unintended consequences for what they really are.

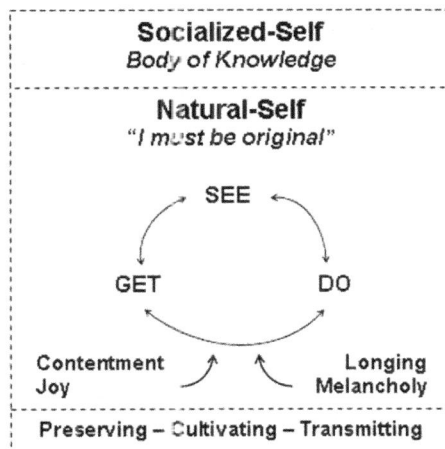

Figure 37

Once the intoxicating energy of Longing and Melancholy subsides, Fours will settle back down to the normal state-of-equilibrium of their dominant type. But over time, this cycle of behaviors and emotional responses *solidifies* into a well-defined pattern of interaction that goes on autopilot and slips below the surface of conscious awareness. These patterns-of-interactions are commonly called "hot buttons" or defense routines.

The philosophy of *originality as the road to individual existence* powerfully shapes the day-to-day preferences of Fours about the people, relationships, careers, hobbies, and lifestyles they are attracted to (and repulsed by), and over time these myriad choices are woven into the fabric of their lives. By the time Fours are young adults, they have identified with the Tacit Creed of "being original" to the point where they are locked into a cognitive, emotional, social, and contextual configuration that solidifies, reaches a state-of-equilibrium, and *becomes* their day-to-day reality. The inner mandate to be "original" becomes externalized, objectified, and ultimately reified into a social mirror that seems to objectively affirm the belief that the Four's way of seeing themselves, others, and the world is *the* way that life should be lived. We described this earlier as the Self-Sealing Process of forming Personality in Context.

But the *false sense* of individual existence that comes from being "original," the *validation* that comes from the social mirror, and the *stability* of the day-to-day reality that Fours construct – *come* at an enormous price, because they deeply divide them at the very core of their being. *Secretly*, Fours know that they're not as original as they claim to be, and the fear of this being discovered by others only *fuels* the autopilot, insatiable, destructive power of their Tacit Creed. Think about it – if the Tacit Creed of "being original" isn't true for Fours like Thomas – then what is? If Fours are wrong about how they see themselves, others, and the world, then they may be wrong about almost everything in life.

Growth-Motivated

We've spent a significant amount of time discussing the Tacit Creed and underlying mechanisms of the deficiency-driver of type Fours like Thomas because without a correct understanding of the process by which these underlying mechanisms bind and limit the choices, personal freedom, and self-determination of type Fours, there is little or no hope of ever escaping the pernicious entanglements of Personality in Context. In this section, I'd like to focus on the *single point of leverage* that will address the question, "So what should type Fours *do* about the negative characteristics and effects of their personality?" I will also discuss the concrete changes that Fours can expect to see in their actions and interactions when they choose the Upward Path of Becoming. As shown in Figure 38, when Fours are at their best Contentment and Joy become the growth-motivators for the Tacit Creed – "I must be original."

Growth-motivated Fours are original, creative, self-revealing, authentic (different from others) and express their own way of seeing the world "indirectly" by creating tangible representations like art, music, literature, technology, architecture, or innovative products and services.

While the Four's Blind Spots, defense routines, and the inner mandate to be "original" *combine* with the social mirror and the edicts of their socio-cultural context to form barriers to deep change, they all rest on the foundation of the Four's core assumption that they lack individual existence in life. Fours experience this "lack of individual existence in life" as a self-evident truth that cannot (and should not)

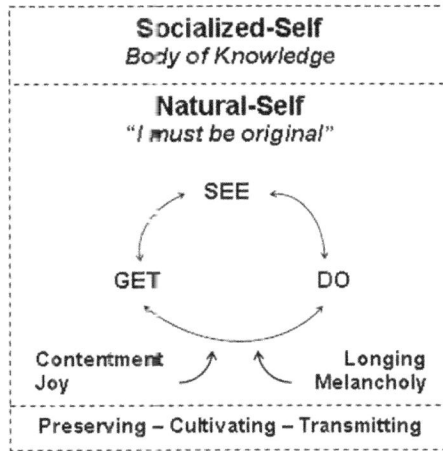

Figure 38

be questioned or tested, *but this is precisely what Fours must do*: face their fear of self-knowledge by questioning, and publicly testing, the truth of this claim. They must come to "see" themselves as having the tools to unlearn these *biased, misguided*, and *erroneous* ways of seeing themselves, others, and the world. Like the story of the Mulla, looking for the key in the *right* place becomes the *single point of leverage* that will enable Fours to ignite deep personal change.

Focusing on the *single point of leverage* acts like a *solvent* that begins to dissolve the *hidden inauthentic layers* of cognitive, emotional, social, and contextual strata from which the Four's life has been built. Using the single point of leverage enables Fours to begin living more authentically in terms of their actions, interactions, and decision-making within the current context of their lives. It helps them to do the right things, for the right reasons. There are a number of very concrete indicators that emerge when Fours like Thomas begin the journey on the Upward Path of Becoming:

- Fours are free to question their default way of seeing themselves as having to be "original" and having others see them as being different, special, and unique.
- Their hyper-sensitivity toward identifying ways to express their originality and individualism gives way to Contentment, Joy and a deep sense of equanimity, inner calm, and emotional balance where the experience of authentic love comes from loving others and making meaningful contributions to their lives.
- They begin to see that true originality comes from being an open, receptive conduit for the original, archetypal, collective source of all life and creative

power in the universe, and concretizing their own way of seeing the world in natural, spontaneous, authentic ways.

- Over time, Fours gain new confidence in their ability to transcend the constraints of their personality and cultural context as they see the concrete evidence of change indicated by their ability to act-out the 80-20 Rule – where eight out of ten interactions are motivated by Contentment and Joy, rather than being driven by Longing and Melancholy.

Connecting Points

As we saw in the case of Thomas, Fours intentionally alter their actions and inter-actions to "fit" the requirements and norms of a specific social or cultural context because doing otherwise might be inappropriate and could have negative conse-quences on them personally and professionally. In a previous section, I referred to this as the Socialized-Self. But buried deep beneath the Four's Socialized-Self, family background, life experiences, and body of knowledge is a unique under-lying *signature pattern* of connecting points that identifies what it means to be a type Four – their Natural-Self.

Connecting Points
(Conflicting Inner Mandates and Mixed Emotions)

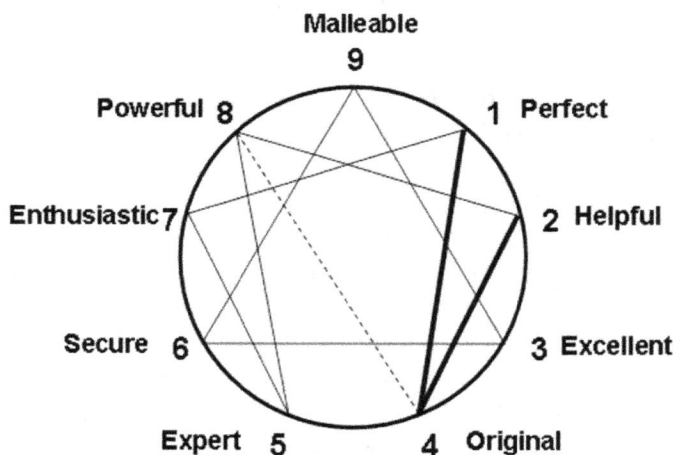

Figure 39

The underlying pattern and characteristics of the connecting points remain relatively constant over time and with changes in context. They are a well-defined intra-psy-chic pattern of interaction that shapes and defines Four's behaviors and responses in day-to-day discourse, especially in situations where they face *embarrassment* or *threat*. The patterns-of-interaction associated with the connecting points are also an indicator of whether or not the overall direction of the Four's life tends toward the Downward Spiral of Striving or the Upward Path of Becoming.

The Four's dominant type anchors them to the Enneagram and is a necessary element of verifying a person's Enneagram type. The signature pattern for type Four consists of four connecting points: types 4, 2, 1, and 8.

- Type Four is the Tacit Creed which we've already discussed in detail.

- Type Two is the Striving Point which is referred to by some Enneagram theorists as the point that indicates the direction of disintegration.

- Type One is the Becoming Point which is referred to by some Enneagram theorists as the point that indicates the direction of integration.

- Type Eight is the Paradox point. Although type Fours and Eights exhibit very different surface traits, Tacit Creeds, and underlying motivations; they are paradoxical opposites around the issue of *emotions* and *sensitivity*. Whereas type Fours tend to be the most emotionally sensitive of the Enneagram types and seek *intensity* through the deeper (and often darker) emotions of life rather than action, type Eights tend to be the least emotionally sensitive of the Enneagram types (turning their emotions off) and instead seek *intensity* through action and dominating their world.

- While the connecting points for Fours represent the *natural* pattern, process, and structure of this Enneagram type, they should not be viewed as rigid and determined. Given sufficient pressure and influence from family or the social-cultural context, these natural tendencies can be powerfully shaped and defined in other ways, with the original signature pattern of the type Four being hidden (or buried) beneath other configurations of Enneagram points.

What is most important to note is that the foundation of the type Four's personality is an *interdependent configuration* of conflicting inner mandates and mixed emotions that includes four types, their Tacit Creeds, and their destructive and constructive emotions. In other words, the type Four's personality is not a homogeneous set of beliefs; instead it is a portfolio of interdependent, complementary, competing, and conflicting ways of seeing themselves, others, and the world.

So when Fours like Thomas are stressed and facing embarrassment and threat, the autopilot patterns-of-interaction between their tacit, Striving, Becoming, and Paradox points can (and often do) create inner conflict and mixed emotions. This is especially true when Fours are faced with a problem that requires a *single* solution. In other words, Thomas would find himself wondering, "Should I do this, or should I do that? Should I be original or helpful?" This inner conflict is *intensified* when external pressures force Fours to act, interact, or make decisions *now*!

There are some key concepts that I'd like to review to define the psychological patterns, processes, and structure of the connecting points for type Fours in more detail.

- The actions and interactions of the other eight Enneagram types are done *in the service of* following the inner mandate to be "original" and maintaining the equilibrium of the cognitive, emotional, social, and contextual configuration that the Four builds as their life – their Personality in Context.

- When they are growth-motivated, the connections between type Four, Two, One, and Eight can help to balance some of the symmetries by giving Fours an Enneagram point in two out of the three triads, thus straddling the emotional and sensory parts of the human brain. The Four's connecting points also help to balance the left-right and top-bottom symmetries, where type Eight provides a left-side balance for Fours, and the types One and Eight provide Enneagram points that help to balance the top-bottom symmetry.

- Another key concept centers on the *combining* of the Tacit Creeds and underlying emotions into what is referred to as conflicting inner mandates and mixed emotions for type Fours. People rarely act univocally. Rather, actions, interactions (and eventually patterns-of-interaction) come in complex, interdependent bundles, where the Tacit Creeds and underlying emotions of the Four's connecting points *combine* and *co-mingle* to form extremely complex packages of emotional messages that are communicated to others.

A solid understanding of the signature pattern is the key to *unbundling* the complex packages of emotional messages and patterns-of-interaction that type Fours often exhibit in day-to-day interactions.

Type Four Summary Profile

Figure 40 provides an overall summary of the key patterns, structures, and processes that were described in this section and that typify the Enneagram type Four.

Type Summary Profile - Type Four	
Core Assumption	I lack an individual existence in life
Tacit Creed (Mulla)	I must be original
Unconscious Appraisal	Opportunities to be original and Somatic Instincts
Impose Meaning	My unique, suffering self entitles me to special treatment
Move Into Action	Long for love, envy others, express inner turmoil
Deficiency Drivers	Longing, Melancholy
Growth Motivators	Contentment, Joy
Striving Point	Type Two
Becoming Point	Type One
Paradox Point	Type Eight
Group (Triad)	Heart, leads with the emotional part of the brain (Amygdala)
Existential Question	How do I find an identity?
Conflict Processing Strategy	Reactive
Attitude Towards Socio-Cultural Change	Move Away/Withdrawn
Single Point of Leverage	Question and publicly test the core assumption

Figure 40

In keeping with the overall approach of the Breckenridge Enneagram, the characteristics and dynamics shown in Figure 40 are not surface-traits or behaviors. Rather, the content of Figure 40 describes the underlying patterns, structures, and processes that define what makes type Fours like Thomas different from the other eight Enneagram types.

Examples and Movies

While Fours are found in every area of life and all professional fields, the list below shows some famous examples of people who are probably type Fours. How many names do you recognize? Which ones are you interested enough in to learn more about by reading a biography or autobiography?

- *Examples* – Famous examples who exhibit Four traits: Joni Mitchell, Edgar Allen Poe, Thomas Merton, Judy Garland, George Harrison, James Dean, Neil Diamond, Judy Collins, Nicholas Cage, Nick Nolte.

Another way to see Enneagram type in action is through the characters and story lines in movies. Select some of the movies listed below and take some time to watch Fours in action.

- *Movie Characters* – Roles in movies that exemplify Four traits: Kate Winslet as Rose (Titanic), Sean (Good Will Hunting), Salieri (Amadeus), Nicholas Cage (Moonstruck and Leaving Las Vegas), Meryl Streep (Out of Africa).

To deepen your understanding of this Enneagram type, identify people who you *know* that embody this personality type and become more observant about their behaviors, attitudes, and decision-making strategies. Ask them to share their thoughts, views, and perspectives on key issues and criteria for decision-making and see how closely the descriptions in this section describe and predict their responses. To further solidify and deepen your understanding, log your insights and observations about this personality type in a journal. You can use this exercise for the other eight types as well.

Head Group

This section describes the three types that form the Head Group: Fives, Sixes, and Sevens. The types in the Head Group emerge from the Cognitive Brain which is localized in the Neocortex and other related neurophysiologic and sensory structures. The head types tend to "lead" with the cognitive rational part of their being, with the neuropsychological functions of the Heart and Action Groups playing key support roles. Head types tend to be future-oriented because their ideas and intellectual concepts are not bound to the realities of the past or present (space and time) and consequently they can travel far into the future.

Head Group
(Cognitive Brain, Neocortex, Future-Oriented)

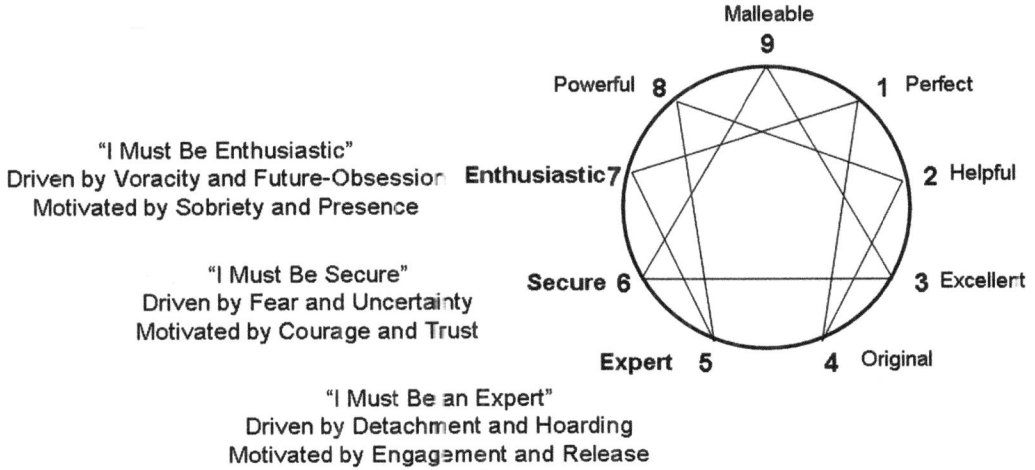

Malleable
9

Powerful **8**

1 Perfect

"I Must Be Enthusiastic"
Driven by Voracity and Future-Obsession
Motivated by Sobriety and Presence

Enthusiastic7

2 Helpful

Secure 6

3 Excellent

"I Must Be Secure"
Driven by Fear and Uncertainty
Motivated by Courage and Trust

Expert **5**

4 Original

"I Must Be an Expert"
Driven by Detachment and Hoarding
Motivated by Engagement and Release

Figure 41

The Tacit Creed for Five is, "I must be an expert" and can be either deficiency-driven by Detachment and Hoarding or growth-motivated by Engagement and Release. The look and feel of this personality type, and our *experience* of it, are very different when it is growth-motivated by Engagement and Release, rather than deficiency-driven by Detachment and Hoarding.

The Tacit Creed for Six is, "I must be secure" and can be either deficiency-driven by Fear and Uncertainty or growth-motivated by Courage and Trust. The look and feel of this personality type, and our *experience* of it, are very different when it is growth-motivated by Courage and Trust, rather than deficiency-driven by Fear and Uncertainty.

The Tacit Creed for Seven is, "I must be enthusiastic" and can be either deficiency-driven by Voracity and Future-Obsession or growth-motivated by Sobriety and Presence. The look and feel of this personality type, and our *experience* of it, are very different when it is growth-motivated by Sobriety and Presence, rather than deficiency-driven by Voracity and Future-Obsession.

The neocortex region of the brain exists only in mammals; and is most developed in humans where it contains an estimated 100 billion cells (each with up to 10,000 synapses) and roughly 100 million yards of wiring all packed into a structure the size and thickness of a formal dinner napkin.[32] The cells in the neocortex are arranged in six layers and, for humans, form the center of higher mental functions for humans such as sensory perception; generation of motor commands; spatial reasoning; high-level analytic and cognitive reasoning; and complex language processes. Our cognitive functions powerfully shape our ability to model, represent, understand, and ultimately control much of what goes on in our world and to navigate our way into the future. In many ways, who we are *cognitively* reveals something very deep about who we are as human beings *regardless* of what our dominant Enneagram type is. The ability to evaluate, analyze, and map-out the patterns, processes, and structures in our world is *universal* and Head types are tuned-in to the constant mental activity (and endless cognitive processing) that typifies this part of the human experience. It is important to remember that the Head space where types Fives, Sixes, and Sevens live, is known to (and experienced by) all nine types, and is an inner capacity that powerfully shapes and defines how we see ourselves, others, and the world through the See-Do-Get Process.

Key Question

Fives, Sixes, and Sevens tend to be overly-preoccupied with the key question of human existence, "How do I face the future?", although the three types tend to answer this same question in a very different way. It's not that the other types don't care about facing the future, it's just *not* the central concern of their lives and the focus of their values.

**Head Group
(Key Question: How Do I Face the Future?)**

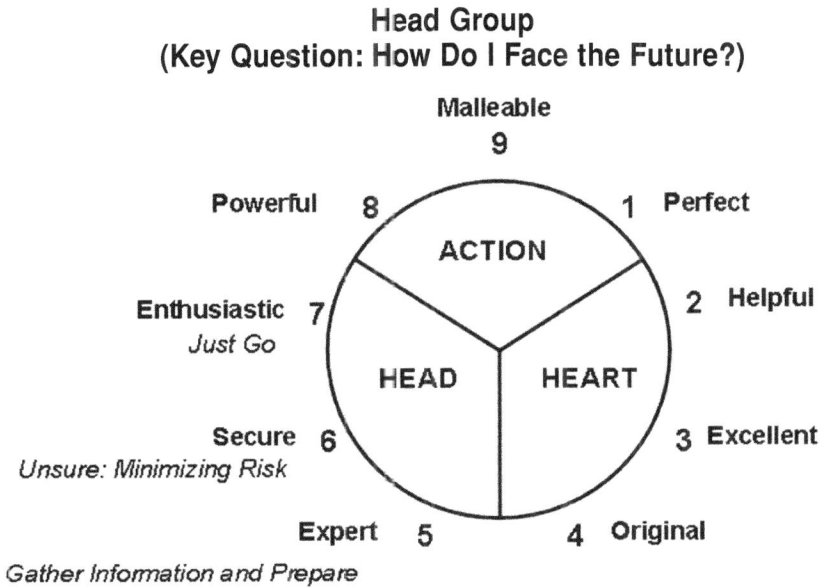

Figure 42

Fives tend to face the future by gathering information, preparing, and trying to think through every possible scenario that might occur. Sixes tend to face the future by minimizing all possible risks in order to ease their fear and uncertainty. Sevens tend to face the future by just moving into the future without much planning or thought of risk mitigation – they just go. The head types also ask the existential question that's common to all nine types, "How do I get the results that I want from my one-trip through life?" This key question compounds their natural tendency to focus on the future, and forces types Fives, Sixes, and Sevens to see the *outcome* of their lives within the context of its long-term implications.

Conflict Processing Strategies

All three conflict processing strategies are represented in the Head Group. Type Fives tend to use the *objective* strategy where they deal with conflict in relationships by putting their emotions and subjective feelings on the back burner, and resolving their differences by being objective, logical, effective, and rejecting the structures, systems and established rules of the context and relationship and work outside the boundaries.

**Head Group
(Conflict Processing Strategies)**

Malleable
9

Challenger 8   1 Perfect

ACTION

Enthusiastic 7   2 Helpful
Reframing

HEAD   HEART

Secure 6   3 Excellent
Reactive

Expert 5   4 Original
Objective

Figure 43

Type Sixes tend to use the *reactive* strategy where they deal with conflict by react-ing emotionally and then looking for an emotional response that mirrors their con-cern. They have strong opinions and emotional reactions and want to vent their feelings *before* moving on in relationships, so they both look for understanding and support and also deny that they need it. Type Sevens tend to use the *reframing* strategy where they deal with conflict and disappointment in relationships by "reframing" them in some positive way that emphasizes a brighter, more uplifting way of "seeing" life, and tend to have a problem balancing their own needs with the needs of others. More specifically, Sevens focus on their own needs rather than the needs of others.

Attitude toward Socio-Cultural Change

Each of the types in the Head Group tends to embody a different attitude toward socio-cultural change. Fives tend to be Withdrawn types that move away from others in their interactions, while Sixes are Compliant types and tend to move toward people in interactions, and Sevens tend to be Aggressive types who move against people in interactions.

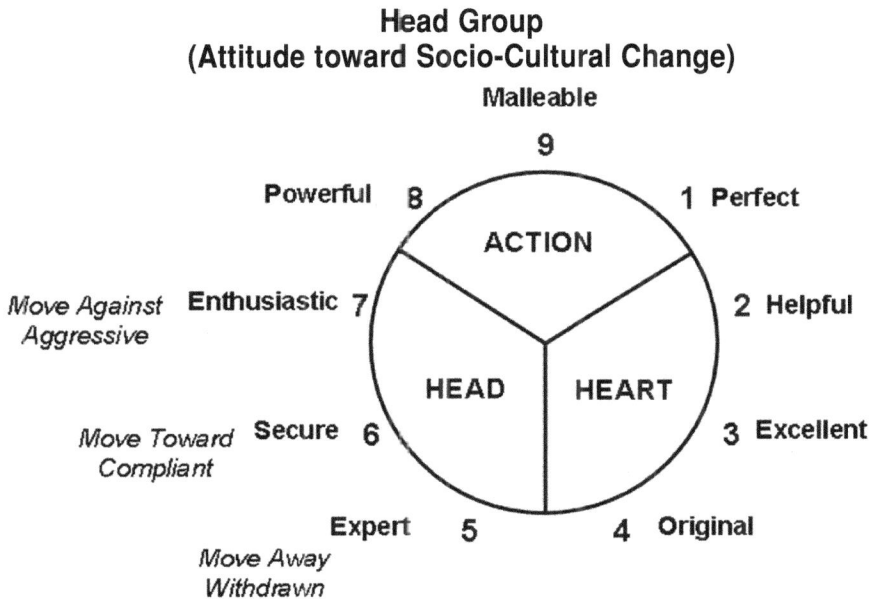

**Head Group
(Attitude toward Socio-Cultural Change)**

Malleable

Powerful 8   9   1 Perfect

ACTION

Move Against Enthusiastic 7   2 Helpful
Aggressive

HEAD | HEART

Move Toward Secure 6   3 Excellent
Compliant

Expert 5   4 Original

*Move Away
Withdrawn*

Figure 44

Type Fives tend to withdraw and disengage from socio-cultural change that they don't agree with or support because their Tacit Creed "I must be an expert" drives them to analyze and evaluate the change model and process. They inwardly disengage from people who support (or lead) the change process and outwardly exhibit an iconoclastic attitude toward the change process. Type Sixes tend to be compliant with socio-cultural change that they don't agree with or support because their Tacit Creed "I must be secure" drives them to minimize the risk and uncertainty of surviving in that context; and they tend to move toward people who support (or lead) the change process to identify hidden meanings and intentions. Type Sevens tend to be aggressive toward socio-cultural change that they don't agree with or support because their Tacit Creed "I must be enthusiastic" drives them to consider myriad alternatives to the proposed changes; and they tend to move against people who support (or lead) the change process because they believe their own needs are not being met.

Type Five (I Must Be an Expert)

When Fives are at their best, they are reflective, analytical, curious, pioneering, open-minded, independent thinkers with deep insight into the connections between complex and seemingly unrelated concepts, bodies of knowledge, and human and natural phenomena. When under pressure, they detach from the arena of life's problems and become provocative, iconoclastic, and apathetic; stoically resigned to life's "cosmic" meaninglessness, and accumulate knowledge and understanding in order to ignore and repress their profound and deeply hidden sense of neediness, inner-poverty, isolation, and alienation from themselves, others, and the world around them.

Figure 45

The very top of Figure 45 is made up of a person's Socialized-Self and body of knowledge, which form a major portion of the knowledge-base of their personal paradigm.

Tacit Creed

Fives live by the Tacit Creed "I must be an expert" – a belief that solidifies early in life through countless cycles through the See-Do-Get Process. When they are deficiency-driven they are hyper-sensitive to identifying areas where they lack knowledge, expertise, and the resources to face life, they constantly evaluate their relationships and environment for situations that require commitment and perceived demands (both internal and external) because they fear they will be overwhelmed by life's activities. Detachment and Hoarding are *inflamed* when under pressure or when they don't get the result they want; e.g., people either object to, or don't respond to, their insatiable desire for knowledge and understanding, and their lack of empathy and meanness, cynical-critical attitude, retentiveness, stonewalling, and their tendency to placate others about commitments they have made but not kept. When under stress, they become "intoxicated" by the power of these emotions and have a *Blind Spot* about the extent to which Detachment and Hoarding dominate their lives and create decision-making bias and predictable errors in judgment. While the perfectionism of Ones is *externally* focused on people and the environment, Fives exhibit an *internal* perfectionism where their knowledge and expertise are increased, deepened, and refined to higher and higher levels.

When they are growth-motivated, they are free to question their default way of seeing, and their hyper-sensitivity gives way to Engagement, Release, and a strong desire to experience, confront and move beyond their deeply hidden sense of neediness, inner-poverty, isolation, and alienation from self, others, and the world, rather than trying meeting these basic needs by accumulating and hoarding expertise. They begin to see that true knowledge and wisdom connect the underlying structures, patterns, and processes of how the world works to the concrete experiences of everyday life and common-sense strategies for solving life's problems. For Fives, the key element of personal growth and building effective relationships is to follow the 80-20 Rule – where eight out of ten interactions with others are characterized by Engagement and Release, rather than Detachment and Hoarding.

Joel's Story

Joel Booker's story is an example of what the Tacit Creed "I must be an expert" looks like when it's solidified in the life of a type Five. Even as a child, Joel Booker's family and friends always viewed him as living in his own little world. Inwardly, he was afraid of being engulfed by the collective demands of people and life so he just stayed to himself. Joel came to believe that he lacked material existence to face the future, so he set out to create a material existence by hoarding knowledge and being an expert at anything he set his mind to. He was the "smart kid" in class. As an adult, Joel pretty much knew that when he walked into a room full of people, he would probably be smarter than 95 percent of them, and he took pleasure in this fact. Joel's style was to be an inside-out observer of a world that he never quite felt he belonged in.

This was probably why Joel fit in so naturally as a bio-physicist at Los Alamos National Laboratory, the place where Robert Oppenheimer and a secluded and heavily guarded band of physicists invented the atomic bombs that were dropped on Japan. His top-secret clearance meant there were parts of Joel's job that he could not talk about. With a jet black ponytail, a plaid shirt, and a tweed jacket, in a town that had one of the highest per capita densities of Ph.D.s in the country, Joel was one of the "cone-heads" up on the hill. Like their predecessors during the war years, the Los Alamos scientists were the protected few who kept our nation's defense strong by pouring their creativity and technical prowess into weapons of greater and greater sophistication and destructive power.

Joel's intellectual arrogance and emotional detachment caused serious interpersonal conflicts with his last two secretaries, who filed grievances against him for creating a hostile work environment. His division leader was forced by the laboratory's HR Office to reprimand him and require that he attend a workshop on building his communication and interpersonal skills. Joel viewed this as another kind of "charm school" being taught by a not-so-bright business consultant. When cynically quizzed by one of his colleagues over lunch, "So how was it?" Joel responded, "It was like the revenge of the 'C' students."

It was not that Joel didn't *have* emotions and desires; he hid them from others under a persona of intellectual distance and indifference to matters of the heart. Joel had become a master at appearing detached and uninvolved when he actually had powerful emotions and desires on issues of life. Rather than take precious time and psychological energy away from his research, if he suspected that his hidden views might cause conflict with someone that he would have to stop and damp down, he didn't give them a straight answer. "Well," he'd say with a long pondering pause, "It's just more complicated than that." That was often the end of the discussion and people never knew where they stood with him.

In the part of his job that Joel could talk about, he had been doing radiation measurement studies in the Marshall Islands for the last twenty-five years. Some of the islands where the U.S. tested nuclear weapons, like Eniwetok, had already been resettled based partly on the scientific rigor of Joel's work. But over fifty years after the U.S. removed the natives of Bikini Atoll and detonated thirty-nine thermonuclear devices, Joel and his team of scientists were still studying the radioactive levels of cesium and plutonium on this tiny atoll. In a sense, the goal of the research was to help answer scientific questions about when people could return home. But for Joel, he just loved doing the research and hoped it would go on forever. He had published his results in the top scientific journals, and was viewed as a world-renowned expert in his field. The scientific community had long recognized Joel to be a person with extraordinary technical insight who had charted his own scientific course at Bikini. Joel was able to see the seemingly unrelated connections between the physics problems of residual radiation levels, and the biological and environmental problems of vegetation and rainfall levels in this secluded ecosystem.

The isolation of Los Alamos, high on the fingered mesas of northern New Mexico, mirrored Joel's deep need for isolation. Joel always had more research projects than he possibly could handle. He complained about being over-worked and having so little time to relax, but he constantly took on more and more projects as if they were satisfying some insatiable hunger that he had. He worked constantly and was stingy with his time, his emotional life, his psychological energy, and his willingness to meet with and communicate even with his colleagues and associates at the laboratory. His latest secretary, Gena, was under strict orders to protect him from the demands of everyone, even the laboratory director.

The only thing he enjoyed more than his work at the laboratory were his field trips to that isolated speck of sand that rose three feet above the Pacific Ocean, five thousand miles west of California, Bikini Atoll. For over a month at a time, Joel and his team lived in a primitive base-camp that was funded by his research project. Other than a scuba diving concession owned by a businessman in Majuro where Joel learned to dive years earlier, the base camp was the only thing on the island. The shadowy figures of aircraft carriers, battle ships, and destroyers that were brought to Bikini, moored in the lagoon, and sunk as part of the U.S. nuclear testing program lay on the sandy floor of the lagoon almost two hundred feet below the surface of the crystal clear water. Because of the historical link between Los Alamos and the war in the Pacific, Joel had often done the 185-foot deep decompression dive to see the 780-foot battleship Nagato, the boat from which Admiral Yamamoto gave the order to bomb Pearl Harbor. It's not that Joel particularly liked wreck diving, it's just that these ships were not "boringly" sunk by airplanes and torpedoes during the war like those at Truk Lagoon. The ships at Bikini are the only ones in the world that were sunk by thermonuclear detonation.

Joel normally felt compelled to debate the merits and shades-of-gray of almost every situation with whoever he was talking to. When he felt pressed for time or psychological energy, as he almost always was, he would appear to go along with what his wife or a project leader wanted, but secretly he would just continue to do exactly what he wanted to do and then let them figure it out. He often substituted thinking about something for actually doing it. In reflective moments when he was brutally honest with himself, he knew that this was what he did in his relationships because intellectualizing a relationship was much less threatening than actually having one. Joel knew that he should buy his wife flowers once in a while, take some time off for a family vacation, and spend more time with his daughter who was growing up right before his eyes. But he had enormous difficulty initiating action on even the smallest things in life without thinking it to death. At least part of his experience had taught him that if he could just ignore the problems he had in life and stick them into some mental drawer in his mind, six months from now, 80 percent of them would no longer be a problem. Unfortunately, Joel would ignore people even when *he knew* they were asking him to do something that was in his best interest. Joel wanted to work on these issues at some level, but he just didn't know where to start.

Joel's story is only one of many that could be told to show what the Tacit Creed "I must be an expert" looks like in the life of an individual. While the surface traits; natural talents and abilities; life-experiences; relationships; socio-cultural setting; ethnicity; gender; and level of psychological health defined by the 80-20 Rule may vary dramatically from person-to-person, the underlying patterns, processes and structures of the stories of all type Fives will be similar.

Emergence of the Tacit Creed

The Five's Natural-Self occupies the bottom portion of Figure 45 where the Tacit Creed (I must be an expert) *emerges* from their innate, inborn temperament and the deep fear associated with the core assumption that they *lack the material existence to face the future.* The emphasis is on the word "material" and the tacit conviction (and near certainty) that they lack the physical and financial resources, available time, psychological energy, and other sources of physical and corporeal supplies needed to face the challenges that life presents. Fives *experience* this core assumption with an inner sense of *certainty* as a *self-evident* truth that cannot (and ought not) be: a) questioned, b) objectively or publicly tested, or c) even verbalized. This belief that Fives hold about themselves is a *secret* truth that they hide from themselves, others, and the world. It's undiscussible and even its un-discussibility cannot be discussed. The *deep fear* of experiencing the emotions, pain and rejection that surround this core assumption creates a sense of psychological survival in Fives that threatens their *existence* to the point where the gate-keeping function *blocks* these emotions from conscious awareness. But life goes on, and so must the Five. Over time, the emotional and cognitive memories associated with this core assumption are *buried* deeper and deeper within the psyche of type Fives to the point where they become largely inaccessible to conscious awareness and are only experienced at pivotal (*kairos*) moments in life. This *forces* a shift in the Five's focus in order to avoid the embarrassment and threat that the reality of the core assumption creates, so rather than face (or test) the *truth* of not having a material existence in life, they *displace* the problem by "being an expert." But trying to be an "expert" can never fill the deep inner need of type Fives because it tries to address an *inner* (existential) issue with *outer* behavior.

Notice how the Tacit Creed can either be *deficiency-driven* by Detachment and Hoarding or *growth-motivated* by Engagement and Release and has a very different look and feel depending on whether it's driven or motivated – with the ratio of driven-to-motivated actions and interactions being defined as the 80-20 Rule. When Fives like Joel are at their best and are growth-motivated, they are reflective, analytical, curious, pioneering, open-minded, independent thinkers with deep insights into the connections between complex and seemingly unrelated concepts, bodies of knowledge, and human and natural phenomena. When they face embarrassment, threat or are deficiency-driven, Fives detach from the arena of life's problems and become provocative, iconoclastic, and apathetic; stoically resigned to life's cosmic meaninglessness, and accumulate knowledge and understanding in order to ignore and repress their profound and deeply hidden sense of neediness, inner-poverty, isolation, and alienation from themselves, others, and the world around them.

The three Somatic Instincts shown at the very bottom of Figure 45 are the first three levels of Maslow's Hierarchy and form the inner core and foundation upon which the type Five's personality is built. The Somatic Instincts powerfully shape the overall direction of a Five's life in the sense that their deep inner yearnings and desires unconsciously draw them to people, experiences, careers, relationships, and life situations that will gratify these basic human needs. So the *autopilot needs* of deficiency-driven Preserving Fives can only be gratified by being an "expert" in areas associated with home, nurture and comfort, while Cultivating Fives are unconsciously drawn to gratify their need for "expertise" in areas associated with belonging and affiliation with groups, and the autopilot needs of Transmitting Fives must be gratified by gaining "expertise" in situations that revolve around love, affection, caring, and communicating their ideas.

Deficiency-Driven

As shown in Figure 45, when Fives are under pressure or facing embarrassment or threat, Detachment and Hoarding become the deficiency-drivers, and the Tacit Creed for people like Joel:

- Is like a hyper-sensitivity or allergic reaction to situations that fit the underlying pattern of having to be an expert, which for type Fives means identifying areas where they lack knowledge, expertise, and the resources to face life.

- Creates a narrowing of focus in their attention that is driven by a yearning and desire to gratify the fourth level of Maslow's Hierarchy – the esteem needs. So how Fives "esteem" themselves is powerfully shaped and defined by their need to "see" themselves as being an expert, and by having other people *confirm* this self-perception by also "seeing" them as an expert.

- Becomes a cognitive and emotional angle or perspective on life that singles-out specific underlying patterns in relationships, interactions, and situations that will gratify the Five's basic need to be an expert.

- Causes them to constantly evaluate their relationships and the environment for opportunities to gain "expertise," even when situations don't require it (or people state that they do not need it), which indicates that their need to be an "expert" often satisfies *their own needs*, not the needs of other people or the situations they face.

Unconscious Appraisal and Selection

This section *links* the unconscious, autopilot cognitive and emotional appraisal and selection process for type Fives, to the See-Do-Get Process and the Downward Spiral of Striving. Notice in Figure 46, that when the Tacit Creed "I must be an expert" is unpacked *as* the autopilot doing and learning process, Fives like Joel tend to be unconsciously drawn to specific people, relationships, situations, and events in the world that will gratify: a) their need to be an expert, and b) the basic needs of their dominant Somatic Instinct.

Unconscious Appraisal and Selection

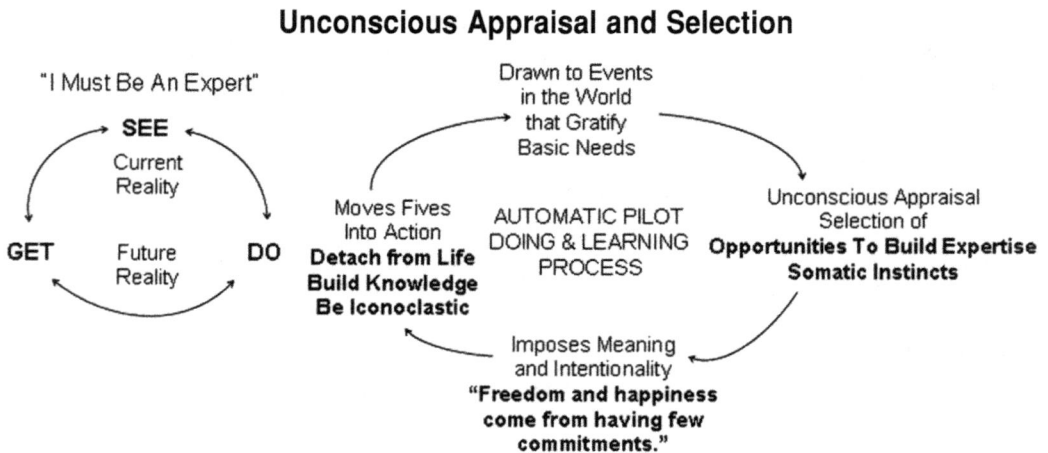

Figure 46

In the second step, Fives unconsciously *appraise* situations and *select* opportunities to get their basic needs met by gaining "expertise" in areas that are shaped and defined by their dominant Somatic Instinct – whether preserving, cultivating, or transmitting. They unconsciously choose very specific cognitive and emotional data from the world because they "match" the underlying patterns and basic need to develop the material existence to face the future by acting out the *inner mandate* to be an expert.

In the third step, the Five's Tacit Creed *imposes* meaning and intentionality on the actions and interactions of people *and* the situations they're involved in. A typical tacit belief that Fives might impose on a situation from their Left-Hand Column is, "Freedom and happiness come from having few commitments to people or life – it's always better to go it alone." This reveals the Five's tendency to *project* their own needs and beliefs onto the world around them.

In the final step, the momentum and psychological force of the first three steps move Fives *into action* and these actions will tend to follow the pattern just described, where they detach from the problems of day-to-day life, build (and even hoard) knowledge, and exhibit an iconoclastic attitude, all with the unconscious goal of gratifying their own needs, but under the pretense of being an "expert."

The entire process shown in Figure 46 happens beneath the surface of conscious awareness – in the blink of an eye. It's important to remember that the process can be growth-motivated where the four steps produce positive, constructive actions and interactions along the Upward Path of Becoming. Fives like Joel who want to move from being deficiency-driven to growth-motivated must consciously raise this autopilot process back into conscious awareness; deconstruct and reconfigure it by running the See-Do-Get Process backwards in the counter clockwise direction; and then migrate the new growth-motivated actions and interactions back to autopilot operation by embedding them through repetition. When Fives succeed in using this change process, the new growth-motivated actions and interactions begin to happen as naturally and automatically as the previous deficiency-driven ones once did. When eight out of ten behaviors are growth-motivated by Engagement and Release, rather than deficiency-driven by Detachment and Hoarding, this is an indication that a Five is embodying the 80-20 Rule.

Blind Spots

When Fives are under pressure or facing embarrassment or threat, Detachment and Hoarding become the deficiency-drivers for the Tacit Creed – "I must be an expert." Mounting evidence produced by countless cycles through the See-Do-Get Process gives Fives a *false sense* that being an "expert" has actually given them the resources and material existence needed to face the future, but this breeds an even deeper sense of detachment because of how alienated and isolated their iconoclasm, apathy, and stoic resignation about life's meaninglessness make them feel from other people (see Figure 47).

Figure 47

Much like Joel, Fives tend to have "Blind Spots" about the *extent* to which Detachment and Hoarding dominate their lives and create decision-making bias and predictable errors in judgment. Deficiency-driven Fives tend to "see" themselves as growth-motivated, while the people they interact with tend to "see" them as more deficiency-driven. The emotions of Detachment and Hoarding are *inflamed* when Fives are under pressure or they don't get the results they want because people either object to (or don't respond to) their insatiable desire for knowledge and understanding and their lack of empathy, cynical-critical attitude, and stonewalling (and placating) others about commitments they have made, but not kept. Fives become "intoxicated" by the emotional power of Hoarding and Detachment, which makes it more difficult for them to see their Blind Spots and unintended consequences for what they really are. Once the intoxicating energy of Hoarding and Detachment subsides, Fives will settle back down to the normal state-of-equilibrium of their dominant type. But over time, this cycle of behaviors and emotional responses *solidifies* into a well-defined pattern of interaction that goes on autopilot and slips below the surface of conscious awareness. These patterns-of-interactions are commonly called "hot buttons" or defense routines.

The philosophy of *building expertise and resources as the road to building a material existence* powerfully shapes the day-to-day preferences of Fives about the people, relationships, careers, hobbies, and lifestyles they are attracted to (and repulsed by), and over time these myriad choices are woven into the fabric of their lives. By the time Fives are young adults, they have identified with the Tacit Creed of "being an expert" to the point where they are locked into a cognitive, emotional, social, and contextual configuration that solidifies, reaches a state-of-equilibrium, and *becomes* their day-to-day reality. The inner mandate to be "an expert" becomes externalized, objectified, and ultimately reified into a social mirror that seems to objectively affirm the belief that the Five's way of seeing themselves, others, and the world is *the* way that life should be lived. We described this earlier as the Self-Sealing Process of forming Personality in Context.

But the *false sense* of material existence that comes from being an "expert," the *validation* that comes from the social mirror, and the *stability* of the day-to-day reality that Fives construct – *come at* an enormous price, because they deeply divide them at the very core of their being. *Secretly*, Fives know that they don't have the level of expertise that they claim to have, and the fear of this being discovered by others only *fuels* the autopilot, insatiable, destructive power of their Tacit Creed. Think about it – if the Tacit Creed of "being an expert" isn't true for Fives like Joel – then what is? If Fives are wrong about how they see themselves, others, and the world, then they may be wrong about almost everything in life.

Growth-Motivated

We have spent a significant amount of time discussing the Tacit Creed and under-lying mechanisms of the deficiency-driver of Fives like Joel because without a correct understanding of the process by which these underlying mechanisms bind and limit the choices, personal freedom, and self-determination of type Fives, there is little or no hope of ever escaping the pernicious entanglements of Personality in Context. In this section, I'd like to focus on the *single point of leverage* that will address the question, "So what should type Fives *do* about the negative characteristics and effects of their personality?" I will also discuss the concrete changes that Fives can expect to see in their actions and interactions when they choose the Upward Path of Becoming. As shown in Figure 48, when Fives are at their best Engagement and Release become the growth-motivators for the Tacit Creed – "I must be an expert."

Socialized-Self
Body of Knowledge

Natural-Self
"I must be an expert"

SEE

GET   DO

Engagement   Detachment
Release   Hoarding

Preserving – Cultivating – Transmitting

Figure 48

Growth-motivated Fives are reflective, analytical, curious, pioneering, open-minded, independent thinkers with deep insights into the connections between complex and seemingly unrelated concepts, bodies of knowledge, and human and natural phenomena.

While the Five's Blind Spots, defense routines, and the inner mandate to be "an expert" *combine* with the social mirror and the edicts of their socio-cultural context to form barriers to deep change, they all rest on the foundation of the Five's core assumption that they lack the resources and material existence to face the future. Fives experience this "lack of resources and material existence" as a self-evident truth that cannot (and ought not) be questioned or tested, *but this is precisely what Fives must do*: face their fear of self-knowledge by questioning, and publicly testing, the truth of this claim. They must come to "see" themselves as having the tools to unlearn these *biased, misguided,* and *erroneous* ways of seeing themselves, others, and the world. Like the story of the Mulla, looking for the key in the *right* place becomes the *single point of leverage* that will enable Fives to ignite deep personal change.

Focusing on the single point of leverage acts like a *solvent* that begins to dissolve the *hidden inauthentic layers* of cognitive, emotional, social, and contextual strata from which the Five's life has been built. Using the single point of leverage enables Fives to begin living more authentically in terms of their actions, interactions, and decision-making within the current context of their lives. It helps them to do the right things, for the right reasons. There are a number of very concrete indicators that emerge when Fives like Joel begin the journey on the Upward Path of Becoming:

- Fives are free to question their default way of seeing themselves as having to be an "expert" and having others "see" them as being an expert.
- Their hyper-sensitivity toward identifying areas where they lack knowledge, expertise, and the resources to face life gives way to the experience of Engagement and Release, and a strong desire to experience, confront, and move beyond their deeply hidden sense of neediness, inner-poverty, isolation, and alienation from self, others, and the world around them, rather than trying to gratify these basic needs by accumulating expertise.
- They begin to see that true knowledge and wisdom *connect* the underlying structures, patterns, and processes of how the world works to the concrete, mundane, pedestrian experiences of day-to-day life, and to common-sense strategies for solving life's problems.
- Over time, Fives gain new confidence in their ability to transcend the constraints of their personality and cultural context, as they see the concrete evidence of change indicated by their ability to act-out the 80-20 Rule – where eight out of ten interactions are motivated by Engagement and Release, rather than being driven by Detachment and Hoarding.

Connecting Points

Much like the story of Joel, Fives intentionally alter their actions and interactions to "fit" the requirements and norms of a specific social or cultural context because doing otherwise might be inappropriate and could have negative consequences on them personally and professionally. In a previous section, I referred to this as the Socialized-Self. But buried deep beneath the Five's Socialized-Self, family background, life experiences, and body of knowledge is a unique underlying signature pattern of connecting points that identifies what it means to be a type Five – their Natural-Self.

The underlying pattern and characteristics of the connecting points remain relatively constant over time and with changes in context. They are a well-defined intra-psychic pattern of interaction that shapes and defines Five's behaviors and responses in day-to-day discourse, especially in situations where they face *embarrassment* or *threat*. The patterns-of-interaction associated with the connecting points are also an indicator of whether or not the overall direction of the Five's life tends toward the Downward Spiral of Striving or the Upward Path of Becoming.

Connecting Points
(Conflicting Inner Mandates and Mixed Emotions)

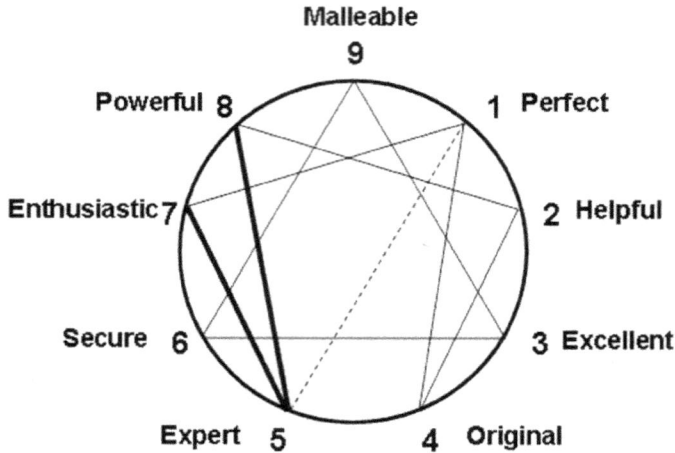

Figure 49

The Five's dominant type anchors them to the Enneagram and is a necessary element of verifying a person's Enneagram type. The signature pattern for type Five consists of four connecting points: types Five, Seven, Eight, and One.

- Type Five is the Tacit Creed which we've already discussed in detail.

- Type Seven is the Striving Point which is referred to by some Enneagram theorists as the point that indicates the direction of disintegration.

- Type Eight is the Becoming Point which is referred to by some Enneagram theorists as the point that indicates the direction of integration.

- Type One is the Paradox Point. What could be more different than the perfectionistic rule-keeping of type Ones and the intense desire for knowledge and expertise of the type Five personality? But on closer examination type Ones exhibit an externally focused perfectionism on people and the environment, while type Fives exhibit an internally focused perfectionism where they deepen and refine their knowledge in an endless search for intellectual perfectionism.

- While the connecting points for Fives represent the *natural* pattern, process, and structure of this Enneagram type, they should not be viewed as rigid and determined. Given sufficient pressure and influence from family or the social-cultural context, these natural tendencies can be powerfully shaped and defined in other ways, with the original signature pattern of the type Five being hidden (or buried) beneath other configurations of Enneagram points.

What is most important to note is that the foundation of the type Five's personality is an *interdependent configuration* of conflicting inner mandates and mixed emotions that includes four types, their Tacit Creeds, and their destructive and constructive emotions. In other words, the Five's personality is not a homogeneous set of beliefs; instead it is a portfolio of interdependent, complementary, competing, and conflicting ways of seeing themselves, others, and the world.

So when Fives like Joel are stressed and facing embarrassment and threat, the auto-pilot patterns-of-interaction between their tacit, Striving, Becoming, and Paradox points can (and often do) create inner conflict and mixed emotions. This is especially true when Fives are faced with a problem that requires a *single* solution. In other words, Joel would find himself wondering, "Should I do this, or should I do that? Should I be an expert or powerful?" This inner conflict is *intensified* when external pressures force Fives to act, interact, or make decisions *now*!

There are some key concepts that I'd like to review to define the psychological patterns, processes, and structure of the connecting points for type Fives in more detail.

- The actions and interactions of the other eight Enneagram types are done *in the service of* following the inner mandate to being an "expert" and maintaining the equilibrium of the cognitive, emotional, social, and contextual configuration that the Five builds as their life – their Personality in Context.

- When they are growth-motivated, the connections between type Five, Seven, Eight, and One can help to balance some of the symmetries by giving Fives an Enneagram point in two out of the three triads, thus straddling the cognitive and sensory parts of the human brain. The Five's connecting points also help to balance the left-right and top-bottom symmetries, where type One provides a left-side balance for Fives, and the types One and Eight provide Enneagram points that help to balance the top-bottom symmetry.

- Another key concept centers on the *combining* of the Tacit Creeds and underlying emotions into what is referred to as conflicting inner mandates and mixed emotions for type Fives. People rarely act univocally. Rather, actions, interactions (and eventually patterns-of-interaction) come in complex, interdependent bundles, where the Tacit Creeds and underlying emotions of the Five's connecting points *combine* and *co-mingle* to form extremely complex packages of emotional messages that are communicated to others.

A solid understanding of the signature pattern is the key to *unbundling* the complex packages of emotional messages and patterns-of-interaction that type Fives often exhibit in day-to-day interactions.

Type Five Summary Profile

Figure 50 provides an overall summary of the key patterns, structures, and processes that were described in this section and that typify the Enneagram type Five.

Type Summary Profile - Type Five	
Core Assumption	I lack the material substance to face the future
Tacit Creed (Mulla)	I must be an expert
Unconscious Appraisal	Opportunities to build expertise and Somatic Instincts
Impose Meaning	Freedom and happiness come from having few commitments
Move Into Action	Detach from life, build knowledge, be iconoclastic
Deficiency Drivers	Detachment, Hoarding
Growth Motivators	Engagement, Release
Striving Point	Type Seven
Becoming Point	Type Eight
Paradox Point	Type One
Group (Triad)	Head, leads with the cognitive part of the brain (Neocortex)
Existential Question	How do I face the future?
Conflict Processing Strategy	Objective
Attitude Towards Socio-Cultural Change	Move Away/Withdrawn
Single Point of Leverage	Question and publicly test the core assumption

Figure 50

In keeping with the overall approach of the Breckenridge Enneagram, the characteristics and dynamics shown in Figure 50 are not surface-traits or behaviors. Rather, the content of Figure 50 describes the underlying patterns, structures, and processes that define what makes type Fives like Joel different from the other eight Enneagram types.

Examples and Movies

While Fives are found in every area of life and all professional fields, the list below shows some famous examples of people who are probably type Fives. How many names do you recognize? Which ones are you interested enough in to learn more about by reading a biography or autobiography?

- *Examples* – Famous examples who exhibit Five traits: John Lennon, Bill Gates, Amelia Earhart, Albert Einstein, Bobby Fischer, Charles Darwin, Rene Descartes, Isaac Asimov, Stephen King, Jane Goodall, Alfred Hitchcock, Anthony Hopkins, T.S. Eliot, Warren Buffett.

Another way to see Enneagram type in action is through the characters and story lines in movies. Select some of the movies listed below and take some time to watch Fives in action.

- *Movie Characters* – Roles in movies that exemplify Five traits: Will (Good Will Hunting), C.S. Lewis (Shadowlands), Alastair Sim as Ebenezer Scrooge in Dickens' Christmas Carol, Gena Rowlands (Another Woman), Robin Williams (Awakenings), Data (Star Trek), Tommy Lee Jones (Lonesome Dove), Alex Rover (Jodie Foster) in Nim's Island.

To deepen your understanding of this Enneagram type, identify people who you *know* that embody this personality type and become more observant about their behaviors, attitudes, and decision-making strategies. Ask them to share their thoughts, views, and perspectives on key issues and criteria for decision-making and see how closely the descriptions in this section describe and predict their responses. To further solidify and deepen your understanding, log your insights and observations about this personality type in a journal. You can use this exercise for the other eight types as well.

Type Six (I Must Be Secure)

When Sixes are at their best, they are cautious, responsible, hard-working and vigilant about identifying potential problems in order to create a reliable and safe environment for themselves and others. When under pressure, they are hyper-alert, suspicious, chronically uncertain, looking for hidden meanings and underlying patterns of intention, and filled with anxiety in the absence of real threats.

Figure 51

The very top of Figure 51 is made up of a person's Socialized-Self and body of knowledge, which form a major portion of the knowledge-base of their personal paradigm.

Tacit Creed

Sixes live by the Tacit Creed "I must be secure" – a belief that solidifies early in life through countless cycles through the See-Do-Get Process. When they are Deficiency Driven, they are hyper-sensitive to identifying potential threats, harm, or danger, they constantly evaluate and remain vigilant for hidden motives, special meanings, ulterior motives, and trickery because they see themselves as living in a dog-eat-dog world of people who are out for themselves. Fear and Uncertainty are *inflamed* when under pressure or when they don't get the result they want; e.g., people either object to, or don't respond to, their insatiable desire to test and probe others' motives and intentions, being overly-cautious, compulsively checking and rechecking, avoiding decisions, and being paralyzed by doubt. When under stress, they become "intoxicated" by the power of these emotions and have a *Blind Spot* about the extent to which Fear and Uncertainty dominate their lives and create decision-making bias and predictable errors in judgment.

When they are Growth Motivated, they are free to question their default way of see-ing and their hyper-sensitivity gives way to Courage, Trust, and a deep sense of inner guidance and direction combined with discernment that helps differentiate between actual instances of potential threats and harm, and those that are an artifact of their basic need to be secure. They begin to see that they can put their welfare in the hands of others and are no longer bound by indecision, doubt, and ambiguity because they experience an inner gyroscopic sense of orientation and direction that enables them to face the problems and challenges of life effectively. For Sixes, the key ele-ment of personal growth and building effective relationships is to follow the 80-20 Rule – where eight out of ten interactions with others are characterized by Courage and Trust, rather than Fear and Uncertainty.

Bethany's Story

Bethany Wringer's story is an example of what the Tacit Creed "I must be secure" looks like when it's solidified in the life of a type Six. Bethany has always been dominated by anxiety, sometimes to the point where people were afraid to tell her things they feared she would worry about. For as long as she could remember, she felt like she couldn't trust her ability to make decisions and cope with life. Bethany came to believe that she lacked the inner discernment needed to face the future, so she tried to create a sense of discernment by being secure in all that she had and did. More than anything, she was ambivalent about life.

Bethany was a caseworker for the Social Services Department of the city and county of Myrtle Beach, South Carolina. She had a passion for helping children who came from dysfunctional families and her job allowed her to do just that. But after a few years, Bethany had become increasingly cynical about the seriousness of the prob-lems she encountered in the families she and her fellow caseworkers confronted every day. What she was unaware of was that her passion and her growing cynicism resulted from her unconscious attempts to use her job as a way to work through her own childhood issues.

Bethany's father, Jerry, was an ultra-fundamentalist preacher who sermonized long and hard about sin and repentance, with a judgmental tone that came through even when he tried to talk about God's love. Her mother, Nadine, was a stay-at-home pastor's wife who had raised Bethany and four other children in a meager country parsonage. They were dedicated to their ministry, and times were often hard. The fundamentalist guidelines and "truth" that Bethany had gotten drummed into her head all her life were what she looked to for guidance, but paradoxically they did nothing to ease her anxiety and worry about this life or the next. If anything, they made things worse. Her parents insisted that she go to a Christian school, and given how well she had done academically in high school, Bethany won a scholarship to attend the Midwest Bible Institute in Chicago, where she studied child psychology.

Bethany found it hard to make decisions, especially ones that had long-term impact. When she finally did make a decision, she would worry herself sick about it and manufacture potential problems that "might" happen as a result. More than most people, she was dominated by a fear of her ability to survive in life, and she responded to the world reactively and with a sense of urgency and alarm. In the very deepest part of who she was, Bethany lived at the level of her animal instincts, but these could not be trusted because they not only detected real danger in life, but also found danger where there was none. Her friends and parents alike knew her to be lovable, friendly and hardworking – the kind of person who would be committed to getting any job done she was given. But beneath this veneer of compliance was a woman who was out of touch with herself in a serious way, and found it difficult or impossible to act independently of the views and opinions of others because she so thoroughly distrusted her own thoughts and emotions. But at the same time, she would routinely play the devil's advocate with those same people she claimed she trusted.

Her fundamentalist faith became even more calcified at the Midwest Bible Institute, where she was required to sign a doctrinal statement about her faith in God, plus a lengthy laundry list of things she promised not to do while she was at the school. Students were required to attend chapel three times a week, and conservative theology was a significant lens through which all disciplines were interpreted. But compared with the fundamentalism of her upbringing, Bethany was confronted for the first time with defining what she thought about the issues of life and her faith. The combination of the pressure of schoolwork, her part-time job, and her new freedom stressed Bethany to the point where she began seeing Dr. Paula Jones, a local Christian psychologist. Paula was an open and direct person, and for Bethany, a breath of fresh air. Dr. Jones tried to explain to Bethany that rigid forms of fundamentalism could be psychologically damaging to people through guilt and manipulation. Many people like Paula still believed in God, but did not have such rigid views. With Paula as her guide, Bethany began to realize that her religious beliefs were creating many of her psychological problems, and to the degree that Paula was able to help her see this, Bethany began the long journey toward freedom from this misplaced religious guilt and bondage.

Bethany met Dave at the Midwest Bible Institute and after graduation they moved back to Myrtle Beach and got married. Dave found a job as the manager of a large hotel and golf course resort. Bethany accepted a position with the Social Services Department. Two years later, they had their first child, whom they named Samuel.

After her maternity leave, Bethany returned to work and brought Samuel to the day care run by her father's church where she and Dave attended. One day, she picked Samuel up from day care, drove home, and walked into the hallway of their apartment building where she found Dave and their neighbor Betty talking in the hallway. They weren't doing anything amiss and both Dave and Betty casually greeted her, but Bethany sensed something was going on between them. As they walked to their apartment, Dave explained how he had gotten off of work early that day and just happened to run into Betty in the hallway. Bethany pressed him for answers because her suspicion was running wild. But the more she pressured him, the more he insisted that there was nothing going on between them. It was just a chance meeting and that was all there was to it.

Bethany never took things at face value, and always suspected that there was a contradictory side of the story that was just waiting to reveal itself. In instances when this actually happened, it validated her fears, but ironically it also made those fears deeper and more profound. This inner life of total uncertainty was terrifying to her. But she lacked the courage to begin the journey down what she viewed as the slippery slide that led to facing her *total* uncertainty and inner doubt about all of life, including the fundamentalist faith of her parents. On the rare occasions she had ventured this way, she was horrified about how little she actually knew about herself, her feelings, beliefs, other people and the world. She had almost no confidence in her ability to clearly know and trust her own instincts, and even doubted her perceptions about everyday interactions with friends, colleagues, and family. And that's why she soon began to question whether her suspicions about Dave and Betty were fact or fiction. Maybe nothing was happening, and *she* was creating a problem where there really was none.

Bethany had been pleasant, but never "friends" with Betty previous to the hallway incident. Now there was a wide chasm between them that Bethany could not easily cross. She kept a close eye on Betty constantly, trying to peer below the surface of Betty's life from down the hallway. She found nothing she could put her hands on, but this did not alleviate her suspicion. The lack of hard evidence did nothing to change the way Bethany constantly ragged Dave about this single incident even years later. Lurking on the fringe of Bethany's consciousness was the hardened belief that people were somehow out to get her, or wanted to undermine her attempts at living her life in peace. Bethany had learned early on that the world was a dog-eat-dog place where people were struggling to survive, most times at the expense of others.

Four years after the hallway incident, Bethany came home from work with Samuel to discover that Dave had moved out. His note said that her non-stop accusations had finally driven him to do what he was being accused of, and that he and Betty had taken an apartment together across town. When she finally called Dave several days later in an attempt to work things out, he again insisted that there had been nothing between him and Betty until very recently, and that it was Bethany's nagging that drove him into Betty's arms. Dave made it clear that he would have no part of a reconciliation attempt, and Bethany had no choice but to move on with her life. Her parents helped her purchase a small house near the church after the divorce was final, and Bethany set about the task of trying to put this trauma behind her. That was ten years ago and since that time she'd finished a Masters degree and had turned down a promotion to Department Director because she worried about taking on too much responsibility.

Because Dave had run off with Betty, her father felt justified in claiming that she had "scriptural" grounds for the divorce and thus could remarry. They were pressuring her to marry another person from their congregation. By this time, Bethany was just about fed up with the fundamentalist faith and how much her parents had dominated her life. She'd had it with her parents' brand of religion, and had moved on to attend a church that was more open, and tolerant. Her parents blamed the liberalism of her psychologist, Paula, and the Midwest Bible Institute for this change in Bethany, but she knew it was a necessary move to maintain her sanity and protect her from a religious framework that would crush her psychologically with mindless, heartless, legalism.

Bethany's is only one of myriad possible stories that could be told to show what the Tacit Creed "I must be secure" looks like in the life of an individual. While the surface traits; natural talents and abilities; life-experiences; relationships; socio-cultural setting; ethnicity; gender; and level of psychological health defined by the 80-20 Rule may vary dramatically from person-to-person, the underlying patterns, processes and structures of the stories of all type Sixes will be similar.

Emergence of the Tacit Creed

The Six's Natural-Self occupies the bottom portion of Figure 51 where the Tacit Creed (I must be secure) *emerges* from their innate, inborn temperament and the deep fear associated with the core assumption that they *lack the discernment to face the future*. The emphasis is on the word "discernment" and the tacit conviction (and near certainty) that they lack the ability to judge, discriminate and make the distinctions needed to tease apart the difference between threatening from non-threatening situations and navigate their way through the waters of day-to-day life. Sixes experience this core assumption emotionally as a deep and abiding sense that, "I don't trust my own ability to make decisions and cope with life. I lack inner guidance and the inner gyroscopic sense of orientation that I need to face life's challenges and make the choices that life requires of me." They *experience* the core assumption with an inner sense of *certainty* as a *self-evident* truth that cannot (and ought not) be: a) questioned, b) objectively or publicly tested, or c) even verbalized. This belief that Sixes hold about themselves is a *secret* truth that they hide from themselves, others, and the world. It's undiscussible and its un-discussibility is itself undiscussible. The fear of self-knowledge creates a sense of psychological survival in Sixes that threatens their *existence* to the point where the gate-keeping function *blocks* these emotions from conscious awareness. But life goes on, and so must the Six. Over time, the emotional and cognitive memories associated with this core assumption are *buried* deeper and deeper within the psyche of type Sixes to the point where they become largely inaccessible to conscious awareness and are only experienced at pivotal (*kairos*) moments in life. This *forces* a shift in the Six's focus in order to avoid the embarrassment and threat that the reality of the core assumption creates, so rather than face (or test) the *veracity* of not having the discernment needed to face life, they *displace* the problem by avoiding all risks and thus "being secure." But trying to be "secure" can never fill the deep inner need of type Sixes because it tries to address an *inner* (existential) issue with *outer* behavior.

Notice how the Tacit Creed can either be *deficiency-driven* by Fear and Uncertainty or *growth-motivated* by Courage and Trust and has a very different look and feel depending on whether it's driven or motivated – with the ratio of driven-to-motivated actions and interactions being defined as the 80-20 Rule. When Sixes like Bethany are at their best and are growth-motivated, they are cautious, responsible, hard-working and vigilant about identifying potential problems in order to create a reliable and safe environment for themselves and others. When they face embarrassment, threat or are deficiency-driven, Sixes become hyper-alert, suspicious, chronically uncertain, looking for hidden meanings and underlying patterns of intention, and filled with anxiety in the absence of real threats. They constantly evaluate and remain vigilant for hidden motives, special meanings, ulterior motives, and trickery because they see themselves as living in a dog-eat-dog world of people who are out for themselves.

The three Somatic Instincts shown at the very bottom of Figure 51 are the first three levels of Maslow's Hierarchy and form the inner core and foundation upon which the type Six's personality is built. The Somatic Instincts powerfully shape the overall direction of a Six's life in the sense that their deep inner yearnings and desires unconsciously draw them to people, experiences, careers, relationships, and life situations that will gratify these basic human needs. So the *autopilot needs* of deficiency-driven Preserving Sixes can only be gratified by becoming "secure" in areas associated with home, nurture and comfort, while Cultivating Sixes are unconsciously drawn to gratify their need to be "secure" in areas associated with belonging and affiliation with groups, and the autopilot needs of Transmitting Sixes must be gratified by being "secure" in situations that revolve around love, affection, caring, and communicating their ideas.

Deficiency-Driven

As shown in Figure 51, when Sixes are under pressure or facing embarrassment or threat, Fear and Uncertainty become the deficiency-drivers, and the Tacit Creed for people like Bethany:

- Is like a hyper-sensitivity or allergic reaction to situations that fit the underlying pattern of having to be secure, which for type Sixes means identifying potential threats, harm, or danger.
- Creates a narrowing of focus in their attention that is driven by a yearning and desire to gratify the fourth level of Maslow's Hierarchy – the esteem needs. So how Sixes "esteem" themselves is powerfully shaped and defined by their need to "see" themselves as being secure, and by having other people *confirm* this self-perception by also "seeing" them as being secure.
- Becomes a cognitive and emotional angle or perspective on life that singles-out specific underlying patterns in relationships, interactions, and situations that will gratify the Six's basic need to be secure.
- Causes them to constantly evaluate their relationships and the environment for opportunities to identify potential threats, harm, or danger, even when other people don't want them to (or flatly refuse it) and in the absence of actual threats indicates that their need to be "secure" often satisfies *their own needs*, not the needs of other people.

Unconscious Appraisal and Selection

This section *links* the unconscious, autopilot cognitive and emotional appraisal and selection process for type Sixes, to the See-Do-Get Process and the Downward Spiral of Striving. Notice in Figure 52, that when the Tacit Creed "I must be secure" is unpacked *as* the autopilot doing and learning process, Sixes like Bethany tend to be unconsciously drawn to specific people, relationships, situations, and events in the world that will gratify: a) their need to be secure, and b) the basic needs of their dominant Somatic Instinct.

In the second step, Sixes unconsciously *appraise* situations and *select* opportunities to get their basic needs met by being "secure" in ways that are shaped and defined by their dominant Somatic Instinct – whether preserving, cultivating, or transmitting. They unconsciously choose very specific cognitive and emotional data from the world because they "match" the underlying patterns and basic need to create a sense of having the discernment to face the future by acting out the *inner mandate* to be secure.

Unconscious Appraisal and Selection

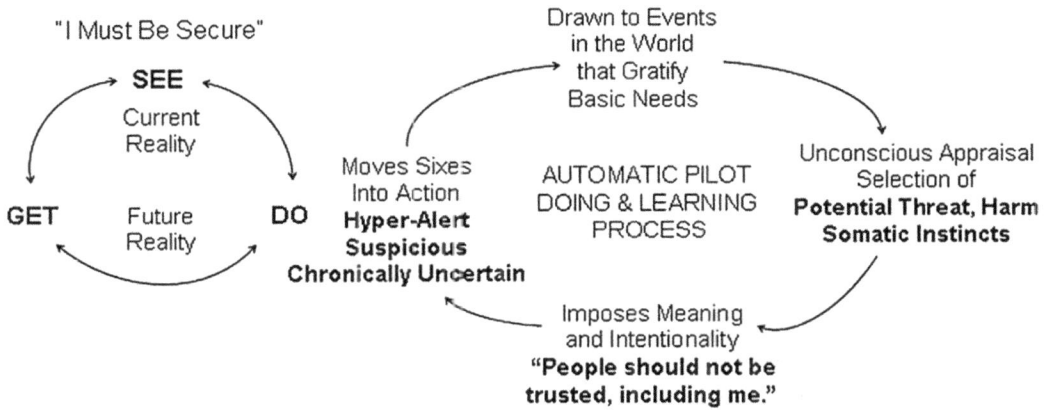

"I Must Be Secure"

Drawn to Events
in the World
that Gratify
Basic Needs

SEE
Current
Reality

GET   Future
Reality   **DO**

Moves Sixes
Into Action
**Hyper-Alert
Suspicious
Chronically Uncertain**

AUTOMATIC PILOT
DOING & LEARNING
PROCESS

Unconscious Appraisal
Selection of
**Potential Threat, Harm
Somatic Instincts**

Imposes Meaning
and Intentionality
**"People should not be
trusted, including me."**

Figure 52

In the third step, the Six's Tacit Creed *imposes* meaning and intentionality on the actions and interactions of people *and* the situations they're involved in. A typical tacit belief that Sixes might impose on a situation from their Left-Hand Column is, "People should be questioned and not be trusted – including my own thoughts, intuitions, and desires." This reveals the Six's tendency to *project* their own needs and beliefs onto the world around them.

In the final step, the momentum and psychological force of the first three steps move Sixes *into action* and these actions will tend to follow the pattern just described, where they become hyper-alert, suspicious, chronically uncertain, looking for hidden meanings and underlying patterns of intention, and filled with anxiety in the absence of real threats – all with the unconscious goal of gratifying their own needs, but under the pretense of being "secure."

The entire process shown in Figure 52 happens beneath the surface of conscious awareness – in the blink of an eye. It's important to remember that the process can be growth-motivated where the four steps produce positive, constructive actions and interactions along the Upward Path of Becoming. Sixes like Bethany who want to move from being deficiency-driven to growth-motivated must consciously raise this autopilot process back into conscious awareness; deconstruct and recon-figure it by running the See-Do-Get Process backwards in the counter clockwise direction; and then migrate the new growth-motivated actions and interactions back to autopilot operation by embedding them through repetition. When Sixes succeed in using this change process, the new growth-motivated actions and interactions begin to happen as naturally and automatically as the previous deficiency-driven ones once did. When eight out of ten behaviors are growth-motivated by Courage and Trust, rather than deficiency-driven by Fear and Uncertainty, this is an indica-tion that a Six is embodying the 80-20 Rule.

Blind Spots

When Sixes are under pressure or facing embarrassment or threat, Fear and Uncer-tainty become the deficiency-drivers for the Tacit Creed – "I must be secure." Mounting evidence produced by countless cycles through the See-Do-Get Process gives Sixes a *false sense* that being "secure" has actually given them discernment to face the future, but this breeds an even deeper sense of Fear about their *actual* level of safety and security (see Figure 53).

Figure 53

As in the case of Bethany, Sixes tend to have "Blind Spots" about the *extent* to which Fear and Uncertainty dominate their lives and create decision-making bias and pre-dictable errors in judgment. Deficiency-driven Sixes tend to "see" themselves as growth-motivated, while the people they interact with tend to "see" them as more deficiency-driven. The emotions of Fear and Uncertainty are *inflamed* when Sixes are under pressure or they don't get the results they want because people either object to (or don't respond to) their *insatiable desire* to test and probe other people's motives and intentions, and to be overly cautious, compulsively checking and rechecking, avoiding decisions, and paralyzed by doubt even about day-to-day decisions. Sixes become "intoxicated" by the emotional power of Fear and Uncertainty, which makes it more difficult for them to see their Blind Spots and unintended consequences for what they really are. Once the intoxicating energy of Fear and Uncertainty subsides, Sixes will settle back down to the normal state-of-equilibrium of their dominant type. But over time, this cycle of behaviors and emotional responses *solidifies* into a well-defined pattern of interaction that goes on autopilot and slips below the surface of conscious awareness. These patterns-of-interactions are commonly called "hot buttons" or defense routines.

The philosophy of *being secure as a way to create a sense of discernment about facing the future* powerfully shapes the day-to-day preferences of Sixes about the people, relationships, careers, hobbies, and lifestyles they are attracted to (and repulsed by), and over time these myriad choices are woven into the fabric of their lives. By the time Sixes are young adults, they have identified with the Tacit Creed of "being secure" to the point where they are locked into a cognitive, emotional, social, and contextual configuration that solidifies, reaches a state-of-equilibrium, and *becomes* their day-to-day reality. The inner mandate to be "secure" becomes externalized, objectified, and ultimately reified into a social mirror that seems to objectively affirm the belief that the Six's way of seeing themselves, others, and the world is *the* way that life should be lived. We described this earlier as the Self-Sealing Process of forming Personality in Context.

But the *false sense* of discernment about the future that emerges from being "secure," the *validation* that comes from the social mirror, and the *stability* of the day-to-day reality that Sixes construct – *come* at an enormous price, because they deeply divide them at the very core of their being. *Secretly*, Sixes know that they're not as secure as they claim to be, and the fear of this being discovered by others (and by themselves) only *fuels* the autopilot, insatiable, destructive power of their Tacit Creed. Think about it – if the Tacit Creed about "being secure" isn't true for Sixes like Bethany – then what is? If Sixes are wrong about how they see themselves, others, and the world, then they may be wrong about almost everything in life.

Growth-Motivated

We have spent a significant amount of time discussing the Tacit Creed and underlying mechanisms of the deficiency-driver of type Sixes like Bethany because without a correct understanding of the process by which these underlying mechanisms bind and limit the choices, personal freedom, and self-determination of type Sixes, there is little or no hope of ever escaping the pernicious entanglements of Personality in Context. In this section, I'd like to focus on the *single point of leverage* that will address the question, "So what should type Sixes *do* about the negative characteristics and effects of their personality?" I will also discuss the concrete changes that Sixes can expect to see in their actions and interactions when they choose the Upward Path of Becoming. As shown in Figure 54, when Sixes are at their best Courage and Trust become the growth-motivators for the Tacit Creed – "I must be secure."

Figure 54

Growth-motivated Sixes are cautious, responsible, hard-working and vigilant about identifying potential problems in order to create a reliable and safe environment for themselves and others.

While the Six's Blind Spots, defense routines, and the inner mandate to be "secure" *combine* with the social mirror and the edicts of their socio-cultural context to form barriers to deep change, they all rest on the foundation of the Six's core assumption that they lack the discernment to face the future. Sixes experience this "lack of discernment about the future" as a self-evident truth that cannot (and should not) be questioned or tested, *but this is precisely what Sixes must do*: face their fear of self-knowledge by questioning, and publicly testing, the truth of this claim. They must come to "see" themselves as being *unacceptable* through the active, tacit, and cultural teaching imprinted on their unscripted and malleable hearts and minds by their family, social and cultural context as children – as adults they must come to "see" themselves as having the tools to unlearn these *biased*, *misguided*, and *erroneous* ways of seeing themselves, others, and the world. Like the story of the Mulla, looking for the key in the *right* place becomes the *single point of leverage* that will enable Sixes to ignite deep personal change.

Focusing on the single point of leverage acts like a *solvent* that begins to dissolve the *hidden inauthentic layers* of cognitive, emotional, social, and contextual strata from which the Six's life has been built. Using the single point of leverage enables Sixes to begin living more authentically in terms of their actions, interactions, and decision-making within the current context of their lives. It helps them to do the right things, for the right reasons. There are a number of very concrete indicators that emerge when Sixes like Bethany begin the journey on the Upward Path of Becoming:

- Sixes are free to question their default way of seeing themselves as having to be "secure" and others as also needing to be secure.
- Their hyper-sensitivity toward identifying potential threats, harm and danger gives way to Courage, Trust, and a deep sense of inner guidance and direction, combined with discernment that helps differentiate between actual instances of potential threats and harm, and those that are an artifact of their basic need to be secure.
- They begin to see that they can put their welfare in the hands of others and are no longer bound by indecision, doubt, and ambiguity because they experience an inner gyroscopic sense of orientation and direction that enables them to face the problems and challenges of life effectively.
- Over time, Sixes gain new confidence in their ability to transcend the constraints of their personality and cultural context, as they see the concrete evidence of change indicated by their ability to act-out the 80-20 Rule – where eight out of ten interactions are motivated by Courage and Trust, rather than being driven by Fear and Uncertainty.

Connecting Points

As we saw in the case of Bethany, Sixes intentionally alter their actions and interactions to "fit" the requirements and norms of a specific social or cultural context because doing otherwise might be inappropriate and could have negative consequences on them personally and professionally. In a previous section, I referred to this as the Socialized-Self. But buried deep beneath the Six's Socialized-Self, family background, life experiences, and body of knowledge is a unique underlying *signature pattern* of connecting points that identifies what it means to be a type Six – their Natural-Self.

Connecting Points
(Conflicting Inner Mandates and Mixed-Emotions)

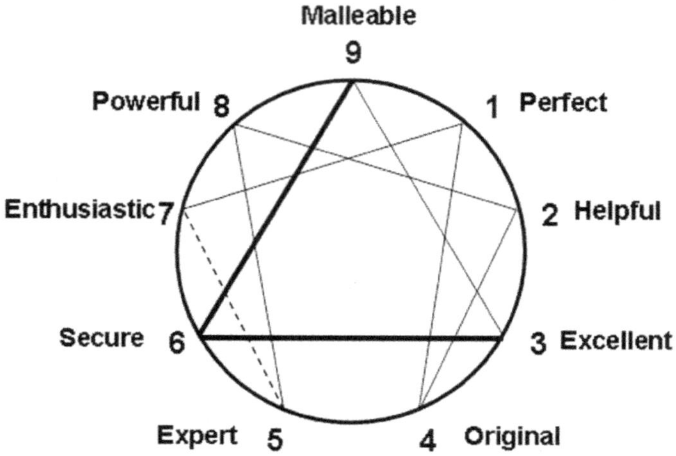

Figure 55

The underlying pattern and characteristics of the connecting points remain relatively constant over time and with changes in context. They are a well-defined intra-psychic pattern of interaction that shapes and defines Six's behaviors and responses in day-to-day discourse, especially in situations where they face *embarrassment* or *threat*. The patterns-of-interaction associated with the connecting points are also an indicator of whether or not the overall direction of the Six's life tends toward the Downward Spiral of Striving or the Upward Path of Becoming.

The Six's dominant type anchors them to the Enneagram and is a necessary element of verifying a person's Enneagram type. The signature pattern for type Six consists of five connecting points: types 6, 3, 9, 5 and 7.

- Type Six is the Tacit Creed which we've already discussed in detail.
- Type Three is the Striving Point which is referred to by some Enneagram theorists as the point that indicates the direction of disintegration.
- Type Nine is the Becoming Point which is referred to by some Enneagram theorists as the point that indicates the direction of integration.

- The Seven-Five Paradox straddles type Six, where Sevens and Fives are iso-morphic images of each other, with type Sevens exhibiting too much doing and not enough thinking-through the consequences of their actions, and type Fives exhibiting too much thinking and not enough doing and acting in the world. Type Sixes tend to be pulled along the axis of this paradox and can embody either set of characteristics if their uncertainty in facing the future forces them to.

- While the connecting points for Sixes represent the *natural* pattern, process, and structure of this Enneagram type, they should not be viewed as rigid and determined. Given sufficient pressure and influence from family or the social-cultural context, these natural tendencies can be powerfully shaped and defined in other ways, with the original signature pattern of the type Six being hidden (or buried) beneath other configurations of Enneagram points.

What is most important to note is that the foundation of the type Six's personality is an *interdependent configuration* of conflicting inner mandates and mixed emo-tions that includes five types, their Tacit Creeds, and their destructive and construc-tive emotions. In other words, the type Six's personality is not a homogeneous set of beliefs; instead it is a portfolio of interdependent, complementary, competing, and conflicting ways of seeing themselves, others, and the world.

So when Sixes like Bethany are stressed and facing embarrassment and threat, the autopilot patterns-of-interaction between their tacit, Striving, Becoming, and Paradox points can (and often do) create inner conflict and mixed emotions. This is espe-cially true when Sixes are faced with a problem that requires a *single* solution. In other words, Bethany would find herself wondering, "Should I do this, or should I do that? Should I be secure or malleable?" This inner conflict is *intensified* when external pressures force Sixes to act, interact, or make decisions *now*!

There are some key concepts that I'd like to review to define the psychological patterns, processes, and structure of the connecting points for type Sixes in more detail.

- The actions and interactions of the other eight Enneagram types are done *in the service of* following the inner mandate to be "secure" and maintaining the equilibrium of the cognitive, emotional, social, and contextual configuration that the Six builds as their life – their Personality in Context.

- When they are growth-motivated, the connections between type Six, Three, Nine, Five and Seven can help to balance some of the symmetries by giving Sixes at least one Enneagram point in each of the three triads, thus straddling the emotional, cognitive, and sensory parts of the human brain. The Six's connecting points also help to balance the left-right and top-bottom symmetries, where type Three provides a left-side balance for Sixes, and the type Nine provides an Enneagram point that helps to balance the top-bottom symmetry.

- Another key concept centers on the combining of the Tacit Creeds and underlying emotions into what is referred to as conflicting inner mandates and mixed emotions for type Sixes. People rarely act univocally. Rather, actions, interactions (and eventually patterns-of-interaction) come in complex, interdependent bundles, where the Tacit Creeds and underlying emotions of the Six's connecting points combine and co-mingle to form extremely complex packages of emotional messages that are communicated to others.

A solid understanding of the signature pattern is the key to unbundling the complex packages of emotional messages and patterns-of-interaction that type Sixes often exhibit in day-to-day interactions.

Type Six Summary Profile

Figure 56 provides an overall summary of the key patterns, structures, and processes that were described in this section and that typify the Enneagram type Six.

Type Summary Profile - Type Six	
Core Assumption	I lack the discernment to face the future
Tacit Creed (Mulla)	I must be secure
Unconscious Appraisal	Potential threat, harm, and Somatic Instincts
Impose Meaning	People should not be trusted, including me
Move Into Action	Hyper-alert, suspicious, chronically uncertain
Deficiency Drivers	Fear, Uncertainty
Growth Motivators	Courage, Trust
Striving Point	Type Three
Becoming Point	Type Nine
Paradox Point	Type Five, Type Seven
Group (Triad)	Head, leads with the cognitive part of the brain (Neocortex)
Existential Question	How do I face the future?
Conflict Processing Strategy	Reactive
Attitude Towards Socio-Cultural Change	Move Toward/Compliant
Single Point of Leverage	Question and publicly test the core assumption

Figure 56

In keeping with the overall approach of the Breckenridge Enneagram, the characteristics and dynamics shown in Figure 56 are not surface-traits or behaviors. Rather, the content of Figure 56 describes the underlying patterns, structures, and processes that define what makes type Sixes like Bethany different from the other eight Enneagram types.

Examples and Movies

While Sixes are found in every area of life and all professional fields, the list below shows some famous examples of people who are probably type Sixes. How many names do you recognize? Which ones are you interested enough in to learn more about by reading a biography or autobiography?

- *Examples* – Famous examples who exhibit Six traits: Jay Leno, J. Edgar Hoover, Richard Nixon, Julia Roberts, Harrison Ford, Clint Eastwood, Tom Hanks, Mel Gibson, Rodney Dangerfield, Dustin Hoffman, Diane Keaton, George W. Bush.

Another way to see Enneagram type in action is through the characters and story lines in movies. Select some of the movies listed below and take some time to watch Sixes in action.

- *Movie Characters* – Roles in movies that exemplify Six traits: Woody Allen (Hannah and Her Sisters), Bill Murray as Bob (What About Bob), Meg Ryan (When Harry Met Sally and You've Got Mail), Jane Fonda (On Golden Pond), Teri Garr (Tootsie), Marlin (Finding Nemo).

To deepen your understanding of this Enneagram type, identify people who you *know* that embody this personality type and become more observant about their behaviors, attitudes, and decision-making strategies. Ask them to share their thoughts, views, and perspectives on key issues and criteria for decision-making and see how closely the descriptions in this section describe and predict their responses. To further solidify and deepen your understanding, log your insights and observations about this personality type in a journal. You can use this exercise for the other eight types as well.

Type Seven (I Must Be Enthusiastic)

When Sevens are at their best, they are a limitless source of thoughts and ideas – they are spontaneous, curious, and adventurous, with quick, agile minds that focus on the positive aspects of life. When under pressure, they become restless, easily bored, overcommitted, stifled by stability and continuity in life, addicted to excitement, narcissistic with a subtle attitude of superiority and "entitlement" clothed beneath a calm, relaxed, confident exterior.

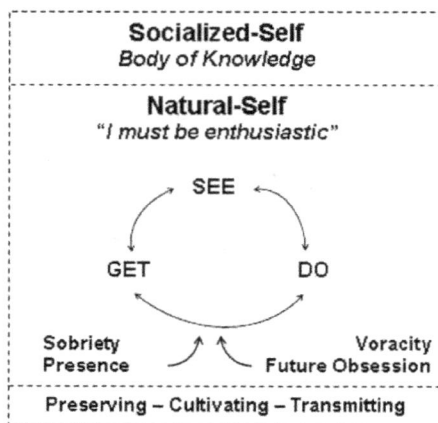

Figure 57

The very top of Figure 57 is made up of a person's Socialized-Self and body of knowledge, which form a major portion of the knowledge-base of their personal paradigm.

Tacit Creed

Sevens live by the Tacit Creed "I must be enthusiastic" – a belief that solidifies early in life through countless cycles through the See-Do-Get Process. When they are Deficiency Driven, they are hyper-sensitive to identifying things that don't stimulate their enthusiasm, they constantly evaluate their relationships and environment for things that are boring, mundane, unexciting, unadventurous, and lack novelty. Voracity and Future-Obsession are *inflamed* when under pressure or when they don't get the results they want; e.g., people either object to, or don't respond to, their *insatiable desire* for stimulation and excitement, their lack of discipline, seductive pleasing, narcissism, and tendency to confuse their imagination and reality. When under stress, they become "intoxicated" by the power of these emotions and have a *Blind Spot* about the extent to which Voracity and Future-Obsession dominate their lives and create decision-making bias and predictable errors in judgment. While Twos manipulate and seduce people through warm, helpful, generosity designed to build dependencies, Sevens manipulate and seduce others through their myriad ideas, smooth words, and intellect.

When they are Growth Motivated, they are free to question their default way of seeing and their hyper-sensitivity gives way to Sobriety, Presence, and a deep desire to become grounded and centered, enjoying the mundane aspects of life for their own sake, rather than to meet their basic need to be enthusiastic. They begin to find a deep sense of fulfillment in the ongoing stability and continuity of day-to-day life. For Sevens, the key element of personal growth and building effective relationships is to follow the 80-20 Rule – where eight out of ten interactions with others are characterized by Sobriety and Presence, rather than Voracity and Future-Obsession.

Nikki's Story

Nikki Salem's story is an example of what the Tacit Creed "I must be enthusiastic" looks like when it's solidified in the life of a type Seven. From the time she was a little girl, Nikki always seemed to be carefree, optimistic and always looked on the positive side of life. But deep below the surface of this positive outlook, her world felt like a desolate, dry desert that was devoid of life. She came to believe that she lacked the inner-vitality to face the future, so she had to create inner-vitality by being enthusiastic. Nikki needed constant stimulation, so she would read a book, watch TV, and write a letter to a friend all at the same time. For as long as she could remember, she had an insatiable desire for life, things, relationships, and new experiences.

Nikki's father was in the military and she had lived more places and had more friends than she could remember. The constant moving bothered her brother Erick, but Nikki seemed to like it. She did her last two years of high school in Sacramento, where her parents finally settled down. She kept in touch with many of the friends she made, and one of them, Mike, was living on the south side of Manhattan. He invited her to come out and stay with him. With only a few courses to go toward her two-year degree in general studies, Nikki moved to New York in the hopes of finishing school and becoming an actor.

Nikki was always over-committed and trying to do too much, and often let people and tasks alike fall through the cracks of her commitments. Whether it was relationships, school, or a conversation she was having with a colleague, Nikki could not focus on one thing without being distracted by other more interesting things that she feared she would miss out on. The beat and pace of New York City were a constant stimulation for her. She worked as a waitress in a small French restaurant in Greenwich Village where she learned a lot about wine and food, and three years later she graduated from NYU with a degree in fine arts. Nikki's life was a constant blur of activity as she auditioned for acting parts during the day, waited tables at night, and sandwiched in more social life than most people could handle in a lifetime.

But underneath her smile, and happy-go-lucky manner, was an inner psychological landscape that was a dry, barren, emotionally parched land. She was a walking contradiction – she was one of the most accomplished people you would ever meet, but she was also one of the most vacuous people you would ever meet. Nikki could not connect to her experiences in a way that would ground her, so she constantly stayed in motion as a way of distracting herself from experiencing the inner wilderness of her life. Nikki was never able to make enough money to even marginally support her lifestyle as an actor. She was ready for a change from the humdrum routine of waiting tables and chasing ephemeral parts in second-rate plays, so she took a job in a small publishing company on the Upper East Side where she was able to do everything from editing to marketing and sales. She quickly secured a senior position with the company, and met Todd, who was the lead book editor for fiction offerings. Nikki and Todd moved in together, and at the age of thirty-five, she was the happiest she had ever been in a relationship. Maybe Todd would finally be the one she would settle down with?

Six months after her promotion at the publishing company, Nikki was feeling like she needed a change, so rather than just leave the job like she'd always done before, Nikki applied for an executive MBA program at Yale and just reduced her hours at work. The train ride to and from New Haven once a week gave her time to read and work on homework, and she was able to use the business aspect of the publishing company as a case study for many of the workshops and seminars she had to write papers on. Nikki had little patience for the realities of what it actually took to get through the MBA program, but it was Todd who had a stabilizing effect on her. When the mundane grind of writing papers, or reading books she wasn't interested in, combined with the long commute every week, got her to the point where she was ready to quit, Todd gave Nikki the support she needed to go on and finish. She really loved Todd and wanted the relationship part of her life to settle down, but she knew that once she got her MBA, she would feel the urge to move on to other things.

Nikki was quick on her feet. When one of her professors would ask a question, her hand would first go up, and then she would begin to formulate her answer. Nikki could read the Cliffs Notes version of any topic, then instantly pass herself off as an expert in that area. Occasionally, when one of her professors or classmates who really was an expert saw beyond this veneer and pressed her to thoroughly substantiate her opinion or her facts, it became clear that her seemingly endless wellspring of wisdom and knowledge did not go that deep after all. But Nikki would adroitly move on to the next topic or point of discussion. Moving on was her middle name.

Even before she graduated, Nikki was recruited by an international cosmetics company as their field manager for distribution in Europe. In her first year, she was overseas 150 days with no sign that this schedule would let up. While Todd loved Nikki, he didn't want to have to live at this pace for the rest of his life. Todd had heard Nikki discuss her own compulsion for new experiences often enough that he could see there was no settling down in sight. He discussed this with her over and over again, sometimes on costly long distance calls while she was overseas, and she agreed that she needed to slow down. But Todd knew that she was addicted to staying in motion. Secretly, she had plans for her and Todd and she was trying to smooth things over so that she could make these plans happen. Nikki would tell Todd that all she wanted was to be happy with him, but Todd knew that her idea of "happy" was actually a kind of frenetic escapism of which he wanted no part.

Tired of constantly talking with no resolution, Todd began seeing someone else during the time Nikki was away. When he finally told Nikki he was leaving her, she was devastated. It was the first time Nikki had ever been left in a relationship. She had always done the leaving. The break up with Todd forced Nikki to face herself and what she truly wanted out of life like she had never done before. But even before he left, her discussions with Todd had sparked more pressing inner questions about leaving a legacy with her life.

Nikki's story is only one of many that could be told to show what the Tacit Creed "I must be enthusiastic" looks like in the life of an individual. While the surface traits; natural talents and abilities; life-experiences; relationships; socio-cultural setting; ethnicity; gender; and level of psychological health defined by the 80-20 Rule may vary dramatically from person-to-person, the underlying patterns, processes and structures of the stories of all type Sevens will be similar.

Emergence of the Tacit Creed

The Seven's Natural-Self occupies the bottom portion of Figure 57 where the Tacit Creed (I must be enthusiastic) *emerges* from their innate, inborn temperament and the deep fear associated with the core assumption that they *lack the inner-vitality to face the future.* The emphasis is on the words "inner-vitality" and the tacit conviction (and near certainty) that they lack the capacity to survive, live, grow, and develop in the face of the mundane, pedestrian activities of day-to-day life. Sevens *experience* this core assumption emotionally as a deep and abiding sense that, "My inner world is a desolate, dry desert that's devoid of life so I lack the capacity to live, grow, develop, and enjoy the simple, everyday things of life in any meaningful way." They experience the core assumption with an inner sense of *certainty* as a *self-evident* truth that cannot (and ought not) be: a) questioned, b) objectively or publicly tested, or c) even verbalized. This belief that Sevens hold about themselves is a *secret* truth that they hide from themselves, others, and the world. Like the other types, it's undiscussible and its un-discussibility cannot be discussed. The fear of self-knowledge creates a sense of psychological survival in Sevens that threatens their *existence* to the point where the gate-keeping function *blocks* these emotions from conscious awareness. But life goes on, and so must the Seven so they just stay in motion. Over time, the emotional and cognitive memories associated with this core assumption are *buried* deeper and deeper within the psyche of type Sevens to the point where they become largely inaccessible to conscious awareness and are only experienced at pivotal (*kairos*) moments in life. This *forces* a shift in the Seven's focus in order to avoid the embarrassment and threat that the reality of the core assumption creates, so rather than face (or test) the *truth* of not having the inner-vitality to face the future, they *displace* the problem by creating inner-vitality by being "enthusiastic." But trying to be "enthusiastic" can never fill the deep inner need of type-Sevens because it tries to address an *inner* (existential) issue with *outer* behavior.

Notice how the Tacit Creed can either be *deficiency-driven* by Voracity and Future-Obsession or *growth-motivated* by Sobriety and Presence and has a very different look and feel depending on whether it's driven or motivated – with the ratio of driven-to-motivated actions and interactions being defined as the 80-20 Rule. When Sevens like Nikki are at their best and are growth-motivated, they are a limitless source of thoughts and ideas – they are spontaneous, curious, and adventurous, with quick agile minds that focus on the positive aspects of life. When they face embarrassment, threat or are deficiency-driven, they become restless, easily bored, overcommitted, stifled by stability and continuity in life – addicted to excitement, narcissistic – with a subtle attitude of superiority and "entitlement" clothed beneath a calm, relaxed, confident exterior.

The three Somatic Instincts shown at the very bottom of Figure 57 are the first three levels of Maslow's Hierarchy and form the inner core and foundation upon which the type Seven's personality is built. The Somatic Instincts powerfully shape the overall direction of a Seven's life in the sense that their deep inner yearnings and desires unconsciously draw them to people, experiences, careers, relationships, and life situations that will gratify these basic human needs. So the *autopilot needs* of deficiency-driven Preserving Sevens can only be gratified by being "enthusiastic" in areas associated with home, nurture and comfort, while Cultivating Sevens are unconsciously drawn to gratify their need to be "enthusiastic" in areas associated with belonging and affiliation with groups, and the autopilot needs of Transmitting Seven's must be gratified by being "enthusiastic" in situations that revolve around love, affection, caring, and communicating their ideas.

Deficiency-Driven

As shown in Figure 57, when Sevens are under pressure or facing embarrassment or threat, Voracity and Future-Obsession become the deficiency-drivers, and the Tacit Creed for people like Nikki:

- Is like a hyper-sensitivity or allergic reaction to situations that fit the underlying pattern of having to be enthusiastic, which for type Sevens means identifying things that are boring and don't stimulate their need for novel experiences.

- Creates a narrowing of focus in their attention that is driven by a yearning and desire to gratify the fourth level of Maslow's Hierarchy – the esteem needs. So how Sevens "esteem" themselves is powerfully shaped and defined by their need to "see" themselves as being enthusiastic, and by having other people *confirm* this self-perception by also "seeing" them as enthusiastic.

- Becomes a cognitive and emotional angle or perspective on life that singles-out specific underlying patterns in relationships, interactions, and situations that will gratify the Seven's basic need to be enthusiastic.

- Causes them to constantly evaluate their relationships and the environment for opportunities to be "enthusiastic," even when other people don't want their enthusiasm (or flatly refuse it), which indicates that their need to be "enthusiastic" often satisfies *their own needs*, not the needs of other people.

Unconscious Appraisal and Selection

This section *links* the unconscious, autopilot cognitive and emotional appraisal and selection process for type Sevens, to the See-Do-Get Process and the Downward Spiral of Striving. Notice in Figure 58, that when the Tacit Creed "I must be enthusiastic" is unpacked *as* the autopilot doing and learning process, Sevens like Nikki tend to be unconsciously drawn to specific people, relationships, situations, and events in the world that will gratify: a) their need to be enthusiastic, and b) the basic needs of their dominant Somatic Instinct.

Unconscious Appraisal and Selection

Figure 58

In the second step, Sevens unconsciously *appraise* situations and *select* opportunities to get their basic needs met by becoming "enthusiastic" in ways that are shaped and defined by their dominant Somatic Instinct – whether preserving, cultivating, or transmitting. They unconsciously choose very specific cognitive and emotional data from the world because they "match" the underlying patterns and basic need to create a sense of inner-vitality by acting out the *inner mandate* to be enthusiastic.

In the third step, the Seven's Tacit Creed *imposes* meaning and intentionality on the actions and interactions of people *and* the situations they're involved in. A typical tacit belief that Sevens might impose on a situation from their Left-Hand Column is, "I can do whatever I like because people are dazzled by my many talents and my personal charm." This reveals the Seven's tendency to *project* their own needs and beliefs onto the world around them.

In the final step, the momentum and psychological force of the first three steps move Sevens *into action* and these actions will tend to follow the pattern just described, where they become easily bored, overcommitted, stifled by stability and continuity in life, addicted to excitement, narcissistic with a subtle attitude of superiority and "entitlement" – all with the unconscious goal of gratifying their own needs, but under the pretense of being "enthusiastic."

The entire process shown in Figure 58 happens beneath the surface of conscious awareness – in the blink of an eye. It's important to remember that the process can be growth-motivated where the four steps produce positive, constructive actions and interactions along the Upward Path of Becoming. Sevens like Nikki who want to move from being deficiency-driven to growth-motivated must consciously raise this autopilot process back into conscious awareness; deconstruct and reconfigure it by running the See-Do-Get Process backwards in the counter clockwise direction; and then migrate the new growth-motivated actions and interactions back to auto-pilot operation by embedding them through repetition. When Sevens succeed in using this change process, the new growth-motivated actions and interactions begin to happen as naturally and automatically as the previous deficiency-driven ones once did. When eight out of ten behaviors are growth-motivated by Sobriety and Presence, rather than deficiency-driven by Voracity and Future-Obsession, this is an indication that a Seven is embodying the 80-20 Rule.

Blind Spots

When Sevens are under pressure or facing embarrassment or threat, Voracity and Future-Obsession become the deficiency-drivers for the Tacit Creed – "I must be enthusiastic." Mounting evidence produced by countless cycles through the See-Do-Get Process gives Sevens a *false sense* that being "enthusiastic" has actually given them the inner-vitality to face the future, and this only increases the level of Voracity as they consume more and more experiences, resources, and human inter-actions (see Figure 59).

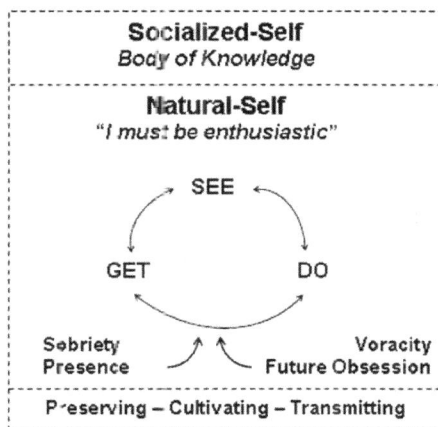

Figure 59

Much like Nikki, Sevens tend to have "Blind Spots" about the *extent* to which Voracity and Future-Obsession dominate their lives and create decision-making bias and predictable errors in judgment. Deficiency-driven Sevens tend to "see" themselves as growth-motivated, while the people they interact with tend to "see" them as more deficiency-driven. The emotions of Voracity and Future-Obsession are *inflamed* when Sevens are under pressure or they don't get the results they want because people either object to (or don't respond to) their insatiable desire for stimulation and excitement, their lack of discipline, seductive pleasing, narcissism, and tendency to confuse imagination with reality. Sevens become "intoxicated" by the emotional power of Voracity and Future-Obsession which makes it more difficult for them to see their Blind Spots and unintended consequences for what they really are. Once the intoxicating energy of Voracity and Future-Obsession subsides, Sevens will settle back down to the normal state-of-equilibrium of their dominant type. But over time, this cycle of behaviors and emotional responses *solidifies* into a well-defined pattern of interaction that goes on autopilot and slips below the surface of conscious awareness. These patterns-of-interactions are commonly called "hot buttons" or defense routines.

The philosophy of *being enthusiastic as the road to the inner-vitality to face the future* powerfully shapes the day-to-day preferences of Sevens about the people, relationships, careers, hobbies, and lifestyles they are attracted to (and repulsed by), and over time these myriad choices are woven into the fabric of their lives. By the time Sevens are young adults, they have identified with the Tacit Creed of "being enthusiastic" to the point where they are locked into a cognitive, emotional, social, and contextual configuration that solidifies, reaches a state-of-equilibrium, and *becomes* their day-to-day reality. The inner mandate to be "enthusiastic" becomes externalized, objectified, and ultimately reified into a social mirror that seems to objectively affirm the belief that the Seven's way of seeing themselves, others, and the world is *the* way that life should be lived. We described this earlier as the Self-Sealing Process of forming Personality in Context.

But the false sense of inner-vitality that comes from being "enthusiastic," the *validation* that comes from the social mirror, and the *stability* of the day-to-day reality that Sevens construct – *come* at an enormous price, because they deeply divide them at the very core of their being. *Secretly*, Sevens know that they're not as enthusiastic as they claim to be, and the fear of this being discovered by others only *fuels* the autopilot, insatiable, destructive power of their Tacit Creed. Think about it – if the Tacit Creed of "being enthusiastic" isn't true for Sevens like Nikki – then what is?

If Sevens are wrong about how they see themselves, others, and the world, then they may be wrong about almost everything in life.

Growth-Motivated

We have spent a significant amount of time discussing the Tacit Creed and underlying mechanisms of the deficiency-driver of type Sevens like Nikki because without a correct understanding of the process by which these underlying mechanisms bind and limit the choices, personal freedom, and self-determination of type Sevens, there is little or no hope of ever escaping the pernicious entanglements of Personality in Context. In this section, I'd like to focus on the *single point of leverage* that will address the question, "So what should type Sevens *do* about the negative characteristics and effects of their personality?" I will also discuss the concrete changes that Sevens can expect to see in their actions and interactions when they choose the Upward Path of Becoming. As shown in Figure 60, when Sevens are at their best Sobriety and Presence become the growth-motivators for the Tacit Creed – "I must be enthusiastic."

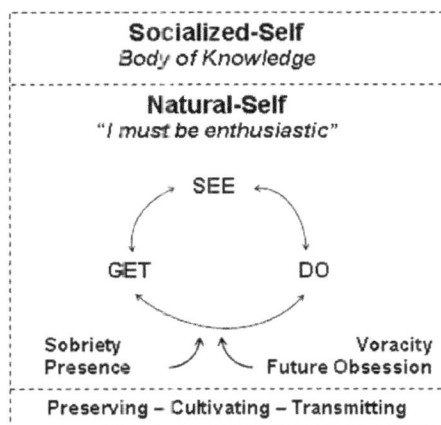

Figure 60

Growth-motivated Sevens are a limitless source of thoughts and ideas – they are spontaneous, curious, and adventurous, with quick agile minds that focus on the positive aspects of life.

While the Seven's Blind Spots, defense routines, and the inner mandate to be "enthusiastic" *combine* with the social mirror and the edicts of their socio-cultural context to form barriers to deep change, they all rest on the foundation of the Seven's core assumption that they lack the inner-vitality to face the future. Sevens experience this "lack of inner-vitality to face the future" as a self-evident truth that cannot (and ought not) be questioned or tested, *but this is precisely what Sevens must do*: face their fear of self-knowledge by questioning, and publicly testing, the truth of this claim. They must come to "see" themselves as having the tools to unlearn these *biased*, *misguided*, and *erroneous* ways of seeing themselves, others, and the world. Like the story of the Mulla, looking for the key in the *right* place becomes the *single point of leverage* that will enable Sevens to ignite deep personal change.

Focusing on the single point of leverage acts like a *solvent* that begins to dissolve the *hidden inauthentic layers* of cognitive, emotional, social, and contextual strata from which the Seven's life has been built. Using the single point of leverage enables Sevens to begin living more authentically in terms of their actions, interactions, and decision-making within the current context of their lives. It helps them to do the right things, for the right reasons. There are a number of very concrete indicators that emerge when Sevens like Nikki begin the journey on the Upward Path of Becoming:

- Sevens are free to question their default way of seeing themselves as having to be "enthusiastic" and having to stay in constant motion.
- Their hyper-sensitivity toward identifying things that are boring and don't stimulate them gives way to Sobriety, Presence, and a deep desire to become grounded and centered, enjoying the mundane aspects of life for their own sake, rather than to meet their need to be enthusiastic.
- They begin to find a deep sense of fulfillment in the ongoing stability and continuity of day-to-day life and this insight and new way of "seeing" gives Sevens a deep sense of inner freedom and personal growth.
- Over time, Sevens gain new confidence in their ability to transcend the constraints of their personality and cultural context, as they see the concrete evidence of change indicated by their ability to act-out the 80-20 Rule – where eight out of ten interactions are motivated by Sobriety and Presence, rather than being driven by Voracity and Future-Obsession.

Connecting Points

Much like the story of Nikki, Sevens intentionally alter their actions and interactions to "fit" the requirements and norms of a specific social or cultural context because doing otherwise might be inappropriate and could have negative consequences on them personally and professionally. In a previous section, I referred to this as the

Socialized-Self. But buried deep beneath the Seven's Socialized-Self, family background, life experiences, and body of knowledge is a unique underlying *signature pattern* of connecting points that identifies what it means to be a type Seven – their Natural-Self.

The underlying pattern and characteristics of the connecting points remain relatively constant over time and with changes in context. They are a well-defined intra-psychic pattern of interaction that shapes and defines Seven's behaviors and responses in day-to-day discourse, especially in situations where they face *embarrassment* or *threat*. The patterns-of-interaction associated with the connecting points are also an indicator of whether or not the overall direction of the Seven's life tends toward the Downward Spiral of Striving or the Upward Path of Becoming.

Connecting Points
(Conflicting Inner Mandates and Mixed Emotions)

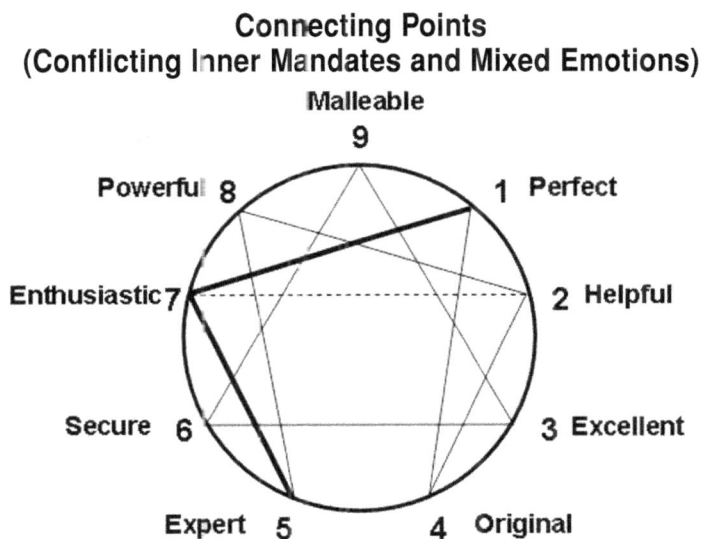

Figure 61

The Seven's dominant type anchors them to the Enneagram and is a necessary element of verifying a person's Enneagram type. The signature pattern for type Seven consists of four connecting points: types 7, 1, 5, and 2.

- Type Seven is the Tacit Creed which we've already discussed in detail.
- Type One is the Striving Point which is referred to by some Enneagram theorists as the point that indicates the direction of disintegration.
- Type Five is the Becoming Point which is referred to by some Enneagram theorists as the point that indicates the direction of integration.

- Type Two is the Paradox point and reveals an underlying paradoxical relationship between Twos and Sevens around the issues of seduction and manipulation, where Sevens manipulate and seduce people through their myriad ideas, smooth words, and intellect, and Twos manipulate and seduce others through warm, helpful, generosity designed to build dependencies.

- While the connecting points for Sevens represent the *natural* pattern, process, and structure of this Enneagram type, they should not be viewed as rigid and determined. Given sufficient pressure and influence from family or the social-cultural context, these natural tendencies can be powerfully shaped and defined in other ways, with the original signature pattern of the type Seven being hidden (or buried) beneath other configurations of Enneagram points.

What is most important to note is that the foundation of the type Seven's personality is an *interdependent configuration* of conflicting inner mandates and mixed emotions that includes four types, their Tacit Creeds, and their destructive and constructive emotions. In other words, the type Seven's personality is not a homogeneous set of beliefs; instead it is a portfolio of interdependent, complementary, competing, and conflicting ways of seeing themselves, others, and the world.

So when Sevens like Nikki are stressed and facing embarrassment and threat, the autopilot patterns-of-interaction between their tacit, Striving, Becoming, and Paradox points can (and often do) create inner conflict and mixed emotions. This is especially true when Sevens are faced with a problem that requires a *single* solution. In other words, Nikki would find herself wondering, "Should I do this, or should I do that? Should I be enthusiastic or perfect?" This inner conflict is *intensified* when external pressures force Sevens to act, interact, or make decisions *now*!

There are some key concepts that I'd like to review to define the psychological patterns, processes, and structure of the connecting points for type Sevens in more detail.

- The actions and interactions of the other eight Enneagram types are done *in the service of* following the inner mandate to be "enthusiastic" and maintaining the equilibrium of the cognitive, emotional, social, and contextual configuration that the Seven builds as their life – their Personality in Context.

- When they are growth-motivated, the connections between type Seven, One, Five and Two can help to balance some of the symmetries by giving Sevens at least one Enneagram point in each of the three triads, thus straddling the emotional, cognitive, and sensory parts of the human brain. The Seven's connecting points also help to balance the left-right and top-bottom symmetries, where types One and Two provide a left-side balance for Sevens, and the type Five provides an Enneagram point that balances the top-bottom symmetry.

- Another key concept centers on the *combining* of the Tacit Creeds and underlying emotions into what is referred to as conflicting inner mandates and mixed emotions for type Sevens. People rarely act univocally. Rather, actions, interactions (and eventually patterns-of-interaction) come in complex, interdependent bundles, where the Tacit Creeds and underlying emotions of the Seven's connecting points *combine* and *co-mingle* to form extremely complex packages of emotional messages that are communicated to others.

A solid understanding of the signature pattern is the key to *unbundling* the complex packages of emotional messages and patterns-of-interaction that type Sevens often exhibit in day-to-day interactions.

Type Seven Summary Profile

Figure 62 provides an overall summary of the key patterns, structures, and processes that were described in this section and that typify the Enneagram type Seven.

Type Summary Profile - Type Seven	
Core Assumption	I lack the inner-vitality to face the future
Tacit Creed (Mulla)	I must be enthusiastic
Unconscious Appraisal	Boring, mundane, lack stimulation and Somatic Instincts
Impose Meaning	I can do whatever I like, people are dazzled by my personal charm
Move Into Action	Overcommitted, narcissistic, seductive
Deficiency Drivers	Voracity, Future-Obsession
Growth Motivators	Sobriety, Presence
Striving Point	Type One
Becoming Point	Type Five
Paradox Point	Type Two
Group (Triad)	Head, leads with the cognitive part of the brain (Neocortex)
Existential Question	How do I face the future?
Conflict Processing Strategy	Reframing
Attitude Towards Socio-Cultural Change	Move Against/Aggressive
Single Point of Leverage	Question and publicly test the core assumption

Figure 62

In keeping with the overall approach of the Breckenridge Enneagram, the characteristics and dynamics shown in Figure 62 are not surface-traits or behaviors. Rather, the content of Figure 62 describes the underlying patterns, structures, and processes that define what makes type Sevens like Nikki different from the other eight Enneagram types.

Examples and Movies

While Sevens are found in every area of life and all professional fields, the list below shows some famous examples of people who are probably type Sevens. How many names do you recognize? Which ones are you interested enough in to learn more about by reading a biography or autobiography?

- *Examples* – Famous examples who exhibit Seven traits: Steven Spielberg, Jim Carrey, Goldie Hawn, Benjamin Franklin, Carol Burnett, Jack Nicholson, Joan Rivers, Richard Feynman, Chevy Chase, Eddie Murphy, Jonathan Winters, Jimmy Buffett.

Another way to see Enneagram type in action is through the characters and story lines in movies. Select some of the movies listed below and take some time to watch Sevens in action.

- *Movie Characters* – Roles in movies that exemplify Seven traits: Robin Williams (Good Morning Viet Nam), Mozart (Amadeus), Leonardo DiCaprio as Jack (Titanic), Robert Duvall (Lonesome Dove), Brad Pitt (A River Runs Through It), Greg Kinnear (Sabrina), Dory (Finding Nemo).

To deepen your understanding of this Enneagram type, identify people who you *know* that embody this personality type and become more observant about their behaviors, attitudes, and decision-making strategies. Ask them to share their thoughts, views, and perspectives on key issues and criteria for decision-making and see how closely the descriptions in this section describe and predict their responses. To further solidify and deepen your understanding, log your insights and observations about this personality type in a journal. You can use this exercise for the other eight types as well.

The Action Group

This section describes the three types that form the Action Group: Eights, Nines, and Ones. The types in the Action Group emerge from the Sensory Brain which is localized in the Brainstem and other related neurophysiologic and sensory structures.

These Action types tend to "lead" with the action-oriented-part of their being, with the neuropsychological functions of the Head and Heart Groups playing key support roles. Action types tend to be present-oriented because they are inextricably bound to the immediate context of what's going on in the world around them, including where things are happening and who's involved.

Action Group
(Sensory Brain, Brainstem, Present-Oriented)

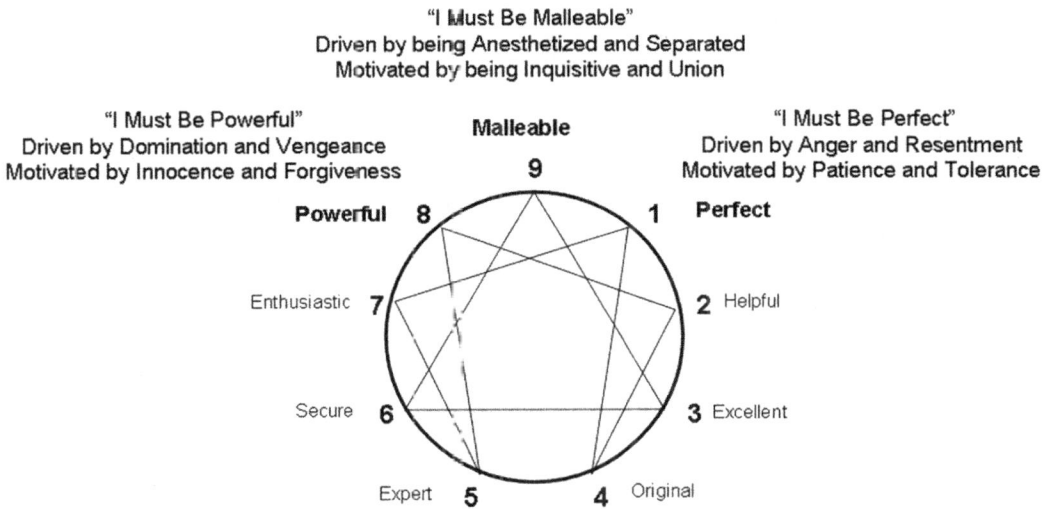

"I Must Be Malleable"
Driven by being Anesthetized and Separated
Motivated by being Inquisitive and Union

"I Must Be Powerful"   "I Must Be Perfect"
Driven by Domination and Vengeance   **Malleable**   Driven by Anger and Resentment
Motivated by Innocence and Forgiveness   Motivated by Patience and Tolerance

                                              9

Powerful 8   1 **Perfect**

Enthusiastic 7   2 Helpful

Secure 6   3 Excellent

Expert 5   4 Original

Figure 63

The Tacit Creed for Eight is, "I must be powerful" and can be either deficiency-driven by Domination and Vengeance or growth-motivated by Innocence and Forgiveness. The look and feel of this personality type, and our *experience* of it, are very different when it is growth-motivated by Innocence and Forgiveness, rather than deficiency-driven by Domination and Vengeance.

The Tacit Creed for Nine is, "I must be malleable" and can be either deficiency-driven by being Anesthetized and Separated, or growth-motivated by being Inquisitive and in Union with self, others, and the world. The look and feel of this personality type, and our *experience* of it, are very different when it is growth-motivated by being Inquisitive and in Union, rather than deficiency-driven by being Anesthetized and Separated.

The Tacit Creed for One is, "I must be perfect" and can be either deficiency-driven by Anger and Resentment or growth-motivated by Patience and Tolerance. The look and feel of this personality type, and our *experience* of it, are very different when it is growth-motivated by Patience and Tolerance, rather than deficiency-driven by Anger and Resentment.

All sensory information from the body that goes to the other parts of the brain must first traverse the brainstem which provides neurological control for functions that are necessary for survival such as, breathing, digestion, heart rate, blood pressure, and arousal. The brainstem also plays a crucial role in maintaining alertness and generating the capacity for conscious awareness, where the *capacity* for consciousness is not the same thing as the sensory *content* of consciousness which is thought (by most researchers) to be in the lateral-prefrontal cortex. In other words, the functions of the brainstem create the essential *precondition* for conscious awareness and without a functioning brainstem there is no meaningful activity in the higher parts of the brain – no cognitive or emotional life, no sensory activity, no thoughts or feelings, no introspection or social interaction with the environment. Our sensory experience of our bodies and what's going on in the world around us powerfully shape our physical sense of self. In many ways, who we are *corporeally* reveals something very deep about who we are as human beings *regardless* of what our dominant Enneagram type is. These bodily functions (and our experience of them) are *universal* and are experienced by all people, in all times, in all cultures; and the Action types are tuned-in to the constant flow of sensory stimulus because of their connection to their own bodies and the immediate context of what's going on in the world, where things are happening, and who's involved in doing them. It is important to remember that the action-space where types Eights, Nines, and Ones live, is known to (and experienced by) all nine types, and powerfully shapes and defines how we see ourselves, others, and the world through the See-Do-Get Process.

Key Question

Eights, Nines, and Ones tend to be overly preoccupied with the key question of human existence, "How do I deal with the environment?", although the three types tend to answer this same question in a very different way. It's not that the other types don't care about dealing with the environment, it's just *not* the central concern of their lives and the focus of their values.

**Action Group
(Key Question: How Do I Deal with the Environment?)**

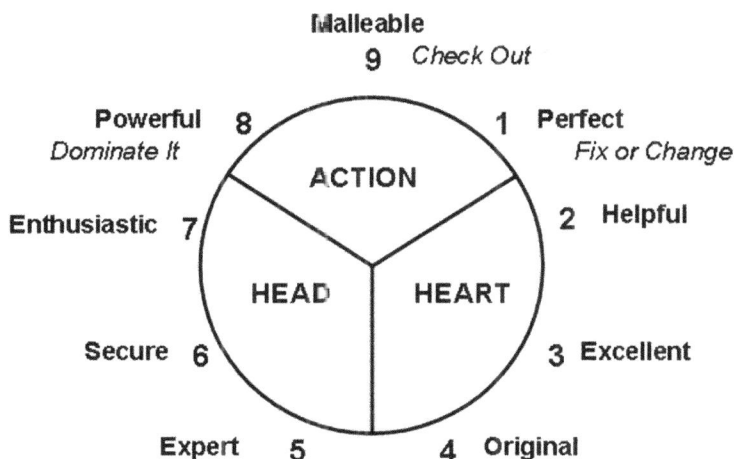

Malleable

9   *Check Out*

Powerful 8   1   Perfect
Dominate It   *Fix or Change*

ACTION

Enthusiastic 7   2   Helpful

HEAD   HEART

Secure 6   3   Excellent

Expert   5   4   Original

Figure 64

Eights tend to deal with the environment by dominating it by expanding their sphere of control and influence over the people and situations around them. Nines tend to deal with the environment by not dealing with it or checking out, especially when they encounter conflict or when their involvement in a situation might "rock the boat." Ones tend to deal with the environment by trying to fix and improve it as they stand apart from life's circumstances and critique them. The Action types also ask the existential question that's common to all nine types, "How do I get the results that I want from my one-trip through life?" This key question forces types Eight, Nine, and One to see the *outcome* of their lives as anchored to (and in the context of) their present experiences and sensations.

Conflict Processing Strategies

All three conflict processing strategies are represented in the Action Group. Type Eights tend to use the *reactive* strategy where they deal with conflict by reacting emotionally and then looking for an emotional response that mirrors their concern. They have strong opinions and emotional reactions and want to vent their feelings *before* moving on in relationships, but they often deny their need for understanding and support.

Action Group
(Conflict Processing Strategies)

Malleable
9   *Reframing*

Powerful **8**   **1** **Perfect**
Reactive   **ACTION**   *Objective*

Enthusiastic 7   **2 Helpful**

HEAD   **HEART**

Secure 6   **3   Excellent**

Expert   5   **4 Original**

Figure 65

Type Nines tend to use the *reframing* strategy where they deal with conflict and disappointment in relationships by "reframing" them in some positive way that emphasizes a brighter, more uplifting way of "seeing" life and tend to have a problem balancing their own needs with the needs of others. More specifically, type Nines tend to focus on both their own needs and the needs of others with neither getting filled adequately. Type Ones use the *objective* strategy where they deal with conflict in relationships by putting their emotions and subjective feelings on the back burner, and resolving their differences by being objective, logical, effective, and working within the structures, systems and established rules of the context and relationship.

Attitude toward Socio-Cultural Change

Each of the types in the Action Group tends to embody a different attitude toward socio-cultural change. Eights tend to be Aggressive types that move against others in interactions, while Nines tend to be Withdrawn types and move away from others, and Ones tend to be Compliant types and move toward people.

Action Group
(Attitude toward Socio-Cultural Change)

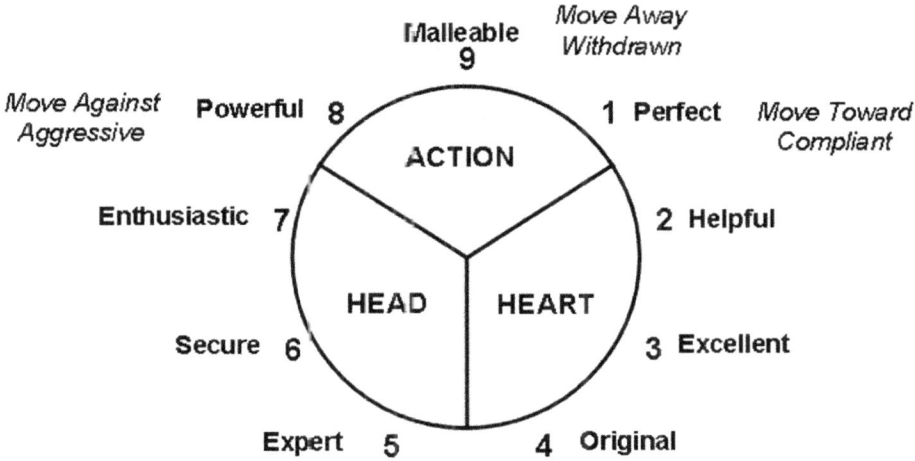

Figure 66

Type Eights tend to be aggressive toward socio-cultural change that they don't agree with or support because their Tacit Creed "I must be powerful" drives them to dominate their environment, and they tend to move against people who support (or lead) the change process to directly oppose their authority and leadership. Type Nines tend to withdraw from socio-cultural change that they don't agree with or support because their Tacit Creed "I must be malleable" drives them to just go through the motions, avoid conflict, and not "rock the boat." They *inwardly* disengage from people who support (or lead) the change process, but outwardly create the impression that they'll go along with the change process by not outwardly opposing or supporting it. Type Ones tend to be compliant with socio-cultural change that they don't agree with or support because their Tacit Creed "I must be perfect" drives them to keep the rules defined by external contexts; and they tend to move toward people who support (or lead) the change process to try to improve and correct them.

Type Eight (I Must Be Powerful)

When Eights are at their best, they are strong, assertive, persistent, tenacious, seeking challenges, action-oriented with a take-charge attitude and enormous determination and will power to triumph over all obstacles and be influential in their world. When under pressure, they become hostile, vindictive, defiant, emotionally insensitive, desiring to control and dominate people and situations to get what they want, or exploiting people and situations by taking what they want by force or cunning.

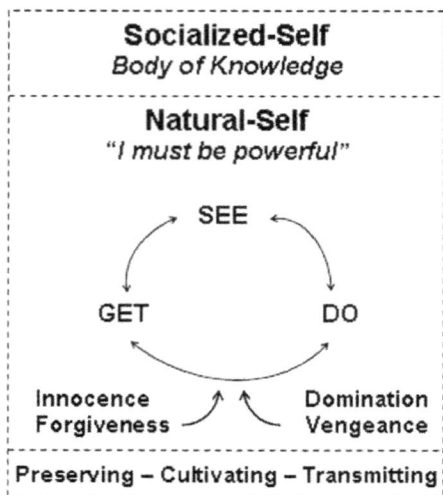

Figure 67

The very top of Figure 67 is made up of a person's Socialized-Self and body of knowledge, which form a major portion of the knowledge-base of their personal paradigm.

Tacit Creed

Eights live by the Tacit Creed "I must be powerful" – a belief that solidifies early in life through countless cycles through the See-Do-Get Process. When they are Deficiency Driven, they are hyper-sensitive to identifying areas in which they can expand their span of domination and control, they constantly evaluate their relationships and environment for opportunities to assert their primitive-instinctual lust for life, thirst for intensity, oppose authority, conquer and vindictively triumph over people and situations. Domination and Vengeance are *inflamed* when under pressure or when they don't get the results they want; e.g., people either object to, or don't respond to, their *insatiable desire* to expand their control over their environment through intimidation, humiliation, and fighting for pleasure. When under stress, they become "intoxicated" by the power of these emotions and have a *Blind Spot* about the extent to which Domination and Vengeance control their lives and create decision-making bias and predictable errors in judgment. While Fours are the most *sensitive* of the nine types, thirsting for intensity through their emotions, Eights are the most *insensitive* and thirst for intensity through action.

When they are Growth Motivated, they are free to question their default way of seeing and their hyper-sensitivity gives way to Innocence, Forgiveness, and a deep desire to develop inner strength, self-mastery, and no longer see vulnerability and child-like innocence as something to be stamped out in order to meet their basic need to be powerful. They begin to see how they can have enormous positive influence and impact on their world by using their strengths and abilities for constructive, not destructive ends. For Eights, the key element of personal growth and building effective relationships is to follow the 80-20 Rule – where eight out of ten interactions with others are characterized by Innocence and Forgiveness, rather than Domination and Vengeance.

James' Story

James Tuffs' story is an example of what the Tacit Creed "I must be powerful" looks like when it's solidified in the life of a type Eight. Although his parents never came right out and said it to him, their cold and distant relationship gave him the clear message that he was on his own in life. This made him feel weak and vulnerable when trying to get his needs met naturally by the world around him. He came to believe that because he lacked the ability to get his needs met naturally, that he would gratify them by being powerful. If life wouldn't give him what he wanted, he would take it. Even in his teen years, James honestly believed that given the right circumstances anyone, even his closest friend or a family member, would screw him over. James trusted no one. He rarely let people get too close to him, and when he didn't really know and trust someone, he sent out the loud message that they should just *stay away*. He also got very uncomfortable about giving out too much information about himself to people he didn't know well.

James got his undergraduate degree in structural engineering from Texas A&M and then decided to go on to law school in Austin. Just after graduation, he was recruited by a well-established law firm in Dallas and within five years he was told that they were considering making him a partner. James' case load focused primarily on high-stakes, high dollar divorce and custody cases where he quickly earned the reputation of being a hired gun – a verbally abusive, in-your-face kind of guy who could get his clients the blacktop off the opponent's driveway if they wanted it. James always made sure that he dominated the people in his professional life, and even used his power and strength to control the direction of his personal relationships. James was always uncomfortable if he was not in the power position, and the life he had built for himself was hammered into existence by the sheer force of his will.

Paul Henderson, the senior partner who had recruited James and had told him about the firm's intention to make him a partner, found a summer job for his daughter Tonya as a paralegal. When Tonya started flirting with James, he didn't hesitate in asking her out. They were together as much as possible. Tonya even convinced James to take her to the Cayman Islands for a week where they both got certified to scuba dive. After the trip, they had a falling out. Tonya demanded that James stay away from her, but James rarely capitulated to demands of any kind. Three weeks later, Tonya left for school, which she hoped would solve her "James problem" and allow her move on with her life.

Two years had passed since James had been told about the prospect of becoming a partner in the firm, but there was no sign of any movement in this direction. James had asked around about it a few times, and finally was able to pry the secret loose that Paul had lobbied the other senior partners not to extend the offer to James as pay-back for what had happened with his daughter, Tonya. James felt he had been betrayed. With full-on vengeance, he turned his verbally abusive, in-your-face attitude on Paul in meetings within the firm and even in front of clients. Weeks of this turned into months, and the tension in the firm was so thick you could cut it with the proverbial knife. Other senior partners began challenging James on his behavior and attitude toward Paul. But James refused to back down – they'd promised him a partnership and then reneged because of something that was totally unrelated to his performance. When some of their largest and longest-standing clients began to complain to Paul and the other senior partners about James, the partners decided they had to begin the process of building a file of objective evidence against James, and then show him to the door.

James had developed a tightly woven and small group of friends and confidants in Dallas who he allowed to see below the turbulent, often violent, surface of his life. They knew him to be a natural born leader who people wanted to follow, and an honorable person who would use his strength, control, and power to help them and even protect them if necessary. Once you were in the inner circle, James would go against all odds to make sure the world did not take advantage of or harm you.

But once you betrayed him, there was no going back, and James made it very difficult not to cross him at some point in time. People who had known him for years described James as a loose cannon who went off without warning, a guy who would fight at the drop of a hat and wore it tipped to start with, like he had some hidden score to settle with life. He kept an unbridgeable psychological moat between him and people outside the inner circle because James figured the less they knew about him, the less they could use against him. Finally, the senior partners unanimously voted to eject James from the firm by buying him off with an overly liberal separation package effective immediately. The speed of their action took James by surprise, and after trying to sabotage as many client relationships as he could, he turned his case load over to the others in the firm, and stormed out of the building, knocking over anything within his reach. Paul was just glad to be rid of him.

James wiped the dust off his feet and got a real change of lifestyle by moving to a place he had been camping near for the last few summers, Alma, Colorado. Alma is a town of two hundred people. It's two blocks wide, four blocks long and at an elevation of 10,587 feet above sea level, it is the highest town in North America. Alma is pure, ungentrified Colorado, only fifteen miles south of the world-class ski resort at Breckenridge. When James got to Alma, he rented a small house about a mile off the main road that ran through town. It was quiet there, so quiet that the only thing James heard when he sat on his front porch in the evening was the thunderous sound of his own breath. He picked up a copy of the *Fairplay Flume* in the Alma post office where he had to go to get his mail, and scoured the half page want ads looking for a job. He wanted to do anything but be a lawyer. With his background in engineering, he easily landed a job as one of Park County's two building inspectors.

James had his share of trouble as an inspector. Park County was like a different universe from the world he had just left. Nobody cared who he was, what he knew, or where he went to law school. In Alma, how much you knew was more closely tied to how long you'd been in town and whether you remembered when Main Street was still a dirt road. James was no respecter of persons in a rural mountain setting that was all about nepotism, old friendships and how many generations a family had been ranching in Park County. One day over a beer at the South Park Saloon, his neighbor, Bobby, told James that he had been living in Alma for twenty-five years, and the old-timers still didn't consider him a "local." Whether he was dealing with contractors, county commissioners, long-time locals, or his small group of new friends, James tried to dominate them and force his opinions and views on them. He would push, and push, and push some more until he had totally alienated people. Occasionally, someone who cared about him even less than he cared about them would push him back with equally abusive, intimidating, and streetwise force. James accepted this for what it was. He always respected a worthy adversary on the few occasions that he found one.

Ten years of the quiet, solitary, reflective life in the high country began to change James. Over the years, he flirted with the idea of opening a law office, but was increasingly taunted by remorse and inner conflict about the families he had helped to tear apart in the courtroom. He was also taunted by how abusive and vengeful he had been to people, but he had been that way for as long as he could remember. He had little prospect for real change. James left a broad, long trail of psychologically damaged people and shameful situations behind him. In the quietness and peace of the mountains, when the normal distractions of life were not there to drown them out, the inner voices of shame and remorse haunted him and became harder and harder to push out of conscious awareness.

James' is only one of many possible stories that could be told to show what the Tacit Creed "I must be powerful" looks like in the life of an individual. While the surface traits; natural talents and abilities; life-experiences; relationships; socio-cultural setting; ethnicity; gender; and level of psychological health defined by the 80-20 Rule may vary dramatically from person-to-person, the underlying patterns, processes and structures of the stories of all type Eights will be similar.

Emergence of the Tacit Creed

The Eight's Natural-Self occupies the bottom portion of Figure 67 where the Tacit Creed (I must be powerful) *emerges* from their innate, inborn temperament and the deep fear associated with the core assumption that they *lack the ability to receive their needs from the environment naturally*. The emphasis is on the words *receive* and *naturally* and the tacit conviction (and near certainty) that they are incapable of having their needs met through the natural, spontaneous, ordinary course of life. Eights experience this core assumption emotionally as a deep and abiding sense that, "I'm weak and vulnerable when getting my needs met by people and the world." They *experience* the core assumption with an inner sense of *certainty* as a *self-evident* truth that cannot (and ought not) be: a) questioned, b) objectively or publicly tested, or c) even verbalized. This belief that Eights hold about themselves is a *secret* truth that they hide from themselves, others, and the world. It's undiscussible and its un-discussibility is itself undiscussible. The fear of self-knowledge creates a sense of psychological survival in Eight's that threatens their *existence* to the point where the gate-keeping function *blocks* these emotions from entering conscious awareness. But life goes on, and so must the Eight. Over time, the emotional and cognitive memories associated with this core assumption are *buried* deeper and deeper within the psyche of type Eights to the point where, they become largely inaccessible to conscious awareness and are only experienced at pivotal (*kairos*) moments in life. This primal fear *forces* a shift in the Eights focus in order to avoid the embarrassment and threat that the reality of the core assumption creates, so rather than face (or test) the *veracity* of lacking the ability to receive their needs from the environment, they *displace* the problem by being "powerful." But trying to be "powerful" can never fill the deep inner need of type Eights because it tries to address an *inner* (existential) issue with *outer* behavior.

Notice how the Tacit Creed can either be *deficiency-driven* by Domination and Vengeance or *growth-motivated* by Innocence and Forgiveness and has a very different look and feel depending on whether it's driven or motivated – with the ratio of driven-to-motivated actions and interactions being defined as the 80-20 Rule. When Eights like James are at their best and are growth-motivated, they are strong, assertive, persistent, tenacious, seeking challenges, action-oriented with a take-charge attitude and enormous determination and will power to triumph over all obstacles and be influential in their world. When they face embarrassment, threat or are deficiency-driven, Eights become hostile, vindictive, defiant, emotionally insensitive, desiring to control and dominate people and situations to get what they want, or exploiting people and situations by taking what they want by force or cunning.

The three Somatic Instincts shown at the very bottom of Figure 67 are the first three levels of Maslow's Hierarchy and form the inner core and foundation upon which the type Eight's personality is built. The Somatic Instincts powerfully shape the overall direction of an Eight's life in the sense that their deep inner yearnings and desires unconsciously draw them to people, experiences, careers, relationships, and life situations that will gratify these basic human needs. So the *autopilot needs* of deficiency-driven Preserving Eights can only be gratified by "being powerful" in areas associated with home, nurture and comfort, while Cultivating Eights are unconsciously drawn to gratify their need to "be powerful" in areas associated with belonging and affiliation with groups, and the autopilot needs of Transmitting Eight's must be gratified by "being powerful" in situations that revolve around love, affection, caring, and communicating their ideas.

Deficiency-Driver

As shown in Figure 67, when Eights are under pressure or facing embarrassment or threat, Domination and Vengeance become the deficiency-drivers for the Tacit Creed – "I must be powerful." When deficiency-driven, the Tacit Creed for Eights is like:

- A hyper-sensitivity or allergic reaction to situations that fit the underlying pattern of the Tacit Creed and the dominant Somatic Instinct, which for type Eights means identifying areas in which they can expand their span of domination and control.

- Another way to describe the deficiency-driven Tacit Creed of Eights is that it creates a narrowing of focus in their attention that is driven by a yearning and desire to gratify the fourth level of Maslow's Hierarchy – the esteem needs. So how Eights "esteem" themselves is powerfully shaped and defined by their need to "see" themselves as being powerful, and by having other people *confirm* this self-perception by also "seeing" them as powerful.

- The Tacit Creed of type Eights can also be described as a cognitive and emotional angle-or-perspective-on-life that singles-out specific underlying patterns in relationships, interactions, and situations that will gratify the Eight's basic need to be powerful.

- The fact that Eights constantly evaluate their relationships and the environment for opportunities to expand their span of domination and control, even when other people don't want it, indicates that their drive to be "powerful" often satisfies *their own needs*, not the needs of other people or the situations they face.

Unconscious Appraisal and Selection

This section *links* the unconscious, autopilot cognitive and emotional appraisal and selection process for type Eights, to the See-Do-Get Process and the Downward Spiral of Striving. Notice in Figure 68, that when the Tacit Creed "I must be powerful" is unpacked *as* the autopilot doing and learning process, Eights like James tend to be unconsciously drawn to specific people, relationships, situations, and events in the world that will gratify: a) their need to be powerful, and b) the basic needs of their dominant Somatic Instinct.

Unconscious Appraisal and Selection

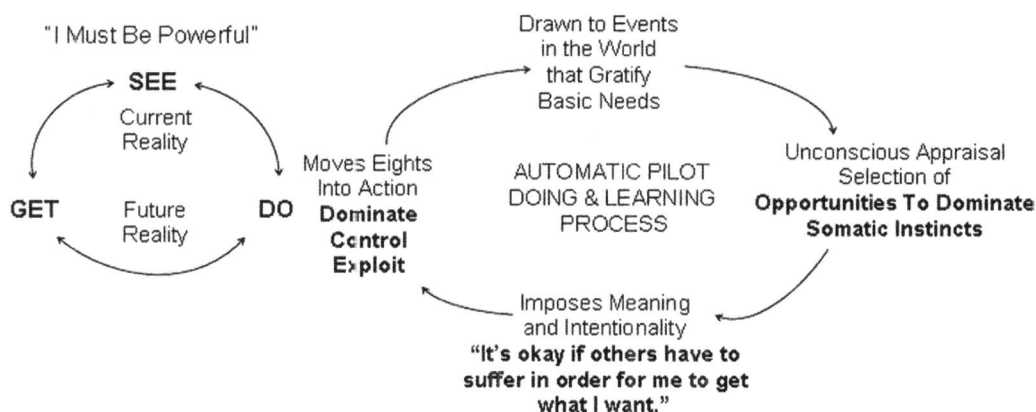

"I Must Be Powerful"

SEE
Current Reality

GET   Future   DO
Reality

Moves Eights Into Action
Dominate Control Exploit

Drawn to Events in the World that Gratify Basic Needs

AUTOMATIC PILOT DOING & LEARNING PROCESS

Unconscious Appraisal Selection of **Opportunities To Dominate Somatic Instincts**

Imposes Meaning and Intentionality
"It's okay if others have to suffer in order for me to get what I want."

Figure 68

In the second step, Eights unconsciously *appraise* situations and *select* opportunities to get their basic needs met by "dominating" others in ways that are shaped and defined by their dominant Somatic Instinct – whether preserving, cultivating, or transmitting. They unconsciously choose very specific cognitive and emotional data from the world because they "match" the underlying patterns and basic need to gratify their needs by acting out the *inner mandate* to be powerful.

In the third step, the Eight's Tacit Creed *imposes* meaning and intentionality on the actions and interactions of people *and* the situations they're involved in. A typical tacit belief that Eights might impose on a situation from their Left-Hand Column is, "It's okay if others have to suffer for me to get what I want – this is pay-back for when I was forced to suffer." This reveals the Eight's tendency to *project* their own needs and beliefs onto the world around them.

In the final step, the momentum and psychological force of the first three steps move Eights *into action* and these actions will tend to follow the pattern just described, where they become hostile, vindictive, and defiant, exploiting people and situations by taking what they want by force or cunning – all with the unconscious goal of gratifying their own needs, but under the pretense of being "powerful."

The entire process shown in Figure 68 happens beneath the surface of conscious awareness – in the blink of an eye. It's important to remember that the process can be growth-motivated where the four steps produce positive, constructive actions and interactions along the Upward Path of Becoming. Eights like James who want to move from being deficiency-driven to growth-motivated must consciously raise this autopilot process back into conscious awareness; deconstruct and reconfigure it by running the See-Do-Get Process backwards in the counter clockwise direction; and then migrate the new growth-motivated actions and interactions back to autopilot operation by embedding them through repetition. When Eights succeed in using this change process, the new growth-motivated actions and interactions begin to happen as naturally and automatically as the previous deficiency-driven ones once did. When eight out of ten behaviors are growth-motivated by Innocence and Forgiveness, rather than deficiency-driven by Domination and Vengeance, this is an indication that an Eight is embodying the 80-20 Rule.

Blind Spots

When Eights are under pressure or facing embarrassment or threat, Domination and Vengeance become the deficiency-drivers for the Tacit Creed – "I must be powerful." Mounting evidence produced by countless cycles through the See-Do-Get Process gives Eights a *false sense* that being "powerful" has actually given them the ability to receive their needs from the environment naturally, and this only deepens their sense of Domination and Vengeance (see Figure 69).

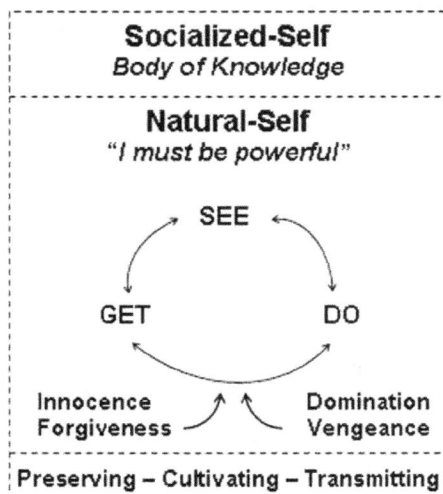

Figure 69

As in the case of James, Eights tend to have "Blind Spots" about the *extent* to which Domination and Vengeance dominate their lives and create decision-making bias and predictable errors in judgment. Deficiency-driven Eights tend to "see" themselves as growth-motivated, while the people they interact with tend to "see" them as more deficiency-driven. The emotions of Domination and Vengeance are *inflamed* when Eights are under pressure or they don't get the results they want because people either object to (or don't respond to) their insatiable desire to expand their control over their environment through intimidation, humiliation, and fighting for pleasure. Eights become "intoxicated" by the emotional power of Domination and Vengeance, which makes it more difficult for them to see their Blind Spots and unintended consequences for what they really are. Once the intoxicating energy of Domination and Vengeance subsides, Eights will settle back down to the normal state-of-equilibrium of their dominant type. But over time, this cycle of behaviors and emotional responses *solidifies* into a well-defined pattern of interaction that goes on autopilot and slips below the surface of conscious awareness. These patterns-of-interactions are commonly called "hot buttons" or defense routines.

The philosophy of *power as the road to receiving their needs naturally* powerfully shapes the day-to-day preferences of Eights about the people, relationships, careers, hobbies, and lifestyles they are attracted to (and repulsed by), and over time these myriad choices are woven into the fabric of their lives. By the time Eights are young adults, they have identified with the Tacit Creed of "being powerful" to the point where they are locked into a cognitive, emotional, social, and contextual configuration that solidifies, reaches a state-of-equilibrium, and *becomes* their day-to-day reality. The inner mandate to be "powerful" becomes externalized, objectified, and ultimately reified into a social mirror that seems to objectively affirm the belief that the Eight's way of seeing themselves, others, and the world is *the* way that life should be lived. We described this earlier as the Self-Sealing Process of forming Personality in Context.

But the *false sense* of being able to receive their needs naturally that comes from "being powerful," the *validation* that comes from the social mirror, and the *stability* of the day-to-day reality that Eights construct – *come* at an enormous price, because they deeply divide them at the very core of their being. *Secretly*, Eights know that they're not as powerful as they claim to be, and the fear of this being discovered by others only *fuels* the autopilot, insatiable, destructive power of their Tacit Creed. Think about it – if the Tacit Creed of "being powerful" isn't true for Eights like James – then what is? If Eights are wrong about how they see themselves, others, and the world, then they may be wrong about almost everything in life.

Growth-Motivated

We have spent a significant amount of time discussing the Tacit Creed and underlying mechanisms of the deficiency-driver of type Eights like James because without a correct understanding of the process by which these underlying mechanisms bind and limit the choices, personal freedom, and self-determination of type Eights, there is little or no hope of ever escaping the pernicious entanglements of Personality in Context. In this section, I'd like to focus on the *single point of leverage* that will address the question, "So what should type Eights *do* about the negative character-istics and effects of their personality?" I will also discuss the concrete changes that Eights can expect to see in their actions and interactions when they choose the Upward Path of Becoming. As shown in Figure 70, when Eights are at their best Innocence and Forgiveness become the growth-motivators for the Tacit Creed – "I must be powerful."

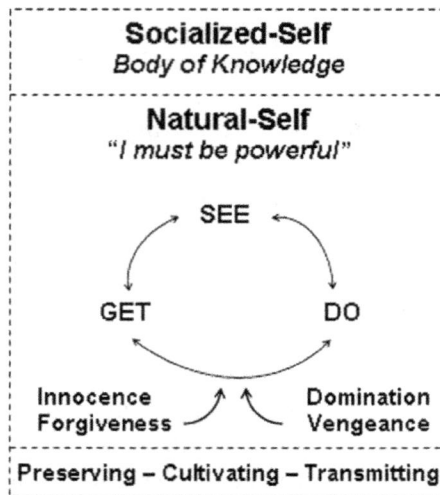

Figure 70

Growth-motivated Eights are strong, assertive, persistent, tenacious, seeking chal-lenges, action-oriented with a take-charge attitude and enormous determination and will power to triumph over all obstacles and be influential in their world.

While the Eight's Blind Spots, defense routines, and the inner mandate to be "pow-erful" *combine* with the social mirror and the edicts of their socio-cultural context to form barriers to deep change, they all rest on the foundation of the Eight's core assumption that they lack the ability to receive their needs from the environment naturally. Eights experience this "lack of ability to receive their needs naturally" as a self-evident truth that cannot (and should not) be questioned or tested, *but this is precisely what Eights must do*: face their fear of self-knowledge by questioning, and publicly testing, the truth of this claim. They must come to "see" themselves as having the tools to unlearn these *biased*, *misguided*, and *erroneous* ways of seeing themselves, others, and the world. Like the story of the Mulla, looking for the key in the *right* place becomes the *single point of leverage* that will enable Eights to ignite deep personal change.

Focusing on the single point of leverage acts like a *solvent* that begins to dissolve the *hidden inauthentic layers* of cognitive, emotional, social, and contextual strata from which the Eight's life has been built. Using the single point of leverage enables Eights to begin living more authentically in terms of their actions, interactions, and decision-making within the current context of their lives. It helps them to do the right things, for the right reasons. There are a number of very concrete indicators that emerge when Eights like James begin the journey on the Upward Path of Becoming:

- Eights are free to question their default way of seeing themselves as having to be "powerful" and having to dominate others to get what they want.
- Their hyper-sensitivity toward identifying ways to expand their control and domination over their world gives way to Innocence, Forgiveness, and a deep desire to develop inner strength, self-mastery, and no longer see vulnerability and child-like innocence as something to be stamped out in order to meet their basic need to be powerful.
- They begin to see how they can have an enormous positive influence and impact on their world by using their strengths and abilities for constructive, not destructive ends
- Over time, Eights gain new confidence in their ability to transcend the constraints of their personality and cultural context, as they see the concrete evidence of change indicated by their ability to act-out the 80-20 Rule – where eight out of ten interactions are motivated by Innocence and Forgiveness, rather than being driven by Domination and Vengeance.

Connecting Points

As we saw in the case of James, Eights intentionally alter their actions and interactions to "fit" the requirements and norms of a specific social or cultural context because doing otherwise might be inappropriate and could have negative consequences on them personally and professionally. In a previous section, I referred to this as the Socialized-Self. But buried deep beneath the Eight's Socialized-Self, family background, life experiences, and body of knowledge is a unique underlying *signature pattern* of connecting points that identifies what it means to be a type Eight – their Natural-Self.

Connecting Points
(Connecting Inner Mandates and Mixed Emotions)

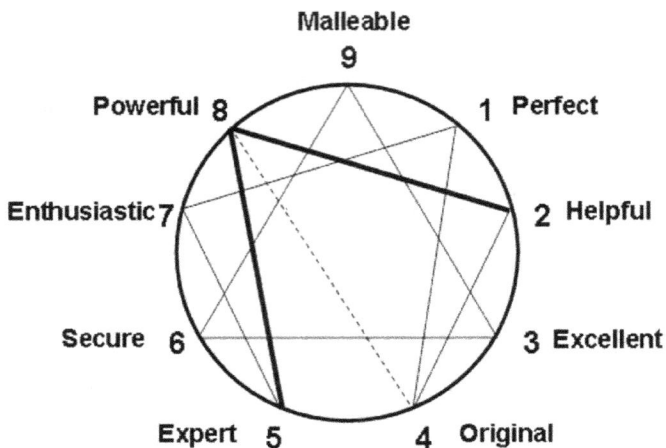

Figure 71

The underlying pattern and characteristics of the connecting points remain relatively constant over time and with changes in context. They are a well-defined intra-psychic pattern of interaction that shapes and defines Eight's behaviors and responses in day-to-day discourse, especially in situations where they face *embarrassment* or *threat*. The patterns-of-interaction associated with the connecting points are also an indicator of whether or not the overall direction of the Eight's life tends toward the Downward Spiral of Striving or the Upward Path of Becoming.

The Eight's dominant type anchors them to the Enneagram and is a necessary element of verifying a person's Enneagram type. The signature pattern for type Eight consists of four connecting points: types 8, 5, 2, and 4.

- Type Eight is the Tacit Creed which we've already discussed in detail.
- Type Five is the Striving Point which is referred to by some Enneagram theorists as the point that indicates the direction of disintegration.
- Type Two is the Becoming Point which is referred to by some Enneagram theorists as the point that indicates the direction of integration.
- Type Four is the paradox point. While type Fours and Eights exhibit very different surface traits, Tacit Creeds, and underlying motivations; they are paradoxical opposites around the issue of *emotions* and *sensitivity*. Whereas type Fours tend to be the most emotionally sensitive of the Enneagram types and seek *intensity* through the deeper (and often darker) emotions of life rather than action, type Eights tend to be the least emotionally sensitive of the

Enneagram types (turning their emotions off) and instead seek *intensity* through action and dominating their world.

- While the connecting points for Eights represent the *natural* pattern, process, and structure of this Enneagram type, they should not be viewed as rigid and determined. Given sufficient pressure and influence from family or the social-cultural context, these natural tendencies can be powerfully shaped and defined in other ways, with the original signature pattern of the type Eight being hidden (or buried) beneath other configurations of Enneagram points.

What is most important to note is that the foundation of the type Eight's personality is an *interdependent configuration* of conflicting inner mandates and mixed emotions that includes four types, their Tacit Creeds, and their destructive and constructive emotions. In other words, the type Eight's personality is not a homogeneous set of beliefs; instead it is a portfolio of interdependent, complementary, competing, and conflicting ways of seeing themselves, others, and the world.

So when Eights like James are stressed and facing embarrassment and threat, the autopilot patterns-of-interaction between their tacit, Striving, Becoming, and Paradox points can (and often do) create inner conflict and mixed emotions. This is especially true when Eights are faced with a problem that requires a *single* solution. In other words, James would find himself wondering, "Should I do this, or should I do that? Should I be powerful or helpful?" This inner conflict is *intensified* when external pressures force Eights to act, interact, or make decisions *now*!

There are some key concepts that I'd like to review to define the psychological patterns, processes, and structure of the connecting points for type Eights in more detail.

- The actions and interactions of the other eight Enneagram types are done *in the service of* following the inner mandate to be "powerful" and maintaining the equilibrium of the cognitive, emotional, social, and contextual configuration that the Eight builds as their life – their Personality in Context.

- When they are growth-motivated, the connections between type Eight, Five, Two and Four can help to balance some of the symmetries by giving Eights at least one Enneagram point in each of the three triads, thus straddling the emotional, cognitive, and sensory parts of the human brain. The Eight's connecting points also help to balance the left-right and top-bottom symmetries, where types Two and Four provide a left-side balance for Eights, and types Five and Four provide Enneagram points that balance the top-bottom symmetry.

- Another key concept centers on the *combining* of the Tacit Creeds and underlying emotions into what is referred to as conflicting inner mandates and mixed emotions for type Eights. People rarely act univocally. Rather, actions, interactions (and eventually patterns-of-interaction) come in complex, interdependent bundles, where the Tacit Creeds and underlying emotions of the Eight's connecting points *combine* and *co-mingle* to form extremely complex packages of emotional messages that are communicated to others.

A solid understanding of the signature pattern is the key to *unbundling* the complex packages of emotional messages and patterns-of-interaction that type Eights often exhibit in day-to-day interactions.

Type Eight Summary Profile

Figure 72 provides an overall summary of the key patterns, structures, and processes that were described in this section and that typify the Enneagram type Eight.

Type Summary Profile - Type Eight	
Core Assumption	I lack the ability to receive my needs from the environment naturally
Tacit Creed (Mulla)	I must be powerful
Unconscious Appraisal	Opportunities to dominate and Somatic Instincts
Impose Meaning	It's okay if others have to suffer in order for me to get what I want
Move Into Action	Dominate, control, exploit
Deficiency Drivers	Domination, Vengeance
Growth Motivators	Innocence, Forgiveness
Striving Point	Type Five
Becoming Point	Type Two
Paradox Point	Type Four
Group (Triad)	Action, leads with the sensory part of the brain (Brain Stem)
Existential Question	How do I deal with the environment?
Conflict Processing Strategy	Reactive
Attitude Towards Socio-Cultural Change	Move Against/Aggressive
Single Point of Leverage	Question and publicly test the core assumption

Figure 72

In keeping with the overall approach of the Breckenridge Enneagram, the characteristics and dynamics shown in Figure 72 are not surface-traits or behaviors. Rather, the content of Figure 72 describes the underlying patterns, structures, and processes that define what makes type Eights like James different from the other eight Enneagram types.

Examples and Movies

While Eights are found in every area of life and all professional fields, the list below shows some famous examples of people who are probably type Eights. How many names do you recognize? Which ones are you interested enough in to learn more about by reading a biography or autobiography?

- *Examples* – Famous examples who exhibit Eight traits: Donald Trump, John Wayne, Golda Meir, Franklin D. Roosevelt, Frank Sinatra, Roseanne, Martin Luther King Jr., Charles Bronson, Ernest Hemingway, Zorba the Greek, Darth Vader, Johnny Cash, Dixy Lee Ray.

Another way to see Enneagram type in action is through the characters and story lines in movies. Select some of the movies listed below and take some time to watch Eights in action.

- *Movie Characters* – Roles in movies that exemplify Eight traits: George C. Scott (Patton), Molly Brown (Titanic), Don Vito Corleone (Godfather), William Hurt (The Doctor), Denzel Washington (Remember the Titans), Robert Duvall (The Great Santini), Al Pacino (Scent of a Woman), Judd Hirsch (Ordinary People), Gil (Finding Nemo).

To deepen your understanding of this Enneagram type, identify people who you *know* that embody this personality type and become more observant about their behaviors, attitudes, and decision-making strategies. Ask them to share their thoughts, views, and perspectives on key issues and criteria for decision-making and see how closely the descriptions in this section describe and predict their responses. To further solidify and deepen your understanding, log your insights and observations about this personality type in a journal. You can use this exercise for the other eight types as well.

Type Nine (I Must Be Malleable)

When Nines are at their best, they are self-aware, seekers of self-actualization, engaged and connected to life, good-natured, friendly, easy-going, patient, tolerant, creative, imaginative, excellent mediators and communicators, emotionally stable, non-confrontational, and focused on life's simple pleasures. When under pressure, they become overly submissive and agreeable (peace at any price), distractible, mechanically going through the motions in life and desensitized to the point where their capacity for psychological insight is diminished substantially – they long not to long, to stay blind to their Blind Spots.

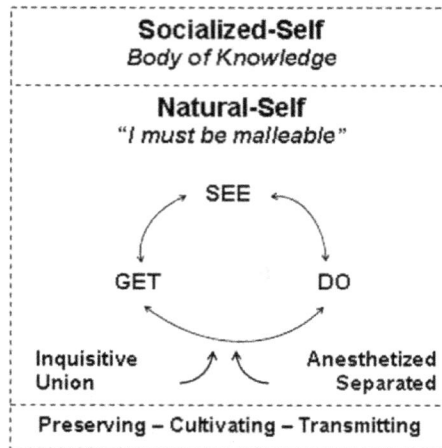

Figure 73

The very top of Figure 73 is made up of a person's Socialized-Self and body of knowledge, which form a major portion of the knowledge-base of their personal paradigm.

Tacit Creed

Nines live by the Tacit Creed "I must be malleable" – a belief that solidifies early in life through countless cycles through the See-Do-Get Process. When they are Deficiency Driven, they are hyper-sensitive to identifying situations in which asserting their desires could "rock the boat" and create conflict, they become anesthetized to their true desires, inner life, personal views and go along with what others want too easily. The downward pull (undertow) of being Anesthetized and Separated are *accelerated* when under pressure or when they don't get the result they want; e.g., people either object to, or don't respond to, their psychological inertia, distractibility, and their desensitized, indirect approach to relationships and life. When under stress, they become "narcotized" by the power of these emotions and have a *Blind Spot* about the extent to which being Anesthetized and a profound sense of being Separated dominates their lives and create decision-making bias and predictable errors in judgment.

When they are Growth Motivated, they are free to question their default way of seeing and their hyper-sensitivity gives way to Inquisitiveness, a sense of being in Union with self, others, and a deep desire to be directly and authentically connected to their inner world, other people, situations, and the opportunities for personal growth and self-actualization that life brings their way. They begin to see themselves, the human race, and the natural world as an interdependent whole to which they are vitally connected (in Union) For Nines, the key element of personal growth and building effective relationships is to follow the 80-20 Rule – where eight out of ten interactions with others are characterized by being Inquisitive and in Union with self, others, and the world, rather than being Anesthetized and Separated.

Rick's Story

Rick Flowton's story is an example of what the Tacit Creed "I must be malleable" looks like when it's solidified in the life of a type Nine. Rick had always been an easy-going guy who didn't like to make waves. He was raised in a family whose philosophy was that children should be seen, but not heard. As a child, he felt that his presence made no tangible difference in his family and the world around him. He came to believe that he lacked the ability to act on the environment, so he had to just go through the motions and be malleable.

He learned to scuba dive as a teenager, not because he wanted to, but because his family pressured him into it. Despite this, he came to like the sport. Whenever he tried to assert himself, people responded with a pressure for him to remain invisible – seen, but not heard. Life just went on without him almost like his presence didn't make a difference to the course of life. Rick had lived with his wife Linda and three young children in a house he owned in Evanston, Illinois. He had gone to Northwestern, earned a degree in business, and had been the CFO of the Stonewall corporation, a small, family run business on the north side of Chicago. About six years ago, the founder of the company retired and gave control of the operation to his grandson Josh who was bright and energetic and breathed new life and enthusiasm into a small business that had been maintaining the status quo for years. Josh's gung-ho approach paid off in bottom-line results as the company grew from $5 million per year to $80 million over a five-year period. Josh set his sights on managed growth that was driven by new marketing strategies, customer focus, and quantitative measures of employee performance to push productivity to the bottom-line.

Rick hated conflict more than anything and did everything he could to avoid it. His image of "the good life" was peace and harmony in all his relationships, a Norman Rockwell view of life. But he never quite learned the lesson that when he put conflict off, it magnified, intensified, and only got worse. Time after time with professional, family, and friendship relationships, Rick would withdraw from facing difficulties whenever he could. In the end, putting conflict off forced him to deal with much more conflict than if he had just faced issues directly from the beginning.

When Stonewall was first started, Rick was the lead man in a four-person accounting office. Eight years later, Rick was promoted to CFO by Josh's grandfather and Rick's staff grew to over twenty people. From the very beginning, Josh had serious questions about Rick's ability to handle the bigger operation, but his grandfather had confidence that Rick could grow with the company and should be given more and more responsibility. Rick was given assignments and goals, which he never completed on time. When Josh confronted him about his poor performance, Rick would insist that he was overworked and that he needed more staff. In the old days, this type of diversionary whining worked, and Rick would get more staff. But in the new performance-based culture that Josh was trying to establish, these cries fell on deaf ears. A desk audit that Josh asked the HR manager to conduct of Rick's actual day-to-day activities revealed that he was seriously under-employed. Casual, day-to-day observations of Rick showed that he spent more time gossiping with the "old timers" about how unhappy he was about the changes Josh was making in the company, and passive-aggressively undermining those changes at every turn. After discussing these issues with Rick informally on a number of occasions, Josh told the HR manager to begin documenting Rick's lack of performance on deliverables, as well as his duplicitous attempts to undermine the new organizational culture Josh was trying to bring to the company.

Rick was a strange mixture of a really nice guy who chatted with his employees over coffee in an approachable demeanor, and someone who had to maintain control by ensuring that he was involved in every decision that was made in his department. Many of his people liked him, but a few hated him because they were always cleaning up the organizational messes that he left behind. His in-box was like a black hole, everything went in – nothing ever came out. Often quiet and unassuming in staff meetings, Rick was very subtly interested in his image, how big his office was, whether he got free parking privileges, and all the other trappings of organizational power. Out of loyalty to Rick, and a desire to see the company succeed, the staff who liked him worked around him and covered for him just to get the job done. The people who were terminally frustrated by his passive-aggressive undermining of Josh's new culture, and Rick's duplicitous support for Josh in meetings, would tell Josh what was really going on. Josh continued to build the paper file of Rick's poor performance. He tolerated Rick while his grandfather was still involved in the transition of the company, but once the responsibility for the company was fully his, firing Rick was the first high-level administrative decision that Josh would make.

Frank and Connie, Linda's parents, also had questions about Rick's level of motivation even before he got fired, lost his house, and moved Linda and the kids into their basement in the south west suburbs of Chicago. Their moving in was only supposed to be until "things got straightened out," but Frank and Connie both had a bad feeling about how long this would take. Living with Rick allowed Frank to watch Rick's coming and going more closely, and he only made intermittent attempts to look for a job. It was a buyer's market for employers at that time where there were many more applicants than there were jobs. Most potential employers were able to see through the smoke screen of Rick's inflated history of titles, promotions, and "accomplishments." Others got the picture quickly when they called his former employer as a reference check. Rick even applied for government positions where he knew he could trade a reduction in his former salary for job security, but nothing turned up. Every rejection letter and unreturned phone call just drove Rick's self-esteem further into the ground. Beneath his nice guy exterior, Rick was depressed and felt like he was sinking into the muck and mire of the pressure and demands of a world that he just couldn't keep up with.

Rick would "check out" as a way of dealing with problematic situations or when the pressure of everyday life grew too intense. Unfortunately for the people in his life, when Rick didn't deal with his problems, *they* had to pick up the pieces as he just stood there with an unknowing, faraway stare in his eyes. Most people looked beyond his shortcomings because Rick was an open, easy-going person. In many ways, Rick actually had a kind of calming influence on difficult situations. But for those who were closest to him and saw him at his worst, he was an overly agreeable, too submissive doormat who feared and resisted almost all change, regardless of the cost to himself or others.

Connie had been pushing Frank to do something to take the pressure off, but Frank was torn about getting involved. From the perspective of a CPA who owned an accounting firm, there was *no way* that Frank would give Rick a job working for him. But as a father who was concerned about the welfare of Linda and his grand-children, he stewed over scenario after scenario of how he could help, without being one more enabler to Rick's indolence. Frank had been observing a trend of how clients who lived up to thirty minutes north of his current location were traveling to use his services because there were no accounting firms in that immediate area. Connie was pushing Frank to open another location to the north, and to let Rick run that operation. They could rent office space, transfer some of the current staff and the more northern clients to that location, and let Rick build up the rest of the business. Given the fact that Rick was not a CPA, the northern branch would do bookkeeping, accounting, and taxes, and Frank would still do the CPA tasks. It sounded good on paper, but Frank was worried about the reality of it all.

Because Frank had chosen an excellent location in an area where there were no other accountants, and transferred three of his best staff and $175 thousand in existing client revenues to the new location, the business grew to about a quarter of a million dollars in a little over eighteen months. The growth was due primarily to the word of mouth marketing that happened because of the lead person on Rick's staff, Joanne. Joanne was an aggressive, competent, go-getter who had worked for Frank for over ten years and handled some of the larger accounts that were trans-ferred to the northern location. Clients who worked with Joanne liked her and told others, which served to make the business grow more rapidly. In fact, the growth happened despite Rick who was back into the flow of the management style that had gotten him fired only two years earlier.

Joanne wanted to please Frank, but soon saw through the contradictions of Rick's management style. Rick would say yes, when he meant no. His words rarely matched his deeds. When Rick disagreed with Joanne, rather than confront the conflict, he would play dumb and say he didn't understand. Joanne learned quickly that when Rick said he didn't understand, what he was really saying was that he didn't agree. She was ready to strangle him because she hated the duplicity of his passive-aggressive style. As far as Joanne was concerned, passive aggression was still aggression, and she spent a major portion of her time doing damage control with the other two people in the office who also saw through Rick's behavior. Joanne tried to broach the topic with Frank on numerous occasions, but this put them both in the difficult position of sharing issues that were uncomfortable. As the conflict in the office grew, Rick predictably ignored it, hoping it would go away and painted nothing but rosy pictures in his weekly reports to Frank, who knew better. Frank didn't want to confront the situation directly because Rick, Linda, and the children had finally moved out and into a new house and Frank didn't want them moving back in with them. So the real depth and magnitude of the problem were almost completely masked by the increase in clients and revenues and the only question was when would Joanne simply quit out of utter frustration.

About a year later, Joanne's non-compete agreement with the firm expired and Rick, who was responsible for renewing employee contracts, failed to notice this. Things had gone from bad to worse, and despite her continued discussions with Frank, nothing was being done and there was no change in sight. Joanne knew she was the backbone of the business because the clients she serviced were about 60 percent of the total revenues of the northern location, plus her reputation had brought in most of the new clients. She decided it was time for a showdown. She began confronting Rick on a regular basis in memos about his mismanagement of the business, with copies going to Frank. Rick would meet with her, admit that he needed to do better, but then nothing would change or he'd tell her he didn't completely understand what she wanted from him.

When Joanne could take it no more, she walked in, dropped her resignation on Frank's desk, and said, "I told you it was either Rick or me." Frank was speechless, and tried to smooth things over by taking her out for a farewell lunch to wish her well. Rather than rehash the problems about Rick yet one more time, they both decided to just chat about the good old days and things that were happening outside of the office. At one point close to the end of their meal, Frank asked Joanne what she planned to do next. Joanne replied that she was going to do some accounting work out of her house. Frank wished her well, having no idea what this would mean for him.

Within two weeks of Joanne's leaving, the majority of the big clients that she serviced had called Rick to tell him they were changing accountants. Although they didn't say why, it didn't take Frank long to figure out where the clients were going. Frank called and threatened Joanne with legal action, claiming she had a non-compete agreement that stated she could not run off with his clients. But the letter that Joanne's lawyer sent in response included a copy of the expired non-compete agreement, proving it had been out of force for almost a year, thus Frank had no legal recourse.

Rick's story is only one of many that could be told to show what the Tacit Creed "I must be malleable" looks like in the life of an individual. While the surface traits; natural talents and abilities, life-experiences; relationships; socio-cultural setting; ethnicity; gender; and level of psychological health defined by the 80-20 Rule may vary dramatically from person-to-person, the underlying patterns, processes and structures of the stories of all type Nines will be similar.

Emergence of the Tacit Creed

The Nine's Natural-Self occupies the bottom portion of Figure 73 where the Tacit Creed (I must be malleable) *emerges* from their innate, inborn temperament and the deep fear associated with the core assumption that they *lack the ability to act on (and make tangible differences in) the environment*. The emphasis is on the word "act" and the tacit-conviction (and near certainty) that they lack the ability to make a physical difference in the world with their own energy and force, so they just go through the motions. Nines experience this core assumption emotionally as a deep and abiding sense that, "My presence makes no tangible difference in life – relationships, events, good-times, bad-times, victories, and defeats all happen without any substantive input from me." They *experience* the core assumption with an inner sense of *certainty* as a *self-evident* truth that cannot (and ought not) be: a) questioned, b) objectively or publicly tested, or c) even verbalized. This belief that Nines hold about themselves is a *secret* truth that they hide from themselves, others, and the world. It's undiscussible and its un-discussibility cannot be discussed. The fear of self-knowledge creates a sense of psychological survival in Nines that threatens their *existence* to the point where the gate-keeping function *blocks* these emotions from conscious awareness. But life goes on, and so must the Nine. Over time, the emotional and cognitive memories associated with this core assumption are *buried* deeper and deeper within the psyche of type Nines to the point where they become largely inaccessible to conscious awareness and are only experienced at pivotal (*kairos*) moments in life. This *forces* a shift in the Nine's focus in order to avoid the embarrassment and threat that the reality of the core assumption creates, so rather than face (or test) the *truth* of lacking the ability to act on the environment, they *displace* the problem by being "malleable" and just going through the motions. But trying to be "malleable" can never fill the deep *inner* need of type Nines because it tries to address an inner (existential) issue with *outer* behavior.

Notice how the Tacit Creed can either be *deficiency-driven* by being Anesthetized and Separated, or *growth-motivated* by being Inquisitive and in Union with self and others, and has a very different look and feel depending on whether it's driven or motivated – with the ratio of driven-to-motivated actions and interactions being defined as the 80-20 Rule. When Nines like Rick are at their best and are growth-motivated, they are self-aware, seekers of self-actualization, engaged and connected to life, good-natured, friendly, easy-going, patient, tolerant, creative, imaginative, excellent mediators and communicators, emotionally stable, non-confrontational, and focused on life's simple pleasures. When they face embarrassment, threat or are deficiency-driven, Nines become overly submissive and agreeable (pursing peace at any price), and become distractible, mechanically going through the motions in life and desensitized to the point where their capacity for psychological insight is diminished substantially – they long not to long, and to stay blind to their Blind Spots.

The three Somatic Instincts shown at the very bottom of Figure 73 are the first three levels of Maslow's Hierarchy and form the inner core and foundation upon which the type Nine's personality is built. The Somatic Instincts powerfully shape the overall direction of a Nine's life in the sense that their deep inner yearnings and desires unconsciously draw them to people, experiences, careers, relationships, and life situations that will gratify these basic human needs. So the *autopilot needs* of deficiency-driven Preserving Nines can only be gratified by "being malleable" in areas associated with home, nurture and comfort, while Cultivating Nines are unconsciously drawn to gratify their need to "be malleable" in areas associated with belonging and affiliation with groups, and the autopilot needs of Transmitting Nines must be gratified by "by being malleable" in situations that revolve around love, affection, caring, and communicating their ideas.

Deficiency-Driven

As shown in Figure 73, when Nines are under pressure or facing embarrassment or threat, being Anesthetized and Separated become the deficiency-drivers, and the Tacit Creed for people like Rick:

- Is a hyper-sensitivity or allergic reaction to situations that fit the underlying pattern of having to be malleable, which for type Nines means identifying situations that involve conflict or the potential to "rock the boat."

- Creates a narrowing of focus in their attention that is driven by a yearning and desire to gratify the fourth level of Maslow's Hierarchy – the esteem needs. So how Nines "esteem" themselves is powerfully shaped and defined by their need to "see" themselves as being malleable, and by having other people *confirm* this self-perception by also "seeing" them as being malleable.

- Becomes a cognitive and emotional angle or perspective on life that singles-out specific underlying patterns in relationships, interactions, and situations that will gratify the Nine's basic need to be malleable.

- Causes them to constantly evaluate their relationships and the environment for opportunities to "be malleable" and not rock the boat, even when other people want their input, which indicates that their need to be "malleable" often satisfies *their own needs*, not the needs of other people or the situation they're in.

Unconscious Appraisal and Selection

This section *links* the unconscious, autopilot cognitive and emotional appraisal and selection process for type Nines, to the See-Do-Get Process and the Downward Spiral of Striving. Notice in Figure 74, that when the Tacit Creed "I must be malleable" is unpacked *as* the autopilot doing and learning process, Nines like Rick tend to be unconsciously drawn to specific people, relationships, situations, and events in the world that will gratify: a) their need to be malleable, and b) the basic needs of their dominant Somatic Instinct.

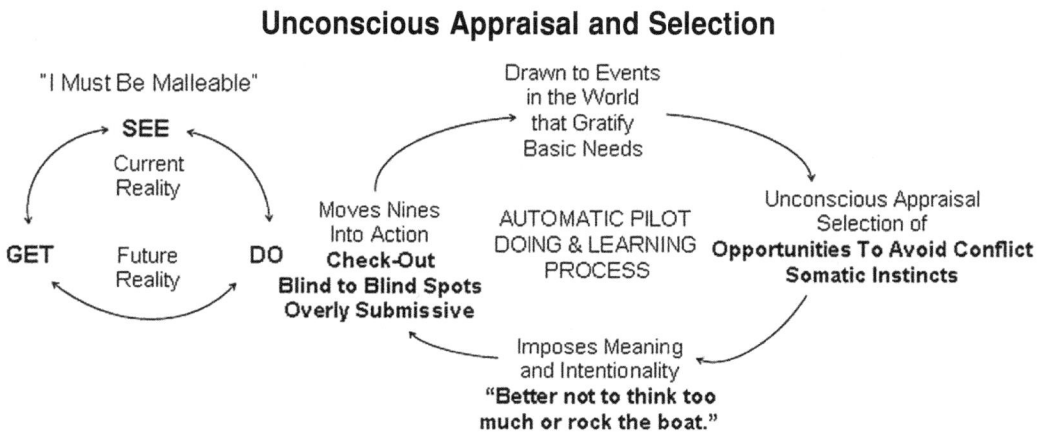

Unconscious Appraisal and Selection

Figure 74

In the second step, Nines unconsciously *appraise* situations and *select* opportunities to get their basic needs met by "being malleable" in ways that are shaped and defined by their dominant Somatic Instinct – whether preserving, cultivating, or transmitting. They unconsciously choose very specific cognitive and emotional data from the world because they "match" the underlying patterns and basic need to act on the environment by going through the motions and acting out the *inner mandate* to be malleable.

In the third step, the Nine's Tacit Creed *imposes* meaning and intentionality on the actions and interactions of people *and* the situations they're involved in. A typical tacit belief that Nines might impose on a situation from their Left-Hand Column is, "It's better not to think too much about things and not rock the boat." This reveals the Nine's tendency to *project* their own needs and beliefs onto the world around them.

In the final step, the momentum and psychological force of the first three steps move Nines *into a kind of action* (that is actually in-action) and these will tend to follow the pattern just described where they are overly submissive and agreeable, mechanically going through the motions of life, check-out of life's reality, and blind to their Blind Spots – all with the unconscious goal of gratifying their own needs, but under the pretense of being "malleable" for others and just going through the motions.

The entire process shown in Figure 74 happens beneath the surface of conscious awareness – in the blink of an eye. It's important to remember that the process can be growth-motivated where the four steps produce positive, constructive actions and interactions along the Upward Path of Becoming. Nines like Rick who want to move from being deficiency-driven to growth-motivated must consciously raise this autopilot process back into conscious awareness; deconstruct and reconfigure it by running the See-Do-Get Process backwards in the counter clockwise direction; and then migrate the new growth-motivated actions and interactions back to autopilot operation by embedding them through repetition. When Nines succeed in using this change process, the new growth-motivated actions and interactions begin to happen as naturally and automatically as the previous deficiency-driven ones once did. When eight out of ten behaviors are growth-motivated by being Inquisitive and in Union with self and others, rather than deficiency-driven by being Anesthetized and Separated, this is an indication that a Nine is embodying the 80-20 Rule.

Blind Spots

When Nines are under pressure or facing embarrassment or threat, being Anesthetized and Separated become the deficiency-drivers for the Tacit Creed – "I must be malleable." Mounting evidence produced by countless cycles through the See-Do-Get Process gives Nines a false sense that being "malleable" has actually given them the ability to act on their environment, but this only deepens their level of being Anesthetized and separated from others (see Figure 75).

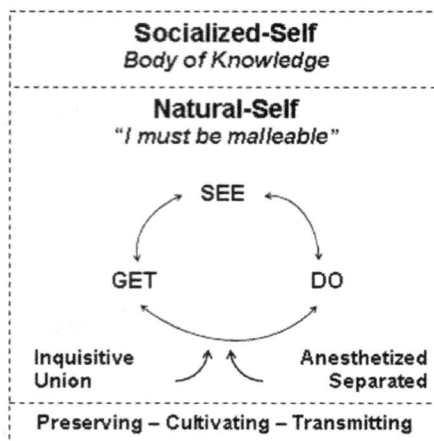

Figure 75

Much like Rick, Nines tend to have "Blind Spots" about the *extent* to which being Anesthetized and Separated dominate their lives and create decision-making bias and predictable errors in judgment. Deficiency-driven Nines tend to "see" themselves as growth-motivated, while the people they interact with tend to "see" them as more deficiency-driven. The experiences of being Anesthetized and Separated are *intensified* when Nines are under pressure or they don't get the results they want because people either object to (or don't respond to) their insatiable desire to their psychological inertia, distractibility, and their desensitized, indirect approach to relationships and life. Nines become "intoxicated" by the emotional power of being Anesthetized and Separated which makes it more difficult for them to see their Blind Spots and unintended consequences for what they really are. Once the intoxicating energy of being Anesthetized and Separated subsides, Nines will settle back down to the normal state-of-equilibrium of their dominant type. But over time, this cycle of behaviors and emotional responses *solidifies* into a well-defined pattern of interaction that goes on autopilot and slips below the surface of conscious awareness. These patterns-of-interactions are commonly called "hot buttons" or defense routines.

The philosophy of *being malleable as the road to acting on the environment* powerfully shapes the day-to-day preferences of Nines about the people, relationships, careers, hobbies, and lifestyles they are attracted to (and repulsed by), and over time these myriad choices are woven into the fabric of their lives. By the time

Nines are young adults, they have identified with the Tacit Creed of "being mal-leable" to the point where they are locked into a cognitive, emotional, social, and contextual configuration that solidifies, reaches a state-of-equilibrium, and *becomes* their day-to-day reality. The inner mandate to be "malleable" becomes externalized, objectified, and ultimately reified into a social mirror that seems to objectively affirm the belief that the Nine's way of seeing themselves, others, and the world is *the* way that life should be lived. We described this earlier as the Self-Sealing Process of forming Personality in Context.

But the *false sense* of having the ability to act on the environment that comes from being "malleable" and going through the motions, the *validation* that comes from the social mirror, and the *stability* of the day-to-day reality that Nines construct – *come* at an enormous price, because they deeply divide them at the very core of their being. *Secretly*, Nines know that they're not as malleable as they claim to be, and the fear of this being discovered by others only *fuels* the autopilot, insatiable, destructive power of their Tacit Creed. Think about it – if the Tacit Creed of "being malleable" isn't true for Nines like Rick – then what is? If Nines are wrong about how they see themselves, others, and the world, then they may be wrong about almost everything in life.

Growth-Motivated

We have spent a significant amount of time discussing the Tacit Creed and under-lying mechanisms of the deficiency-driver of type Nines like Rick because without a correct understanding of the process by which these underlying mechanisms bind and limit the choices, personal freedom, and self-determination of type Nines, there is little or no hope of ever escaping the pernicious entanglements of Personality in Context. In this section, I'd like to focus on the *single point of leverage* that will address the question, "So what should type Nines *do* about the negative character-istics and effects of their personality?" I will also discuss the concrete changes that Nines can expect to see in their actions and interactions when they choose the Upward Path of Becoming. As shown in Figure 76, when Nines are at their best being Inquisitive and in Union with themselves and others become the growth-motivators for the Tacit Creed – "I must be malleable."

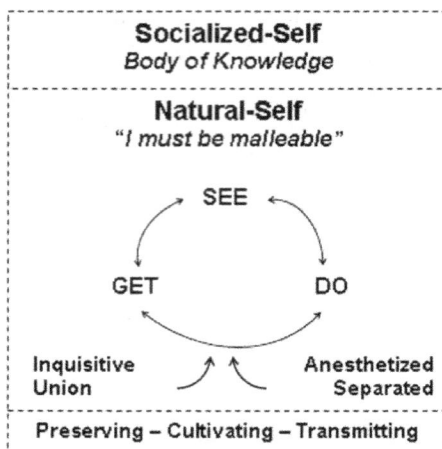

Figure 76

Growth-motivated Nines are self-aware, seekers of self-actualization, engaged and connected to life, good-natured, friendly, easy-going, patient, tolerant, creative, imaginative, excellent mediators and communicators, emotionally stable, non-confrontational, and focused on life's simple pleasures.

While the Nine's Blind Spots, defense routines, and the inner mandate to be "malleable" *combine* with the social mirror and the edicts of their socio-cultural context to form barriers to deep change, they all rest on the foundation of the Nine's core assumption that they lack the ability to act tangibly on their environment. Nines experience this "lack of ability to act tangibly on life" as a self-evident truth that cannot (and ought not) be questioned or tested, *but this is precisely what Nines must do*: face their fear of self-knowledge by questioning, and publicly testing, the truth of this claim. They must come to "see" themselves as having the tools to unlearn these *biased*, *misguided*, and *erroneous* ways of seeing themselves, others, and the world. Like the story of the Mulla, looking for the key in the *right* place becomes the *single point of leverage* that will enable Nines to ignite deep personal change.

Focusing on the single point of leverage acts like a *solvent* that begins to dissolve the *hidden inauthentic layers* of cognitive, emotional, social, and contextual strata from which the Nine's life has been built. Using the single point of leverage enables Nines to begin living more authentically in terms of their actions, interactions, and decision-making within the current context of their lives. It helps them to do the right things, for the right reasons. There are a number of very concrete indicators that emerge when Nines like Rick begin the journey on the Upward Path of Becoming:

- Nines are free to question their default way of seeing themselves as having to be "malleable" and going through the motions in order not to rock the boat.
- Their hyper-sensitivity toward identifying and avoiding conflict gives way to Inquisitiveness, a sense of being in Union with themselves and others, and a deep desire to be directly and authentically connected to their inner world, other people, situations, and the opportunities for personal growth and self-actualization that life brings their way.
- They begin to see themselves, the human race, and the natural world as an interdependent whole to which they are vitally connected with a sense of union.
- Over time, Nines gain new confidence in their ability to transcend the constraints of their personality and cultural context, as they see the concrete evidence of change indicated by their ability to act-out the 80-20 Rule – where eight out of ten interactions are motivated by being Inquisitive and with a sense of being in Union with self and others, rather than being driven by being Anesthetized and Separated.

Connecting Points

Much like the story of Rick, Nines intentionally alter their actions and interactions to "fit" the requirements and norms of a specific social or cultural context because doing otherwise might be inappropriate and could have negative consequences on them personally and professionally. In a previous section, I referred to this as the Socialized-Self. But buried deep beneath the Nine's Socialized-Self, family background, life experiences, and body of knowledge is a unique underlying *signature pattern* of connecting points that identifies what it means to be a type Nine – their Natural-Self.

The underlying pattern and characteristics of the connecting points remain relatively constant over time and with changes in context. They are a well-defined intra-psychic pattern of interaction that shapes and defines Nine's behaviors and responses in day-to-day discourse, especially in situations where they face *embarrassment* or *threat*. The patterns-of-interaction associated with the connecting points are also an indicator of whether or not the overall direction of the Nine's life tends toward the Downward Spiral of Striving or the Upward Path of Becoming.

**Connecting Points
(Conflicting Inner Mandates and Mixed Emotions)**

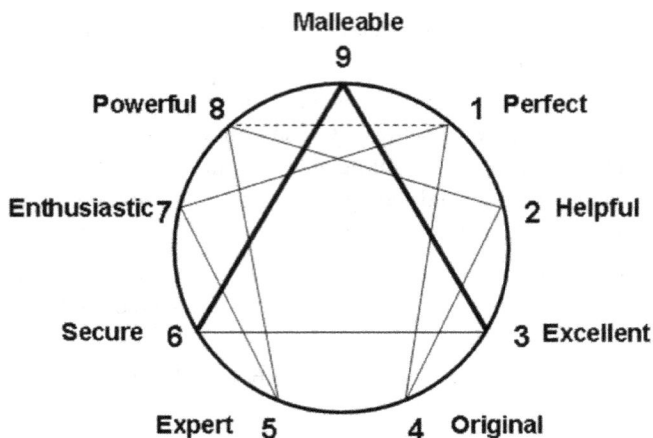

Figure 77

The Nine's dominant type anchors them to the Enneagram and is a necessary element of verifying a person's Enneagram type. The signature pattern for type Nine consists of five connecting points: types 9, 6, 3, 8 and 1.

- Type Nine is the Tacit Creed which we've already discussed in detail.
- Type Six is the Striving Point which is referred to by some Enneagram theorists as the point that indicates the direction of disintegration.
- Type Three is the Becoming Point which is referred to by some Enneagram theorists as the point that indicates the direction of integration.
- The Eight-One Paradox straddles type Nine, where Eights and Ones are isomorphic images of each other, with type Ones being too moral and type Eights being too anti-moral like laws unto-themselves. Type Nines tend to be pulled along the axis of this paradox and can embody either set of characteristics if the environment forces them to.
- While the connecting points for Nines represent the *natural* pattern, process, and structure of this Enneagram type, they should not be viewed as rigid and determined. Given sufficient pressure and influence from family or the social-cultural context, these natural tendencies can be powerfully shaped and defined in other ways, with the original signature pattern of the type Nine being hidden (or buried) beneath other configurations of Enneagram points.

What is most important to note is that the foundation of the type Nine's personality is an *interdependent configuration* of conflicting inner mandates and mixed emotions that includes five types, their Tacit Creeds, and their destructive and constructive emotions. In other words, the type Nine's personality is not a homogeneous set of beliefs; instead it is a portfolio of interdependent, complementary, competing, and conflicting ways of seeing themselves, others, and the world.

So when Nines like Rick are stressed and facing embarrassment and threat, the autopilot patterns-of-interaction between their tacit, Striving, Becoming, and Paradox points can (and often do) create inner conflict and mixed emotions. This is especially true when Nines are faced with a problem that requires a *single* solution. In other words, Rick would find himself wondering, "Should I do this, or should I do that? Should I be malleable or secure?" This inner conflict is *intensified* when external pressures force Nines to act, interact, or make decisions *now*!

There are some key concepts that I'd like to review to define the psychological patterns, processes, and structure of the connecting points for type Nines in more detail.

- The actions and interactions of the other eight Enneagram types are done *in the service of* following the inner mandate to be "malleable" and maintaining the equilibrium of the cognitive, emotional, social, and contextual configuration that the Nine builds as their life – their Personality in Context.

- When they are growth-motivated, the connections between type Nine, Six, Three, Eight and One can help to balance some of the symmetries by giving Nines at least one Enneagram point in each of the three triads, thus straddling the emotional, cognitive, and sensory parts of the human brain. The Nine's, where types Eight and Six and One and Three provide a left-right side balance for Nines and type Six and Three provide two Enneagram points that help to balance the top-bottom symmetry.

- Another key concept centers on the *combining* of the Tacit Creeds and underlying emotions into what is referred to as conflicting inner mandates and mixed emotions for type Nines. People rarely act univocally. Rather, actions, interactions (and eventually patterns-of-interaction) come in complex, interdependent bundles, where the Tacit Creeds and underlying emotions of the Nine's connecting points *combine* and *co-mingle* to form extremely complex packages of emotional messages that are communicated to others.

A solid understanding of the signature pattern is the key to *unbundling* the complex packages of emotional messages and patterns-of-interaction that type Nines often exhibit in day-to-day interactions.

Type Nine Summary Profile

Figure 78 provides an overall summary of the key patterns, structures, and processes that were described in this section and that typify the Enneagram type Nine.

Type Summary Profile - Type Nine	
Core Assumption	I lack the ability to act on the environment
Tacit Creed (Mulla)	I must be malleable
Unconscious Appraisal	Opportunities to avoid conflict and Somatic Instincts
Impose Meaning	Better not to think too much or "rock the boat"
Move Into Action	Check-out, blind to blind-spots, overly submissive
Deficiency Drivers	Anesthetized, Separation
Growth Motivators	Inquisitive, Connection
Striving Point	Type Six
Becoming Point	Type Three
Paradox Point	Type Eight, Type One
Group (Triad)	Action, leads with the sensory part of the brain (Brain Stem)
Existential Question	How do I deal with the environment?
Conflict Processing Strategy	Reframing
Attitude Towards Socio-Cultural Change	Move Away/Withdrawn
Single Point of Leverage	Question and publicly test the core assumption

Figure 78

In keeping with the overall approach of the Breckenridge Enneagram, the characteristics and dynamics shown in Figure 78 are not surface-traits or behaviors. Rather, the content of Figure 78 describes the underlying patterns, structures, and processes that define what makes type Nines like Rick different from the other eight Enneagram types.

Examples and Movies

While Nines are found in every area of life and all professional fields, the list below shows some famous examples of people who are probably type Nines. How many names do you recognize? Which ones are you interested enough in to learn more about by reading a biography or autobiography?

- *Examples* – Famous examples who exhibit Nine traits: Ronald Reagan, Walt Disney, Ringo Starr, George Lucas, Norman Rockwell, Dwight D. Eisenhower, Abraham Lincoln, Carl Rogers, Roy Rogers, Peter Falk as Columbo.

Another way to see Enneagram type in action is through the characters and story lines in movies. Select some of the movies listed below and take some time to watch Nines in action.

- *Movie Characters* – Roles in movies that exemplify Nine traits: Kevin Costner (Dances with Wolves), Captain (Titanic), Anne Hathaway (Princess Diaries), James Stewart (It's a Wonderful Life), Martin Sheen (American President), Jeff Bridges (K-Pax), Donald Sutherland (Ordinary People).

To deepen your understanding of this Enneagram type, identify people who you *know* that embody this personality type and become more observant about their behaviors, attitudes, and decision-making strategies. Ask them to share their thoughts, views, and perspectives on key issues and criteria for decision-making and see how closely the descriptions in this section describe and predict their responses. To further solidify and deepen your understanding, log your insights and observations about this personality type in a journal. You can use this exercise for the other eight types as well.

Type One (I Must Be Perfect)

When Ones are at their best, they are conscientious, proper, correct, rational, self-disciplined, placing a high value on integrity, objectivity which gives them an extremely keen sense of what's right and wrong. When under pressure, they become overly critical, demanding, rigid, intolerant, overly detailed, methodical, afraid to make mistakes, and too focused on rule-keeping.

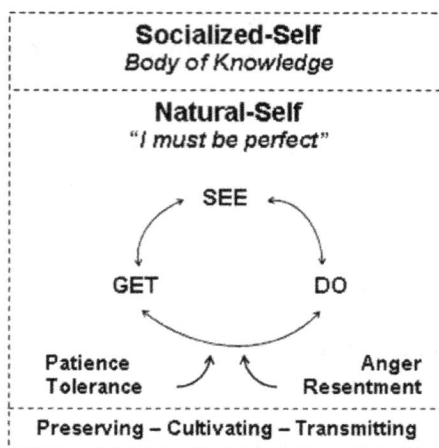

Figure 79

The very top of Figure 79 is made up of a person's Socialized-Self and body of knowledge, which form a major portion of the knowledge-base of their personal paradigm.

Tacit Creed

Ones live by the Tacit Creed "I must be perfect" – a belief that solidifies early in life through countless cycles through the See-Do-Get Process. When they are Deficiency Driven, they are hyper-sensitive to identifying errors, mistakes, broken rules, and imperfections, they constantly evaluate their relationships and environment for opportunities to critique and correct through criticism, over-control, discipline, and demanding that others comply with their standards and values. Anger and Resentment are *inflamed* when under pressure or when they don't get the result they want; e.g., people either object to, or don't respond to, their *insatiable desire* for perfectionism, criticism, discipline, value judgments, and being too demanding. When under stress, they become "intoxicated" by the power of these emotions and have a *Blind Spot* about the extent to which Anger and Resentment dominate their lives and create decision-making bias and predictable errors in judgment. While Fives exhibit an *internal* perfectionism where their knowledge and expertise are increased, deepened, and refined to higher and higher levels, Ones exhibit an *external* perfectionism that is focused on people and the environment.

When they are Growth Motivated, they are free to question their default way of seeing and their hyper-sensitivity gives way to Patience, Tolerance, and a deep desire to help others increase their competencies and grow for their own sake, not just to meet their own basic need to be perfect. They begin to see life and relationships as a glass that is half full, not half empty, where duty is enriched by pleasure, work balanced by play, and maturity deepened by child-like spontaneity and they experience this insight and new perspective as inner freedom and personal growth. For Ones, the key element of personal growth and building effective relationships is to follow the 80-20 – Rule where eight out of ten interactions with others are characterized by Patience and Tolerance, rather than Anger and Resentment.

Dan's Story

Dan Wright's story is an example of what the Tacit Creed "I must be perfect" looks like when it's solidified in the life of a type One. Dan had always been a perfectionist who had a hard time just loosening up and having fun. From the time he was a child, Dan got a loud and clear message that mistakes would not be tolerated, and he felt like he was fundamentally flawed and lacked the ability to do what was correct. His father, Jake, was a strict authoritarian who hammered into Dan's senses the edict that he was only good when he did what was right, and what was right was defined exclusively by his father's standards and measuring sticks. He came to believe that he lacked the ability to do what was right in the world, so he had to bear down and be perfect.

Dan and his wife Susan met Cindy Reeder in graduate school at MIT where he finished an undergraduate degree in physics, and went straight into an MS program in electrical engineering. Cindy was a graduate assistant finishing up her Ph.D. Susan remembers the days in Cambridge fondly. The university world was an easy place to make friends because everyone had such a common focus. They were young, without children, and would travel and enjoy life on school breaks. Susan remembered dinner parties, holiday celebrations, and even bold, daring and exotic trips such as when Cindy, Dan and she went scuba diving in the Red Sea during the mid-1970s while Israel was still occupying the Sinai.

When Dan was not being inwardly hammered by his fixation about perfection, he displayed a deep and abiding sense of conscientiousness and an objective sense of right and wrong, even in situations that were difficult for most people to figure out. But once Dan got up on his self-righteous high horse, he became rigid and intolerant of others. He went out of his way to point out and try to correct the flaws he saw in others, even in areas that were none of his business and over their protests for him to leave them alone.

After graduate school, Cindy stayed on in Cambridge to finish her degree. Cindy always liked the creative stimulation of the university and decided to take a post doc at Harvard rather than go into the frenetic world of business. Dan landed a good job in Connecticut with a company that was a defense contractor doing work at the Navy base in Groton. Dan was a careful, conservative, and insightful engineer who always did quality work and quickly established himself as a team leader and then became a regional manager for the West Coast division of the company. Dan passed through a lot of airports traveling a hundred days a year, and was always interested in the metal detectors and X-ray scanning equipment because they related to some of the work that he was doing for the Navy.

Dan began wondering if he could produce more cost-effective, high-resolution airport X-ray equipment that would be more computer automated, and would remove more human error in scanning baggage. He had the seed money to start a company and a three-car garage behind his house he could use as an office and fabrication facility. But he wasn't sure if the current technology could really support his idea. He drove to Cambridge to meet with Cindy, who had just accepted a position at MIT as an assistant professor. After passing the feasibility test with Cindy, Dan wrote a business plan for what became the SciTech Corporation. He secured a loan from a bank in Boston, hired Cindy as his first employee, and set about the task of hammering their ideas into a technology that could be packaged, produced, and sold around the world.

The company grew to the point where, after two years, Dan had purchased some land and broke ground on a ten thousand square foot facility, which could expand to fifty thousand if continued business growth required it. Revenues continued the typical pattern of rising then leveling off, but after ten years the company had seventy-five employees and was generating gross revenues of over $100 million per year. The grueling development years had taken their toll on Dan both professionally and in his family life. He was feeling like he had to push harder and harder as the business grew just to get people to toe the line of quality and service that he demanded. He worked sixty to seventy hours a week and felt like he had the world on his shoulders. But if he were to cut back, who would fill the gap?

Those who knew him best, like Cindy Reeder, had seen Dan's own duplicity where he would follow his inner convictions about what was right and wrong to the point where he set a standard so high that even he could not keep it. Once Dan was confronted by the fact that he had violated his own standards, he would spiral down into a state of guilt, shame, self-reproach, and depression, or become erratic in his behavior, moving on to another issue just to escape the condemnation. Dan had always lived with this darker side of his personality, but he always had enough psychological energy to "manage" it and keep it under control. In a less overt way, Dan siphoned off his anger against himself and the imperfections of life by constant faultfinding, nit picking, and commenting only on the one out of a hundred things that was not done correctly. When Dan felt justified (which was most of the time), there was nothing that could stop the storm of relentless criticism and chastising that followed. Dan once hired a consultant in New York. While finalizing the scope of work, he called the consultant and emphatically told her to correct the letter of agreement. He insisted that he wanted the date on the letter to match the date on the fax. "Sure," the consultant replied. After an uncomfortable period of silence, Dan said, "This is why my people hate me isn't it?" The consultant didn't respond, because she knew better.

Dan tried to avoid any experience of being wrong at all costs. One of the most difficult challenges for him was to keep his anger and rage concealed from people outside the inner circle of his friends and family. He even tried to hide it from himself. His disgust with the imperfections of his staff, and of life itself, was like a pressure cooker ready to blow. Dan would show this mean side of himself to his staff and his family because he knew they would take it. At work, he threw temper tantrums, pounding his desk, and demanding that things be done his way, immediately. At home, Dan and Susan's marriage was littered with broken dishes, slammed doors, and meals that had gone uneaten because Dan had stormed out of the house.

Dan was a hard-driving man at all times, but he was hardest on his line managers, from whom he had a zero tolerance for rework situations, quality problems, and a lack of response to customer suggestions for improvement. Dan expected his managers to stay on top of the finest details of their operation. But when he came around looking for a real-time status report on how things were going, he totally undermined his managers' authority One manager who Dan had publicly embarrassed numerous times liked to joke sardonically that Dan wasn't a micro-manager – he was a nano-manager and a pico-manager. Some people are dead wrong. Dan was almost always dead right, but he made himself wrong through his harsh, critical delivery and caustic style, even when he began by being right in the first place.

The demands of running the business, along with family issues, had worn Dan down to the point where he was beginning to wonder about how he could get out of the business and move on to doing other less stressful things. Dan didn't want to sell SciTech to an outsider because a few of his employees, such as Cindy Reeder, had become friends over the years and for their sakes he was afraid of losing total control of the company. He thought about an employee buy-out plan where he could issue stock and those employees who were able could purchase a portion of the corporation, but both his lawyer and accountant had advised him against this.

With the coming and passing of September 11, 2001, SciTech's business more than doubled as even the smallest airports began buying and installing the most sophisticated baggage screening equipment they could find. SciTech was the top of the line in terms of this technology, but was more affordable long-term than even less sophisticated screening packages. Dan had mixed feelings about this boom in business. First, he was glad the company was financially solvent and had bright prospects for the future. But in Dan's mind, his psychological clock was ticking and it was high time for him to get out of SciTech. With each passing day he was feeling more and more trapped by his own success. With the departure of Dan's daughter Carol, his last hope for moving in another direction in his life without totally having to give up control of the company went out the window. His resentment continued to grow toward her and toward his employees because he felt that his loyalty to them was forcing him to keep running the company. His resentment toward himself was also growing because he wasn't smart enough to figure his way out of this mess.

Dan's is only one of myriad possible stories that could be told to show what the Tacit Creed "I must be perfect" looks like in the life of an individual. While the surface traits; natural talents and abilities; life-experiences; relationships; sociocultural setting; ethnicity; gender; and level of psychological health defined by the 80-20 Rule may vary dramatically from person-to-person, the underlying patterns, processes and structures of the stories of all type Ones will be similar.

Emergence of the Tacit Creed

The One's Natural-Self occupies the bottom portion of Figure 79 where the Tacit Creed (I must be perfect) *emerges* from their innate, inborn temperament and the deep fear associated with the core assumption that they *lack the ability to do what's right in the environment*. The emphasis is on the words "right" and the tacit-conviction (and near certainty) that they lack the ability to know, and do, what is right in the context they're in. Ones experience this core assumption emotionally as a deep and abiding sense that, "I'm fundamentally flawed and lack the ability to do what's correct, just, and moral. They *experience* the core assumption with an inner sense of *certainty* as a *self-evident* truth that cannot (and ought not) be: a) questioned, b) objectively or publicly tested, or c) even verbalized. This belief that Ones hold about themselves is a *secret* truth that they hide from themselves, others, and the world. It's undiscussible and its un-discussibility is itself undiscussible. The fear of self-knowledge creates a sense of psychological survival in Ones that threatens their *existence* to the point where the gate-keeping function *blocks* these emotions from conscious awareness. But life goes on, and so must the One. Over time, the emotional and cognitive memories associated with this core assumption are *buried* deeper and deeper within the psyche of type Ones to the point where they become largely inaccessible to conscious awareness and are only experienced at pivotal (*kairos*) moments in history. This *forces* a shift in the One's focus in order to avoid the embarrassment and threat that the reality of the core assumption creates, so rather than face (or test) the *veracity* of lacking the ability to do what's right, they *displace* the problem by bearing down and being "perfect." But trying to be "perfect" can never fill the deep inner need of type Ones because it tries to address an *inner* (existential) issue with *outer* behavior.

Notice how the Tacit Creed can either be *deficiency-driven* by Anger and Resentment or *growth-motivated* by Patience and Tolerance and has a very different look and feel depending on whether it's driven or motivated – with the ratio of driven-to-motivated actions and interactions being defined as the 80-20 Rule. When Ones like Dan are at their best and are growth-motivated, they are conscientious, proper, correct, rational, self-disciplined, placing high value on integrity and objectivity which gives them an extremely keen sense of what's right and wrong within a cultural context. When they face embarrassment, threat or are deficiency-driven, Ones become overly critical, demanding, rigid, intolerant, overly detailed, methodical, afraid to make mistakes and too focused on rule-keeping.

The three Somatic Instincts shown at the very bottom of Figure 79 are the first three levels of Maslow's Hierarchy and form the inner core and foundation upon which the type One's personality is built. The Somatic Instincts powerfully shape the overall direction of a One's life in the sense that their deep inner yearnings and desires unconsciously draw them to people, experiences, careers, relationships, and life situations that will gratify these basic human needs. So the *autopilot needs* of deficiency-driven Preserving Ones can only be gratified by "being perfect" in areas associated with home, nurture and comfort, while Cultivating Ones are unconsciously drawn to gratify their need to "be perfect" in areas associated with belonging and affiliation with groups, and the autopilot needs of Transmitting Ones must be gratified by "being perfect" in situations that revolve around love, affection, caring, and communicating their ideas.

Deficiency-Driven

As shown in Figure 79, when Ones are under pressure or facing embarrassment or threat, Anger and Resentment become the deficiency-drivers, and the Tacit Creed for people like Dan:

- Is like a hyper-sensitivity or allergic reaction to situations that fit the underlying pattern of having to be perfect, which for type Ones means identifying errors, mistakes, and broken rules.

- Creates a narrowing of focus in their attention that is driven by a yearning and desire to gratify the fourth level of Maslow's Hierarchy – the esteem needs. So how Ones "esteem" themselves is powerfully shaped and defined by their need to "see" themselves as being perfect, and by having other people *confirm* this self-perception by also "seeing" them as perfect.

- Becomes a cognitive and emotional angle or perspective on life that singles-out specific underlying patterns in relationships, interactions, and situations that will gratify the One's basic need to be perfect.

- Causes them to constantly evaluate their relationships and the environment for opportunities to "improve and correct" others, even when other people don't want their advice (or flatly refuse it), which indicates that their need to be "perfect" often satisfies *their own needs*, not the needs of other people or the situations they're in.

Unconscious Appraisal and Selection

This section *links* the unconscious, autopilot cognitive and emotional appraisal and selection process for type Ones, to the See-Do-Get Process and the Downward Spiral of Striving. Notice in Figure 80, that when the Tacit Creed "I must be perfect" is unpacked *as* the autopilot doing and learning process, Ones like Dan tend to be unconsciously drawn to specific people, relationships, situations, and events in the world that will gratify: a) their need to be perfect, and b) the basic needs of their dominant Somatic Instinct.

In the second step, Ones unconsciously *appraise* situations and *select* opportunities to get their basic needs met by "being perfect" in ways that are shaped and defined by their dominant Somatic Instinct – whether preserving, cultivating, or transmitting. They unconsciously choose very specific cognitive and emotional data from the world because they "match" the underlying patterns and basic need to create a sense that they can do what's right by acting out the *inner mandate* to be perfect.

Unconscious Appraisal and Selection

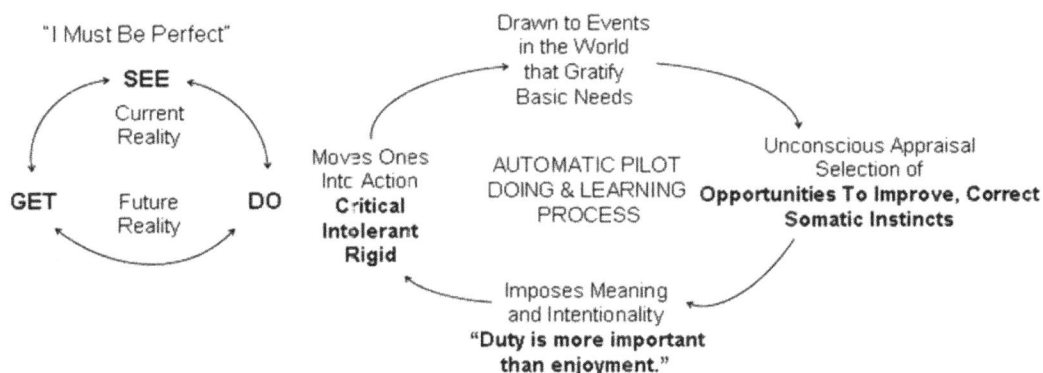

Figure 80

In the third step, the One's Tacit Creed *imposes* meaning and intentionality on the actions and interactions of people and the situations they're involved in. A typical tacit belief that Ones might impose on a situation from their Left-Hand Column is, "Duty is more important than enjoyment so emotions and natural impulses should be controlled, not trusted." This reveals the One's tendency to *project* their own needs and beliefs onto the world around them.

In the final step, the momentum and psychological force of the first three steps move Ones *into action* and these actions will tend to follow the pattern just described, where they become overly critical, demanding, intolerant, and afraid to make mistakes – all with the unconscious goal of gratifying their own needs, but under the pretense of helping others improve.

The entire process shown in Figure 80 happens beneath the surface of conscious awareness – in the blink of an eye. It's important to remember that the process can be growth-motivated where the four steps produce positive, constructive actions and interactions along the Upward Path of Becoming. Ones like Dan who want to move from being deficiency-driven to growth-motivated must consciously raise this autopilot process back into conscious awareness; deconstruct and reconfigure it by running the See-Do-Get Process backwards in the counter clockwise direction; and then migrate the new growth-motivated actions and interactions back to autopilot operation by embedding them through repetition. When Ones succeed in using this change process, the new growth-motivated actions and interactions begin to happen as naturally and automatically as the previous deficiency-driven ones once did. When eight out of ten behaviors are growth-motivated by Patience and Tolerance, rather than deficiency-driven by Anger and Resentment, this is an indication that a One is embodying the 80-20 Rule.

Blind Spots

When Ones are under pressure or facing embarrassment or threat, Anger and Re-sentment become the deficiency-drivers for the Tacit Creed – "I must be perfect." Mounting evidence produced by countless cycles through the See-Do-Get Process gives Ones a *false sense* that being "perfect" has actually given them the ability to do what's right in their environment, and this only deepens their sense of Anger and Resentment when other people don't do what's right and keep the rules (see Figure 81).

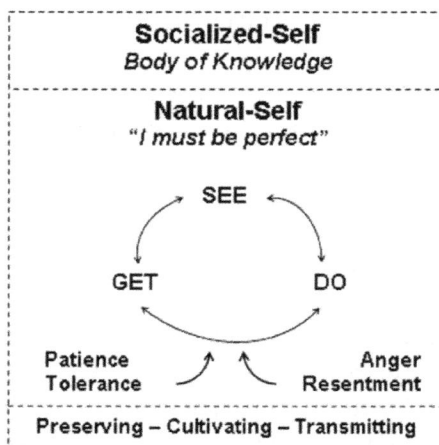

Figure 81

As in the case of Dan, Ones tend to have "Blind Spots" about the *extent* to which Anger and Resentment dominate their lives and create decision-making bias and predictable errors in judgment. Deficiency-driven Ones tend to "see" themselves as growth-motivated, while the people they interact with tend to "see" them as more deficiency-driven. The emotions of Anger and Resentment are *inflamed* when Ones are under pressure or they don't get the results they want because people either object to (or don't respond to) their insatiable desire for perfectionism and to be overly critical, rigidly disciplined, and too demanding about what they view as being the right thing to do in a situation. Ones become "intoxicated" by the emotional power of Anger and Resentment which makes it more difficult for them to see their Blind Spots and unintended consequences for what they really are. Once the intoxicating energy of Anger and Resentment subsides, Ones will settle back down to the normal state-of-equilibrium of their dominant type. But over time, this cycle of behaviors and emotional responses *solidifies* into a well-defined pattern of interaction that goes on autopilot and slips below the surface of conscious awareness. These patterns-of-interactions are commonly called "hot buttons" or defense routines.

The philosophy of *perfection as the road to being able to do what's right* powerfully shapes the day-to-day preferences of Ones about the people, relationships, careers, hobbies, and lifestyles they are attracted to (and repulsed by), and over time these myriad choices are woven into the fabric of their lives. By the time Ones are young adults, they have identified with the Tacit Creed of "being perfect" to the point where they are locked into a cognitive, emotional, social, and contextual configuration that solidifies, reaches a state-of-equilibrium, and becomes their day-to-day reality. The inner mandate to be "perfect" *becomes* externalized, objectified, and ultimately reified into a social mirror that seems to objectively affirm the belief that the One's way of seeing themselves, others, and the world is *the* way that life should be lived. We described this earlier as the Self-Sealing Process of forming Personality in Context.

But the *false sense* of having the ability to do what's right that comes from "being perfect," the *validation* that comes from the social mirror, and the *stability* of the day-to-day reality that Ones construct – come at an enormous price, because they deeply divide them at the very core of their being. *Secretly*, Ones know that they're not as perfect as they claim to be, and the fear of this being discovered by others only *fuels* the autopilot, insatiable, destructive power of their Tacit Creed. Think about it – if the Tacit Creed of "being perfect" isn't true for Ones like Dan – then what is? If Ones are wrong about how they see themselves, others, and the world, then they may be wrong about almost everything in life.

Growth-Motivated

We have spent a significant amount of time discussing the Tacit Creed and underlying mechanisms of the deficiency-driver of type Ones like Dan because without a correct understanding of the process by which these underlying mechanisms bind and limit the choices, personal freedom, and self-determination of type One, there is little or no hope of ever escaping the pernicious entanglements of Personality in Context. In this section, I'd like to focus on the *single point of leverage* that will address the question, "So what should type Ones *do* about the negative characteristics and effects of their personality?" I will also discuss the concrete changes that Ones can expect to see in their actions and interactions when they choose the Upward Path of Becoming. As shown in Figure 82, when Ones are at their best Patience and Tolerance become the growth-motivators for the Tacit Creed – "I must be perfect."

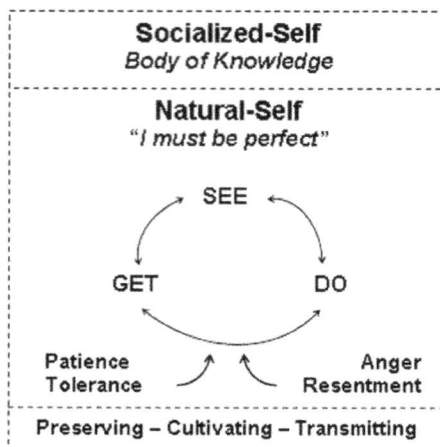

Figure 82

Growth-motivated Ones are conscientious, proper, correct, rational, self-disciplined, placing high value on integrity and objectivity which gives them an extremely keen sense of what's right and wrong within a cultural context.

While the One's Blind Spots, defense routines, and the inner mandate to be "perfect" *combine* with the social mirror and the edicts of their socio-cultural context to form barriers to deep change, they all rest on the foundation of the One's core assumption that they lack the ability to do what's right in their environment. Ones experience this "lack of ability to do what's right" as a self-evident truth that cannot (and should not) be questioned or tested, *but this is precisely what Ones must do*: face their fear of self-knowledge by questioning, and publicly testing, the truth of this claim. They must come to "see" themselves as having the tools to unlearn these *biased, misguided,* and *erroneous* ways of seeing themselves, others, and the world. Like the story of the Mulla, looking for the key in the *right* place becomes the *single point of leverage* that will enable Ones to ignite deep personal change.

Focusing on the single point of leverage acts like a *solvent* that begins to dissolve the *hidden inauthentic layers* of cognitive, emotional, social, and contextual strata from which the One's life has been built. Using the single point of leverage enables Ones to begin living more authentically in terms of their actions, interactions, and decision-making within the current context of their lives. It helps them to do the right things, for the right reasons. There are a number of very concrete indicators that emerge when Ones like Dan begin the journey on the Upward Path of Becoming:

- Ones are free to question their default way of seeing themselves as having to be "perfect" and being responsible to correct and improve others.
- Their hyper-sensitivity toward identifying errors and mistakes gives way to Patience, Tolerance, and a deep desire to help others increase their competencies and grow for their own sake, not just to meet the One's own basic need to be perfect.
- They begin to see life and relationships as a glass that's half-full, not half-empty, where duty is enriched by pleasure, work balanced by play, and maturity deepened by child-like spontaneity; and they experience this insight and new perspective as inner freedom and personal growth.
- Over time, Ones gain new confidence in their ability to transcend the constraints of their personality and cultural context, as they see the concrete evidence of change indicated by their ability to act-out the 80-20 Rule – where eight out of ten interactions are motivated by Patience and Tolerance, rather than being driven by Anger and Resentment.

Connecting Points

As we saw in the case of Dan, Ones intentionally alter their actions and interactions to "fit" the requirements and norms of a specific social or cultural context because doing otherwise might be inappropriate and could have negative consequences on them personally and professionally. In a previous section, I referred to this as the Socialized-Self. But buried deep beneath the One's Socialized-Self, family background, life experiences, and body of knowledge is a unique underlying *signature pattern* of connecting points that identifies what it means to be a type One – their Natural-Self.

Connecting Points
(Conflicting Inner Mandates and Mixed Emotions)

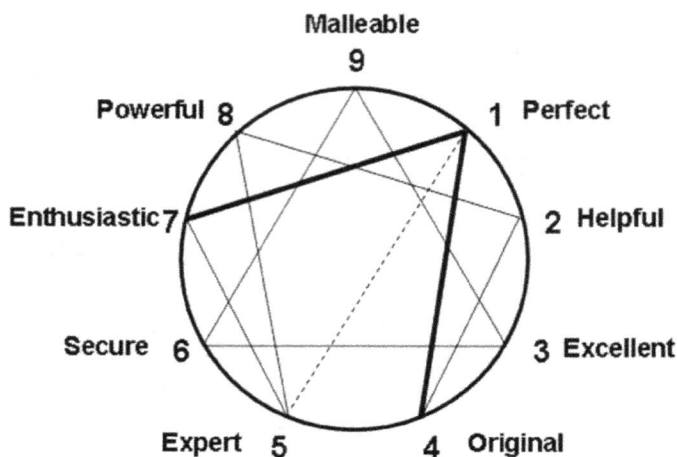

Figure 83

The underlying pattern and characteristics of the connecting points remain relatively constant over time and with changes in context. They are a well-defined intra-psychic pattern of interaction that shapes and defines One's behaviors and responses in day-to-day discourse, especially in situations where they face *embarrassment* or *threat*. The patterns-of-interaction associated with the connecting points are also an indicator of whether or not the overall direction of the One's life tends toward the Downward Spiral of Striving or the Upward Path of Becoming.

The One's dominant type anchors them to the Enneagram and is a necessary element of verifying a person's Enneagram type. The signature pattern for type Ones consists of four connecting points: types 1, 4, 7, and 5.

- Type One is the Tacit Creed which we've already discussed in detail.
- Type Four is the Striving Point which is referred to by some Enneagram theorists as the point that indicates the direction of disintegration.
- Type Seven is the Becoming Point which is referred to by some Enneagram theorists as the point that indicates the direction of integration.
- Type Five is the Paradox point. What could be more different than the perfectionistic rule-keeping of type Ones and the intense desire for knowledge and expertise of the type Five personality? But on closer examination type Ones exhibit an externally focused perfectionism on people and the environment,

while type Fives exhibit an internally focused perfectionism where they deepen and refine their knowledge in an endless search for intellectual perfectionism.

- While the connecting points for Ones represent the *natural* pattern, process, and structure of this Enneagram type, they should not be viewed as rigid and determined. Given sufficient pressure and influence from family or the social-cultural context, these natural tendencies can be powerfully shaped and defined in other ways, with the original signature pattern of the type One being hidden (or buried) beneath other configurations of Enneagram points.

What is most important to note is that the foundation of the type One's personality is an *interdependent configuration* of conflicting inner mandates and mixed emotions that includes four types, their Tacit Creeds, and their destructive and constructive emotions. In other words, the type One's personality is not a homogeneous set of beliefs; instead it is a portfolio of interdependent, complementary, competing, and conflicting ways of seeing themselves, others, and the world.

So when Ones like Dan are stressed and facing embarrassment and threat, the auto-pilot patterns-of-interaction between their tacit, Striving, Becoming, and Paradox points can (and often do) create inner conflict and mixed emotions. This is especially true when Ones are faced with a problem that requires a *single* solution. In other words, Dan would find himself wondering, "Should I do this, or should I do that? Should I be Perfect or Original?" This inner conflict is *intensified* when external pressures force Ones to act, interact, or make decisions *now*!

There are some key concepts that I'd like to review to define the psychological patterns, processes, and structure of the connecting points for type Ones in more detail.

- The actions and interactions of the other eight Enneagram types are done *in the service of* following the inner mandate to be "perfect" and maintaining the equilibrium of the cognitive, emotional, social, and contextual configuration that the One builds as their life – their Personality in Context.

- When they are growth-motivated, the connections between type One, Four, Seven and Five can help to balance some of the symmetries by giving Ones at least one Enneagram point in each of the three triads, thus straddling the emotional, cognitive, and sensory parts of the human brain. The One's connecting points also help to balance the left-right and top-bottom symmetries, where types Five and Seven provide a right-side balance for One, and types Four and Five provide an Enneagram point that balances the top-bottom symmetry.

- Another key concept centers on the *combining* of the Tacit Creeds and underlying emotions into what is referred to as conflicting inner mandates and mixed emotions for type Ones. People rarely act univocally. Rather, actions, interactions (and eventually patterns-of-interaction) come in complex, interdependent bundles, where the Tacit Creeds and underlying emotions of the One's connecting points *combine* and *co-mingle* to form extremely complex packages of emotional messages that are communicated to others.

A solid understanding of the signature pattern is the key to *unbundling* the complex packages of emotional messages and patterns-of-interaction that type Ones often exhibit in day-to-day interactions.

Type One Summary Profile

Figure 84 provides an overall summary of the key patterns, structures, and processes that were described in this section and that typify the Enneagram type One.

Type Summary Profile - Type One	
Core Assumption	I lack the ability to do what's right in the environment
Tacit Creed (Mulla)	I must be perfect
Unconscious Appraisal	Opportunities to improve, correct, and Somatic Instincts
Impose Meaning	Duty is more important than enjoyment
Move Into Action	Critical, intolerant, rigid
Deficiency Drivers	Anger, Resentment
Growth Motivators	Patience, Tolerance
Striving Point	Type Four
Becoming Point	Type Seven
Paradox Point	Type Five
Group (Triad)	Action, leads with the sensory part of the brain (Brain Stem)
Existential Question	How do I deal with the environment?
Conflict Processing Strategy	Objective
Attitude Towards Socio-Cultural Change	Move Toward/Compliant
Single Point of Leverage	Question and publicly test the core assumption

Figure 84

In keeping with the overall approach of the Breckenridge Enneagram, the characteristics and dynamics shown in Figure 84 are not surface-traits or behaviors. Rather, the content of Figure 84 describes the underlying patterns, structures, and processes that define what makes type Ones like Dan different from the other eight Enneagram types.

Examples and Movies

While Ones are found in every area of life and all professional fields, the list below shows some famous examples of people who are probably type Ones. How many names do you recognize? Which ones are you interested enough in to learn more about by reading a biography or autobiography?

- *Examples* – Famous examples who exhibit One traits: Margaret Thatcher, Hillary Clinton, Stephen Covey, Al Gore, Ralph Nader, Gandhi, St. Augustine, John Calvin, Leonard Nimoy as Mr. Spock, Julie Andrews.

Another way to see Enneagram type in action is through the characters and story lines in movies. Select some of the movies listed below and take some time to watch Ones in action.

- *Movie Characters* – Roles in movies that exemplify One traits: Mohandas Gandhi (Gandhi), Mr. Andrews (Titanic), Sidney Poitier (To Sir with Love), Alec Guinness (The Bridge Over the River Kwai), Gary Cooper (High Noon), Henry Fonda (On Golden Pond), Wall-E (the robot), Karl Malden as Omar Bradley (Patton), Tom Skerritt as father (A River Runs Through It).

To deepen your understanding of this Enneagram type, identify people who you *know* that embody this personality type and become more observant about their behaviors, attitudes, and decision-making strategies. Ask them to share their thoughts, views, and perspectives on key issues and criteria for decision-making and see how closely the descriptions in this section describe and predict their responses. To further solidify and deepen your understanding, log your insights and observations about this personality type in a journal. You can use this exercise for the other eight types as well.

MORE COMMON REASONS
WHY PEOPLE MISTYPE

This section describes common reasons why some people may mistype when trying to identify their dominant Enneagram type:

- They live closer to one or the other ends of their connecting points (Striving, Becoming, or Paradox); e.g., type Ones who resemble Fours, Sevens, or Fives.

- They live out of the low side of the Striving point (disintegration) and they "see" themselves, others, and the world through that lens; or they live out of the low side of the Becoming point (integration) and "see" in that way.

- They resemble other members of a larger grouping of types: a) heart, head, action groups, b) key question groups focus on identity, the future, or the environment, c) conflict processing strategy of reactive, objective, or reframing, or d) attitude toward socio-cultural change; e.g., aggressive, withdrawn, or compliant.

- They resemble their dominant hybrid-type on either side of the dominant point (wing).

- They are influenced and shaped by the power of their dominant Somatic Instinct and the fact that the underlying deficiency-drivers of a person's Enneagram type tend to express themselves (and be most pronounced) in the area in which the dominant Somatic Instinct is focused. For example, a type One with Cultivating as their dominant instinct will experience Anger and Resentment around issues having to do with social networks and social status, while a One with Transmitting as their dominant instinct will experience Anger and Resentment around issues having to do with relationships and getting their ideas across. In some cases, the influencing and shaping power of the instinct may even mask, or obscure, our experience of the deficiency-drivers in much the same way hunger masks or obscures our higher psychological needs; e.g., it's hard to think about self-actualization on an empty stomach. Understanding how the deficiency-drivers are *linked* to the instincts through day-to-day behaviors is a powerful way to tease apart cases of apparent mistyping.

- Some of the surface traits or characteristics of their Tacit Creed are similar to other Enneagram types and these differences can only be "resolved" by a careful evaluation of the underlying deficiency-drivers, growth-motivators, and the core assumption, for example Nines and Fives, Ones and Sixes, Threes and Eights.

- They are influenced by the various aspects of their four-dichotomy Jungian type code; e.g., dominant function, Interaction Style, Temperament. For example, an ENTJ, INTJ, INFP, ENFP who is also a type Four or an ESTJ, INTJ, ENFP, ISFP who is a type Eight.

- They are influenced and shaped by the power of the See-Do-Get Process where they may have come to an incorrect conclusion about what their dominant type is because of: a) the influence and views of an influential teacher, coach, friend, or relative, or b) having received incorrect scores from an assessment instrument that was either not psychometrically validated, or had questionable levels of reliability and validity.

- They are under either episodic or long-term stress and they "see" themselves, others, and the world through this lens.

- They have a well-developed Socialized-Self and answer the questions from that part of their personality. For example, if a person has been pressing hard in their professional life, beginning (or ending) a relationship, experiencing significant external pressures in their personal or professional life, they may embody the beliefs, assumptions, values, strategies, surface traits needed to face these challenges and "see" themselves, others, and the world from that perspective.

- They lack the depth of self-awareness needed to answer: a) the questions on an instrument like the BTI, or b) the questions in a typing session in a way that describes their true self. This is often more typical of types Nine, Three, and Six.

- They purposely do not answer the questions on an instrument like the BTI or questions in a typing session truthfully and honestly for a variety of reasons.

THE THREE SOMATIC INSTINCTS

As humans, we have a biological heritage that powerfully affects us. The Somatic Instincts are a subtle, but profound, remnant of this heritage.[33] While the patterns and dynamics of the nine Enneagram types are primarily intra-psychic (psychological) interactions that occur within the human brain and associated sensory apparatus, the Somatic Instincts are the part of the human organism that *links* people to key aspects of survival within a given environment. In other words, our physiological needs, psychological needs, and the resources available to us in our context are *interdependent*; e.g., our bodily needs, psychological needs, and contextual resources all interact together at the same time. This is not unlike what Maslow suggested in his Hierarchy of Needs.[34] We experience this mind-body-contextual interaction through the Somatic Instincts.

The Somatic Instincts are largely shaped and defined during the first year of life; e.g., prior to (and independent of) the Tacit Creed and the cognitive elements, and are a key element of our overall psychology and personality. In terms of our over-all well-being, quality of life, and sense of purpose, the instincts are probably *more important* than our Tacit Creed because they describe the fundamental goals and underlying objectives of all human behavior, and are the arena within which the underlying emotions of the Tacit Creed express themselves and are most pronounced. Claudio Naranjo proposed a model that took the complexity and importance of human instinctual life proposed by Marx, Freud, and Object-Relations theorists and integrated them into a model of sexual, social, and self-preserving instincts (see list below).[35]

- For Karl Marx, the goal and objective of human behavior was *survival*, so his views described psychological and cultural factors from a largely Darwinian (biological) perspective.
- Freud argued that the overall goal and objective of human behavior was to seek *pleasure*, with his formulation of the psychic structure as being composed of the Id, ego, and super-ego.
- Object-Relations theorists proposed that *relationships* with others are the overall goal and objective of human behavior and the focus of all of life.

As described earlier, the Breckenridge Enneagram reformulates Naranjo's view into the Somatic Instincts and maps them to the first four levels of Maslow's Hier-archy as shown in Figure 85. The preserving instinct is Level-1 of Maslow's Hier-archy, cultivating is Level-2, transmitting is Level-3, and the Tacit Creeds are the "esteem" needs found at Level-4.

Maslow's Hierarchy of Needs

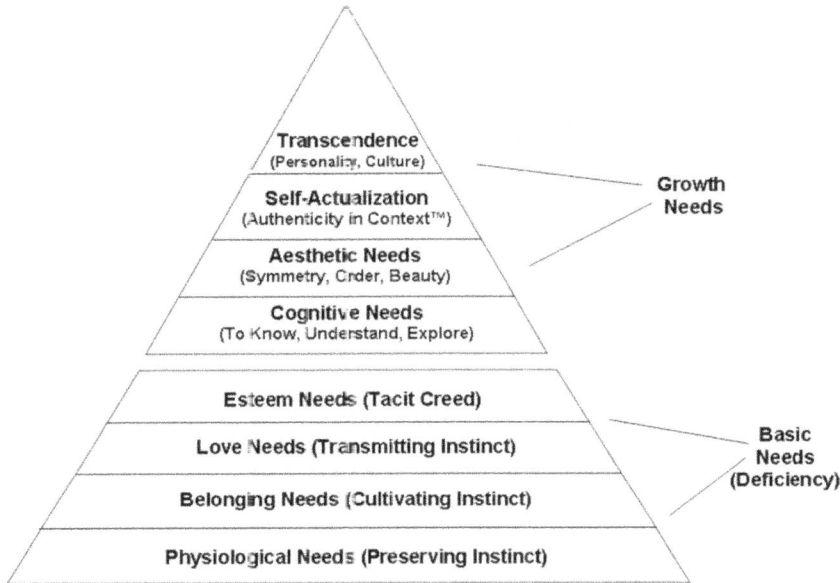

Figure 85

Figure 86 shows the belief structure of our personal paradigm; e.g., how we see ourselves, others, and the world through the See-Do-Get Process. The knowledge that comes from the Somatic Instincts is the deepest thing that we know about ourselves psychologically, and we experience this knowledge with a deep and profound sense of meaning, purpose, and calling. When we are disconnected from this part of ourselves, we experience life as being shallow, lacking rootedness, without meaning and significance, and many people have a deep urge to "get back to the basics" of life and human existence.

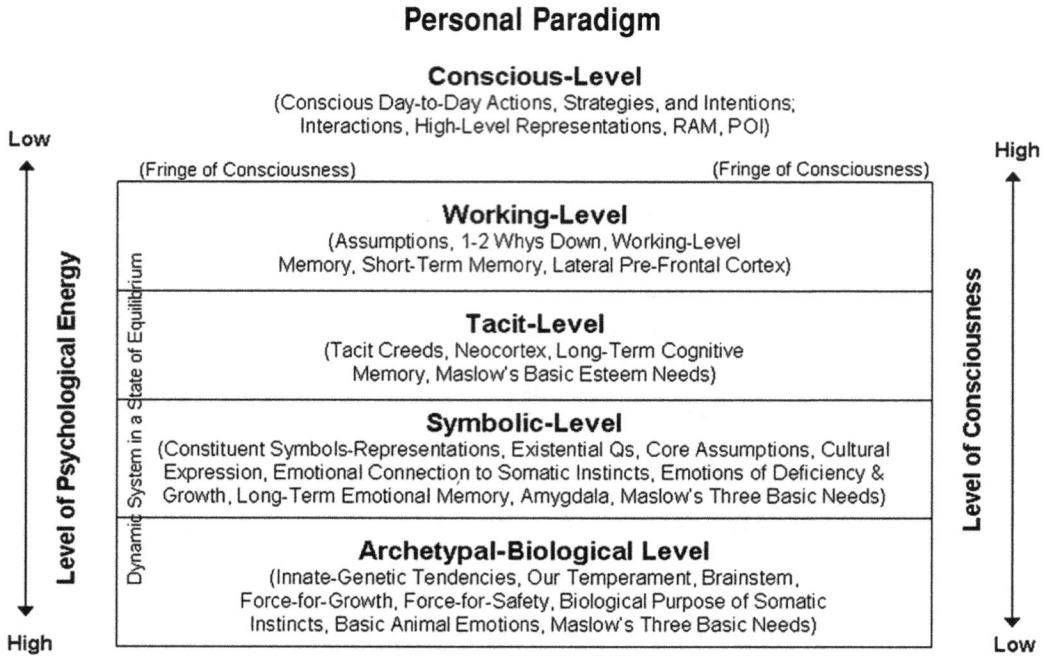

Personal Paradigm

Conscious-Level
(Conscious Day-to-Day Actions, Strategies, and Intentions;
Interactions, High-Level Representations, RAM, POI)

Low   High

(Fringe of Consciousness)   (Fringe of Consciousness)

Working-Level
(Assumptions, 1-2 Whys Down, Working-Level
Memory, Short-Term Memory, Lateral Pre-Frontal Cortex)

Tacit-Level
(Tacit Creeds, Neocortex, Long-Term Cognitive
Memory, Maslow's Basic Esteem Needs)

Symbolic-Level
(Constituent Symbols-Representations, Existential Qs, Core Assumptions, Cultural
Expression, Emotional Connection to Somatic Instincts, Emotions of Deficiency &
Growth, Long-Term Emotional Memory, Amygdala, Maslow's Three Basic Needs)

Archetypal-Biological Level
(Innate-Genetic Tendencies, Our Temperament, Brainstem,
Force-for-Growth, Force-for-Safety, Biological Purpose of Somatic
Instincts, Basic Animal Emotions, Maslow's Three Basic Needs)

Left axis: Level of Psychological Energy — Low (top), High (bottom)
Inner left axis: Dynamic System in a State of Equilibrium
Right axis: Level of Consciousness — High (top), Low (bottom)

Figure 86

Notice that the levels in Figure 86 have been "mapped" to Maslow's Hierarchy, key neurophysiologic structures in the human brain, and key elements of the Breckenridge Enneagram like the key existential questions. A more detailed description of the five levels is presented on page 257 in Chapter 2.

The instincts have three dimensions, including an underlying *biological purpose* (human survival), a *cultural expression* (human survival within a given context), and the *emotional connection* that people have to the biological and cultural dimensions based on early childhood experiences. So the *biological purpose* of the Somatic Instincts is a constant, underlying driving force of human behavior for all people, in all times, in all places. This is shown as Level-5 in Figure 86. The *cultural expression* of the instincts is dependent on the physical, geographical, and cultural context in which people live, and the *emotional connection* that they develop toward the instincts is powerfully shaped by the subjective experience of their biology, culture, and personality working together interdependently through the See-Do-Get Process. This is shown as Level-4 in Figure 86. Probably the best way to see the relationship between the biological purpose and cultural expression of the Somatic Instincts is to do a simple "thought" experiment with people living in Papua New Guinea and Boulder, Colorado.

Snap your fingers and imagine that you've been transported to a primitive jungle tribe in Papua New Guinea where people live without electricity, clean running water, cars, computers, the Internet, indoor toilets, airplanes, supermarkets, modern medicine, or myriad other things that modern science and technology make possible. In this setting, the relationship between the biological purpose and the cultural expression of the Somatic Instincts is clear because the context is so close to nature or what I would call a "natural" culture. A "natural" culture is one in which the natural forces and biological processes of nature are seamlessly woven into the active, tacit, and cultural teaching of how people "see" themselves, others, and the world around them through the See-Do-Get Process. The setting in Papua New Guinea clearly reflects the context in which our ancestors lived for tens of thousands of years prior to the modern era of science and technology. In this natural context:

- The *preserving* instincts will be focused on the daily gathering and preparation of food, securing a supply of clean water, patterns of sleep and relaxation, making clothing, building shelter from the elements, nurturing of children, and overall safety from harm. The basic human emotions of nurture, comfort, and biological-safety are associated with this cluster of instincts. The preserving instincts are a short-term survival strategy,

- The *cultivating* instincts will be focused on finding strength in numbers by building alliances within the social structure of a tribe or between tribes, using gift-giving to create reciprocity (putting others in our debt), observing tribal rituals, ceremonies, and traditions to create and maintain common purpose and common identity, and other ways of banding together with groups of people who can provide help or defense in time of need. The basic human emotions of belonging, affiliation, and physical-social-safety are associated with this cluster of instincts. The cultivating instincts are a mid-term survival strategy.

- The *transmitting* instincts will be focused on producing large numbers of progeny by the literal passing on of genes through reproduction. In addition, this Somatic Instinct has the social value of carrying on specific blood lines, and the ability of grown children to carry out the functions of the preserving and cultivating instincts. The basic human emotions of love, affection, caring, and emotional-safety are associated with this cluster of instincts. The transmitting instincts are a long-term survival strategy.

Describing what Naranjo called the sexual sub-type can be problematic in the 21st Century because of the cultural prohibitions against discussing human sexuality, especially in the workplace, so we refer to these as the transmitting instincts. While a main focus of this Somatic Instinct is on love and intimacy in one-on-one relationships (rather than groups and social networks), the cluster of instincts that make up the *transmitting* instinct were named as an adaptation of Richard Dawkins' metaphor for explaining the development and transmission of culture by cultural-units called *memes*, which is a play on the word *genes*.[36] While *genes* are *replicators* that transmit genetic information from person-to-person, *memes* are units of cultural information such as words, ideas, concepts, metaphors, tunes, images, beliefs, values, interest areas, stereotypes, and worldviews held by individuals or groups that can be passed from brain-to-brain through the See-Do-Get Process. Transmitting memes causes other people to become carriers of these units and powerfully shapes how they "see" themselves, others, and the world. Dawkins argues that when we die, the only things that we leave on earth are *genes* and *memes*, and our memes can have much more staying power and longevity than our genes. Our genetic contribution and the visual likeness between us, our children, and their progeny may last for two or three generations before returning to the gene pool, but memes can last for thousands of years. I doubt that there is a single intact genetic strand from Alexander the Great left on the earth, but the memes that he spread through Greek culture are with us today almost 2,400 years later in the form of Greek architecture, ways of thinking, and language.

Now snap your fingers again and imagine that you have been transported to present day Boulder, Colorado where the human innovations in science, technology, social structure, and culture have given people all the comforts of modern living in the 21st Century. In modern society, the *connection* between the biological purpose and the cultural expression of the instincts is much less direct, because the "reality" of everyday life is far removed from the natural, more primitive setting just described. In fact, the biological purpose of the instincts operates on autopilot far below the surface of consciousness, which is why it is so difficult for some people to recognize it in their day-to-day lives. Like a person who practices a social or religious ritual without any conscious understanding of what it *means*, people are unconsciously driven to practice the behaviors associated with their Somatic Instincts, without any conscious intention of carrying out their biological purpose.

In terms of the third dimension of the Somatic Instincts, emotional connection, human emotions are universal in the sense that all people, in all times, in all cultural settings have experienced them. Although human emotions are universal, the rules for expressing them within specific cultural contexts vary greatly. So the emotions that are connected with home-nurture, belonging to the group, and expressing and receiving love can vary dramatically from person-to-person, family-to-family, or culture-to-culture. For one person, the feelings associated with "home-nurture" may be linked to hearing the song, "I'll be home for Christmas." For another person, home-nurture-related emotions may be connected to the smell of a fire made from cow dung that is cooking fresh fish that was caught on the reef outside a village in Papua

New Guinea. So while the biological purpose of the Somatic Instincts will be invariant in different cultural settings (human survival) the *cultural expression* and *emotional connection* in Boulder or any other modern city will look very different than they did in the example of the tribe in Papua New Guinea. For example:

Preserving Instincts

- The *cultural expression* of the preserving instincts in modern society would manifest themselves as a strong tendency to: a) have a conservative attitude toward money and financial matters (spending, saving, and credit cards), b) focus on home-related activities (comfortable furniture, well-stocked cupboards and refrigerator, comfortable climate and surroundings, home-related hobbies), c) dress more for comfort than for style, d) focus on food and health issues, and e) family and home-related traditions with sentimental associations (memorabilia, pictures, knick-knacks).

- The *emotional connection* of the preserving instincts in modern society would manifest themselves as the basic human emotions of maternal and paternal nurture, comfort, and a sense of biological-safety. When *preserving* is the dominant instinct, people find themselves preoccupied by the thought of having a home, even when they have a place to live, because having a home where they can nurture those they love (and be nurtured) matters more to them than almost anything in life. Their need to build a home for themselves and those they love is like a deep inner emptiness that needs to be filled. Their physical comfort and having an abundant supply of material resources matter deeply to them and they are happiest when they have a plentiful supply of these things. In addition, having their own space where they can keep their personal things is very important to them. This is the most basic level of physiological needs on Maslow's Hierarchy.

Cultivating Instincts

- The *cultural expression* of the cultivating instincts in modern society would manifest themselves as a strong tendency to: a) cultivate a strong network of the "right" kind of people, b) cultivate a large number of friendly yet casual acquaintances as social connections, c) understand and orchestrate group dynamics, d) help connect people to what's going on in the world, e) build alliances and create reciprocity through fair dealings with people and repayment for favors, f) use of public rituals, ceremonies, and traditions to create and maintain common purpose and common identity, and g) have a good understanding of their own role in group dynamics and social interactions.

- The *emotional connection* of the cultivating instincts in modern society would manifest themselves as the basic human emotions of belonging, affiliation, and a sense of physical-social safety. When *cultivating* is the dominant instinct, people have a deep need to belong that's like an inner emptiness that needs to be filled, and "belonging" and knowing where they fit in the group matter more to them than almost anything in life. They find themselves preoccupied by the thought of belonging, even when they're part of a group. In fact, being accepted by the group is a key to their happiness. Given a choice, they prefer being with a group of people to intimate one-on-one connection, and they long to have the respect and admiration of the group. This is the second level of needs on Maslow's Hierarchy.

Transmitting Instincts

- The *cultural expression* of the transmitting instincts in modern society would manifest themselves as a strong tendency to: a) reproduce, create a family, and communicate emotions, ideas, and beliefs using literal and metaphorical sexual expressions, b) seek conversations where people are deeply connected with others about interests and views they hold in common, c) be passionate and intense about getting others to understand and adopt our ideas and world view with the goal of making others the carriers and vehicles of that information.[37]

- The *emotional connection* of the transmitting instincts in modern society would manifest themselves as the basic human emotions of love, affection, caring, and a sense of emotional-relational safety. When *transmitting* is the dominant instinct, people find themselves preoccupied by the thought of giving and receiving love and affection, even when they are in a relationship because they have a deep need for love that's like an inner emptiness that needs to be filled. Given a choice, they prefer intimate one-on-one connection to being with a group of people. Being deeply loved matters more to them than almost anything in life, and they long to be deeply loved by a special someone. In fact, being deeply loved by someone is a key to their happiness. This is the third level of needs on Maslow's Hierarchy.

Figure 87 shows another way to connect the three dimensions of the Somatic Instincts described in the "thought experiment" to the five levels of the personal paradigm (Figure 86) and the profoundly alienated experience of the cultural chasm between how we live in the 21st Century, and a natural culture like the one described in Papua New Guinea.

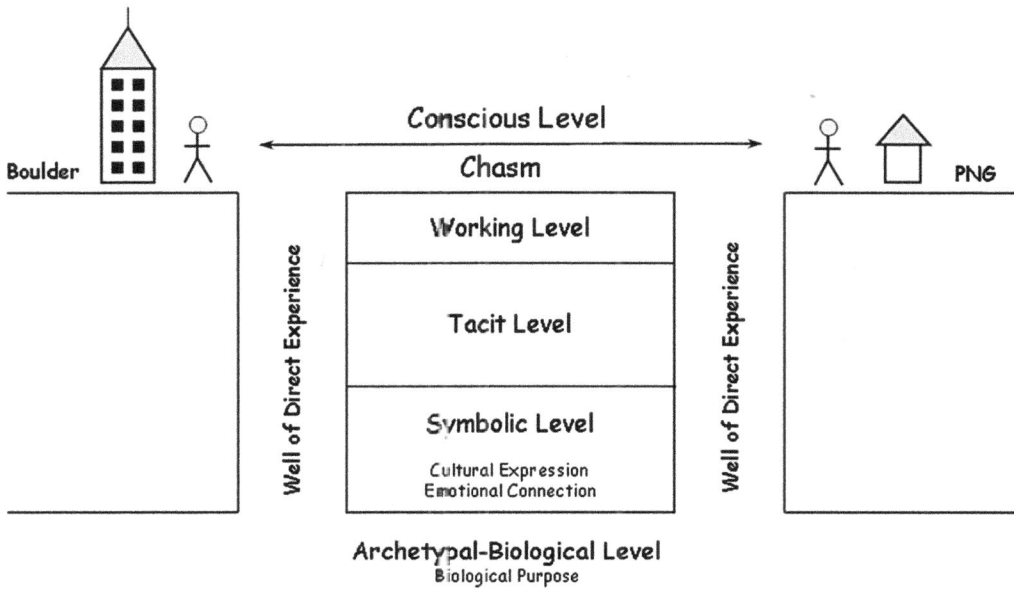

Figure 87

Notice how the two people represented in Figure 87 each have a well of direct experience that goes down the levels of the personal paradigm to the Archetypal-Biological Level where the biological purpose of the instincts resides. This collective human level is common to all people, in all times, in all cultures; so people in Boulder and PNG *share* the direct experience of this part of their humanity. The Symbolic-Level is powerfully shaped and defined by the cultural context and the long-term emotional memory of childhood and can vary significantly from person-to-person and culture-to-culture. Figure 87 shows why two people from such radically different cultures would look across the enormous chasm of the Somatic Instincts at the Conscious-Level and sense a strange, paradoxical kinship toward each other that is largely unconscious and difficult or impossible to explain or put into words.

In terms of how the instincts develop over time, when a person is a child, unable to control their environment, and they lack direct access to the resources needed to sustain life, the Somatic Instincts manifest themselves much more *literally*. As a child, the focus is on "me," trying to obtain "my" survival needs in day-to-day life because children are unable to survive on their own. These instinctual behaviors may appear "selfish" because children focus on preserving their own comfort and physical well-being (Preserving), establishing and cultivating groups and social networks (Cultivating), and convincing others to give them the love and attention that they want (Transmitting). As children gain the ability to control their environment and have direct access to resources, the instinct-driven behaviors become less literal and focused on themselves and increasingly shaped by the edicts and demands of their cultural context. As Maslow's Hierarchy of Needs suggests, when your *literal* survival needs are taken care of, you start attending to: a) matters of home and health (Preserving), b) social consciousness and creating a sense of community (Cultivating), and c) finding ways to deeply connect with and influence others and leave a legacy (Transmitting).[38] To reiterate – it's hard to think about self-actualization or leaving a legacy on an empty stomach. The Somatic Instincts become like a three-legged stool, but we tend to be focused primarily on one of them as our dominant instinct. Balance comes from an ability to consciously use all three instinct clusters to shape your decisions, choices, and preferences about personal, interpersonal, family, and professional matters. One way to do this is to use the See-Do-Get Process.

Not surprisingly, the Somatic Instincts have the greatest impact on the lifestyle of people in close, personal relationships because lifestyle often reflects the deeper attitudes, values, and preferences of the overall personality, not just the Tacit Creed and underlying emotions. Lifestyle can be described as a "bundle" of behaviors such as habits of consumption, dress, and recreation, common language, attitudes toward how to spend money and time, family, social relations, entertainment, professional versus personal life, and what constitutes a house or home. Lifestyle is often used to forge, develop, or maintain a sense of identity for people in a relationship, so understanding lifestyle is an important aspect of understanding the shared values and the social space (sub-culture) that people create, and within which they live in families and other close relationships.[39] Significant differences in the Somatic Instincts can cause people to *disdain* each other's lifestyle preferences and personal habits. This attitude almost guarantees that destructive emotional messages will dominate the relationship.

The Somatic Instincts are inextricably bound to the nine types of the Breckenridge Enneagram in very important and specific ways. As mentioned earlier, the Tacit Creeds and their underlying emotions are influenced and shaped by the power of a person's dominant Somatic Instinct. More specifically, the underlying deficiency-drivers of the nine types tend to express themselves (and be most pronounced) in the area in which the dominant Somatic Instinct is focused. For example, a type One with Cultivating as their dominant instinct will experience Anger and Resentment around issues having to do with social networks and social status. When Transmitting is the dominant instinct, Ones will experience Anger and Resentment around issues having to do with relationships and getting their ideas across. In some cases, the influencing and shaping power of the instinct may even mask, or obscure, our experience of the deficiency-drivers in much the same way hunger can mask or obscure our higher-level psychological needs. Understanding how the deficiency-drivers are *linked* to the Somatic Instincts through day-to-day behaviors is a powerful way to see the Breckenridge Enneagram as an integrated system that provides deep insight into how we actually *experience* the first four levels of Maslow's Hierarchy psychologically.

Eleven Characteristics of the Somatic Instincts [40]

The Somatic Instincts form the very *heart* of the concept of Personality in Context because they are that part of the human organism that links us to our environment and the socio-cultural context in which we live, so we tend to experience differences in how the Somatic Instincts are expressed most profoundly when we find ourselves in cultural settings other than our own. In fact, I developed some of the material on the Somatic Instincts while working in a small cottage in the woods on an island off the west coast of Sweden where my wife's family has lived since the 11th Century. While the ways in which family nurturing is expressed and homes are constructed have changed over the last 1,000 years (as have the political structures, social networks, and the focus on "royal" bloodlines, and ways in which love, affection, and ideas are expressed) the collective aspects of the three Somatic Instincts form an underlying continuity back to the dawn of human history.

In fact, when the *preserving* instinct is viewed more broadly as land, gold, riches, natural resources; and the *cultivating* instinct is viewed as political alliances and political marriages; and the *transmitting* instinct is viewed as royal bloodlines, triangular love relationships, or the transmission of cultural ideas; it becomes clear that many of the wars that have been waged throughout human history have been fought around issues to do with the three Somatic Instincts. The *surface* differences in how people are taught to gratify the basic needs associated with home, nurture, food, clothing, belonging, group affiliation, and the expression of affection and love become a *window* into how common and universal the underlying needs, desires, and motivations of humans actually are in Western civilization – and in entirely different cultures in places like Papua New Guinea. The remainder of this section describes eleven general characteristics of the Somatic Instincts that echo Maslow's view of instincts and form the basis of the theory of human motivation that underlies the Breckenridge Enneagram.

Psycho-Somatic Whole: The higher human needs shown on Maslow's Hierarchy have no known somatic base. More specifically, there is a tendency to assume that "hunger" and other biological drives are the model for the motivational states of the Somatic Instincts, but this assumption is problematic for a number of reasons. While the stomach is the repository of food, "hunger" and the motivations associated with it happen to the *entire person*, not just the stomach. In fact, when a person is hungry, the focus of their *psychological* attention is on finding food, the *memory* of food, and the *emotions* associated with "good meals" are heightened and are at the forefront of conscious awareness. The actual *contents* of awareness change dramatically in the face of hunger and thirst because it's hard to think about self-actualization or solving a scientific problem when these basic needs are not filled. So even if the need to *belong* and the need to be *loved* can someday be localized to a specific anatomical somatic base (like hunger and the stomach, or the emotions in the Amygdala), the Somatic Instincts happen to the *entire person*, not just a specific part of our anatomy. Rather than use hunger or other biological drives as the model for the higher needs and motivations, a more revealing model for the motivation experience of the Somatic Instincts that links these psycho-somatic desires and needs to the context in which they occur is the desire for *money* and the *intangible power* and *capabilities* that this brings within a specific cultural setting. As mentioned above, motivation for money and riches has been the cause of many of the world's wars, and these commodities are directly connected to the Somatic Instincts.

Universal: A second general characteristic of the Somatic Instincts is that they are universal in the sense that the underlying needs, desires, and motivations are *common* to all people, in all times, in all geographic locations as a kind of common wisdom of humanity; but the rules for *expressing* and *gratifying* these desires and needs vary widely from culture to culture. In other words, the *biological purpose* of the instincts is collective and exists at Level-5 in Figure 86, while the *cultural expression* and *emotional connection* manifest themselves symbolically at Level-4. To put it another way, people have a common-set of underlying goals and needs, but take different roads to achieving and gratifying them; and these different roads are powerfully shaped by the cultural setting, point in history, and the geographic location in which they live (weather patterns). In a very real sense, the Somatic Instincts are the "collective wisdom" of the human organism that links us to all other humans that have ever lived, and are the basis of our common humanity. The Somatic Instincts are a key element of what Jung called the "Collective Unconscious," which manifested itself as the life-long process of Individuation.

Interdependent Clusters: Some theorists like Freud and Jung argue that there are as many human instincts as there are human needs, desires, and motivations. A third general characteristic of the Somatic Instincts is that each one is an interdependent cluster of myriad human instincts that have been grouped into three overall instinctual themes (preserving, cultivating, and transmitting) as described above. Consequently, the three dimensions (biological purpose, cultural expression, and emotional connection) often create complementary, competing, conflicting or paradoxical interactions of basic needs, desires, and motivations within a single Somatic Instinct cluster. For example, the human body has an instinctive tendency to crave fats and store body fat as part of its biological purpose of survival. When this aspect of the biological purpose expresses itself in a cultural setting that rewards people who live healthy and are not overweight, this can create enormous inner conflict, which could be further compounded if the person has an emotional connection to the nurturing aspects of food as with the preserving instinct.

Distinctly Human Instincts: A fourth general characteristic of the Somatic Instincts is that they are distinctly human. The concept of "instinct" as a rigidly defined, genetically determined, biological necessity in animals like rats and peacocks becomes increasingly weaker as we go up the phyletic scale, and disappears almost entirely in higher animals like humans who have larger brains and the ability to create powerful cultures as noted by Wexler's notion of *Brain and Culture*. With the humans' ability to create culture, over time it becomes objectified and slips beneath the surface of conscious awareness as a self-referential "social mirror" that defines the acceptable ways for people to *express* and *gratify* the basic underlying needs of the Somatic Instincts. Ultimately, the "social mirror" comes to *define* the very nature of reality in a cultural context, where (as Wexler points out) similarities in the mapping between the inner psychological terrain and the external cultural contextual terrain lessen the level of cognitive dissonance, while differences increase it. The distinctly human nature of the Somatic Instincts is evidenced by the push-pull distinction, where desires, needs, goals, and choices in humans (external-*pulls* from family and culture) can largely *replace* the internal-*pushes* of instincts and drives of animals that are lower on the phyletic scale. In humans, habits, patterns-of-interaction, and cultural norms powerfully shape and define the rules by which the Somatic Instincts are experienced, expressed, and gratified.

Not an Overpowering Force: A fifth general characteristic of the Somatic Instincts is that they are not an overpowering force that cannot be controlled, shaped, masked, suppressed and even modified by goals, desires, habits, patterns-of-interaction and the external-pulls of rules and norms of family culture and the larger socio-cultural context. A common but misguided assumption is that when something is labeled as "genetic" or "innate" that this means it is *determined* – where determined means that it is fixed and tightly controlled, with outcomes that are completely predictable and *cannot* be otherwise. It's hard to overstate how robust this deterministic assumption is for most people. It's not unlike the stubborn tendency toward practicing either-or-thinking as opposed to both-and-thinking.[41] The view espoused by Maslow and the Breckenridge Enneagram is that the Somatic Instincts are "weak" in the sense that they have a subtle, quiet, long-term, persistent power like many other forces in nature – like a flowing river. They certainly do demand gratification, but they are all too easily frustrated and undermined by the competing forces of the nine types and the norms and edicts of our cultural context. When a person's life is dominated by (and founded on) the Tacit Creed and the underlying emotional deficiency-drivers rather than a healthy interaction with the Somatic Instincts, it's not guided by the collective human wisdom of the Somatic Instincts and they experience this as an inauthentic existence.

Instinctual Mosaic: A sixth general characteristic of the Somatic Instincts is that we experience these first three levels of Maslow's Hierarchy as a cluster of basic needs, with one of the three being more dominant as a primary focus or force in life, and the other two functioning as secondary and tertiary functions. The ordering of the three Somatic Instincts into primary, secondary, and tertiary functions emerges from both innate and contextual factors. Often, when the desires and needs of the dominant Somatic Instinct are gratified, the others tend to move to the forefront of conscious awareness and make their presence, desires, and needs increasingly known.

Unconscious Desires and Needs: A seventh general characteristic of the Somatic Instincts is that they exist beneath the surface of conscious awareness as largely unconscious biological, emotional, and cultural desires and needs; e.g., at Level-4 and Level-5 of the personal paradigm (see Figure 86). Even a careful study of *conscious* desires, values, needs, and motivations leaves out many of the most important factors of why people do what they do, because our conscious desires are most often a means to *other* ends, not *ends* in themselves. Asking the questions "why?" and "to what end?" up to five times, is one way to probe beneath the surface of conscious desires, values, needs, and motivations to the underlying tacit, symbolic, and archetypal levels of desires, needs, goals, and choices that are ends-in-themselves. When one succeeds in probing to this deeper level, they often find a direct relationship to the basic needs of the three Somatic Instincts. A life of reflection on (and discernment about) the underlying unconscious motivations of the Somatic Instincts, combined with a conscious decision to live "carefully" by raising our awareness of the ever present pushes and pulls of the somatic dimension, helps to restore the balance between our somatic selves, our psychological selves, and the powerful forces of our family and cultural context.

Constant and Dynamic: An eighth general characteristic of the Somatic Instincts is that they are a complex composite of dynamic, never-ending, constant desires, needs, and motivations that are triggered by our environment and cultural context – human beings almost always want or desire something. As these desires and needs are gratified, new ones emerge and compete for our time, energy, attention, and resources. The Breckenridge Enneagram describes how this constant and dynamic activity tends to be focused around the dominant Somatic Instinct, although all three clusters of instincts make their desires and needs known to us experientially. The fact is that *any* contextual situation or organismic state can become a springboard from which new desires and needs can emerge and move us in new directions. These new directions can have repercussions for the entire person because we are somatic-psychological organisms that are subject to the powerful pulls of our personality and cultural context, as well as the subtle inner forces, inner guidance, and collective wisdom of the Somatic Instincts.

Personal Imbalance: A ninth general characteristic of the Somatic Instincts is that while they should form the foundation and basics of human existence, they are often forced into the service of the Tacit Creed and its underlying emotional deficiency-drivers. This is a kind of personal imbalance where the Tacit Creed and its underlying deficiency-drivers become the ruling factor (and tyrant) over the Somatic Instincts by competing with, dominating, frustrating, and undermining the natural self-regulation of our instinctual life through the powerful See-Do-Get Process, thus disrupting the overall balance of the person as a somatic-psychological whole. As a result, the natural flow of psychological-instinctual energy in the individual is *redirected* by the Tacit Creed and deficiency-drivers and is forced into the service of the more cognitive and emotional aspects of the personality, with the result that life is experienced as being shallow, lacking rootedness, and being without meaning and significance. Over time, we experience this diverted flow of psychological-instinctual energy as an existential problem that can be framed as the four key questions of the *Empirical Existentialism* described in Chapter 2. The key to restoring this personal imbalance is to *rediscover* and *strengthen* the lost instinctual drives, tendencies, and remnants of the Somatic Instincts that were overwhelmed and dominated by the Tacit Creed and its deficiency-drivers through the powerful See-Do-Get Process. We often experience a desire to reconnect to the instincts as a deep and profound desire to "get back to basics." The goal is to free-up the flow of psychological-instinctual energy and allow it to once again flow along the natural pathways defined by our somatic self. This is a necessary, first step toward walking the Upward Path of Becoming, self-actualization, Authenticity in Context, and transcending the constraining forces of personality and culture – the upper part of the pyramid of Maslow's Hierarchy. Rediscovering and strengthening our lost instinctual drives, tendencies, and remnants of the Somatic Instincts do not imply a lack of self-control and self-discipline. Rather, people who live close to the instincts find self-discipline easier than many others because they are free to choose the appropriate response to life's situations, rather than being bound by compulsive, autopilot behaviors and emotional responses. In fact, natural human animal behavior is most clearly seen in psychologically healthy, self-actualized people, not those who are bound by the shackles of personality and the edicts and demands of their cultural context.

Family Context: A tenth general characteristic of the Somatic Instincts is that they are subject to the forces of the family culture in which children are raised, and this powerfully shapes and defines the nature and content of the Somatic Instincts; e.g., how children come to experience the home-nurture, belonging, and love needs. Like the intra-psychic activity of the Tacit Creed and its underlying emotions, family culture can become the ruling factor (and tyrant) over the natural expression and gratification of the instincts in the sense that it competes with, frustrates, and undermines the self-regulation of a child's instinctual life through the powerful See-Do-Get Process. While the active, tacit, and cultural teaching of family culture can, and should, *support* the natural expression of our instinctual life, often they frustrate and undermine it. The family cultural context is the single biggest factor in determining the level of deficiency or growth in the basic needs of home and maternal-paternal nurture, our sense of belonging, and our experience of how affection and love are expressed. This family "social mirror" powerfully shapes and defines what "counts" as a person's "reality" – what counts as nurture-home, belonging, and love. A key factor in shaping the nature and content of family culture is its degree of alignment with (and support for) the larger socio-culture in which the family is embedded, and the degree of permeability of the boundary between the family culture and the larger socio-cultural context.

Cultural Context: An eleventh and final general characteristic of the Somatic Instincts is that they are powerfully shaped by the forces of larger socio-culture within which families are embedded, as was pointed out by Wexler.[42] After reviewing the neuropsychological research on how powerfully a child's environment actually shapes the synaptic structures of their brain during the first years of life, Wexler expands the notion of the "environment" to include the broader influences of the human-created environments that we call "culture." He argues that culture actually shapes the human brain and our natural instincts to a degree that is unprecedented among other animals. Wexler states that it is this ability to shape our environment that in turn shapes our brains and natural instincts, and has allowed human adaptability and capability to develop at a much faster rate than is possible through mutation of the genetic code alone. This trans-generational shaping of our brain-functions and natural instincts through culture also means that processes that govern the evolution of societies and cultures have a great influence on how our individual brains, minds, and instincts work and express themselves. In much the same way, Clotaire Rapaille argues that the cultural imprinting on malleable hearts and minds is so powerful that by the time a child is seven years old, she's not just a seven-year-old girl, she's a seven-year-old French, American, or Japanese girl.[43]

Like the intra-psychic activity of the Tacit Creed and family culture described in the previous section, the larger culture in which we are raised can become the ruling factor (and tyrant) over the natural expression and gratification of the Somatic Instincts in the sense that it competes with, frustrates, and undermines the self-regulation of our instinctual life through the powerful See-Do-Get Process. While the active, tacit, and cultural teaching of culture can, and should, *support* the natural expression of our instinctual life, often they do not. More often, the "social mirror" of cultural edicts and demands powerfully shapes the nature and content of the Somatic Instincts in ways that truncate and redirect the natural flow of our psychological-instinctual energy and forces them out of balance. When the world outside us is "mapped" to (and configured like) our inner mental structures and instinctual responses, we experience a sense of comfort, familiarity and psychological safety about the first three levels of Maslow's Hierarchy. But when the configuration of the world and our cultural context do not "map" to our inner mental and instinctual structures this creates cognitive and emotional dissonance that threatens our sense of safety, identity, and ultimately challenges our view of what "reality" is.

It's important to note that *antagonism* between the Somatic Instincts and the edicts and demands of the larger socio-culture of society *is not necessary* as suggested by some theorists like Freud. Nor is there a required antagonism between the natural expression and gratification of the Somatic Instincts and technology or the human-created cultures found in cities and urbanized areas. In other words, reconnecting to the instincts is not co-extensive with living in a rural area, back-country camping, or even living a "green" lifestyle. A person can *rediscover* and *strengthen* the lost instinctual drives, tendencies, and remnants of the Somatic Instincts while living in New York City or Hong Kong. Rather, the descriptions described by these eleven general characteristics are designed to provide a perspective that can enable people to develop a more holistic and interdependent view of the biological, cultural, and emotional dimensions of human nature that does not artificially "pit" society and its cultural norms against the so-called "animal" within, or automatically reject the advances of science, technology, and human civilization because they shape, define, and often subjugate the forces of nature to human goals, desires, and values.

MORE COMMON REASONS
WHY PEOPLE MISTYPE

This section describes common reasons why some people may mistype on the Somatic Instincts.

- People mistype because the Somatic Instincts are not an overpowering force in the personality – rather they can be controlled, shaped, masked, suppressed, and even modified by goals, desires, habits, patterns-of-interaction and the external-pulls of rules and norms of family culture and the larger cultural context. In reality, the Somatic Instincts are "weak" in the sense that they have a subtle, quiet, long-term, persistent power like many other forces in nature, and demand gratification; but are frustrated and undermined by the competing forces of personality and culture; so life is not guided by the collective human wisdom of the Somatic Instincts.

- People mistype because the Somatic Instincts exist beneath the surface of conscious awareness as largely *unconscious* biological, cultural, and emotional desires and needs. Even a careful study of *conscious* desires, values, and needs leaves out many of the most important factors of why people do what they do. This is because our conscious desires are most often means to other ends, not ends in themselves. In addition, the unconscious needs of the Somatic Instincts can be frustrated or undermined by the forces of personality or culture, which can create multiple causes-motivations of which people remain largely unaware. Asking the questions "why?" and "to what end?" at least five times, is one way to probe beneath the surface of conscious intentions to the underlying tacit, symbolic, and archetypal levels of desires, needs, goals, and choices that are ends in themselves. When trying to clearly establish a person's Somatic Instinct, the key is to explore the deeper level of needs and desires, which are often directly related to the basic needs of the three Somatic Instincts.

- People are influenced and shaped by the power of the See-Do-Get Process where they may have come to an incorrect conclusion about their dominant Somatic Instinct because of: a) the influence and views of an influential teacher, coach, friend, or relative, or b) having received incorrect scores from an assessment instrument that was either not psychometrically validated, or had questionable levels of reliability and validity.

- People lack the depth of self-awareness needed to answer: a) the questions on an instrument like the BTI, or b) the questions in a typing session in a way that describes their true self.

- People purposely do not answer the questions on an instrument like the BTI or the questions in a typing session truthfully and honestly for a variety of reasons.

For these and other reasons, it is important to carefully consider a wide range of possible personal, professional, psychological and contextual influences on a person when they believe they have been mistyped.

CHAPTER 2

DIGGING DEEPER INTO THE HISTORICAL AND THEORETICAL FRAMEWORK

This chapter describes how the theoretical and metaphysical framework of Claudio Naranjo's model of the Enneagram has been deconstructed and rebuilt on new naturalistic foundations. It is designed to provide background information for teachers, type professionals, and serious students of the Enneagram and other personality typologies. People who are unfamiliar with the traditional model of the Enneagram, or those who are interested in the more practical aspects of this typology, are encouraged to skip this chapter, move directly to Chapter 3, and then return here to gain a more thorough understanding of the historical and theoretical development of the Breckenridge Enneagram.

BUILDING NEW FOUNDATIONS

What Causes Things?

Throughout human history in Western civilization, the process of developing knowledge about the world (and the people in it) has been characterized by an interdependent balance between two broad "perspectives" for how people explain the underlying *causes* of events in the world. The first is a *metaphysical-perspective* where causation is seen as the result of spiritual (non-physical) causes – forces and laws that are above or beyond the natural forces that operate in the physical world.[44] The second is a *naturalistic-perspective* where the causes of events in the world are seen as the result of natural patterns, processes, and structures – forces and laws of nature that do not require the existence of metaphysical causation. Most people tend to live in an Essential Tension™ between both perspectives, often with one or the other being more dominant. It's important to note that holding to a *naturalistic-perspective* on the *causes* of things in the world (and the people in it), does not require a person to reject the notion of God and the metaphysical, or the possibility of personally knowing God.[45] But what holding a naturalistic-perspective *does* require is that when constructing a model of what causes events in our world, our relationships, our brain, and our personality, that we do not invoke metaphysical causes to explain phenomena that have a reliable naturalistic explanation.

The beliefs and assumptions upon which the metaphysical and naturalistic perspectives are based are often tacit, unexamined, taken-for-granted beliefs about the way the world "is" – our reality. The tacit (or even unconscious) nature of the metaphysical and naturalistic perspectives that we hold become clear when we are asked to explain the basis of our beliefs, because many people don't really know what they believe and why they believe it. The metaphysical and naturalistic perspectives are like two tacit "lens" through which we "see" ourselves, others, and the world around us. Take a moment and reflect on the interdependent balance of the *metaphysical-perspective* and the *naturalistic-perspective* and how you view the *causes* of events in the world and the people who participate in them.

Why is it important to understand this distinction?

As it is traditionally taught by Claudio Naranjo, the Enneagram is not primarily a personality typology. Rather, its primary purpose and use is as a tool for spiritual enlightenment and spiritual transformation.[46] In other words, becoming more effective in our day-to-day actions and interactions with others only happens by moving beyond the *prison* of our personality in the physical dimension (passions and fixations of the nine types) to a metaphysical dimension of true "being" and "essence" (holy ideas and virtues). On this traditional view, focusing on the personality aspects of the Enneagram makes the walls of our spiritual prison thinner and the bars a little farther apart, but does not get at the underlying, spiritual causes of psychopathology and neurosis.[47] For reasons described in this section, the Breckenridge Enneagram soundly rejects this metaphysical-perspective in favor of a naturalistic-perspective.

The importance of the metaphysical-naturalistic distinction becomes apparent when we ask a series of questions. For example, what is the origin of the nine Enneagram types – do they come from metaphysical or naturalistic sources? Why are the nine types different, and are they formed by metaphysical or naturalistic processes? What exactly *is* the personality and how does it relate to concepts such as personal character and the human heart? Is personality part of the mind, or the brain? How does our personality relate to the rest of our knowledge and beliefs? How does personality relate to advances in neuroscience? If the personality is something other than the mind or the brain, then what exactly is it? Do people have a "spiritual" dimension, and is the personality a part of that dimension? If we do have a "spiritual" dimension, how does this non-material dimension interact with (and have causal efficacy on) the psychological and physical dimensions of who we are as human organisms?

The metaphysical-naturalistic distinction raises equally important questions about how we understand personality, psychopathology, and the nature of psychological health. For example, what are the nature and etiology of psychopathology and psychological health? Are psychopathology and neurosis a deficiency-disease that has naturalistic causes (as Maslow suggests), or are psychopathology and neurosis a deficiency-disorder that has metaphysical causes (as Naranjo and many Enneagram teachers suggest)?[48] Are the causes of psychological health and self-actualization naturalistic, or are psychological health and self-actualization caused by reconnecting to metaphysical constructs like "being" and "essence"? While many people have the experience that "something's missing" in life, does this sense of "deficiency" arise from naturalistic causes (our childhood and life experiences), or does it come from a lost connection with metaphysical constructs like "being" and "essence"?

As will be discussed next, the philosophy and work of G.I. Gurdjieff, Oscar Ichazo, and Claudio Naranjo are dominated by the metaphysical-perspective and these are the sources and traditions from which the Enneagram as we know it today emerged.

Ancient Philosophical Origins

It is common to trace the historical roots of the Enneagram back to ancient Greek sources as evidence that supports a metaphysical-perspective. Some authors suggest that the Enneagram *symbol* has its origins in Pythagoras' teachings on geometry and mathematics, while the notion of the nine types was originally found by Oscar Ichazo in the *Enneads* – the 2nd Century B.C. neo-platonic work of Plotinus that describes nine mystical states.[49] These ancient sources are often read as a confirmation of the historical longevity and reality of the metaphysical-perspective. But the history of philosophy can also be interpreted through the lens of the naturalistic-perspective, where natural philosophers from ancient times have been driven to create *natura-listic* explanations for the patterns, processes, and structures of our physical world and the people in it. From the first philosophers (Thales, Democritus, and other pre-Socratics), to modern particle physics experiments conducted at laboratories like Fermilab, the goal of natural philosophers (later called scientists in the 18th Century) has been to develop explanations of the constituents of the physical world and the forces by which they interact *without* appealing to metaphysical causes. A modern-day example of this type of naturalistic explanation is the Standard Model of particle physics that has shown that the entire universe is composed of six quarks, six leptons, and the four forces by which they interact.[50]

Just because the Enneagram has its roots in the metaphysical-perspectives of G.I. Gurdjieff, Oscar Ichazo, and Claudio Naranjo, does not mean that it can't be viewed from a naturalistic-perspective. In fact, the literature describing the origins and history of the natural sciences shows that many of today's scientific models were originally described as having metaphysical causes, but these references to metaphysical causation were theoretical place-holders because natural philosophers lacked a quantitative, naturalistic framework within which to describe the actions and interactions of natural phenomena. An example of using empirical observations and replacing the underlying metaphysical theories with naturalistic ones is the modern astronomers' and cosmologists' use of the empirical observations of Babylonian astronomy. The precision with which they plotted the positions and trajectories of the stars and planets is extremely high even by modern scientific standards, but this entire body of knowledge was motivated by religious reasons; e.g., the ancient Babylonians viewed the stars and planets as deities.[51]

Let's explore the example of astronomy in more detail. Over 2,400 years ago, Plato issued a challenge to the Academy to construct a mechanical and mathematical model that explained the empirical observations that were documented from the time of Babylonian astronomers.[52] The model had to account for the empirical (observed) facts of various anomalies to do with the motion of the planets (e.g., the retrograde motion of Mercury and Venus, etc.) and be articulated using mathematical formalisms and the current theory of mechanics. This challenge embodied the distinction between: a) the empirical data of what we "see" with our five senses, and b) the underlying mechanical, mathematic, and theoretical models and explanations of those empirical data were also indicative of deep and profound differences between how Plato and his pupil Aristotle saw themselves, others, and the world.

While Aristotle focused on the *visible* empirical data and empirical methods of the five senses as the foundation of reality, Plato argued that reality was reflected in the *invisible*; e.g., underlying mathematical formalisms that were not immediately apparent to the five senses. For readers who are familiar with Jungian typology, Aristotle manifested a strong preference for Sensing (S), while Plato showed a strong preference for Intuition (N). This centuries-old conflict between using empirical data and mathematics as a calculating device (Aristotle, Bacon) or theoretical descriptions (Plato, Pythagoras) was echoed in Descartes' mind-body problem, and then finally resolved by the "mapping" between mathematical formalisms and empirical observations in the work of natural philosophers such as Galileo, Copernicus, and Newton.[53] The ability to tease apart the empirical observations from the underlying theory that describes them is evidenced in the ability to swap-out various explanations of the underlying *causes* of these empirical observations; e.g., Aristarchus of Samos (heliocentric, circular orbits), Ptolemy (geocentric, circular orbits), Copernicus (heliocentric, circular orbits), and finally Kepler (heliocentric, elliptical orbits).[54]

Why is it important to understand this distinction?

Much like the swapping of theoretical foundations of geo-heliocentric models, the Breckenridge Enneagram swaps-out the underlying metaphysical theory and framework of Naranjo and most Enneagram teachers and replaces it with the naturalistic model described in this book.

Some of history's most preeminent natural philosophers such as Galileo and Newton used the concept of metaphysical causes as a "place-holder" for a naturalistic explanation for phenomena such as the force of gravity – a move which had the added benefit of helping them avoid confrontation with the religious leaders of the day. But while the theoretical and empirical evidence that Newton used to unify terrestrial and celestial mechanics and the early theory and experiments conducted by Galileo are still the basis of modern astronomy and mechanics, the metaphysical "place-holders" are long gone.[55] So the fact that the Enneagram was originally created by people who were dominated by the *metaphysical-perspective* need not prevent us from taking a *naturalistic-perspective* and deconstructing and abandoning these metaphysical explanations of our psychology and personality. This is not unlike what Myers, Briggs and others in the type community have done with the MBTI® tool by adopting a naturalistic-perspective on Jungian typology, and at the same time distancing themselves from many of the more esoteric teachings and the metaphysical-perspective of Carl Jung.[56]

From the time of pre-Socratic philosophers such as Thales on, there was a distinction made between "natural" and "supernatural" phenomena in terms of the focus of what *causes* things that is not unlike the *metaphysical-perspective* and the *naturalistic-perspective*. More specifically, most of the greatest ancient philosophers did not view natural phenomena and the causes of events in the world as the random capricious influences of "gods" in the way that the Greek poets who wrote hundreds of years earlier did.[57] Rather, they viewed the causes and outcomes of events in the world as the products of identifiable sequences of cause-and-effect events that could be explained using natural explanations. As G.E.R Lloyd points out, "The first philosophers were far from being atheists. Indeed Thales is reported to have held that 'all things are full of gods.' But while the idea of the divine often figures in their cosmologies, the supernatural plays no part in their explanations."[58] Other examples of ancient natural philosophers' commitment to defining the patterns, processes, and structures of the physical world naturalistically are listed below.[59]

- Pre-Socratic philosophers defined the fundamental constituents of the universe naturalistically; e.g., Thales (water), Anaximenes (air), Xenophanes (earth), and Heraclitus (fire).

- Empedocles' naturalistic model argued that the four elements identified by the pre-Socratics exist together in fixed quantities (fire, air, water, earth).

- Democritus' and Lucretius' naturalistic model of the fundamental constituents of the universe being composed of atoms.

- Hippocrates' naturalistic explanation of disease and a naturalistic explanation of personality as consisting of four temperaments or humors; e.g., cheerful-blood, somber-black bile, enthusiastic-yellow bile, and calm-phlegm.

- Plato's naturalistic explanation of four atomic structures (tetrahedron, octahedron, icosahedron, cube) and the fact that the underlying structure and reality of the world could be defined mathematically.

- Aristotle's naturalistic explanation of the four fundamental elements; e.g., hot-dry, hot-wet, cold-wet, and cold-dry.

- Aristotle's naturalistic explanation of the human mind (psyche), which was the first documented discussion of "introspection" and the belief that there was no "divine mind" controlling natural changes, mechanical causation, and teleology.

- Galen's naturalistic explanation of personality with the four temperaments; e.g., sanguine, melancholic, choleric, and phlegmatic.

While one could still "spiritualize" these ancient works by viewing them through the lens of the metaphysical-perspective, this kind of interpretation misreads the original intent of these ancient philosophers in a serious way.

Enneagram Roots in Gurdjieff and Ichazo

In this section, I'd like to discuss the early roots of the Enneagram in the work of Gurdjieff and Ichazo. G.I Gurdjieff (1877-1949) is commonly believed to have brought the symbol of the Enneagram to the Western world after teaching it to students in Russia beginning around 1915.[60] Gurdjieff lived near the Black Sea in a town called Kars in an area that was permeated by Christian, Islamic, Armenian, Assyrian, and Zoroastrian teachings. He embarked on a search for wisdom and truth and travelled throughout Asia, Afghanistan, the Middle East, and India studying Hindu, Buddhist, Christian, Sufi, Shaman, and various other teachings in the hope of discovering the ultimate truth of human existence, and the place that humans hold in the cosmos. The resulting model that he developed was a complex synthesis of psychology, spirituality, systems theory, complexity theory, and natural (physical and biological) processes that he claimed explained the functioning of the entire universe – a theory of everything. Not surprisingly, Gurdjieff's model was developed from the metaphysical-perspective. It was designed to stimulate creative thinking and problem-solving, with the goal of providing access to higher-levels of wisdom, knowledge, and understanding about the universe and the place of humans in it.

Gurdjieff solidified his massive system of knowledge around the nine-pointed symbol of the Enneagram, which he encountered somewhere in his travels.[61] The knowledge that composed his model was articulated (expressed) through dances and lectures that he conducted in St. Petersburg, Moscow, Paris and other cities around 1915. Two of his most celebrated students were John Bennett and the renowned mathematician P.D. Ouspensky. In keeping with Gurdjieff's focus on developing a cosmology that explained the purpose of humans in the universe, Bennett applied the Enneagram to systems-theory, energy dynamics, biospheric symbiosis, planetary evolution, group dynamics, and the nature of organizational design.[62] From these early sources, Gurdjieff's teachings were probably passed-on from student-to-student through the oral tradition of small groups of people who were in search of wisdom. As Don Riso and Russ Hudson point out, the model of the Enneagram taught by Gurdjieff was primarily a theoretical model of natural processes. It was not a psychological treatise or personality typology.[63] Perhaps the best example of this focus on natural processes like biospheric symbiosis, planetary motion, and the "scientific method" is John Bennett's book, *Enneagram Studies*.[64] The point is that Gurdjieff did not originate the symbol of the Enneagram, and the Enneagram symbol that he used with his students had no words, descriptions, or psychological types associated with it.

Oscar Ichazo was a student of Zen, Sufism, Yoga, Buddhism, Confucianism, I-Ching, the Kabbalah, and was dominated by the metaphysical-perspective. Like Gurdjieff, Ichazo traveled the world in search of ancient wisdom and truth, and then began the process of distilling what he had learned into the model of the Enneagram.[65] By the 1950s, he had discovered the connection between the symbol and the nine personality types and began to place them around the symbol of the Enneagram in the same basic form that he later taught to Claudio Naranjo.[66] In other words, Ichazo labeled the nine points of the Enneagram and its connecting points to describe the interdependent relationships between the nine types as being a "map" of the human psyche that could be verified through oral interviews. The nine types that he placed around the Enneagram symbol emerged from the process of "remembering" the nine divine attributes reflected in human nature as described in Plotinus' 3rd Century A.D. text entitled, *The Enneads*.[67] While some people are still unclear about the relationship between Gurdjieff's model of the Enneagram and Ichazo's, Don Riso and Russ Hudson claim the following: "The seminal work on the Enneagram, as it is now known, is Ichazo's work. Having found no clear antecedents, we support his contentions and wish to give him full credit for the tremendous discovery of combining the core ideas of the nine types with the Enneagram symbol in the correct sequence and combination."[68]

Ichazo conducted a training program on the Enneagram in Arica, Chile in 1970, which was attended by John Lilly and Claudio Naranjo.[69] As mentioned earlier, most people writing about or teaching the Enneagram today trace their roots either directly or indirectly to the work of Naranjo. Consequently, our focus in the rest of this section will be on Naranjo's work and the subsequent work of his students, A.H. Almaas and Sandra Maitri. While Naranjo has written many books on the Enneagram, our main focus will be on his own account of the development of his model as found in the book, *Character and Neurosis*, because it provides a "window" into the process by which Naranjo "mapped" the esoteric enneagon symbol and the descriptions of protoanalysis that he learned from Oscar Ichazo, to a 50-year history and research tradition in academic psychology and personality studies.[70]

Naranjo's Academic Research on Personality

As Linda Berens points out in her article, *A History of Psychological Type and Temperament*, there was an entire movement of psychologists who developed personality typologies during the 1920s based on schools of thought that were prevalent in Europe at the end of the 18th Century.[71] These parallel traditions became the intellectual context from which the modern type community emerged. Consequently, people in today's type community tend to think of personality typologies in terms of the three traditions listed below.[72]

- Jungian models associated with the work of Jung, von Franz, Hillman, and Myers-Briggs.[73]
- Temperament models associated with the work of Kretschmer, Spranger, Keirsey, and Berens.[74]
- Primary emotions models associated with Marston, Geier, Merrill, Bolton and Bolton, and Berens.[75]

But over the past five or six decades, there have been two other major research traditions that have tried to define the structure of personality traits and human emotions.[76] The first research tradition is the Five-Factor Model which originated in the 1940s with the research of Raymond Cattell, H.J. Eysenck, and J.P. Guilford. It was based on using factor analysis techniques to identify a well-defined set of basic underlying dimensions of personality.[77] The five factors in this personality model are:

- Extraversion
- Agreeableness
- Conscientiousness
- Emotional stability
- Openness to experience

The second (less well known) research tradition focused on the Circumplex Model of Personality and Emotions, and has sought to define both the structural characteristics of the personality and human emotions. There are four bodies of research that combined to create the Circumplex Model. The first was the interpersonal theory of psychiatry developed by Harry Stack Sullivan.[78] The second body of research emerged from the 1953 advances in psychometrics made by L.A. Guttmann, who developed the Radex model of factor analysis as a circular ordering of variables within a correlation matrix.[79] This provided personality researchers with the statistical tools needed to study the circular order of personality traits and emotions on a Circumplex graph. The third was the development of a theory of personality for a Circumplex by Timothy Leary, Jerry Wiggins, David Olsen, and others.[80] The fourth body of research was research on emotions conducted by Robert Plutchik, Maurice Lorr, Lorna Benjamin, Richard Lazarus, Nico Frijda, Keith Oatley, and others.[81] The existence of sophisticated psychometric analysis also allowed researchers to create assessment instruments to measure numerous dimensions of the Circumplex Model quantitatively, especially Plutchik, Conte, Maurice Lorr, and L.S. Benjamin.[82]

What is important to understand about the development of Naranjo's work on the Enneagram is the extent to which he was thoroughly familiar with the Five-Factor Model, Circumplex Model and Jungian typology. Naranjo worked in both the Five-Factor and Circumplex research traditions from 1960 on and conducted academic research on personality with some of the intellectual luminaries of this period in both the Five-Factor and Circumplex research traditions. Naranjo actually mentions these bodies of research and collaborators by name in his book, *Character and Neurosis*.[83] More specifically, while working at the Center for Studies in Medical Anthropology at the University of Chile Medical School, Naranjo was engaged in academic personality research where he worked (at a distance) with Raymond Cattell using factor analysis to map-out the structure of the human personality in the tradition of the Five-Factor Model. As Naranjo describes it, "I became immersed in it [factor analysis] as a true believer seeking deeper understanding of the mind through statistics."[84]

In 1962, the University of Chile funded Naranjo to visit Harvard where he worked with Gordon Allport, David McClelland, and Henry Murray at the Center for Studies of Personality, and then at Ohio State University in Columbus working with Samuel Renshaw and Hoyt Sherman in the area of perceptual training and the perception of wholes (gestalts). A year later in 1963, he was awarded a Fulbright Scholarship and worked for six months as a visiting scholar at the Center for Studies of Personality at Harvard where he once again worked with Allport, McClelland, and Murray. Later that year, Naranjo worked with Raymond Cattell at the University of Illinois-Urbana in the Institute of Personality and Ability Testing (IPAT). While at Harvard, he met Frank Barron and two years later became a Guggenheim Fellow working with Barron at the University of California at Berkeley (1965-1966) where he worked as a Research Associate at the Institute of Personality Assessment and Research (IPAR). During this time period, he also worked closely with Fritz Perls (the founder of Gestalt therapy) at Esalen, and by 1969 Perls considered Naranjo one of the second-generation intellectual-heirs of Gestalt psychology.

Within this context, Naranjo states in no uncertain terms that he believed that the Enneagram *is* a Circumplex Model of Personality, purposely linking his Enneagram model to the naturalistic research traditions in academic psychology. I will quote Naranjo at length on this point:

> "It has been an aspiration of modern psychology to organize the known characterological syndromes in what has been called a Circumplex model... This circular continuum with adjoining characters being most similar to each other, while oppositions along the circle correspond to bipolarities; in contrast the Enneagram emphasizes a tripolarity. One Circumplex model was proposed by Leary in connection

with his interpersonal system, another by Schaefer as the way to organize data resulting from his study of parent-child interactions. Lorr and MacNair in 1963 reported an "interpersonal behavior circle," resulting from a factor analysis of clinicians' ratings on various kinds of interpersonal behavior – which was interpreted as reflecting nine clusters of variables. In addition to these theoretically-driven Circumplex models, Conte and Plutchik demonstrated that the Circumplex model maps to main domains of interpersonal personality traits. By two different methods, one an analysis of similarity ratings of terms, another an application of factor analysis to semantic differential ratings of terms, they produced an identical empiric circular ordering of terms on the basis of their loading of the first two factors. A later study by the same authors examines the diagnostic concepts of DSM-II personality disorders. They found that these could also be arranged in a Circumplex order fairly similar to that resulting from the 1967 study. [DSM III Diagram in Original Text]

Perhaps the scheme pictured in Figure 6 below [Enneagram diagram], is the most convincing Circumplex model thus far. Agreeing also with current opinion in terms of the grouping of the DSM III syndromes, the present characterology recognizes three fundamental groups: the schizoid group, with an orientation to thinking (that I will here designate as ennea-types V, VI, and VII), the hysteroid group, with an orientation to feeling (ennea-types II, III, and IV) and another group (which Kretschmer might have called collectively epileptoid) the members of which are constitutionally the lowest ectomorphia and are predominantly oriented to action [ennea-types VIII, IX, and I]."[85]

But to return to the distinction described earlier in this section, despite the fact that he was trained as a physician and psychiatrist and participated in years of academic research in personality, Naranjo was dominated by the metaphysical-perspective. In other words, when Naranjo looked at the data mentioned in the extended quote above and asked, "What causes these things?" he tended to answer this question from the metaphysical-perspective, not a naturalistic-perspective.

As Naranjo describes himself, his search for truth had never been purely intellectual, and during his time at Berkeley he deeply craved a more experiential answer to his questions which he found in part in the theoretical work of Carl Jung and the clinical explorations of Fritz Perls (which were holistic). Naranjo also performed experimental work with psychopharmacology; e.g., using mescaline, LSD and other hallucinogenic drugs for therapeutic purposes, and to create drug-induced paths to spiritual enlightenment. In fact, it was the work of Jung that convinced Naranjo to continue his studies and research into personality after he became disappointed with the search for wisdom and truth through neurophysiology and factor analysis.[86] By 1969, Naranjo stated that the experiential-metaphysical-seeker in him began to take precedence over the intellectual investigator and he found himself at a pivotal crossroad in his life. During this time period, Naranjo

also became part of the Gurdjieff School led by Madame de Salzmann and participated in the gathering of a select group of teachers and disciples, but he became
disillusioned with the Gurdjieff tradition because he didn't find a "living lineage"
in the school that was established after Gurdjieff's death in 1949.[87] He then began
studying Sufism with Idries Shah, which added another dimension to his understanding.[88]

Naranjo recounts that the accidental death of his only son on the eve of Easter 1970
marks the end of one phase of his life, and subsequently he went to Chile to participate in an extended spiritual retreat in the isolation of the desert near Arica with
Oscar Ichazo. As Frank Barron explains, "One day Claudio came into my office and
announced that he was leaving Berkeley a bit earlier than he had planned, because
a call…in the sense of a spiritual demand…had come to him to study with a Sufi
master who had surfaced in Chile and was gathering people together for his teaching in the desert town of Arica. It was, Dr. Naranjo told me, the most important
thing in life for him at that time to go there and learn from the Sufi master."[89]
After this initial visit in 1970, he returned to Chile in 1971 with a personal invita-
tion from Ichazo with about fifty Americans for an extended retreat designed to
lead people to self-realization under Ichazo's direction in Arica. This core group of
people became the original members of the Arica Institute.[90] Naranjo characterizes
the Arica experience as the true beginning of his spiritual experience and rebirth,
his contemplative life, and the source of his inner guidance.[91] After returning, he
abandoned his career as an academic researcher in psychology and devoted himself to the development and teaching of the model of the Enneagram that we have
preserved in *Character and Neurosis* and his other books.

Naranjo's Enneagram

In September of 1971, he began teaching the psycho-spiritual aspects of the Enneagram using therapeutic methods and contemplative methods in study groups called
Seekers After Truth (SAT) in Berkeley. It's important to note that the acronym SAT
not only stands for "Seekers After Truth" but it also is related to the Sanskrit word
for "being." In terms of Naranjo's theoretical development of the Enneagram that
he learned from Ichazo, Don Riso and Russ Hudson argue that, "Naranjo is gener-
ally credited with expanding the descriptions of the Enneagram types and finding
correlations between them and known psychiatric categories."[92] One of the more
prominent students from Naranjo's SAT groups in Berkeley, A.H Almaas, states,
"It is not clear which parts of the Enneagram teaching originated with Ichazo and
which were added to or elaborated upon by Naranjo in the context of his extensive
knowledge of depth psychology. Naranjo, from whom we learned the body of

knowledge associated with the Enneagram, related it to the Middle Eastern school with which Gurdjieff was associated, but clearly stated that he received the basic knowledge of the Enneagram from Oscar Ichazo."[93] What is clear is that Naranjo "mapped" the Enneagram that he had learned from Ichazo to the psychological categories in the DSM III in the form of a Circumplex Model of Personality as described in *Character and Neurosis*.[94]

Naranjo's model of the Enneagram is extremely complex and represents a synthesis of many bodies of knowledge, traditions, and schools of thought. Some of the most important elements include:

- The esoteric teachings of Gurdjieff, Sufism, and Ichazo about the Enneagram.
- A syncretistic merging of Hindu Tantra, Chinese Taoism, and Tibetan Buddhism.
- A transpersonal-spiritual *existential* interpretation of personality (character) that emerges from an "existential vacuum" – an obscuration of our true being.
- A clinical exploration of the same psychological terrain covered by Five-Factor and Circumplex personality theorists, but using the Enneagram as the "map" to define that territory.
- A psychodynamic exploration of the interconnections of personality traits as styles-of-defense and styles-of-values that are based on specific illusions about how our basic needs are fulfilled.
- A clinical exploration of the psychology of Fritz Perls which was holistic.
- Karen Horney's focus on self-diagnosis, self-analysis, and self-healing, hence the sub-title of Naranjo's book, *Ennea-Type Structures: Self Analysis for Seekers*.[95]
- A Freudian theoretical foundation that views "ego" as the enemy of "essence" and the psychic entity that displaces the idealized state of unity, being, and essence in which we are born.[96]

As described by A.H. Almaas, "Naranjo presents the Enneagram as a means for self-observation and study as part of a larger work of spiritual realization... Naranjo's study is the first published account of how each character [personality type] is related to the loss of contact with Being... The transmitted view is that the Enneagram knowledge is an objective knowledge of reality."[97] Another student from that Berkeley SAT group, Sandra Maitri, explains the notion of "being" as, "The ultimate or True Nature of everything. Our individual consciousness is what I will refer to as our soul, and I see it as an individual manifestation of our divine nature, Being. Each of us is a unique arising of Being. When we experience Being within ourselves, we are experiencing the essence of who we are… What I will refer to as Essence then, is Being experienced through our individual soul." [98]

I'd like to return to some of the key questions mentioned at the beginning of this chapter and focus on how Naranjo answered them. For example, what are the nature and etiology of psychopathology and psychological health? Are psychopathology and neurosis a deficiency-disease that has naturalistic causes (as Maslow suggests), or are psychopathology and neurosis a deficiency-disorder that has metaphysical causes (as Naranjo suggests)? Are the causes of psychological health and self-actualization naturalistic, or are psychological health and self-actualization caused by reconnecting to metaphysical constructs like "being" and "essence"? While many people have the experience that "something's missing" in life, does this sense of "deficiency" arise from naturalistic causes (our childhood and life experiences), or does it come from a lost connection between our psychological-biological self and metaphysical constructs like "being" and "essence"? Naranjo's "ontic existentialism" claims that:

- There is no difference between the degradation of consciousness, emotions, motivations seen in neurosis (unconscious deficiency), and our loss of connection with true Being, so at their core neurosis and psychopathology are metaphysical problems. [99]
- The lost connection to Being creates the nagging sense that "something's missing" in life and this is the core-cause of all neurosis and psychopathology. [100]
- The core problem of neurosis and psychopathology is that we look for the "key" to what's missing in the wrong place; e.g., in the day-to-day naturalistic world of "illusions and metaphysical mistakes" rather than the metaphysical realm of Being where our true divine nature lies buried deep within us and undiscovered. [101]

As mentioned earlier, these (and other related questions) are not obtuse intellectual speculations when we begin the process of exploring the historical and theoretical foundation upon which the Breckenridge Enneagram is based. Understanding how the *metaphysical-perspective* and the *naturalistic-perspective* figure into your personal paradigm will help you answer questions about the nature and characteristics of psychology, personality typologies, and the relationships between our biological and psychological selves.

In terms of the actual psycho-spiritual *practice* of the Berkeley SAT groups relative to the Enneagram, the *contemplative* methods used by Naranjo consisted of a practice of meditation that trained people to be "mindful" and to be observers of (and pay attention to) their ongoing inner experience in the present. Through meditation, they developed a sense of inner quiet, and the ability to conduct an inquiry into their inner experience of "being" and ultimately into the nature of ultimate truth. In terms of the *therapeutic* methods, Naranjo used his clinical training as a psychiatrist and his background in Gestalt therapy to conduct clinical interviews from which he gathered information about a person's ennea-type, and then he organized people of confirmed-type into groups based on their ennea-type. This became the basis for the typing panels used by Enneagram teachers in the narrative tradition.

The Gestalt aspect of the therapeutic method involved a transformative reconnecting to childhood memories, emotions, and relationships through therapeutic drama of regression to prenatal experiences using techniques like holotropic breathing.[102] Based on the work of Stanislav Grof, holotropic breathing uses a mild form of oxygen deprivation (like that experienced by climbers) to create altered states of awareness. Etymologically, the word holotropic means moving toward wholeness, where the Greek word *holos* means whole and *trepein* means moving toward something. The process is done in pairs where one person is the breather, and the other is the "sitter" who tends to the breather during the process. The methodology has five components: a) it's a group process, b) it involves intensified breathing (hyperventilating), c) it's accompanied by evocative music, d) it's focused on body work, and subsequently e) it involves expressive drawing of the experiences encountered during the process. Like an ancient shaman, Naranjo used holotropic breathing as the vehicle to conduct deep inner travel into the spiritual dimension of "being" which he claimed was the spiritual dimension of the Enneagram. Using these breathing techniques, inner travelers are said to move through an inner vortex which is the entrance into the spiritual realm of "being" and true reality. Many of these same techniques are still used today by well-known Enneagram teachers like Don Riso and Russ Hudson in their Enneagram-teacher certification programs.[103]

As pointed out by Ken Wilber and some of Naranjo's students, transpersonal states that are beyond the human brain and physical body can also be reached using contemplative meditation and more traditional methods of enlightenment.[104] Naranjo provides an entire section at the end of *Character and Neurosis* entitled, "Suggestions for Further Work on Self" where he describes the process of developing the ability to quiet the mind through meditation and then view ourselves objectively as an impartial observer. Maitri echoes this approach by describing the spiritual practice of presence and inquiry.[105] In many ways, these techniques are not unlike Jung's notion of the Transcendent Function – the mechanism used for inner psychological transformation.[106]

Ichazo and Naranjo taught these and other principles under the condition of utmost secrecy. In fact, people who attended the SAT groups in Berkeley had to sign a statement that they would not teach the principles outside the secrecy of the study groups. In the 1980s, some of Naranjo's students broke secrecy and began offering Enneagram courses in the Berkeley area, and then more broadly. Of the Enneagram teachers today, A.H. Almaas, Sandra Maitri, and Helen Palmer all participated in the Berkeley SAT groups. Several Jesuit priests, including Robert Ochs, also learned the material from Naranjo and the SAT groups. Ochs taught the Enneagram to other Jesuits at Loyola University and from there it was passed on to people like Don Riso, Richard Rohr, Andreas Ebert, and Jerry Wagner. All other teachers of the Enneagram today learned the system from one or more of this small group of people. I received my Enneagram training in the mid-1990s from Don Riso and Russ Hudson, and later attended a three-day workshop at the IEA meeting in Washington DC that was led by Claudio Naranjo.

Enneagram Parallels with a Platonic and Gnostic Ontology

In Ichazo's original work, the nine types emerged from the process of "remembering" the nine divine attributes reflected in human nature described in Plotinus' 3rd Century A.D. text, *The Enneads*, so there is little doubt that the Enneagram symbol and theory of the nine types had their origin in Greek thought.[107] Almaas claims that while Naranjo described the relationship between the ennea-types and "being" in a general way – focusing on how the nine types had an associated passion that perpetuated a person's loss of contact with "being" – he did not describe *where* and *why* the differences between the ennea-types originated in the holy ideas.[108] This further articulation of the model to include the holy ideas was left to two of Naranjo's students from the Berkeley SAT groups – Almaas and Maitri. An evaluation of Almaas' and Maitri's descriptions of the holy ideas as the foundation of the spiritual dimension of the Enneagram reveals that their views echo many of the key elements of Plato's ontology and theory of forms and the ontological structure of Gnosticism.[109] The six key concepts of a Platonic ontology and the theory of Forms (listed below) bear a striking resemblance to the underlying concepts of Naranjo's, Almaas', and Maitri's models of the spiritual dimension of the Enneagram.

- Plato's notion of a previous existence where we were merged with perfect being-essence (true nature) and "forms" which were immutable, timeless, metaphysical truths (holy ideas).
- We lose contact with (become unconscious of) this previous existence of being-essence and our true nature at birth where we cross what Plato calls the "river of forgetfulness," but we have a subtle, but profound, sense that

"something's missing" as we see the imperfect manifestation of "being, essence, forms" in day-to-day life (Plato's Cave).

- Our childhood environment and culture form our personality (instincts, passions, fixations) and bury our true nature and direct experience of being-essence under myriad unconscious layers of defenses and illusions.

- We can move through the inner vortex, passing into the spiritual realm, and reconnect to this metaphysical realm of being-essence and our true divine nature that lies buried deep within us through what Plato called reminiscence-recollection, what Maitri calls open-ended inquiry into our inner experience, as well as meditation practices and other techniques like holotropic breath work.

- Naranjo's Enneagram and the later articulation of the holy ideas are a "map" for making this journey back to true being and essence.

- Over time, our minds are transformed as we come to "see" the world from the nine objective perspectives of the holy ideas and we move from the lower to the upper portion of Naranjo's model shown in Figure 88 as our true essence becomes more and more of who we are.

Naranjo and most Enneagram teachers argue that the human psyche is comprised of the five centers listed below and that a fully developed person has awakened within themselves the two higher centers; e.g., higher emotional and higher cognition.

- Higher Cognition (Holy Ideas)
- Higher Emotional (Virtues)
- Lower Cognition (Fixations)
- Lower Emotion (Passions)
- Instincts (Bound or Freed)

The goal of Naranjo's psycho-spiritual practice was to shift in the focus of control from lower personality-based existence to higher spiritual centers (see Figure 88)[110] or as Don Riso and Russ Hudson state, "One of the profound lessons of the Enneagram is that psychological integration and spiritual realization are not separate processes."[111]

Naranjo's Map of the Psyche

Essence (True Being)

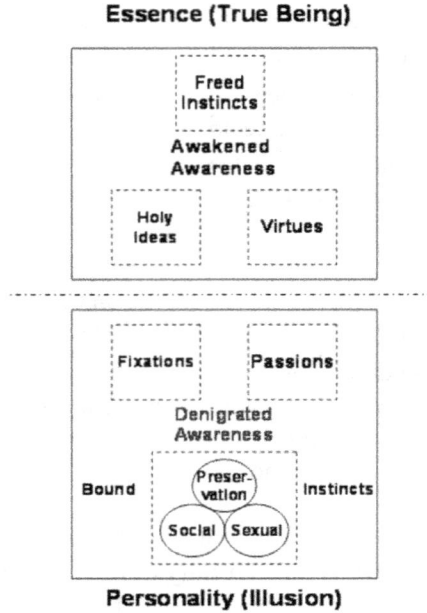

Figure 88

The lower part of Figure 88 represents our personality (the conditioned-self that grew up in our family) that is made up of the mental constructs of our past experiences and historical lives. Our personality supports the illusion that we are a separate self (a discrete physical entity), but the enlightened perspective of the holy ideas on the top part of Figure 88 shows us that we are really one with divine "being" and as such we are inseparable parts of the entire fabric of true reality.[112] Also, the nine types and the three instincts are dominated by their associated passions and fixations, so for Naranjo the true battle (holy war) was not with the animal within (instinct), rather it was with the ways in which the passions contaminate, repress, and stand in the place of the instincts, with the fixations cognitively reinforcing the passions in self-referential ways.[113] For Naranjo, the path to psychological health and the path to spiritual enlightenment were *the same thing* and simply required a shift in focus from the lower to the upper part of Figure 88 through the transformation of our minds using the methods described above.

So to directly address the question of the origin of the nine types and why they are different according to the traditional Enneagram model developed by Naranjo, Almaas, and Maitri, we see that each of the nine types is formed as a direct result of its loss of connection to one of the holy ideas listed below.[114]

- Type Two forms from a loss of connection to Holy Will
- Type Three forms from a loss of connection to Holy Law
- Type Four forms from a loss of connection to Holy Origin
- Type Five forms from a loss of connection to Holy Omniscience
- Type Six forms from a loss of connection to Holy Faith
- Type Seven forms from a loss of connection to Holy Plan
- Type Eight forms from a loss of connection to Holy Truth
- Type Nine forms from a loss of connection to Holy Love
- Type One forms from a loss of connection to Holy Perfection

So given the background presented thus far, let's compare some of the key differences between metaphysical-perspective held by most Enneagram teachers and the naturalistic-perspective of the Breckenridge Enneagram.

Content of the Human Psyche

Metaphysical-Perspective: The human psyche is composed of both our personality (in the physical dimension) and metaphysical essence (being) embodied in the holy ideas and virtues. As shown in Figure 88, "being" and "essence" are in a spiritual dimension that is beyond the physical substance of human brain and the human organism. The *origin* of the nine types is linked to the holy ideas.

Naturalistic-Perspective: The human psyche has a five-level belief structure of innate and learned knowledge that coheres in the human brain in the physical world of space and time (see Figure 91). In terms of the nature-nurture question, whether we learn something or whether it's innate are just two different conduits into the same synaptic registers. The origin of the nine types lies in our innate, inborn tendencies (our temperament) interacting with our experiences and the environment to build underlying patterns of thinking, emotions, and other characteristics that become our Enneagram type and what is commonly called our *personality*.[115]

Origin and Emergence of Personality

Metaphysical-Perspective: The fundamental mechanism by which personality is formed is the Inner Triangle at points Nine, Six and Three where we progressively "fall asleep" to our true nature in being and essence.[116] The nine types are defensive reactions and differing responses to the experiences and wounding of early childhood. Over time, the personality (ego) dominates and ultimately displaces our true essence through its domination and power.

Naturalistic-Perspective: The fundamental mechanism by which personality is formed is the See-Do-Get Process. How we "see" the world develops from our earliest years as our innate, inborn tendencies (our temperament) interact with our experiences and the environment to build underlying patterns of thinking, emotions, and other characteristics that emerge as our Enneagram type. Our Enneagram type has both innate, inborn roots in our temperament, and learned characteristics from the family and socio-cultural context in which we were raised. This contextual process of formation is defined by the Breckenridge Equation™, which is described later in the book.

Methods for Psychological Change

Metaphysical-Perspective: As shown in Naranjo's map of the psyche (Figure 88), we must move from the physical dimension of personality (fixations, passions, and bound instincts) to the spiritual dimension of the holy ideas, virtues, and freed instinct. Authentic change cannot happen on the physical, personality side of the model because the Enneagram is a tool for spiritual transformation – in other words, becoming who we are beyond the prison of our personality in the physical dimension. Focusing only on the dimension of personality (like some Enneagram teachers do) makes the walls of the spiritual prison thinner and the bars farther apart, but does not solve the root-cause problem.[117] The methods used for making this journey to being and essence include Holotropic Breathing, contemplative meditation, objective observation of self (Naranjo), and presence and inquiry into self (Maitri).

Naturalistic-Perspective: We must deconstruct ineffective and inauthentic ways of seeing ourselves, others, and the world that developed through the See-Do-Get Process because they are not addressing the key questions of human existence, or getting us the results we want on our one-trip through life. The methods for making this journey include getting into the Spectator Role and exploring our inner experience with empathic inquiry and constructing new, more effective and authentic ways of seeing ourselves, others, and the world. We do this by running the See-Do-Get Process backwards and following the Upward Path of Becoming rather than the Downward Spiral of Striving; and by deconstructing the contextual elements described by the Breckenridge Equation which is described later in the book.

Mechanism of Psychological Change

Metaphysical-Perspective: The fundamental mechanism in which psychological change happens is through the transformation of the mind through spiritual enlightenment as evidenced by the title of Naranjo's book, *Transformation through Insight* (in Greek, transformation is μεταμορφόομαι).[118] The goal is to be reunited and one with being and essence.

Naturalistic-Perspective: The fundamental mechanism in which psychological change happens is through the transformation (μεταμορφόομαι) of the mind and the deeper regions of the human heart at levels 3, 4, and 5 of our personal paradigm through the See-Do-Get Process. The goal is to learn to see ourselves, others, and the world differently by running the See-Do-Get Process backwards and following the Upward Path of Becoming, rather than the Downward Spiral of Striving.

Outcome of the Transformation Process

Metaphysical-Perspective: The primary purpose of the Enneagram is as a tool of spiritual enlightenment and spiritual transformation, and secondarily it can be used as a personality typology. The outcome is being reconnected with the ultimate truth and reality of all existence in "being" and manifesting our true divine nature as "essence." The transformation process allows people to see the spiritual dimension of truth and reality with increasing clarity from the nine objective perspectives of the holy ideas and the virtues. As mentioned, Riso and Hudson's view, "psychological integration and spiritual realization are not separate processes."[119] Although the existence of life-after-death is not addressed directly by Enneagram teachers, a natural extension of their model seems to imply that when our physical bodies die, the divine part of our "essence" lives-on in a kind of oneness with "being." This can be inferred from comments like Riso and Hudson's, in the dedication of their book, *The Wisdom of the Enneagram*, "We dedicate this book to the Ground of all Being, the One from Whom we have come, and to Whom we shall return, the Font of wisdom and Light of lights, the Maker, Renewer, and Keeper of all things."[120] From this perspective, the Enneagram can be viewed as a path of personal enlightenment and a process of personal salvation.

Naturalistic-Perspective: The Breckenridge Enneagram provides a "window" into the human heart and the depths of human character as described by the five levels of the personal paradigm (see Figure 91). The outcome is to *transcend* the autopilot, tacit, and unconscious forces of our personality with the goal of living life authentically; e.g., Authenticity in Context™, which is described later in the book. Living authentically includes building more effective relationships as well as transcending the inauthentic edicts, demands, and norms of our socio-cultural context. On our view, the extent to which people become self-actualized and transcend the ineffective, inauthentic, autopilot elements of their personality and transcend their culture by living authentically *is not* a path to personal enlightenment or personal salvation. It is a path to psychological health, more effective relationships, and making contributions to humanity.

In what follows, we'll describe a viable alternative to Naranjo's views that takes the empirical-clinical power and predictive ability of the traditional Enneagram and places these empirical elements on a new, naturalistic foundation of the Breckenridge Enneagram.

Empirical Existentialism

As Maslow points out, psychological theories in general, and personality typologies in particular, are not often based on the kind of philosophical foundations that would allow them to raise, systematically explore, and address the key issues that underlie the phenomena within their scope of explanation.[121] Naranjo (correctly) tried to address some of the deepest and most profound issues in life by building his model of the Enneagram on an existentialist framework, but his brand of existentialism reflected a metaphysical-perspective (interpretation) of the abstract categories and concepts of being, essence, and ontology proposed by traditional continental existentialists like Martin Heidegger, Karl Jaspers, Jean-Paul Sartre, and Soren Kierkegaard as well as Platonic, neo-Platonic, and Gnostic thought.[122] We have adopted a naturalistic alternative that echoes a neo-Freudian existentialist psychology. As Maslow points out, existentialist psychology has a deep philosophical underpinning that a number of American psychologists have woven into the fabric of their work. For example, the work of Gordon Allport, Carl Rogers, Kurt Goldstein, Victor Frankl, Eric Fromm, Allen Wheelis, Eric Erickson, H.A. Murray, Karen Horney, Rollo May, and others all have an existentialist framework, but it is based on the naturalistic-perspective.[123] The notions of self-actualization and transcendence found in Maslow and Roger's work are based on a naturalistic, non-metaphysical, neo-Freudian existentialist foundation, with the best examples being, Maslow's *Toward a Psychology of Being*, and Rogers' *On Becoming a Person*.[124]

The Breckenridge Enneagram is also based on an existentialist foundation that is a tangible and concrete philosophical framework and focuses on the conduct of day-to-day life; the creation of our personal history by our choices; the need to make meaningful contributions to life; exploring and ultimately knowing our true identity; facing the future in the light of our one-trip through life; and a deep sense of personal responsibility for living a life of integrity, self-awareness, self-control, and authenticity. I call this philosophical view, *Empirical Existentialism*, which finds its roots in the confluence of the three knowledge clusters listed below.

- The neo-Freudian existentialist focus on human identity, meaning, authentic existence; the primacy of phenomenological-experiential knowledge as a platform upon which to build an existential framework; and the problem of future-time in psychology where each person holds the key to their own future *within them* like the Aristotelian notions of actuality, potentiality, and teleology.[125]

- The kind of "wisdom" found in the Wisdom Literature which is characterized by intellectual acumen, deep insight, and speculative depth, but focuses on exploring the means and ends of life, rather than developing, elaborating, or speculating about esoteric theories or focusing on the complex analysis of facts.[126]

- A view of the creation of human knowledge that echoes Thomas Kuhn's notion of paradigms, anomalies, dialectic, and paradigm shifts; combined with a psychological model that bases the structure and dynamics of human knowledge on the empirical data and studies of neuroscience; and an epistemology and ontology of objective realism and reliability that emerges from the systematic study of experimental science and the history and philosophy of science.[127]

There are four key principles and four key questions that summarize the basic tenets of Empirical Existentialism. Each is described in turn below.

Four Key Principles

Principle 1 (Naturalized Epistemology): This principle forms the basis of a naturalistic view of human knowledge, personality, character, and the human heart of which all personality typologies are sub-sets. It is built on a foundation of realism in the sense that when something is real it makes a physical difference. If it makes no physical difference, then it's not real. It is also built on a foundation of reliability in terms of the ability to describe and predict the actions and interactions of phenomena in our world, including people. Principle 1 is also built on the objective-subjective distinction where something is objective when it exists independent from the knower. If it does not exist independent from the knower, it is *subjective*.

Things like beliefs and assumptions can be subjective, but are very real when they consciously or unconsciously motivate our actions and interactions.[128] Also, things look different depending on whether we view them from the outside-in (objectively) or the inside-out (subjectively); e.g., we see differently when we see from a distance or change perspectives. So the construction of reliable knowledge about ourselves, others, and the world requires us to view things from multiple perspectives.[129] One way to do this is to move into the Spectator Role like Dickens' character Scrooge who watches his life pass before him like an independent observer (outside-in) and then develop an attitude of open-ended, empathic inquiry into our experience and the questions of human existence.[130] Moving into the Spectator Role and exploring the terrain of our inner experience with empathic inquiry (not judgment) ignites a powerful process of inner transformation. So creating reliable knowledge about ourselves, others, and the world is a never-ending process of successive approximations about reality that emerge from this inner exploration.

Principle 2 (Personal Responsibility and Freedom in the Existential Now): This principle states that there are two fundamental human forces: the force-for-safety and the force-for-growth. We experience these human forces as a lifetime of choices between safety (striving) and growth (becoming) and are personally responsible for either proactively choosing or reactively responding to the challenges that life presents. In addition, we live on the cusp of the existential now, where the past exists only in our memory and the future does not yet exist because we must create it daily with the choices that we make within our context. While the past and the future are "real" in the sense that they can (and do) direct and powerfully shape our actions and interactions with people in the *existential now*, the cornerstone and foundation of our sense of personal responsibility and freedom are laid by the cumulative outcome of the dialectic between the force-for-safety and the force-for-growth.

Principle 3 (What is Most Personal, is Most Universal): This principle states that the universal nature of human emotions; the anatomical and operational similarities of the human organism; the biological purpose of the Somatic Instincts; the fact that life is an historical process of birth, infancy, adolescence, maturity, and death within space-and-time; and our concrete and symbolic experiences of these aspects of human existence create the deep and abiding sense that *what is most personal, is most universal*. As Carl Rogers explains, "There have been times when in talking with students or staff, or in my writing, I have expressed myself in ways so personal that I have felt I was expressing an attitude which it was probable no one else could understand, because it was so uniquely my own... In these instances I have almost always found that the very feeling which seemed to me most private, most personal, and hence most incomprehensible by others, has turned out to be an expression for which there is a resonance in many other people. It has led me to believe that what is most personal and unique in each one of us is probably the very element which would, if it were shared or expressed, speak most deeply to others."[131]

Our experience of human existence begins at birth as our innate, inborn tendencies (our temperament) interact with our experiences and the environment to build underlying patterns of emotions that are stored in the long-term emotional memory of the Amygdala long before the neocortex has formed and prior to a child's ability to use language. By the age of four or five, many children can frame penetrating questions about the nature of human existence regarding issues like: a) how they "see" themselves, being themselves, and finding an identity, b) how they should deal with (and face) the future, and c) how they should interact with the people and world around them.[132] As mentioned previously, children aren't "taught" questions of human existence by parents, caretakers, and other adults. Rather, these questions emerge naturally, as do the self-evident conclusions that children come to about life, human existence, and their place in the universe. From my own experience, my son Thomas was able to verbalize and dialogue about the questions of human existence from the time he was five years old without any prompting, and when least expected.

Principle 4 (Authenticity in Context): This principle requires us to overcome our fear of self-knowledge (good or bad) about our emotions, natural impulses, long-term emotional and cognitive memories, natural talents and abilities, potentialities, and our calling and destiny in life.[133] This fear causes us to deal with inner existential issues using outer behaviors. Accepting (and acting out) inauthentic scripts and beliefs about who we are transforms them into deep assumptions – so-called "facts" about ourselves, others, and the world that are reinforced through myriad cycles of the See-Do-Get Process and create a false, inauthentic sense of self. Over time, the inauthentic self becomes a "mask" that increasingly alienates us from ourselves, others, and the world; and which creates a deep inner sense that "something's missing" in life until we become *strangers to ourselves*.[134] Authenticity in Context also requires us to *rediscover* and *strengthen* the natural flow of psychological-instinctual energy from the Somatic Instincts and allow it to once again flow along the natural pathways defined by our somatic self, not the tyranny of our Tacit Creed, underlying emotions, and the edicts and demands of our cultural context. Alienation from the Somatic Instincts creates a deep inner sense of inauthenticity and that "something's missing" in life. This allows the force-for-growth to lead the overall path and direction of our lives, enabling us to move up Maslow's

Hierarchy toward self-actualization and transcendence, where transcendence means moving beyond the autopilot responses of our personality and the inauthentic edicts and demands of our cultural context (transcendence is not a spiritual thing). This principle also requires us to discover our *individual answer* to the four *collective existential questions of life.*

Four Key Questions

The universal nature of human emotions; the anatomical and operational similarities of the human organism; the biological purpose of the Somatic Instincts; the fact that life is an historical process of birth, infancy, adolescence, maturity, and death within space-and-time; and our concrete and symbolic experiences of these aspects of human existence, create the deep and abiding sense that *what is most personal, is most universal.* In the case of the four key questions of Empirical Existentialism, we aren't "taught" these questions of human existence, rather they emerge naturally, as do the self-evident conclusions that we come to about ourselves, others, and the world around us through the See-Do-Get Process and the creation of our personal paradigm. The four key questions are listed below.

- How do I find an identity?
- How do I face the future?
- How do I deal with the environment?
- How do I get the results that I want from my one-trip through life?

It is important to note that these four questions emerge in people who have allowed the path of their lives to be directed by the force-for-growth, self-actualization and transcendence, as well as those who have allowed their path to be directed by the force-for-safety and deficiency-motivation. In growth-motivated people, these four questions lead them on the Upward Path of Becoming where their lives are self-determined, authentic, reunited, autonomous, and trust-based. These same four questions lead those who are deficiency-driven on the Downward Spiral of Striving with lives that are compulsive, inauthentic, alienated, dependent, and fear-based.

While these questions and the conclusions that are associated with them emerge from the Symbolic-Level of the personal paradigm, each one has a wide spectrum of meanings depending on the level at which the question is addressed. The question, "How do I find an identity?" can include *external criteria* like physical appearance, an identification number used to establish a person's individuality, or a set of behavioral and personal characteristics by which a person is recognizable as a member of a specific group. Identity can also include *inner criteria* like a sense of self that distinguishes one person from others in terms of the sameness and continuity of an individual's personality, character, heart, and personal paradigm – how they "see" themselves, others, and the world. The question, "How do I face the future?" can include *external criteria* like dealing with the physical, financial, and relationship challenges of life and trying to age effectively. It can also include *inner criteria* like the fact that our future is contained within us in the sense of our actuality (who we currently are) and potentiality (who we could become). We can powerfully shape our own future by creating it daily through our choices.

The question, "How do I deal with the environment?" can include *external criteria* like the personal and professional challenges that we face day in and day out, navigating the edicts and demands of our culture, and remaining autonomous from people and situations that frustrate and undermine our desired path in life. It can also include *inner criteria* like having the inner force of will, courage, wisdom, and insight to deal effectively with the challenges we face in our personal and professional lives. Finally, the question, "How do I get the results that I want from my one-trip through life?" can include *external criteria* like achieving our personal, professional, financial, social, and cultural goals, accomplishments and aspirations. It can also include *inner criteria* like the desire and commitment to fully understand and utilize our talents, abilities, strengths, weaknesses; and the determination to allow the force-for-growth to lead us on the Upward Path of Becoming, self-actualization, and transcendence.

So given this summary explanation of Empirical Existentialism, let's return to some of the key questions mentioned earlier in this section. What are the nature and etiology of psychopathology and psychological health? Are psychopathology and neurosis a deficiency-disease that has naturalistic causes (as Maslow suggests), or are psychopathology and neurosis a deficiency-disorder that has metaphysical causes (as Naranjo suggests)? Are the causes of psychological health and self-actualization naturalistic, or are psychological health and self-actualization caused by reconnecting to metaphysical constructs like "being" and "essence"? While many people have the experience that "something's missing" in life, does this sense of "deficiency" arise naturalistically from the universal questions of human existence and our childhood and life experiences, or does it come from a lost connection between our psychological-biological self and metaphysical constructs like "being" and "essence"?[135] On our view, we answer these and similar questions as follows:

- We take a naturalistic view of the human mind, brain, and personality that rejects Platonic and Gnostic dualism and Naranjo's metaphysical map of the psyche. Neurosis and psychopathology are a deficiency disease from being deprived of the basic needs and esteem needs described on Maslow's Hierarchy (like a body craves salt).[136]

- The nagging sense that "something's missing" in life comes from a deficiency in not having our basic needs met (home-nurture, belonging, love, esteem of self and others) and a lack of Authenticity in Context.[137]
- The core problem of personality is that we look for the "key" to what's missing in the wrong place (through striving rather than becoming) as a way of avoiding the key existential questions in life.[138]

The concepts and principles of Empirical Existentialism provide a firm foundation upon which to build the Breckenridge Enneagram and a deep understanding of personality as a window into the human heart.

PERSONALITY, CHARACTER, AND THE HUMAN HEART

There were a number of personality typologies developed during the 1920s based on schools of thought that were prevalent in Europe at the end of the 18th Century. In addition, Gurdjieff's work during this time period was later shaped into the traditional model of the Enneagram by Ichazo in the 1950s and 1960s and Naranjo in the 1970s.[139] These parallel traditions were the intellectual context from which the modern discipline of personality type theories emerged as the six traditions listed below.[140]

- Jungian models
- Temperament models
- Primary emotions models
- Five-Factor model
- Circumplex model
- Traditional Enneagram models

But the tendency has been for each tradition to view their model as describing "the" human personality. Our view is that the totality of the human personality is greater than the sum of all possible personality typologies. More specifically, each of the traditions listed above explores a "slice" of our personality, character, and the human heart. An individual's *personality* is defined as the sum of their physical, mental, emotional, and social characteristics – their essential character. This includes organized patterns of action, interaction, and the quality of being a person with an existence – a self-conscious human being with a personal identity. We define a person's *character* as the aggregate of the qualities, traits, and features that distinguishes one person from another and makes that person unique. The *human heart* is the psychological center and unifying fabric of a person's thoughts, emotions, and volition which include the hidden (secret) thoughts, feelings, plans, attitudes, fears, hopes, dreams, and desires of an individual. The psychological model developed by the Breckenridge Institute® views the notions of personality, character, and the human heart as being embodied in an individual's *personal paradigm*, which is described in detail in the next section. Personality typologies like the Breckenridge Enneagram, traditional Enneagram models, Jungian type, Keirsey's four temperaments, the Five-Factor Model, and others are only sub-sets (slices) of the much broader psychic reality of the personal paradigm that are established by identifying and psychometrically validating underlying patterns, processes, and structures that exist within the overall context of an individual's personal paradigm.

The See-Do-Get Process and the Creation of Human Knowledge

We briefly discussed the See-Do-Get Process in Chapter 1. In this section, I'd like to describe it in more detail. The See-Do-Get Process is simple, yet profound. It's a way of describing how our knowledge and beliefs are shaped by how we see ourselves, others, and the world around us (see Figure 89). First, we see the world a certain way and specific behaviors and emotions naturally flow from that worldview because we believe that it is "reality." When we act these behaviors out in relationships, people read our body language and respond to the message they see in us. Their response then reinforces how we see them and create patterns-of-interaction in our relationships.

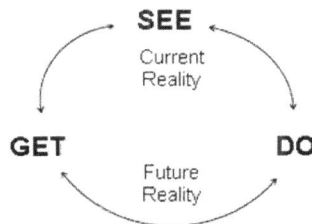

SEE
Current
Reality

GET   DO

Future
Reality

Figure 89

How we learn to "see" the world develops from our earliest years as our innate, inborn tendencies (our temperament) and our experiences and interactions with our environment build and accumulate underlying patterns of thinking, emotions, behavioral responses, biological needs and other characteristics that become what is commonly called our personality, character, or the human heart. Like the seed of a plant that has potentialities but needs good earth, water, and sun to develop, humans have innate tendencies that develop based on the context in which they live and grow. By the time we are two or three years old, these underlying patterns shape and define how we see ourselves, others, and the world around us. They become a *philosophy of life* that powerfully defines the kinds of people, relationships, and experiences to which we are attracted or repulsed, and over time these preferences shape our relationships, families, careers, and lifestyles. The development process is self-referential in that our expectations for how the world *is* powerfully shape our perceptions, so in many ways we "see" exactly what we expect to see – in other words, what you see is what you get. When the See-Do-Get Process runs clockwise, it supports, confirms, and provides additional evidence for our current view of reality. Through countless cycles of the See-Do-Get Process we come to believe that *our* way of seeing *is* reality – the way the world actually *is*.

We begin life as experientially unscripted, malleable creatures with the innate tendencies of our temperament that develop based on the context in which we grow. It's important to remember that children internalize about 93% of communications through emotional messages before they can speak a word because, as research has shown, 55% is visual (body language), 38% is aural (tone of voice), and only 7% is word choice. So our earliest experiences and interactions with our environment build and accumulate underlying patterns of biological needs, emotions, behavioral responses, and thinking that become a governing force in our personality, character, and hearts. The innate, inborn tendencies of our temperament are like the rows and columns in an Excel file that become filled-in with our own unique experiences. This happens through three kinds of learning experiences that powerfully define and shape who we are:

- *Active Teaching:* Active emotional confirmation, rejection, or disconfirmation by parents, family, and other caretakers create intra-psychic patterns-of-interaction in synaptic connections-configurations.

- *Tacit Teaching:* Parents, family, and other caretakers communicate tacit or unconscious emotional confirmation, rejection, or disconfirmation which also creates intra-psychic patterns-of-interaction in synaptic connections-configurations.

- *Cultural Teaching:* Wexler points out in his book, *Brain and Culture*, that the emotional confirmation, rejection, or disconfirmation by the cultural context also creates intra-psychic patterns-of-interaction in synaptic connections-configurations.[141]

But this cognitive efficiency is a double-edged sword. While the underlying patterns free up the psychological energy we need to live our lives, they can become *too* automatic and ultimately self-defeating. They become *Tacit Creeds* that we live by; e.g., unquestioned assumptions and autopilot responses to people and life. For example, one child slowly develops the Tacit Creed "I must be powerful" where he believes that he must dominate the people and situations around him. Another child develops the Tacit Creed "I must be malleable" where she believes that she should go along with others and not rock the boat.

Countless cycles through the See-Do-Get Process deepen the conviction that the view of the world that we have through the lens of our dominant Tacit Creed is actually reality. To quote Maslow once again, "He who is good with a hammer thinks everything is a nail." When we unpack the autopilot operation of the See-Do-Get Process, we discover four distinct, but related autopilot steps that are shown in Figure 90.[142] Let's examine how the four steps happen on autopilot – *in the blink of an eye*.

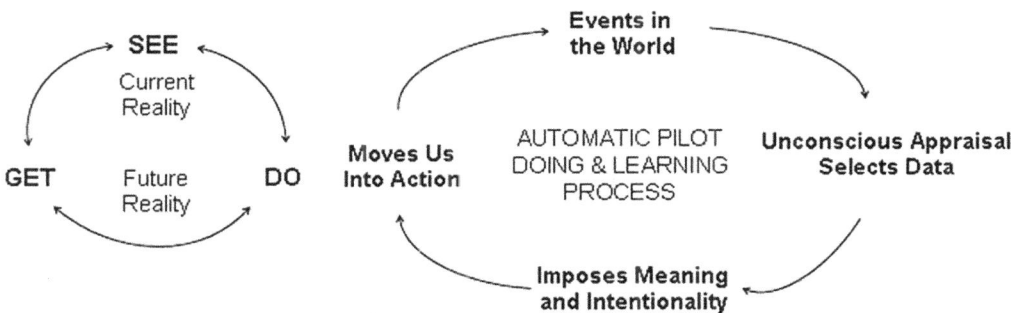

Figure 90

As mentioned in Chapter 1, the interactions between us and others could be recorded with a video camera. Video cameras don't have a personality and don't interpret or impose meaning on situations – they record events as they actually are. Second, when a person has the Tacit Creed (I must be perfect) they are hyper-sensitive to identifying mistakes in themselves and others, so they unconsciously select a small sub-set of data from the total events in the world. These data are selected again and again, regardless of how often others occur, or even how important other data are to the total picture. That's because they have special meaning and significance; e.g., they match the underlying patterns of his way of "seeing" himself, others, and the world, and allow the person to feel more comfortable in a world of constant and frenetic change. Third, we impose meaning and intentionality on what others do; e.g., we automatically interpret the actions of others through the autobiographical lens of *our* dominant Tacit Creed and the broader structures of our personal paradigm. Fourth, personality produces behaviors and emotional responses that have been shaped by, and naturally flow from underlying patterns, often against our best intentions to act otherwise. With most people, all four steps happen on autopilot, without conscious thought or intention – *in the blink of an eye*.

Think about it – a single mom "sees" her child as an unwanted intrusion on her busy life, and then wonders why her kid always gets into trouble. High school teachers "see" students as lazy and unmotivated, then wonder why they drop out. A family "sees" their oldest son as a loser who'll never go anywhere in life, then can't understand why he can't keep a job. You "see" your boss as a moron, and then wonder why he never assigns you to more interesting projects.

The See-Do-Get Process and Thomas Kuhn

The See-Do-Get Process is a simple way to operationalize the work of Thomas Kuhn on paradigms, paradigm shifts, and the creation of human knowledge in his ground-breaking book, *The Structure of Scientific Revolutions*.[143] More importantly for our topic, the See-Do-Get Process is the causal mechanism for the formation of our personal paradigm; e.g., personality, character, and the human heart. In this section, we'll describe Kuhn's model of paradigms and paradigm shifts in scientific activities, and then show how the structure and dynamics of paradigms and paradigm shifts apply to individuals.

The notion of a paradigm comes from the Greek word *paradigma*, which appeared in English in the 15th Century and means a pattern, set of patterns, model, or exemplar. For Kuhn a paradigm is an interdependent-matrix of scientific theories; empirical evidence; scientific tools; instrumentation; measurement methods; beliefs; commitments to specific interpretations of natural phenomena; professional affiliations; and social-and-professional-norms that define "what counts" as being competent in a particular scientific discipline. Students are indoctrinated into a specific way of "seeing" the scientific work conducted within that disciplinary paradigm and their role as a member of that scientific community through their training in college and graduate school, college textbooks, journal publications, and throughout their careers by affiliation with professional societies. The indoctrination of students into a scientific paradigm powerfully shapes how they see themselves, others, and the world through the See-Do-Get Process. So whether we're talking about engineers, physicians, lawyers, film producers, airline pilots, professional athletes, researchers in the physical, biological, and social sciences, or myriad other professions; what it means to become (and remain) a competent member of any disciplinary community is uniquely defined by their paradigm; and new members are indoctrinated into that community-of-practice through the See-Do-Get Process.

Think about a paradigm as an interpretive "lens" that can be used to explain the causes of situations in life. Imagine you're watching two people having an argument. If you pick up a Freudian lens (or Freudian paradigm) and view the argument through that lens, you might conclude that the people are arguing because they are intrinsically bad; e.g., they have Ids that are in conflict with each other. If you were to put that lens aside and pick up a Skinnerian lens, a behaviorist paradigm, and view the same argument through that lens, you might conclude that the people were arguing because they were conditioned to behave that way. Then if you were to put that lens aside and pick up a Rogerian lens, a client-centered therapy paradigm, you might conclude that the people were arguing because they did not grow up in warm supportive environments. If you were to put that lens aside and pick up an E.O. Wilson socio-biological paradigm and view the argument through that lens, you conclude that the people were like two bucks fighting in a field because of a biological reaction to competition. So how we "see" the world, how we interpret the situations that happen around us, and in a sense what reality means to us and how we view reality, is largely a factor of the paradigm or the interpretive lens through which we see ourselves, others, and the world.

One of the key concepts that Kuhn developed for his notion of paradigms was anomalies. Anomalies were phenomena that emerged and couldn't be explained using the existing paradigm. For example Ptolemy's view of the solar system had difficulty explaining the retrograde motion of certain planets (Venus and Mercury). So he accommodated this anomaly by developing circles and epicycles that turned upon other circles and epicycles. Eventually, scientific theories like the one Ptolemy created become so complicated and unaesthetic that scientists know that they can't be right because nature is more elegant than that. This principle of economy, parsimony, and simplicity in scientific theories (called Ocskham's Razor) means that with all other things being equal the simplest solution is normally the best.

The mechanism that Kuhn used to explain changes in paradigms and the creation of new knowledge was the notion of *dialectic*; e.g., thesis versus antithesis equals synthesis. For Kuhn a scientific community's paradigm serves as its thesis – a scientific model for how the world works. As the number of anomalies in a paradigm increases, some scientists, especially the younger ones, begin to question the paradigm's validity, and they begin to construct alternative explanations of the same natural phenomena. As more and more scientists are drawn to this alternative paradigm, it becomes an antithesis to the reigning paradigm in the sense of the thesis versus antithesis equals synthesis formulation shown below.

Thesis-Paradigm versus Antithesis-Paradigm = Synthesis (New Paradigm)

The thesis-paradigm and antithesis-paradigm battle it out in professional journals and talks given at scientific meetings and eventually a synthesis emerges, which ultimately becomes the new reigning paradigm for that scientific discipline. Kuhn called this dialectic mechanism a *scientific revolution*. A scientific revolution occurs when a new paradigm emerges that can explain all the existing scientific data *and* the anomalies in a way that is more precise and reliable than the previous paradigm for that scientific discipline. One example might be the way Copernican astronomy was able to explain everything that Ptolemaic astronomy could, and at the same time provide a systematic explanation for things that the Ptolemaic model could not explain, such as the retrograde motion of certain planets.

As a scientific revolution progresses, more and more scientists and graduate students are converted to the new way of "seeing" the natural world and the experiments that they begin to design and perform are meant to test the parameters of the new paradigm. In other words, scientists "see" the world through the lens of the new paradigm and design ways to test that way of seeing. If the world actually behaves (do) in the way predicted by the new paradigm and scientists "get" the result they anticipate, this reinforces the way of "seeing" inherent in the new paradigm. As empirical evidence from experiments and theoretical calculations of the new model converge and align, the scientific validity of the new paradigm is established to higher and higher levels of reliability. Kuhn points out that every paradigm contains the seed of its own destruction in the form of hidden anomalies – mathematical and empirical descriptions of physical phenomena that do not "map" to how the physical world actually behaves. On this view, the creation of reliable knowledge about the world is the result of a never-ending series of successive approximations that emerge as paradigms morph into new paradigms and move the frontier of scientific knowledge forward.

See-Do-Get Process and Personal Paradigm

In much the same way, the See-Do-Get Process is the mechanism by which our personal paradigm is formed, grows, and is changed. As Stephen R. Covey states, "We see the world as we are, not as it is." In other words, we see the world through our *personal paradigm* – meaning our education, our family upbringing, national and ethnic culture, life experiences, professional training, our personality, character, and our hearts. As children we are indoctrinated by parents, family, friends, and the broader socio-cultural context in which we are raised through the See-Do-Get Process. Our personal paradigm becomes the lens through which we see ourselves, others, and the world around us. In fact, when we are finally old enough to realize that we *have* a personal paradigm, it's too late to have a hand in fashioning it. Who we are has already been largely defined by our innate, inborn tendencies (our temperament) interacting with our environment through experiences that teach us how to see ourselves, others, and the world through the See-Do-Get Process. In other words, our personality, character, and heart have already been powerfully defined and shaped by the time we're five or six years old.

As with scientific disciplines, the key elements of knowledge creation and changes in our personal paradigm are *anomalies* and *dialectic*. Anomalies can be any kind of challenge to how we "see" the world that cannot be explained using our personal paradigm: someone who disagrees with our position in a meeting; a relationship gone bad; interpersonal conflict with a boss or working associate; a difference between your view of your professional abilities and how management sees them; a positive life-altering experience; a negative life-altering experience; moving up the corporate ladder; or achieving a lifetime goal. In other words, an anomaly is anything that challenges us to "see" ourselves, others, and the world in ways that are different than we currently do. Most people have a degree of psychological elasticity, so when small anomalies are encountered in day-to-day life they can confirm, reject, disconfirm, absorb, or assimilate new knowledge and new ways of "seeing" even though they may be inconsistent with the knowledge, beliefs, and assumptions of their personal paradigm. In fact, intellectual, emotional, and experiential learning requires anomalies; e.g., without anomalies there is no intellectual, psychological, emotional or experiential growth.

Our personal paradigm organizes and explains the world, and enables us to develop the problem-solving and decision-making abilities needed to navigate life's situations. Our personal paradigm is our personality, character – our human heart. But sometimes, our interpretations of ourselves, others, and the world don't seem to fit, or we don't get the results we expect or the results we want. We experience these anomalies as stress, pressure, and cognitive dissonance. Our ability to effectively deal with anomalies depends on how *deeply* they challenge the foundations of our personal paradigm and our level of elasticity. When we encounter radically different new knowledge or key moments in our one-trip through life, these profound experiences set up a *dialectic* that can challenge us to the core of our being and reconfigure our personal paradigm in significant ways. When we find ourselves under pressure, or when we face embarrassment or threat, the paradigm's state-of-equilibrium can become destabilized and we experience this psychologically as stress, anxiety, and cognitive dissonance. The larger the number of elements disturbed by the anomaly, the more destabilized our paradigm's state-of-equilibrium becomes, and the more intense the stress, anxiety, and cognitive dissonance we experience. More specifically, our existing way of seeing ourselves, others, and the world functions as our thesis-paradigm as shown below, with the new (conflicting or contradictory) way of "seeing" acting as the antithesis-paradigm in the dialectic.

> Thesis-Paradigm versus Antithesis-Paradigm = Synthesis (New Paradigm)

The process shown above is often an "outer" dialectic when we encounter people, relationships, structures, systems, socio-cultural norms with views that differ from ours. Over time, if the number of anomalies that we experience in life becomes large enough, and if we're not getting the results we want in our lives, we begin to experience an "inner" existential dialectic where alternative, competing, or contradictory ways of seeing, battle it out in our hearts and minds. Much like its counterpart in scientific communities, this *inner revolution* can create intense stress, enormous pressure, and high levels of cognitive dissonance. Given enough time, inner theses and antitheses that are not significantly different often resolve themselves into a new synthesis. We experience this new synthesis as a Gestalt shift or what's commonly called an "Aha" moment of insight. Often this kind of deep personal change or personal paradigm shift happens to us when we least expect it. We wake up one day, see things differently, and wonder how we could ever have held our previous point of view. This becomes our new personal paradigm, which is increasingly confirmed by mounting empirical evidence through the See-Do-Get Process. So much like Kuhn's claim that scientists are "converted" to new scientific paradigms and subsequently use their new knowledge to measure, explore, analyze, and manipulate natural phenomena, individuals are "converted" to embrace new personal paradigms based on what they have learned from others, or by "inner conversions" that reflect deeper and more profound ways of seeing and exploring their one-trip through life.

But like their scientific counterparts, personal paradigms contain the seeds of their own destruction because how we "see" ourselves, others, and the world through the See-Do-Get Process is constantly challenged by other ways of seeing, and by the way the world really is independent of how we see it. Change and conflict in life are an inevitable and necessary part of learning, growth, and psychological health. In fact, the amount of *elasticity* with which a person can absorb and assimilate anomalies into their personal paradigm, can be a powerful indicator of their level of intellectual and emotional development, and their level of psychological health. The issue is not whether people have paradigmatic-conflict from outer and inner dialectics in their lives. Rather, the issue is whether that conflict is experienced as either constructive or destructive, and how well an individual handles the stress, pressure, and cognitive dissonance during the dialectic process that creates personal paradigm shifts. Not only is learning, growth, and the creation of new knowledge and insight a result of paradigm shifts, but obtaining more *reliable* knowledge about the world is a never-ending series of successive approximations where our personal paradigm morphs and transforms into more reliable ways of seeing ourselves, others, and the world around us. In fact, Maslow's notion of walking the path of *striving-and-safety* is typified by people who resist the stress, pressure, and cognitive dissonance required in paradigm shifts by struggling to maintain the configuration of their personal paradigm *at all costs*. Those who walk the path of *growth-and-becoming* know that new and increasingly reliable knowledge, beliefs, and wisdom come only from consciously tolerating the traumatic experiences associated with anomalies, dialectics, and personal paradigm shifts.

The Structure of the Personal Paradigm

So the See-Do-Get Process and the personal paradigms that emerge from day-to-day life are much more complex than a description of our Enneagram type, our Jungian type, our Temperament, our DiSC type, or the combined multitude of all other personality typologies and psychological models. The Breckenridge Enneagram is not a complete "map" or taxonomy of the personality, character, human heart, or the human psyche, as some traditional Enneagram writers claim. The Breckenridge Enneagram and the BTI help us identify a "slice" of the overall complexity of our hearts and minds by identifying a "needle" of underlying patterns, processes, and structures within the "haystack" of our personal paradigm. This becomes clear once we begin the task of establishing *where* the knowledge, beliefs, cognitive processes, and emotions that constitute our personal paradigm "happen" in the human brain and overall organism, because if they don't happen physically, then *they do not happen at all* – they're not *real* in the sense defined by the principles of Empirical Existentialism. Figure 91 shows the structure and dynamics of the personal paradigm.

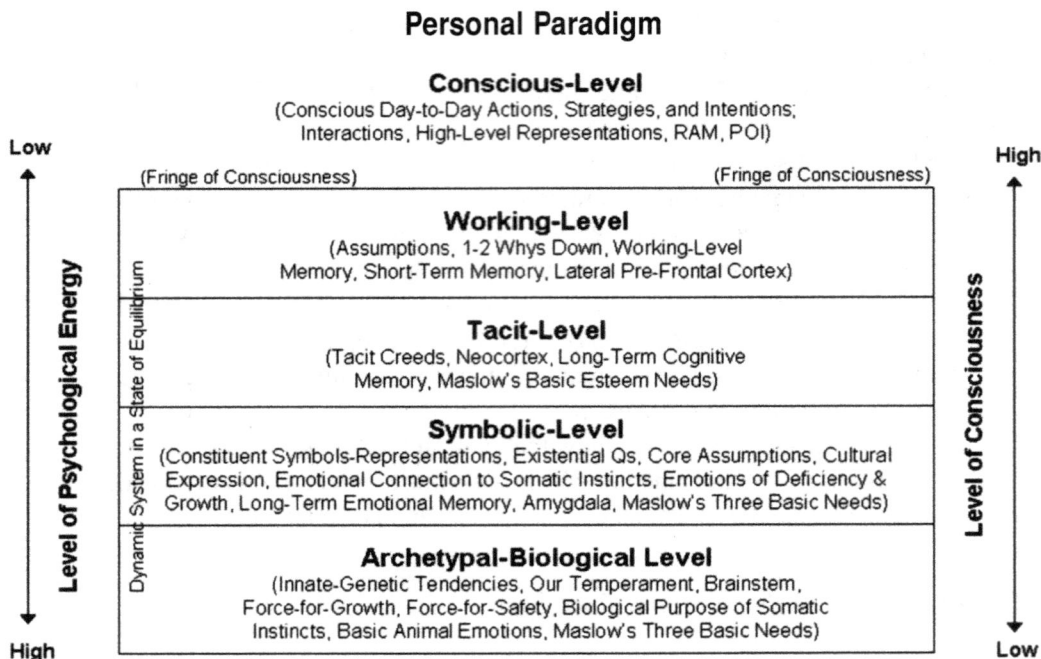

Personal Paradigm

Conscious-Level
(Conscious Day-to-Day Actions, Strategies, and Intentions;
Interactions, High-Level Representations, RAM, POI)

Low

High

(Fringe of Consciousness)   (Fringe of Consciousness)

Level of Psychological Energy

Dynamic System in a State of Equilibrium

Level of Consciousness

Working-Level
(Assumptions, 1-2 Whys Down, Working-Level
Memory, Short-Term Memory, Lateral Pre-Frontal Cortex)

Tacit-Level
(Tacit Creeds, Neocortex, Long-Term Cognitive
Memory, Maslow's Basic Esteem Needs)

Symbolic-Level
(Constituent Symbols-Representations, Existential Qs, Core Assumptions, Cultural
Expression, Emotional Connection to Somatic Instincts, Emotions of Deficiency &
Growth, Long-Term Emotional Memory, Amygdala, Maslow's Three Basic Needs)

Archetypal-Biological Level
(Innate-Genetic Tendencies, Our Temperament, Brainstem,
Force-for-Growth, Force-for-Safety, Biological Purpose of Somatic
Instincts, Basic Animal Emotions, Maslow's Three Basic Needs)

High

Low

Figure 91

Notice how the level of consciousness on the right side of Figure 91 goes from high to low and the line across the top of Figure 91 indicates the fringe of consciousness – the surface of conscious awareness. In practical terms, this means that knowledge and beliefs that exist at the Tacit, Symbolic, and Archetypal Levels are much less accessible to day-to-day awareness even though they are fully present in various parts of the brain. As indicated on the left side of Figure 91, the five levels exist as an interdependent-dynamic system that settles down on a state-of-equilibrium based on their respective contents, with the level of psychological energy becoming higher and more intense as a function of psychic depth. The structure of the personal paradigm can be described metaphorically like the geological strata of the earth, where the deeper the knowledge and belief reside, the older they probably are. The personal paradigm structure can also be compared to a psychological "house" with the Tacit, Symbolic, and Archetypal Levels acting as the oldest and deepest foundation of our knowledge and beliefs – the unquestioned, taken-for-granted basis of our day-to-day actions, interactions, strategies, and intentions. It is important to note that the knowledge and beliefs that reside at the Tacit, Symbolic, and Archetypal Levels form the basis of our personality, character, and heart because they are often conclusions that we came to about ourselves, others, and the world by the time we were five or six years old. The Conscious and Working-Levels are what we have described as the Socialized-Self – that part of our personal identity that morphs to meet the demands and edicts of the socio-culture context that we're in. Let's explore each of the five levels in more detail.

Conscious-Level: This is the arena of conscious day-to-day actions, strategies, intentions, and interactions between ourselves, others, and the world, including patterns-of-interaction (POI) that develop between ourselves and others. Level-1 is about conscious awareness – what's in our minds *right now*.

Working-Level: Working-Level Memory is the platform from which awareness and consciousness emerge. In other words, consciousness is an awareness of the contents that get pieced together and reside in Working-Level Memory. This is one of the most sophisticated and complex functions of the human brain.[144] So our conscious experience of ourselves, others, and the world is the emergent result of algorithms, heuristics, and combinatorial functions performed by Working-Level Memory using data, information, cognitive and emotional beliefs, and assumptions from all parts of the human organism; e.g., Levels 2-5 on Figure 91.[145] Consciousness receives the *results* of these mental computations as high-level representations (symbols) that are created below the surface of awareness at Levels 2-5. So we are only consciously aware of the *outcome* of the mental computations, not the computations themselves. Chris Argyris and Peter Senge referred to this below the surface processing as the "ladder of inference."[146] Direct observation of these mental computations using: a) introspection, b) observation of Red Flags from the Spectator Role, c) external feedback from other people and the world, and d) analysis of long-term trends in our personal history, allows us to begin exploring and understanding the mental computations of personality that occur below the surface of consciousness at Levels 2-5.

Tacit-Level: The Tacit-Level contains knowledge and beliefs that have gone on autopilot, slipped below the surface of consciousness and exist as unquestioned, taken-for-granted assumptions that powerfully shape and motivate behavior. The Tacit Creeds for the nine Enneagram types are at Level-3 (Tacit-Level) and are like an overall philosophy of life that defines how people see themselves, others, and the world around them. While Tacit Creeds are a cognitive-cluster of beliefs and assumptions, they emerge from the interdependent functioning of all parts of the brain and organism, and are related to the three groups of personality types (Head, Heart, and Action). So while the Tacit Creeds for the heart types are a cognitive-cluster of beliefs and assumptions, these three Enneagram types tend to "lead" with the emotional-part of their being, with the neuropsychological functions of the Head and Action Groups playing key support roles. In much the same way, the head types tend to "lead" with the cognitive-rational-part of their being, with the neuropsychological functions of the Heart and Action Groups playing key support roles. And the Action types tend to "lead" with the action-oriented-part of their being, with the neuropsychological functions of the Head and Heart Groups playing key support roles. Level-3 is also the part of our belief structure that corresponds to the esteem needs on Maslow's Hierarchy, how we "see" or esteem ourselves and others, and how they "see" or esteem us in return.

The neocortex region of the brain is a Level-3 function and exists only in mammals. It is most developed in humans where it contains an estimated 100 billion cells (each with up to 10,000 synapses) and roughly 100 million yards of wiring all packed into a structure the size and thickness of a formal dinner napkin.[147] The cells in the neocortex are arranged in six layers and form the center of higher mental functions for humans such as sensory perception; generation of motor commands; spatial reasoning; high-level analytic and cognitive reasoning; and complex language processes. These cognitive functions powerfully shape our ability to model, represent, understand, and ultimately control much of what goes on in our world, and to navigate our way into the future. In many ways, who we are *cognitively* reveals something very deep about who we are as human beings *regardless* of what our dominant Enneagram type is. The ability to evaluate, analyze, and map-out the patterns, processes, and structures in our world is *universal* and Head types are tuned-in to the constant mental activity (and endless cognitive processing) that typifies this part of the human experience.

It is important to note that the use of the word "preference" as a metaphor to describe what personality type *is* can be misleading when thought of as being a *conscious* preference rather than an *unconscious* preference that emerges from the Tacit-Level in Figure 91. Experientially, our personality type *happens to us* from Levels 2 through 5 and is not a moment-by-moment choosing between options. In other words, because beliefs and assumptions at the Tacit-Level are largely unexamined, unquestioned, and taken-for-granted, they tend to manifest themselves in day-to-day actions and interactions at Level-1 and Level-2 in subtle, but profound ways that *are not* conscious "preferences" and represent a loss of freedom-of-choice and self-determination. More specifically, these unconscious preferences create decision-making bias and predictable errors in judgment in strategic and tactical decisions (and choices) in ways defined by the See-Do-Get Process. These tacit, unconscious beliefs and assumptions are also expressed in the choices that people make when answering the questions on the BTI survey. This allows the BTI to measure the characteristics of the Tacit Creed with high precision. The implications of the choices made when answering the BTI questions can be clarified to a high level of confidence by one-on-one verbal assessment during the self-discovery and type verification process

Symbolic-Level: The underlying emotions for deficiency-drivers and growth-motivators associated with the nine Tacit Creeds are at Level-4 (the Symbolic-Level). Level-4 is also the arena for the four existential questions, constituent symbols-representations, and the residue (abstracts) of long term emotional memory in the Amygdala. The cultural expression and emotional connection to the Somatic Instincts are related to Level-4; e.g., the first three levels of Maslow's Hierarchy. The parallel processing and interaction between multiple parts of the brain that occur at Level-4 and higher are performed using representational building blocks (symbols) and are not directly accessible from Level-1 conscious awareness, although the information contained in many dreams are a window into this deep level of processing.

The major center of the emotional brain (the Amygdala) is an almond shaped mass of nuclei located deep within the human brain that appraises situations from an emotional perspective and stores that information in long-term emotional memory as a Level-4 function. More specifically, long-term memories about key situations in life are not formed immediately, (rather) the Amygdala slowly and unconsciously summarizes and assimilates that information into long-term memory as a kind-of-emotional-abstract (or lesson-learned) about that action, interaction, or situation. This emotional-summary becomes a fairly-fixed and permanent part of our recollections about key events in our lives that powerfully defines and shapes how we see ourselves, others, and the world through the See-Do-Get Process. Emotional memory also defines and shapes our personal history, view of life, and our personal identity. In many ways, who we are emotionally (in our hearts) reveals something very deep about who we are as human beings *regardless* of what our dominant Enneagram type is. Neurophysiologic research and studies on the nature of emotions have shown that human emotions are *universal* and can be identified by the facial expressions and body language that people display. Emotions from the emotional-brain at the Symbolic-Level are experienced by all people, in all times, in all cultures; but the heart-types are especially tuned-in to the constant ebb-and-flow of this part of the human experience. While research has shown that these basic emotions are universal, the things that changes from culture-to-culture are the rules for expressing and displaying those emotions.

Archetypal-Biological Level: This is the level which is the biological-psychological interface – where the sandwich you ate for lunch becomes your best ideas in the afternoon. At Level-5 we encounter the biological purpose of the Somatic Instincts (Maslow's first three levels), the Brainstem and our basic animal emotions. Level-5 is also the main arena where our innate, inborn genetic tendencies and temperament reside. The innate aspects of our Enneagram type reside in the innate tendencies of our temperament. It should be noted that I am applying the word "temperament" here in the common use of the word – meaning the combination of cognitive, emotional, sensory, and motivational aspects of human beings that is their innate, inborn disposition toward being who they really are. Or put another way, our temperament is the genetic, biologically inherited foundation from which our personality, character, and heart emerge over time. I am not using the word "temperament" in the sense that David Keirsey used it to mean a specific typology of four temperaments. Rather, our "temperament" is the psycho-biological part of the human organism from which our Enneagram type, Jungian type, and Keirsey's four temperaments emerge.[148]

All sensory information from the body that goes to the other parts of the brain must first traverse the brainstem which provides neurological control for functions that are necessary for survival such as, breathing, digestion, heart rate, blood pressure, and arousal. The brainstem also plays a crucial role in maintaining alertness and generating the *capacity* for conscious awareness; where the capacity for consciousness is not the same thing as the sensory *content* of consciousness, which is thought (by most researchers) to be in the lateral-prefrontal cortex (Level-2 Working-Level Memory). In other words, the functions of the brainstem create the essential *precondition* for conscious awareness, and without a functioning brainstem there is no meaningful activity in the higher parts of the brain – no cognitive or emotional life, no sensory activity, no thoughts or feelings, no introspection and no social interaction with the environment. Our sensory experience of our bodies and what's going on in the world around us powerfully shapes our physical sense of self. In many ways, who we are *corporeally* reveals something very deep about who we are as human beings *regardless* of what our dominant Enneagram type is. These bodily functions (and our experience of them) are *universal* and are experienced by all people, in all times, in all cultures; and the Action-types are tuned-in to the constant flow of sensory stimulus because of their connection to their own bodies and the immediate context of what's going on in the world, where things are happening, and who's involved in doing them.

The Formation of Personal Paradigm

Our approach to the formation of the personal paradigm has an interdependent focus on both innate-inborn and contextual factors where the formation of personality is both: a) an *inside-out* process where innate, inborn tendencies (our temperament) predispose us to behaviors and emotional responses through which we try to influence others, and b) an *outside-in* process where people, organizations, social structures, and the culture we grow up in teach us how to see ourselves, others, and the world through the See-Do-Get Process. The Breckenridge Change Equation™ describes the actual mechanism by which our personal paradigm is formed from infancy through childhood.

Breckenridge Change Equation

$$POI \leftrightarrow CCI \leftrightarrow ROI \times EOI = Desired\ Results™$$

Here's how the five elements of the Breckenridge Change Equation work together to create our personal paradigm. Children are born into a socio-cultural context, and myriad day-to-day patterns-of-interactions (POI) occur between the child, parents, caretakers, and others at the family, social, and cultural levels of the context-of-interaction (COI), both of which occur at Level-1 of the personal paradigm (see Figure 91). Over time, the interaction of POI and COI functions like a socio-psychological learning process that creates a repository-of-interaction (ROI) that begins to form the content of the child's personal paradigm at the Working, Tacit, Symbolic, and Archetypal Levels. Through the embedding mechanisms and repetition (EOI), these first three elements of the equation settle-down on a state-of-equilibrium and the configuration of the ROI begins to solidify and becomes the content of the child's personal paradigm. The first four elements work together to create the desired results, which is a combination of the results that the *child* wants and the desired results of *others* at the family, social, or cultural levels. During the first few years of life, the Desired Results in the equation become a self-referential "social mirror" that is created initially by the actions and interactions of the child within their context. Over time, the edicts and demands of that social mirror become *objectified* and then *reified* as the child's "reality" – the way the world is. The Breckenridge Change Equation also "maps" to the See-Do-Get Process.

- See = ROI
- Do = POI, COI, EOI
- Get = Desired Results

Over time, our deep beliefs and assumptions emerge as the *indirect* product of countless interactions between POI and COI that slip below the surface of consciousness and become tacit and symbolic assumptions. Deep beliefs are inextricably bound to our actions and interactions with the world and they seem to happen *to us*. They emerge naturally from the unconscious "emotional scoreboard" of actions and interactions, they operate on autopilot as tacit and symbolic assumptions that powerfully shape and direct our conscious actions and interactions without us consciously knowing it (in the blink of an eye).

As Bruce Wexler (neuroscientist, psychiatrist, and professor of psychiatry at Yale Medical School) argues in his ground-breaking book, *Brain and Culture*, the power of our socio-cultural context to shape our personal paradigm should not be underestimated.[149] After reviewing the neuropsychological research on how powerfully a child's environment actually shapes the synaptic structures of their brain during the first years of life, Wexler expands the notion of the "environment" to include the broader influences of the human-created environments that we call culture. He argues that "culture" actually shapes the human brain and our natural instincts to a degree that is unprecedented among other animals. Wexler states that it is this ability to shape our environment that in turn shapes our brains and natural instincts, and that has allowed human adaptability and capability to develop at a much faster rate than is possible through mutation of the genetic code alone. This trans-generational shaping of our brain-functions and natural instincts through culture also means that processes that govern the evolution of societies and cultures have a great influence on how our individual brains, minds, and instincts work and express themselves. In much the same way, the process of cultural imprinting on the malleable hearts and minds of children is so powerful that we learn to see ourselves, others, and the world around us through the lens of ethnic cultural norms by the time we are seven years old.[150]

The personal paradigm becomes a self-referential "social mirror" that gets *objectified* and then *reified* as "reality" – the way the world *is* through the See-Do-Get Process. Over time, the configuration of the personal paradigm solidifies and can be described using the Breckenridge Equation shown below.

Breckenridge Equation

POI ←→ COI ←→ ROI = Current Results™

Notice that the embedding-of-interaction (EOI) does not appear in the Breckenridge Equation because our way of "seeing" ourselves, others, and the world has gone on autopilot, slipped below the surface of awareness, and has become a self-reinforcing mechanism through the See-Do-Get Process. As shown below, the Breckenridge Equation also "maps" to the See-Do-Get Process.

- See = ROI
- Do = POI and COI
- Get = Current Results

The four terms of the Breckenridge Equation codify the common-sense intuition that our lives are perfectly aligned to get the results we get. What is also important to note is that these two equations can also be used to describe the mechanisms by which family, organizational, regional, and national culture are created, solidified, objectified, reified, and ultimately changed.[151]

The See-Do-Get Process, Personal Paradigm, and the Socialized Self

This section describes the difference between the Socialized-Self and the Natural-Self, which in many ways is associated with the nature-nurture question. The nature-nurture question asks "To what extent are the characteristics of our personality innate and genetic, and to what extent are they learned and socialized?"

Socialized-Self and Natural-Self

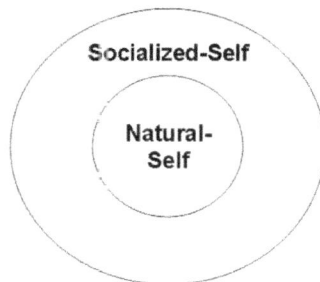

Socialized-Self

Natural-Self

Figure 92

Notice that the center circle of Figure 92 is labeled as our *Natural-Self*. This is the part of our personality that includes behaviors and cognitive or emotional responses that are on autopilot, *regardless* of whether they are innate or learned. The Natural-Self "maps" to the Tacit, Symbolic, and Archetypal Levels of the personal paradigm shown in Figure 91. Our Natural-Self is the part of who we are that happens *to us*; e.g., it occurs "naturally" on autopilot. But there are many situations in which behaving out of our Natural-Self would be inappropriate and would have negative consequences socially, so we act out of our *Socialized-Self*, which is shown as the outer circle of Figure 92. The Socialized-Self "maps" to the Conscious-Level and the Working-Level of the personal paradigm shown in Figure 91. This is the part of our personality that includes conscious, intentional behaviors and emotional responses that have been *shaped* or *required* by our context or environment. Actions and inter-action that come from the Socialized-Self are much more conscious and inten-tional so we can morph our behaviors and emotional responses to "fit" a specific social setting, but the essential elements of our Natural-Self remain unchanged despite these on-the-surface alterations to our behaviors. On this view, we *have* a personal paradigm that is composed of both innate and learned elements that are embodied in the Natural-Self, and paradigm elements that have been *created* over time by the conscious, intentional actions of the Socialized-Self interacting with the environment.

So to address the nature-nurture question more directly, whether a personality characteristic is innate (and hardwired) or *learned* (and socialized) are just *two dif-ferent conduits into the same synaptic registers*. Whether one of my personality traits is innate, or whether I learned it by the time I was two years old is almost impossible to distinguish empirically with any precision. In fact, I have talked to five-year-old children who can hardly remember when they were two years old; so what hope do adults have of performing this type of historical reconstruction with any accuracy? Therefore, the fact that both innate and learned characteristics are simply two different conduits into the same synaptic registers makes any hard-and-fast distinction between nature and nurture operationally and pragmatically mean-ingless.

The concept of the Socialized and Natural-Self, the See-Do-Get Process, and the five levels of the personal paradigm can also be used to describe actions and inter-actions that manifest themselves in the day-to-day activities of our personal and professional lives. In Figure 93, notice how the Socialized-Self is associated with the Action Strategy – our conscious intentions and strategies to see differently and do differently, which is connected to the *Learning Loop*. This is Level-1 (Con-scious-Level) of the personal paradigm shown in Figure 91. The Natural-Self is associated with the Tacit, Symbolic, and Archetypal Levels of the personal para-digm, which includes the Tacit Creed and our Enneagram type, and which can either be deficiency-driven or growth-motivated, and is connected to the *Unlearn-ing Loop*.

Socialized-Self and Natural-Self

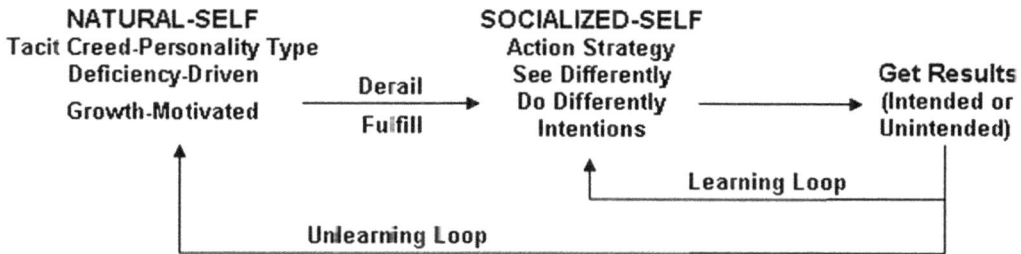

NATURAL-SELF
Tacit Creed-Personality Type
Deficiency-Driven
Growth-Motivated

Derail
Fulfill

SOCIALIZED-SELF
Action Strategy
See Differently
Do Differently
Intentions

Get Results
(Intended or
Unintended)

Learning Loop

Unlearning Loop

Figure 93

When the differential pressure between: a) the social-norms and requirements of our context, and b) our Natural-Self become strong enough, our Natural-Self will begin to "punch through" and increasingly derail the conscious intentions and action-strategy of the Socialized-Self. However, when our Natural-Self is *aligned* with our Socialized-Self, we get a deep sense of fulfillment because the majority of our actions-and-interactions are consistent with the deeper levels of our personal paradigm. In other words, Figure 93 is just another way of formulating and describing the principles associated with the See-Do-Get Process and the five-leveled structure of the personal paradigm.

INTEGRITY, TRUST, AND BECOMING CONSCIOUS OF THE UNCONSCIOUS

This section discusses some of the foundations and principles that provide a broader context for understanding the Breckenridge Enneagram in more practical ways. The four main areas of discussion are: a) Personal Integrity, b) Trust as the Foundation of Individual and Organizational Relationships, c) Surfacing and Managing Conflict, and d) Becoming Conscious of the Unconscious (Red Flags).

Personal Integrity

The principle of *personal integrity* is a key aspect of applying the Breckenridge Enneagram to day-to-day life. We are not using the term "integrity" in the sense of adhering to a moral code or a set of ethical principles. Rather, having personal integrity means that an individual is undivided (whole) in terms of the "mapping" between what they say about themselves and what they actually do. In other words, people who exemplify personal integrity in the sense we're using it here have a deep congruence between the things they *espouse* or claim about themselves and the actions and interactions that they actually live out in day-to-day life. The degree to which an individual has personal integrity is indicated by the Say-Do gap of duplicity; e.g., how wide the "gap" is between what people say and what they do. Personal integrity is not reflected as a perfect one-to-one mapping between Say-Do, rather it is reflected in a deep commitment to course-correction. To use a metaphor, planes that fly between cities are technically off-course about 90% of the time – just slightly off course. In most modern jets, the pilot sets a vector for the city they're flying to in the plane's computer, and then a computerized feedback system adjusts the plane's course when it deviates because of changes in wind and other factors. This course correction brings the plane back onto its plotted trajectory countless times during a flight. In much the same way, personal integrity is a commitment to course correction that enables us to course-correct the actions and interactions in our personal and professional lives – when what we say does not match our actual behavior. Having the self-awareness required to see ourselves *objectively* and catch ourselves in the act of acting in ways that are inconsistent with what we espouse about ourselves, is the necessary first step to developing a foundation of personal integrity and a commitment to course correction.

Trust as the Foundation of Individual and Organizational Relationships

Let's begin by discussing trust as the foundation of individual relationships, because trust in relationships is built through personal integrity and a commitment to course correction; e.g., the extent to which a person's deeds follow their words. Covey uses the metaphor of an "emotional bank account" where doing what we *say* is like a deposit because our deeds follow our words, and a withdrawal occurs when our deeds do not follow our words. Like an emotional "scoreboard" upon which people *unconsciously* keep track of their interactions with others, the building or eroding of trust between individuals is a predictable process of patterns-of-interaction where people either do, or don't do, what they say. Over time, tacit beliefs emerge on the "emotional scoreboard" concerning whether a person can (or cannot) be trusted based on concrete actions and interactions in the relationship. The complex issues surrounding trust, personal integrity, and a commitment to course correction are a key element of using the Breckenridge Enneagram as a reliable explanation for our behavior and the behavior of others. Because each of us learns to see the world so differently, conflict in relationships is inevitable, so the question is not, "Do we experience conflict in our relationships?" rather it is "To what extent is the conflict *constructive* or *destructive*?" and this is vitally related to the level of trust between people. It's the same world out there, but we learn to see it very differently. Consequently, the degree to which we learn to see others' ways of seeing the world as legitimate alternatives to ours is based largely on the level of trust in the relationship.

More specifically, patterns-of-interaction that either build or undermine trust in relationships often consist of multiple issues (bundles) that combine to form extremely complex interactions like the Event, Pattern, and Trust (EPT) Process.[152] Here's how the EPT Process works: The first time a manager has to speak to an employee about a negative attitude toward a customer, inconsistent quality in their work, or destructive conflict displayed toward a coworker, the manager is talking about a single event; e.g., the content of the situation and what was done or left undone. The second or third time the manager has to discuss this issue, a pattern of interaction begins to form. If the problem continues over time, the employee's actions and interactions begin to undermine the manager's trust in the employee's professional capabilities, and eventually these actions and interactions can undermine trust in the overall relationship. The negative effects of these patterns-of-interaction can be exacerbated by differences in personality, whether or not people are familiar with personality frameworks like the one presented by the Breckenridge Enneagram. The key is to remember that the EPT Process is a bundle of separate interactions having different consequences that are tracked on the "emotional scoreboard"; so when one person wants to discuss the current Event rather than the fact that the situation has morphed into a Pattern or Trust issue, destructive conflict often emerges. Over time, the actions and interactions of managers and staff members around the EPT Process are complicated by differences in personality and solidify into autopilot habitual patterns-of-interaction that frustrate and undermine trust in relationships.

This section on trust as the foundation of organizational relationships is being included because the Breckenridge Enneagram and BTI are often used in organizational settings, and people are more likely to mistype when they are in a context that is dominated by fear, rather than trust. Whether a context is driven by fear or motivated by trust is an especially important factor when conducting debriefs and self-discovery in workshops that are attended by managers and staff members. When a manager makes public comments about how much they like (or dislike) a specific Enneagram type, or they publicly dismiss the value-added of using personality typologies in the workplace, these assertions can powerfully script how staff members see their BTI results, and even how they see themselves, others, and the world. More specifically, when managers are publicly critical of the characteristics associated with a given type, their employees are discouraged from self-identifying as that type. A person's day-to-day actions and patterns-of-interaction will tend to emerge more from their Socialized-Self than their Natural-Self in contexts that are driven by fear because they are responding to requirements and norms imposed by that context. This is a powerful drain of psychological energy. Trust is the foundation of all human interactions, and the cornerstone upon which high-performing organizational cultures are built; e.g., organizational culture can either be *motivated* by trust or *driven* by fear. Managers have two choices. They can either consciously build organizational trust by respecting the fact that different personalities "see" the world very differently, or they can allow day-to-day issues, ineffective communication, and misperception to erode trust and develop a fear-based culture.

Trust is often thought of in terms of individual people and one-on-one relationships. But *organizational* trust means that we trust the organizational structures, systems, and culture within which we work. Unlike trusting individuals, the interdependent actions and interactions of structures, systems, and culture can reach a level of combinatorial complexity where the "system" takes on a life of its own and almost no one can change it. As one manager remarked to a direct report's request for more resources to better serve customers, "I know you're disappointed in this decision, Jane, but our system just doesn't allow us to do what you want." The degree to which managers or staff members either *trust* the structures, systems, and culture within which they work, or *fear* them, is a "window" into the underlying patterns of behavior, belief structure, and tacit assumptions of an organization's culture. The degree to which a person "fits" within an organizational culture is powerfully defined by their personality because an individual's personality is like the force field of a magnet within the electromagnetic field of organizational culture.

There are six elements of organizational trust described below: Truth, Integrity, Power, Competency, Values, and Recognition. To more personally connect to the six elements, take a moment to reflect on the following question: "Can you really trust the organization *you* work in?" Now get more specific by reflecting on the six questions listed below relative to your organization.[153]

- *Truth*: Does your organization have a deep commitment to establishing "organizational truth" (what's really going on in the organization), so employees are free to present the unvarnished truth about organizational matters and question the reasoning, assumptions, and attitudes that motivate the organization's decisions?
- *Integrity*: Does your organization have integrity (does it do what it says), does it practice "fair process" (is it fair and objective) and does it base its

evaluations of people and issues on facts and quantitative data, not "politics" and personalities?

- *Power*: Do managers in your organization use their power fairly and effectively to achieve the organization's purpose and goals, and to positively influence people, not out of self-interest?

- *Competency*: Is your organization competent to overcome the challenges it faces, and can leaders make decisions that will ensure the achievement of its strategic and tactical goals (does your organization know exactly what it's doing)?

- *Values*: Does your organization have a well-defined set of core values that it communicates to all employees; does it authentically live by those values (even in difficult situations); and are those values consistent with your own personal values?

- *Recognition*: Does your organization recognize (notice) the contributions that you make in the workplace and does it confirm your own views about your professional abilities? Do you have a clear future in this organization?

As a rule, managers and staff members in for-profit, non-profit, and government organizations do not *consciously* ask these six questions, but they exist invisibly just below the surface of consciousness. The importance of the criteria to individuals in an organization is relative to their position in the organization and their personality type. What a person believes about the six questions can be *made visible* by repetitively asking the question "why" in the face of organizational issues (five-whys). For example, "Why do the managers consistently fail to share information, so the left hand does not know what the right hand is doing, even though they know that it negatively affects the overall performance of the organization?" The answer might be that managers are territorial so they don't share information easily. The next question might be, "But why are managers territorial and why do they fail to share information even when they *know* it's in the best interest of the organization?" Is it because they want to retain their own power? Do they view others as being incompetent to get the job done? Do they have different core values than their coworkers? – And so on. The underlying causes and motivations of ineffective organizational performance are often traceable to an interlocking set of beliefs, tacit assumptions, and patterns of human interaction that emerge from the six questions listed above. The exact nature of this interdependent belief structure will be based on contextual factors, the personality types and level of awareness of the people involved, their level of trust in the organization, and the degree to which the culture is either *motivated* by trust or *driven* by fear.

While some managers believe that fear is a necessary part of achieving goals and objectives, researchers from Abraham Maslow to W. Edwards Deming have warned against the subtle, but profound, effects of management-by-fear (rather than trust) and the devastating affects that fear can have on establishing or maintaining a high-performing organizational culture. Deming argues that fear makes people afraid to share their best ideas; expand their capabilities and skills; admit mistakes; suggest process improvements; question the underlying purpose and reasoning of decisions or procedures; or even to act in the best interest of the company.[154] Managers and staff members fear: a) being the object of real or perceived retribution, b) being passed over for promotion, c) receiving lower performance ratings, d) looking uninformed or like a trouble-maker, e) being assigned to "grunt" work, rather than the more visible projects, and f) being seen as not having sufficient intellectual horsepower to advance beyond one's current position. Fear ultimately leads to padded figures, distorted measures of performance, and the tendency to sanitize, spin, and reinterpret what's really going on in an organization as information moves up through organizational levels to top management. Not surprisingly, fear also leads to mistyping with the BTI and the inability to accurately apply the principles and practices described in this Interpretation Manual when the instrument is used within a fear-based context.

Maslow argues that while each of us has a deep need to know the truth about our capabilities, strengths, areas for improvement, and Blind Spots, many people fear (or even evade) knowing the truth about themselves. Consequently, people may fear (or evade) the powerful insights that the BTI provides into our true selves. We'll discuss this tendency next in the section on Blind Spots and the Red Flags. Fear undermines our courage to speak up, our confidence in our professional abilities, and over time fear erodes our self-esteem. It also can cause people to mistype on the BTI if they are afraid that the results will bring retribution or may be used in a pejorative or negative way. While most managers want to know the truth about what's really going on in their organization in terms of milestones, processes, delivering on commitments to customers, and employee perspectives, these same managers often fear, resist, and evade knowing the truth (the brutal facts) about these same issues. Maslow argues that enlightened managers genuinely *want* their employees to know the truth of what's going on in the workplace (everything relevant to their situation) and that, "…knowing is good for them, that the truth, the facts, and honesty tend to be curative, healing, to taste good, to be familiar…"[155] It's not just a fear of discovering our negative traits and characteristics on a personality indicator like the BTI, as Maslow explains, "To discover in oneself a great talent can certainly bring exhilaration, but it also brings a fear of the dangers and responsibilities and duties of being a leader and of being all alone."[156] The bottom line is that *fear* kills curiosity, exploration, innovation, creativity, growth, high-performance, synergy, teamwork, and morale in organizations. Fear negatively impacts organizational performance in ways that are difficult or impossible to discover because it operates on autopilot, below the surface of organizational awareness, as an undiscussible Invisible Bureaucracy™. Organizational truth is strengthened when the playing field is leveled by a clear knowledge of the personality types of managers and staff members using the Breckenridge Enneagram.

Surfacing and Managing Conflict

Because 55% of communication is non-verbal (body language), 38% is tone of voice, and only 7% is word choice it is almost impossible not to communicate with almost everything we say and do. People communicate on two levels simultaneously – the *conscious* level of what they say (espouse) about themselves, others, and the world, and at an unconscious (or quasi-conscious) level by the body language and tone of voice that form their actions and interactions in day-to-day life. In addition, we often experience a kind of "inner commentary" about our own actions and interactions, and the actions and interactions of others in our context. Like the italicized mental commentary of the characters in Dan Brown's books, our minds become a platform upon which this inner commentary about what we think and feel (but do not say) plays out. Often, it is the commentary of the Natural-Self on the ways in which our Socialized-Self responds to the demands and requirements imposed on us by our context. The model of the Left-Hand Column shown in Figure 94 can be a powerful tool for exploring and understanding this bifurcated communication and the inner commentary of the Natural-Self.

Surfacing and Managing Conflict in Relationships

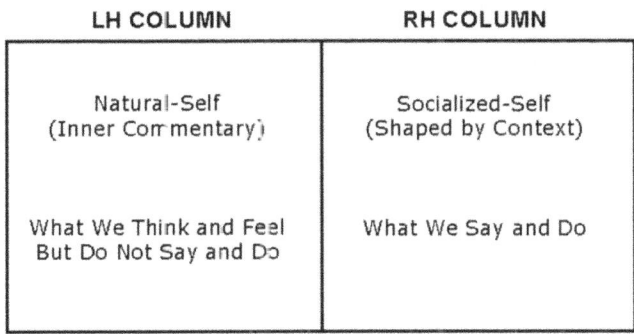

LH COLUMN	RH COLUMN
Natural-Self (Inner Commentary)	Socialized-Self (Shaped by Context)
What We Think and Feel But Do Not Say and Do	What We Say and Do

Figure 94

Based on the work of Chris Argyris and popularized by Peter Senge, the Left-Hand Column can be used as a powerful tool for surfacing and managing conflict in relationships and organizations.[157] But it can also be used as a method for exploring the tacit, unquestioned beliefs and assumptions associated with our personality. The Left-Hand Column is the place in our inner-experience where the tacit beliefs and assumptions of our personality first make their presence known at the fringe of consciousness. It is the psychological place where self-awareness about the strengths, weaknesses, and Blind Spots associated with our personality first emerges into our conscious awareness. As we will discuss in the next section, it is also the first line of defense for people who choose to sensor and block this inner commentary from entering the arena of conscious awareness – a gate-keeping function with which people "manage" the information that they receive about themselves.

Becoming Conscious of the Unconscious

Most people have sophisticated algorithms for managing information that they receive that does not "map" to the way they have learned to see themselves, others, and the world through the See-Do-Get Process. The algorithms are designed to select input that agrees with the image that people have of themselves – the rest of the input is blocked, but often registers as tacit, unconscious input. But like the ostrich hiding its head in the ground (if I can't see them, they can't see me), other people do in-fact see who and what we are. Often, we are the last to know what others have known all along. These beliefs, opinions, assumptions, and views of ourselves and others *build* in the Left-Hand Column of our relationships as inner commentary that people think and feel but do not say. People often have a sense about the issues, beliefs, and assumptions that make-up the content of others' Left-Hand Column because 93% of communication is a combination of non-verbal body language and tone of voice, not what people actually say or espouse. In fact, teasing apart the difference between the non-verbal messages that people send about what they think and feel but do not say, and our tendency to impose (project) our own unconscious views and the biases of personality on their actions and inter-actions, is one of the most sophisticated and complex problems in relationships.

Things that *others* know about us or "see" in us that *we* don't know or "see" about ourselves are called "Blind Spots." One way to picture this is using the Johari Window, which was developed by Joseph Luft as a tool for raising individual self-awareness and for improving the dynamics and communication in groups of people.[158] The Johari window is one of the simplest ways to begin exploring the process of becoming conscious of the unconscious tendencies of our personality (see Figure 95).

Johari Window

OPEN	BLIND SPOT
HIDDEN	UNKNOWN

Figure 95

The "open" quadrant indicates things we know about ourselves, and others also know about us. The "hidden" quadrant represents things that we know about ourselves that others don't. The quadrant marked as "Blind Spots" indicates things that others know about us, but that we are unaware of about ourselves. The quadrant marked as "unknown" is the repository of things that are unknown to others about us, and unknown to ourselves about ourselves. More specifically, the "unknown" quadrant points to things that are so paradoxical that others would not expect them about us, nor would we expect them about ourselves. From the perspective of the Breckenridge Enneagram, the underlying deficiency-drivers, core assumptions and the deeper beliefs and assumptions upon which the Tacit Creed is based are largely in the "unknown" quadrant. For example, type Twos and the people they interact with are largely unaware that their desire to be "helpful" emerges from the core assumption that they lack personal significance in life, or type Sevens and those they interact with are largely unconscious of the fact that their tendency to be "enthusiastic" and stay in constant motion emerges from the core assumption that they lack the inner-vitality to face life now and in the future.

The combination of beliefs, assumptions, and views that are "hidden" from others but known to self on the left side of Figure 95, and our "Blind Spots" and things that are simply "unknown" to all on the right side of Figure 95 are what populate the Left-Hand Column shown in Figure 94. They also represent the "gap" between how we "see" ourselves, how others "see" us, and the reality of who we really are which is a combination of these and other perspectives. The key to achieving personal and professional growth and developing self-awareness about our personality with the Breckenridge Enneagram requires us to take multiple steps to consciously suspend the gate-keeping function of our information algorithms so they can purposely *identify* and *eliminate* Blind Spots. While this normally causes intense inner conflict and cognitive dissonance within the individual, such conflict must be faced *head-on*. If Blind Spots are not dealt with head-on, they distort the knowledge we obtain about ourselves, other people, our relationships, the organizations we work in, and the environment in which those organizations exist.

Red Flags (Mooring Balls)

So how do we become aware of our Blind Spots if they are unconscious? How can we recognize how the unconscious expresses itself in our day-to-day actions and interactions if we are unaware of them? Sometimes insights float to the fringe of consciousness as we "catch ourselves in the act" of being our personality. But there is a natural process that can be used to identify our Blind Spots and the various ways in which the unconscious aspects of personality express themselves in everyday life – follow the Red Flags. One way to describe how the Red Flags work is by using a metaphor from scuba diving and underwater exploration. The vast majority of the ocean is deep blue sea and the majority of underwater topography even around many tropical islands consists of sandy bottoms and no coral reef. So how do you find the coral reef in such an enormous body of water when the total amount of coral reefs in the entire world represent only a tiny fraction of the total area of the ocean? Dive operators find coral reef by exploring the underwater terrain and once they locate a good dive site, they tie a mooring ball to a concrete block on the bottom somewhere near the dive site and let it float just below the surface of the water. The mooring ball allows them to find that dive site every time they return.

Finding coral reef in the vast ocean is not unlike finding the key issues in your life that will yield deep personal change. Of all the experiences you have had in your life, of all the conflicts you are aware of or that press into the fringe of consciousness, all the feedback you've gotten from others, where would you begin to identify *the most important issues* that needed to be changed? How would you have any level of confidence that if you put your shoulder to the wheel and hammered through these issues, that this psychological work would really result in the kind of change we are talking about? The Red Flags are like mooring balls that float near the surface of awareness and indicate an issue below the surface of consciousness that we need to dive down and explore. There are three Red Flags (mooring balls).

- Excess Energy (Inappropriate Levels)
- Unintended Consequences (Unlearning Loop)
- Defense Routines (B, I, C, CC)

Following the Red Flags is a short cut to identifying our Blind Spots – of becoming conscious of the unconscious. When you see one of these Red Flags emerge in your actions or interactions; stop dead in your tracks, tag this situation as a mooring ball, and then dive in and explore this area by getting into the spectator role and using empathic inquiry. We'll discuss each of the Red Flags in more detail.

Excess Energy: The first Red Flag is excess or inappropriate levels of energy. Excess or inappropriate levels of psychological energy mean that your emotional response to a situation *has you*, rather than you having an emotional response to the situation. It's when the level of affect that you display is entirely exaggerated and out of proportion to what was said or done. These enormous levels of psychological energy become stored around some issue or person that we have to deal with and are often linked to the tacit or unconscious beliefs and assumptions of our personality. People get consumed, taken over, grabbed by the scruff of their emotional necks by an issue that an hour earlier or later, even they would admit was not that big of a deal. When your emotions *have you*, your reactions are spring-loaded and toxic about an issue that you normally wouldn't care about, and this is the telltale sign of inappropriate levels of psychological energy. These toxic releases of excess energy can be overt and aggressive, or covert and passive-aggressive. They can be positive, like falling in love, or negative, like conflict between people. Whenever you detect excess inappropriate levels of emotional responses in yourself or others that are just not appropriate to the reality of what happened, this is a Red Flag. Stop dead in your tracks, get curious about what's going on, mark this down as an issue you need to work on, and get into the spectator role using empathic inquiry. Following the path of the Red Flag of excess energy is a natural process for identifying Blind Spots and the tacit and unconscious beliefs and assumptions of our personality.

Unintended Consequences: The second Red Flag is unintended consequences – disruptions of our conscious intentions and actions. Our personality does not exist in a vacuum independent of the relationships and social contexts in which we live. In fact, other people and situations can bring out the very best (or the very worst) in our personalities. For example, John and one of his supervisors, Linda, had an intense conflict over John's cynical attitude about the level of productivity of Linda's direct reports. On the way into work the next day, John reflects on the conflict and wants to make his interactions with Linda more constructive. He decides to discuss his plan to improve their communication when he gets to the office. That morning, Linda also wants to own her part in the conflict and make her interactions with John more constructive, so she gathers her group around her desk for a cup of coffee and discusses how they can increase their productivity. John walks into the department and sees that Linda and her people are standing around drinking coffee when they should be working. He tells her to follow him to his office and words of criticism begin flying out of his mouth before he can stop them, "Must be nice to have the luxury of just standing around drinking coffee with your friends?" Linda responds, "Don't I even get a 'good morning' before you start hammering on me?"

They both intended to improve and create a positive, affirming, conciliatory climate, but they got the *unintended result* of being drawn into a destructive pattern of interaction where they began arguing over the very problem they wanted to solve. As shown by the Learning Loop in Figure 96, John intended to try to "see" the situation differently and to "do" something to show Linda that he really cared for her and valued their work relationship. Linda intended to try to "see" John differently and to "do" something to acknowledge her role in the conflict and to affirm his concerns about productivity. The good intentions of both were motivated by a deep desire to improve their relationship; e.g., the growth-motivator shown in Figure 96.

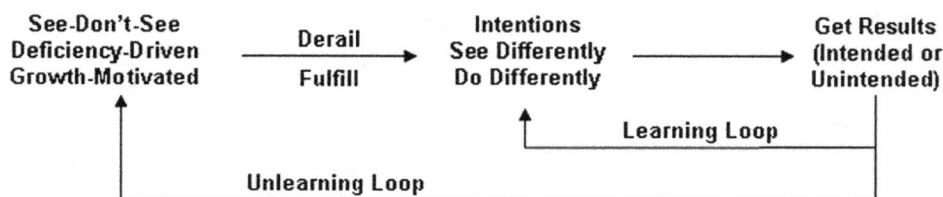

See-Don't-See Deficiency-Driven Growth-Motivated	Derail ———→ Fulfill	Intentions See Differently Do Differently	Get Results (Intended or Unintended)

Learning Loop

Unlearning Loop

Figure 96

But both John and Linda's good intentions were *derailed* by circumstances and the destructive autopilot responses of the patterns-of-interaction that emerged over time through countless cycles through the See-Do-Get Process.[159] Intending to do one thing, but getting an unintended result, is the second Red Flag and is almost always caused by the derailing, autopilot power of our personality and destructive patterns-of-interaction. As long as John and Linda continue to fall into the Learning Loop shown in Figure 96, they will remain the unwitting victims of the same arguments over-and-over again. Using the Learning Loop creates a vicious cycle of trying harder and thinking positively about the relationship, but secretly John and Linda feel helpless to change the powerful, unpredictable derailing forces that are frustrating and undermining their relationship.

Defense Routines: The next Red Flag we need to watch out for is defense routines that are designed to purposely distort and obfuscate our knowledge about ourselves and other people, and prevent us from knowing the psychological "truth" of a situation. We experience the presence of defense mechanisms around two foci of confusion. We can't quite figure out:

- What we are feeling, and
- Whether the source of the problem is in others, or ourselves, or both

Defense routines act like a gate-keeping function that distorts and obfuscates how we see ourselves, others, and the world when we are threatened by embarrassment or threat.[160] They prevent us from objectively interpreting: a) our own experiences and emotions, b) the nature of our interactions with others, and c) the nature and characteristics of issues and situations when they involve embarrassment or threat. So when we ask questions like those listed below, the gate-keeping function of our defense routines can prevent us from honestly knowing the answers.

- What am I am feeling right now?
- Why am I so bound up emotionally?
- Why do I have so much inner tension about this issue?
- Why am I so upset about this issue?

Defense routines are *anti-learning devices* that help people maintain their way of seeing themselves, others, and the world in ways that "map" to the underlying patterns, beliefs, and assumptions of personality. Consequently, they are highly-skilled actions learned early in life which become habitual, occur almost automatically, and operate below the surface of consciousness. A defense routine is a hidden, undiscussible action or series of actions that prevent a person from identifying or eliminating what actually caused the embarrassment or threat. Once hidden, the defense routine is protected by mechanisms such as hot buttons, inflexibility of mind or position, or a seeming inability to make decisions. Argyris claims that "Defense routines... *require* people to communicate inconsistent messages, but act as if they are not doing so. In order for these actions to be effective, they must be covered up while being enacted. In many cases, the cover-ups must also be covered up."[161] More specifically, the sequence that many defense routines manifest is: a) by-pass the real issue, b) give inconsistent messages, c) cover-up the issue and make it undiscussible, and d) cover-up the cover-up by making the undiscussibility undiscussible. For example, an employee knows that his manager is unhappy with his performance and the manager has indicated that she wants to discuss the matter at the employee's convenience; but the employee continually puts off the meeting with the claim that "I'm so busy" when in reality the employee is the one making his schedule. Defense routines protect us from recognizing or dealing with our Blind Spots that frustrate and undermine effective leadership skills. Accurate self-knowledge is the foundation of self-awareness and people cannot obtain accurate self-knowledge unless they understand and control the distortions that result from defense routines and Blind Spots.

Argyris contrasts the defensive reasoning that is often present with defense routines with the productive reasoning that often typifies people who are self-aware. When people use *defensive reasoning*, the premises they use to support their explanations are tacit, their inferences are hidden, and the data they base their arguments on are not easily subjected to objective, public debate. When individuals use defensive reasoning they state their conclusion, claim it is valid, then try to assure others that the only way to test the conclusion is to use *their* logic: "Trust me, I know what I'm talking about." In contrast, a person using *productive reasoning* supplies directly observable data to illustrate the arguments that support their conclusion, makes all inferences explicit, and crafts conclusions so that others can publicly debate and test them. Even when beliefs and conclusions are based on gut-level feeling or intuition, the person using productive reasoning articulates these premises explicitly so that others understand the basis on which the conclusion rests.

CHAPTER 3

THE UPWARD PATH OF PERSONAL AND PROFESSIONAL GROWTH

FINDING OUR CALLING AND DESTINY

Plato claimed that each of us comes into this world with a special calling. We are all meant to do certain things and be someone who is unique unto us. For some people, the calling comes early in life and is like a raging sea that they must navigate. We normally associate this type of calling with famous people like Mozart or Einstein. But for most of us, the calling is like the quiet flow of a river. During the first half of life it cannot be distinguished from many inner and outer things that clamor for our attention – taking guitar lessons, playing sports, doing photography, and most of all meeting the expectations of other people in our lives. Because of the pressure we have early in life to decide, "What do I want to be when I grow up?" most people automatically equate their "calling" with the question of what they want to do for a living. While it can certainly be about this, the calling I am talking about is "How do I become the person I am destined to be?"

The notion of our calling or *destiny* is one of the main themes of the movie *Forrest Gump*. If you recall, the opening and closing scenes of the movie showed a feather floating around in the air, which symbolized the question, "Are we just floating around in life, or is there overall purpose and meaning to what we experience and do?" From early on in the film, Gump wonders if he *has* a destiny like his friend

Lt. Dan claimed, or whether he had to *create* his own destiny like his Momma said: "Life is like a box of chocolates, you never know what you are going to get, so you have to make your own destiny." As the quiet flow of the river of calling proceeds in the first half of life, the pedestrian realities of our lives convince us that Forrest's Momma was right; e.g., that we have to create our own destiny. So we occupy ourselves with the tasks of building a life and a self through the See-Do-Get Process.

During the first half of life, if we are lucky enough to have parents who helped put us through high school and college, we spend our first twelve to sixteen years in school developing ourselves as a human resource that will allow us to assume the responsibilities of adult life. Our overall competencies, gifts, talents, and person-ality, as well as the context in which we find ourselves, vitally affect how much income we can produce, the kind of lifestyle we can live, and our overall position within the socio-economic structure of society. For most people, the struggle between the demands of their lifestyle and their ability to earn revenue dominates their attention and energies during the first half of life. This frenetic pace tends to drown out the quiet flow of the calling as does the deficiency-driven focus of grati-fying our basic needs; e.g., the first four levels of Maslow's Hierarchy. As will be discussed in more detail in the next section, our inner experience of the calling as the force-for-growth and the Upward Path of Becoming is fundamentally different than the nagging empty sense that "something's missing" in life.

But many people who approach the midpoint in life have established themselves in the world and achieved the level of income and assets needed to support the lifestyle they want. As such, the quiet sound of the inner calling becomes louder, stronger, more pressing, more pronounced against the backdrop of their day-to-day existence. After the age of thirty-five or forty, half of our time on this one-trip through life is gone. We begin to face the fact that *life is a currency that we spend one day at a time*, and the question becomes, "How will I spend what I have left?" There's no doubt that our calling is about how we live our day-to-day life and the consequences, outcomes, and end-effects of our decisions. But it's much more than this. The calling has a deep sense of self-actualization, transcendence, and destiny associated with it. And when it begins to press into the fringe of our consciousness more strongly, it can (and often does) create enormous confusion and inner ques-tioning about the overall direction, purpose, and existential meaning of our lives; e.g., whether we're getting the results that we want from our one-trip through life.

Some people come to realize just how tired they are of the daily grind of their per-sonal and professional lives. Others experience an inner restlessness, a hunger for meaning and significance in life, and to leave a legacy. Still others long to live lives of authenticity and integrity – the road less traveled. Yet other people wish they could change, but have no idea where to start because the calling presents itself like a riddle or a parable that makes no practical sense. For example, "I have been working in computing for twenty years, but I don't really enjoy it. If I had a choice, I would quit my job, build a log home up in the mountains of Colorado, get some goats and llamas, sew for fun, stay home and be a full-time mom to my children." In its most poignant and devastating manifestation, not living-out our calling can create a deep and overwhelming sense of futility and desperation where people feel like they are trapped in an inner prison and have no way out.

Over time, the subtle pressure of the calling can forcefully *demand* that we disrupt or dismantle the configuration of our lives; e.g., what we do for a living and how much money we make; our relationships with friends; our marriages and interactions with children and extended family members; our interests, hobbies and the "toys" we need; the kind of car we drive or the house we live in; how we spend our time and money. Sometimes this *is* what people need, but to act-out these demands *literally* is often a mistake because they are trying to communicate a symbolic or archetypal message from Levels 4 and 5 of the personal paradigm shown in Figure 91. We experience the force-for-growth as a prodding, questioning, and probing process that is designed to lead us up the levels of Maslow's Hierarchy on the Upward Path of Becoming, self-actualization, and transcendence. The calling is a common, naturalistic, human experience that comes from the force-for-growth and our innate inborn tendencies, temperament, personality, character, and natural talents and abilities trying to *express* themselves within our historical and cultural context. It is not a spiritual or metaphysical calling – rather it emerges from the Symbolic and Archetypal-Biological Levels of the personal paradigm (Levels 4 and 5). So when a person feels they are being led by the calling to quit their job; sell their house; move to a place like Papua New Guinea; or make other radical changes in life, it's important to ask whether these should be done *literally* or *symbolically*. When the calling leads a person to act-out the inner pressure *symbolically*, but they *literally* quit their job and move to Papua New Guinea, they inevitably regret it.

So in the end, Gump's analysis of the problem of destiny was correct when he said that Momma and Lt. Dan were *both* right. We *have* a destiny that is defined by the force-for-growth and our innate inborn tendencies, temperament, personality, character, and natural talents and abilities trying to express themselves within our historical and cultural context. And we *create* our own destiny by our day-to-day, week-to-week, month-to-month actions, interactions, choices, and decisions within that same context. In other words, the *having* and *creating* of our destiny are both happening together at the same time. It's like we're floating down the river of our calling in life and can choose whether we go with the flow, paddle faster with the flow, paddle upstream, or pull over to the river bank and sit things out for a while.

The principles, practices, and tools of the Breckenridge Enneagram provide pene-trating insights into our personality; character; the hidden recesses of the human heart; and how to find our unique calling and destiny in life.

TEASING APART THE DIFFERENCE BETWEEN DEFICIENCY AND THE CALLING

One of the principles of Empirical Existentialism is, *what is most personal, is most universal*. This section describes some concrete ways for teasing apart the differ-ence between the inner experience of deficiency, and the inner experience of the calling as a force-for-growth. In some ways, it's easier to notice the experience of deficiency because it's so demanding, compulsive, fixated, and outwardly focused on self-gratification. But it's important to note that the experience of the quiet flow of the inner calling exists *at all times* in our life-history, whether or not we are conscious of its presence at any given moment in time. The remainder of this sec-tion compares the inner experience of compulsive deficiency that strives to gratify our basic needs (often at the expense of others), to the quiet flow and urging to follow our calling and destiny in life.[162] People who are deficiency-driven have a qualitatively different look and feel than those who are allowing the calling and the force-for-growth to direct and build their lives. A deficiency-driven existence is much like living on credit – despite the external appearances of material posses-sions, vacations, and social activities, people shovel money into rising credit card balances and the foundation of savings and assets remains an empty hole that is not filled. Analogously, following the calling and force-for-growth is much like living on a cash-basis and building a positive net-worth in terms of savings and other assets.

Being deficiency-driven is experienced as episodic and climactic, with a moment of consummation and an end-state that is goal-oriented – like a person who craves salt or chocolate and finally gratifies that need. We experience the calling as a con-tinuous, steady, upward path and forward movement toward higher and higher levels of Maslow's Hierarchy, with the ultimate goal of transcending the autopilot responses of our personality and the inauthentic edicts and demands of our cultural context. The experience of being deficiency-driven is compulsive, insatiable, fixated, and destructive to self and others, whereas the direction and path of the inner calling are consciously chosen, deeply satisfying, and constructive with a desire to continue to higher and higher levels of self-awareness and freedom to choose that which is deeply satisfying. Not surprisingly, deficiency is characterized by an *instrumental* view of people and life that strives to gratify a person's basic needs at the expense of others, while the inner calling is typified by an *intrinsic* view of people and life that experiences growth as an intrinsically rewarding and exciting process in and of itself.

Being deficiency-driven is past-oriented and based on life experience and our current state of actuality and *who we are*, rather than the future potentiality of who we might become if we could learn to "see" ourselves differently through the See-Do-Get Process. The experience of being deficiency-driven is fear-based with a sense of scarcity (there's not enough to go around so I've got to get mine) and a fear of biological and psychological survival. The quiet flow of the inner calling tends to be future-oriented and impels us forward toward open exploration and the task of seeking our full potentiality in life. Following the inner calling teaches us to be trust-based, with a sense of abundance (there is plenty for everyone), and the tenacity, strength, and courage to face the challenges of life and a basic trust that we will survive biologically and psychologically.

Being deficiency-driven creates an inner experience that "something's missing" in life and an intense desire and craving to eliminate (or get rid of) that need; e.g., "The problem with snacking is that it kills my appetite." When we're deficiency-driven, we feel like there's a deep, empty hole within us that demands to be filled and our tendency is to try to fill it with actions, interactions, activities, or material things (cars, houses, money, popularity, work, status, relationships, etc.). Despite our attempts to the contrary, the inner hole remains empty regardless of how much we stuff into it. Deficiency creates a sense of being *inauthentic* because we try to fill an inner existential void with material things and behaviors, which further alienates us from ourselves, others, and the world. This is accompanied by the fear of self-knowledge and a strong avoidance and indifference to exploring and understanding our inner experience and knowing the psychological truth about ourselves. It's not that deficiency-driven people don't *have* the experience of the calling – it's that they're afraid of it, so they suppress, deny, drown out, turn away from, and "forget" the subtle and easily-silenced leading of the force-for-growth. Being deficiency-driven makes us dependent on others – outer-determined, and need-oriented.

Perhaps the clearest way to tease apart the difference between the inner experience of being deficiency-driven and the experience of the inner calling is by the underlying emotions that are associated with deficiency. Figure 97 shows how the deficiency-driven emotions for the nine types are positioned around the Enneagram, with each pair of emotions bearing the signature of *dependency* on people, resources, and experiences outside of ourselves.

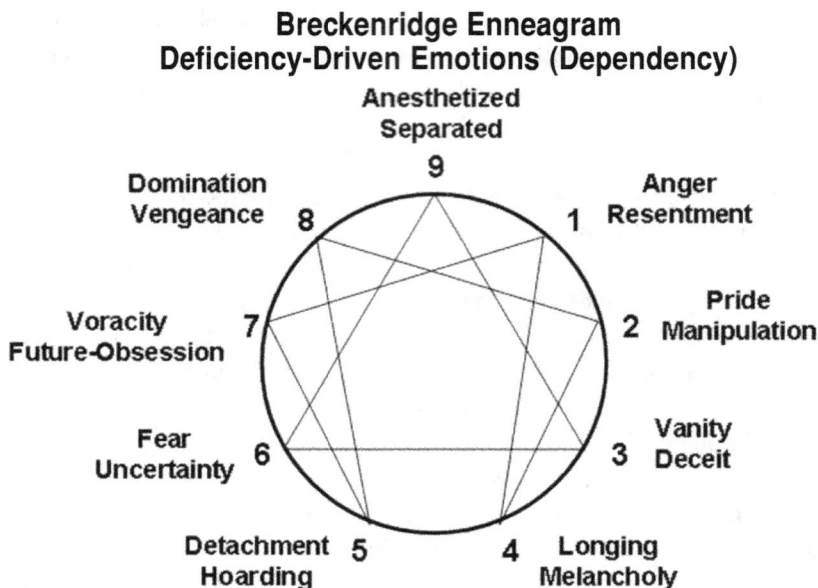

**Breckenridge Enneagram
Deficiency-Driven Emotions (Dependency)**

Anesthetized
Separated

9

Domination
Vengeance   8   1   Anger
                                                Resentment

Voracity   7   2   Pride
Future-Obsession   Manipulation

Fear   3   Vanity
Uncertainty   6   Deceit

Detachment 5   4   Longing
Hoarding   Melancholy

Figure 97

By contrast, the calling is typified by a quiet, ongoing desire for inner fulfillment, wholeness, joy, peace, and equanimity, where the outcomes and end-effects of these endless desires build upon themselves and take us to higher and higher levels of being our best selves, and achieving our true potential which can never be fully attained or satisfied. Unlike the deficiency-driven individual's attempts to fill an empty hole that *remains empty*, the calling and force-for-growth create the basic "substance" of a life at the Symbolic and Archetypal-Levels of the personal para- digm that builds a foundation and accumulates until we are no longer empty. Over time, an inner firmness and foundation rise from our depths and allow us to stand on higher inner ground. This produces deep sustainable growth and a "wider" place in our existence which gives us a better vision of the path and direction of the inner calling. Following the calling creates a sense of being *authentic* because we are in- wardly reunited with ourselves, others, and the world through a desire for veridical self-knowledge and psychological truth, as we openly and honestly explore our inner experience with empathic inquiry from the Spectator Role. This only makes us more autonomous, inner-determined, and abundance-oriented. The clearest way to tease apart the difference between the inner experience of being deficiency- driven (there's "something missing" in life) and the experience of the inner calling is by the underlying emotions that are associated with the calling. Figure 98 shows how the growth-motivated emotions associated with the inner calling are posi- tioned around the Enneagram, with each pair of emotions bearing the signature of *autonomy* from people, resources, and experiences outside of ourselves.

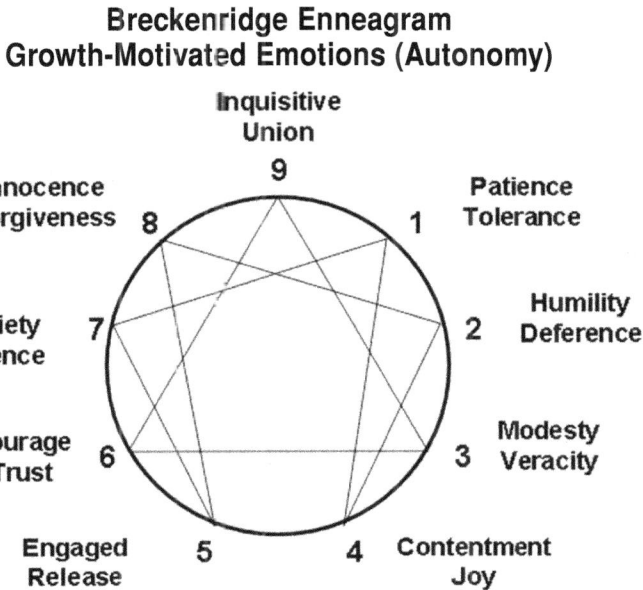

Breckenridge Enneagram
Growth-Motivated Emotions (Autonomy)

Inquisitive
Union

9

Innocence
Forgiveness   8

1   Patience
Tolerance

Humility
2   Deference

Sobriety
Presence   7

Courage
Trust   6

3   Modesty
Veracity

Engaged
Release   5

4   Contentment
Joy

Figure 98

So the difference between being deficiency-driven and following the inner calling is another way to describe the dynamic process that lies beneath the Enneagram and manifests itself as the Downward Spiral of Striving versus the Upward Path of Becoming – what most traditional Enneagram writers call the direction of integration and disintegration. The Downward Spiral of Striving and the Upward Path of Becoming should not be viewed as a description of individual actions and interactions. Rather, they are an indicator of the *overall direction* of our lives in terms of Maslow's two natural-human-forces, and a never-ending series of choices between safety and growth. The two different directions around the Enneagram are also an indicator of the extent to which our lives manifest the 80-20 Rule, where our actions and interactions along the Downward Spiral of Striving will tend to be deficiency-driven, compulsive, inauthentic, alienated, dependent, and fear-based; and actions and interactions along the Upward Path of Becoming will tend to be growth-motivated, self-determined, authentic, reunited, autonomous, and trust-based. Over time, our behaviors and emotional responses to others *solidify* into robust patterns-of-interaction that go on autopilot, slip below the surface of conscious-awareness, and powerfully shape the direction of our relationships and our lives. Deep sustainable change and the process of self-actualization and transcendence *happen to us* in the sense that they emerge *indirectly* as a natural consequence of living out the direction and path of the inner calling. Over time, this becomes an *objective* indicator of our level of psychological health and the extent to which the 80-20 Rule is operating in our lives.

THE METHOD AND MECHANISM
OF DEEP PERSONAL CHANGE

It is important to note that deep sustainable personal change almost always requires a burning platform, and there are two kinds of burning platforms: reactive and proactive. The *reactive* kind is when we wait until our lives lack meaning and significance and when we are overcome by destructive conflict in our key relationships. Alternatively, the *proactive* kind of burning platform is when we realize that whenever our ineffective ways of acting and interacting are still working at some level, we're not living full, satisfying lives and that things will probably get worse if they remain unchanged. When people reach this realization, they often ask the question, "How bad am I hurting?" If the answer is, "Not that bad" then things normally go on as they are – sometimes for a lifetime.

There are three steps that people must take to begin the process of deep change. The *first step* is to use objective feedback from people who we trust, combined with our own observations of our actions and interactions, to begin to cast doubt on the "reality" that was created by us (and for us) through the See-Do-Get Process. The *second step* requires that we begin to see ourselves as being partly *responsible* for not getting the results that we want on our one-trip through life. Once this sense of personal responsibility sufficiently penetrates our denial and defense routines, we will begin to experience *survival anxiety* or *guilt* about the "truth" that we need to take charge of our lives and create positive change.[163] Survival anxiety is another manifestation of our fear of self-knowledge. As our awareness of the need to change increases, the *third step* is for us to use the results of our ineffective ways of acting and interacting as additional *disconfirming evidence* that supports the fact that things cannot continue the way they are. When the weight of evidence from these three steps combines, they become a powerful motivation for people to change – a proactive burning platform.

But as soon as we accept the need to change and our responsibility to create change, most people begin experiencing what Edgar Schein calls *learning anxiety*; e.g., the fear of doing things differently, changing the patterns-of-interaction in relationships, and reconfiguring the world (reality) in which they operate.[164] Learning anxiety creates both cognitive and emotional dissonance.

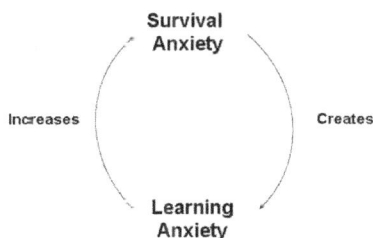

Figure 99

As shown in Figure 99, the self-reinforcing loop of survival anxiety, creating learning anxiety, and in turn increasing survival anxiety, is why most people go on living lives that lack meaning and significance and maintain relationships that are dominated by destructive conflict. Schein claims that there are two principles that summarize a process for moving beyond this self-defeating cycle.

- Initially, survival anxiety and/or guilt must be greater than the learning anxiety in order to penetrate our defenses and begin the process of recognizing and changing destructive ways of acting and interacting.
- Creating change requires that learning anxiety be *reduced* by creating a sense of psychological safety, rather than increasing survival anxiety.

One of the best ways to decrease learning anxiety in the face of survival anxiety is to view our contribution to our current situation in life objectively by depersonalizing the autopilot responses of our personality. This mitigates or eliminates self-blame by showing that the vast majority of our ineffective actions and interactions are not the result of intentional behavior or conscious strategies. Rather, they are the product of the autopilot responses of our personality. In other words, *"It's not personal, it's personality."*[165] Managed properly, the interaction between learning anxiety and survival anxiety can be the first step to creating deep, profound, sustainable change.

So how exactly *do* people who believe that *their* reality is *the* reality come to see the world otherwise? The level of rigidity with which a person holds to their way of "seeing" the world is often directly proportional to their tendency to practice either-or-thinking, rather than *both-and-thinking*.[166] The tendency toward *either-or-thinking* is cultural and emerges from our Western (binary) way of viewing the world. Jim Collins refers to it as "the tyranny of the OR." For example, I can *either* be assertive or passive, I can *either* be rational or emotional, or I can *either* have autonomy *or* be controlled.

Collins calls the counter point "the genius of the AND" and characterizes it as *both-and-thinking*. It emerges from a more Eastern approach to problem-solving and decision-making where we embrace and pursue both extremes at the same time and live in the paradox. Both-and-thinking doesn't seek to strike a balance that is mid-point between two extremes; e.g., a fifty-fifty split. Both-and-thinking pursues two seemingly contradictory or paradoxical concepts at the same time – for example, that we *have* and *create* our calling and destiny in life.

Another way that people come to "see" reality differently is by *unlearning* ineffective or unreliable ways of seeing themselves, others, and the world. Deep learning almost always requires us to "unlearn" ways of seeing that were formed earlier in life. The process of unlearning happens when we run the See-Do-Get Process backwards in the counter-clockwise direction. Acting on these new ways of "seeing" begins to develop a different future reality for our lives and our relationships (see Figure 100). The best way to create our future reality and achieve our full potential in life is to create this future self through our daily choices and decisions.

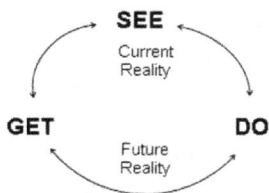

Figure 100

Deep learning and sustainable personal change require that we begin by asking a series of questions that lead us backwards through the See-Do-Get Process:

- *Get (Results)*: Have I identified my calling and destiny in life (to *have* and to *create*)? Is the overall direction of my life on the Upward Path of Becoming, or the Downward Spiral of Striving? Does my life bear the signature of Authenticity in Context? Since my life is a currency that I spend one day at a time, am I getting the results that I want from my one-trip through life?

- *Do (Pattern of Interaction)*: Which of my actions and interactions are creating the results I'm getting, despite the fact that I don't want those results? Am I addressing inner existential questions like finding an identity, facing the future, and dealing with the environment with outer behaviors like the Mulla described? To what extent are my actions and interactions deficiency-driven or growth-motivated, and how far am I from the 80-20 Rule? How wide is the gap between what I *say* and what I actually *do*? To what extent am I allowing the natural

flow of my Somatic Instincts to find expression in my lifestyle? Am I practicing both-and-thinking rather than either-or-thinking? How effectively am I
allowing my competencies, gifts, and natural talents to express themselves
and to concretize my calling and destiny in the overall context of my life?

- *See (Repository of Interactions)*: Am I working through my fear of self-
knowledge? What underlying beliefs, assumptions, and ways of "seeing" are
creating my actions and interactions, even though I don't really want those
results? Am I consciously moving into the Spectator Role and exploring my
inner experience with empathic inquiry as a way of deconstructing old and
ineffective ways of seeing myself, others, and the world? Am I focusing on
the *single point of leverage* and questioning the core assumptions of my life
and subjecting them to objective, public scrutiny?

- *Do (Pattern of Interaction)*: How can I deconstruct, and then reconfigure my
patterns-of-interaction to reflect new ways of seeing myself, others, and the
world? How can I live a more authentic life by narrowing the gap between
what I *say* I'll do and what I *actually* do? How can I be more transparent in
my relationships with others by sharing my thoughts and emotions more
openly? How do I develop the discipline, self-control, focus, force-of-will,
and tenacity needed to move from increased self-awareness to concrete day-
to-day action? How do I develop the ability to commit to course correction
when I deviate from the Upward Path of Becoming?

- *Get (Results)*: What changes can I predict will happen if I begin to see and
live differently? Over time, positive changes will begin to *disconfirm* old
ways of seeing and doing, as we begin to get new results, which will
subsequently reinforce the new ways of seeing and doing.

While the process listed above is presented in a sequential order, the key to using
the See-Do-Get Process in the counter clockwise direction is: a) to work on the
See and Do steps at the same time, and b) to embed changes in the day-to-day
realities of life until the new, more effective ways of seeing, acting, and interacting happen as automatically as the old, ineffective ones did. This creates hope
that deep personal change is actually possible and that we can become who we
were meant to be. Another way to visualize this process of unlearning is shown in
Figure 101. The process begins by hitting the interrupt button, which disrupts the
equilibrium of the upper loops and moves an individual into the lower loop.

Deep Learning Requires Unlearning

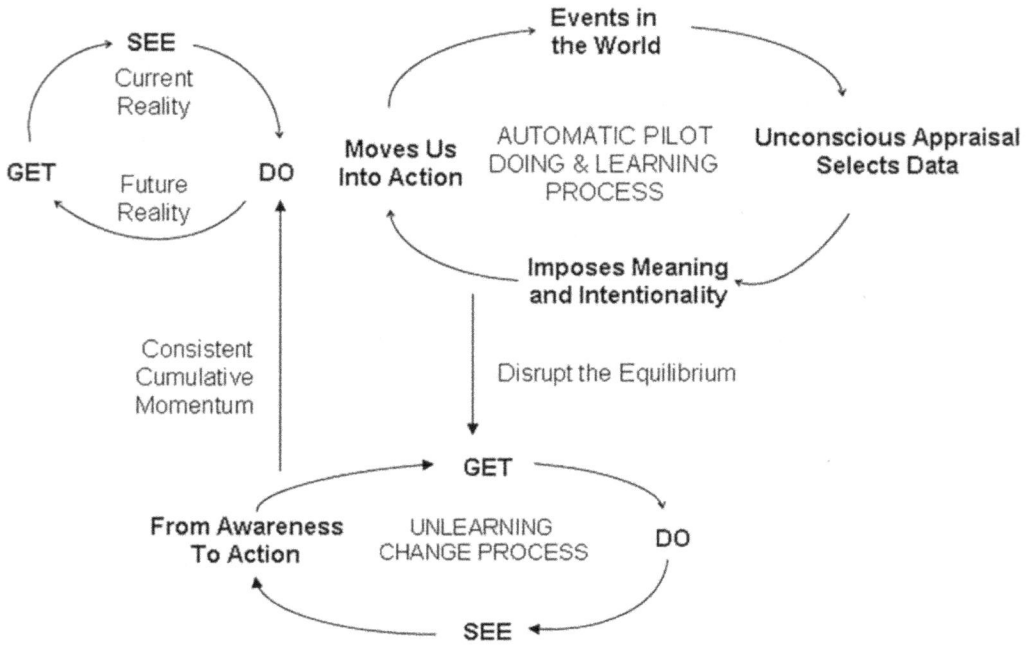

Figure 101

Moving to the lower loop begins the process of running the See-Do-Get Process backward, which deconstructs the autopilot ways of "seeing" that develop over the years and produces new results. It is important to note that the fundamental mechanism of deep personal change is the transformation (μεταμορφόομαι) of the mind and the deeper regions of the human heart at Levels 3, 4, and 5 of the personal paradigm. The goal is to learn to see ourselves, others, and the world differently by running the See-Do-Get Process backwards and following the Upward Path of Becoming, rather than the Downward Spiral of Striving.

Living in the Essential Tension between Striving and Becoming means to allow both to happen together at the same time through both-and-thinking. It also means that our freedom to choose has been restored; e.g., we *consciously* strive rather than being driven by deficiency and we consciously move toward becoming and being more growth-motivated. *Striving* means moving clockwise through endless cycles of the See-Do-Get Process as we strive to "see" differently, we strive to "do" differently, and we strive to "get" different results; e.g., the learning loop. This is a pragmatic, means-oriented, instrumental, way of moving through life that is focused on getting the results we want, using our current configuration of the See-Do-Get Process.[167] Striving to see differently produces small, incremental changes in how we act and interact and is a necessary part of life, especially when we are living out of our Socialized-Self. *Becoming* means moving counter-clockwise through the See-Do-Get Process as we allow new ways of "seeing" and "doing" and "getting" to emerge and define who we are. This is a truly creative, end-oriented, intrinsic, way of exploring and discovering life, regardless of the pragmatic value of what we find; e.g., the unlearning loop. Becoming creates deep sustainable change that reshapes the autopilot responses of our Natural-Self.

The See-Do-Get Process biases us toward Striving because our way of seeing, doing, and getting what we want becomes so habitual. Walking the path of personal and professional growth means consciously developing the practice of Becoming by reflecting on (and questioning) whether we're *really* getting what we want out of life, then running the See-Do-Get Process backwards in the counter-clockwise direction. The practice of Becoming returns us to a place of child-like learning where we become increasingly unafraid to reconfigure ourselves and the world we live in, knowing that this kind of child-like learning will ultimately produce wisdom and maturity.

Learning to live in the Essential Tension between Striving and Becoming is not a quick-fix, band-aide solution to life's problems. Rather, it is the road that is less traveled.[168] Consistent application of the principles and practices of the Breckenridge Enneagram will show that deep personal change can (and does) happen to people everyday. On this view, self-actualization and psychological health are defined as a constructive, synergistic alignment between our Socialized-Self and our Natural-Self, where 100% of our actions and interactions are *growth-motivated* toward autonomy, abundance, and trust, rather than *deficiency-driven* by dependency, need, and fear.

THE OUTCOME OF THE TRANSFORMATION PROCESS

We began this chapter by describing how to identify our calling and destiny in life, where we *have* a destiny that is defined by our innate, inborn tendencies, temperament, and natural talents and abilities trying to express themselves within our historical and cultural context. And we *create* our own destiny by our day-to-day, week-to-week, month-to-month actions, interactions, choices, and decisions within that same context. More specifically, the *having* and *creating* of our destiny are both happening together at the same time. A key element of identifying our calling is the ability to tease apart the inward phenomenological difference between the experience of deficiency-driven emotions and the Downward Spiral of Striving; and the growth-motivated emotions associated with the inner calling and the Upward Path of Becoming. In the previous section, we discussed the method and mechanism of personal change where we learn to run the See-Do-Get Process backwards in the counter-clockwise direction. This is a method for deep learning that requires us to first unlearn deeply entrenched ways of seeing ourselves, others, and the world. Finally, in this section we'll discuss three outcomes of the personal transformation process described by the Breckenridge Enneagram; e.g., the path toward Authenticity in Context.

The first outcome is overcoming our fear of self-knowledge about our emotions, natural impulses, long-term emotional and cognitive memories, natural talents and abilities, potentialities, and our calling and destiny in life.[169] We become unafraid of self-knowledge that reveals our "weaknesses" and areas for improvement; and knowledge that reveals our "strengths" and natural talents, and we accept the fact that both require personal responsibility, discipline, and self-control to act on. We no longer deal with our inner existential issues with outer behaviors and material things. We refuse to accept (and act out) inauthentic scripts and beliefs about who we are, and can truthfully question the deep assumptions and scripts that we have accepted as "facts" about ourselves, others, and the world. Over time, we learn to deconstruct the inauthentic self that became a "mask" that alienated us from ourselves, others, and the world and we discover who we really are and who we were meant to be. Overcoming this deep fear of knowing the truth about ourselves, and learning to face life with a sense of excitement and courage, is a product and key outcome of the transformation process.

The second outcome of the transformation process is *rediscovering* and *strengthening* the natural flow of psychological-instinctual energy from the Somatic Instincts and allowing it to once again flow along the natural pathways defined by our somatic self; not the tyranny of our Tacit Creed, underlying emotions, and the edicts and demands of our family or cultural context. Rediscovering and strengthening the natural flow from the Somatic Instincts allows the force-for-growth to lead the over-all path and direction of our lives. This enables us to move up Maslow's Hierarchy toward self-actualization and transcendence, where transcendence means moving beyond the autopilot responses of our personality and the inauthentic edicts and demands of our cultural context. It's important to remember that in the way the Breckenridge Enneagram defines it, transcendence is not a spiritual thing.

The third outcome of the transformation process is moving toward Authenticity in Context, where we discover and concretize our *individual answer* to the *collective existential questions of life*. As mentioned earlier, the universal nature of human emotions; the anatomical and operational similarities of the human organism; the biological purpose of the Somatic Instincts; the fact that life is an historical process of birth, infancy, adolescence, maturity, and death within space-and-time; and our concrete and symbolic experiences of these aspects of human existence create the deep and abiding sense that *what is most personal, is most universal*. In the case of the four key questions of Empirical Existentialism, we aren't "taught" these questions of human existence. Rather, they emerge naturally, as do the self-evident conclusions that we come to about ourselves, others, and the world around us through the See-Do-Get Process, and the creation of our personal paradigm. The four key questions are listed below:

- How do I find an identity?
- How do I face the future?
- How do I deal with the environment?
- How do I get the results that I want from my one-trip through life?

It is important to note that these four questions emerge in people who have allowed the path of their lives to be directed by the force-for-growth, self-actualization and transcendence – as well as those who have allowed their path to be directed by the force-for-safety and deficiency-motivation. In growth-motivated people, these four questions lead them on the Upward Path of Becoming, where their lives are self-determined, authentic, reunited, autonomous, and trust-based. These same four questions lead those who are deficiency-driven on the Downward Spiral of Striving with lives that are compulsive, inauthentic, alienated, dependent, and fear-based.

While these questions and the conclusions that are associated with them emerge from the Symbolic-Level of the personal paradigm, each one has a wide spectrum of meanings depending on the level at which the question is addressed. The question, "How do I find an identity?" can include *external criteria* like physical appearance, an identification number used to establish a person's individuality, or a set of behavioral and personal characteristics by which a person is recognizable as a member of a specific group. Identity can also include *inner criteria* like a sense of self that distinguishes one person from others in terms of the sameness and continuity of an individual's personality, character, heart, and personal paradigm – how they "see" themselves, others, and the world. Our individual answer to the collective existential question of identity emerges naturally from the life-long task of following the path of our unique calling and destiny.

The question, "How do I face the future?" can include *external criteria* like dealing with the physical, financial, and relationship challenges of life and trying to age effectively. It can also include *inner criteria* like the fact that our future is contained within us in the sense of our actuality (who we currently are) and potentiality (who we could become). We learn that we can actually shape our own future by creating it daily through our choices. When we walk the path of Authenticity in Context, our individual answer to the collective existential question of facing the future emerges naturally from the force-for-growth and the Upward Path of Becoming.

The question, "How do I deal with the environment?" can include *external criteria* like the personal and professional challenges that we face day in and day out, navigating the edicts and demands of our culture, and remaining autonomous from people and situations that frustrate and undermine our desired path in life. It can also include *inner criteria* like having the inner force of will, courage, wisdom, and insight to deal effectively with the challenges we face in our personal and professional lives. Our individual answer to the collective existential question of dealing with the environment emerges naturally from the life-long task of following the path of our unique calling and destiny.

Finally, the question, "How do I get the results that I want from my one-trip through life?" can include *external criteria* like achieving our personal, professional, financial, social, and cultural goals, accomplishments, and aspirations. It can also include *inner criteria* like the desire and commitment to fully understand and utilize our talents, abilities, strengths, weaknesses; and the determination to allow the force-for-growth to lead us on the Upward Path of Becoming, self-actualization, and transcendence. Understanding the deepest desires of our heart, and being able to articulate and act on them is one of our key existential challenges because life is a currency that we spend one day at a time.

The Breckenridge Enneagram provides a "window" into the human heart and the depths of human character as described by the five levels of the personal paradigm. The goal is to *transcend* the autopilot, tacit, and unconscious forces of our personality with the goal of living life authentically. This includes building more effective relationships as well as transcending the edicts, demands, and norms of our family and cultural context, especially when they emerge from inauthentic foundations. On our view, the process of psychological integration is not the same process as spiritual transformation. The extent to which people become self-actualized and transcend the ineffective and inauthentic aspects of their personality and transcend their culture by living authentically *is not* a path to personal enlightenment or personal salvation. It is a path to psychological health, more effective relationships, and making contributions to humanity.

END NOTES

1   I am using the word "temperament" here in the common use of the word –
meaning the combination of cognitive, emotional, sensory, and motivational
aspects of human beings that is their innate, inborn disposition toward being
who they really are. Or put another way, our temperament is the genetic,
biologically inherited foundation from which our personality emerges over
time. I am not using the word "temperament" in the sense that David Keirsey
used it to mean a specific typology of four temperaments. Rather, our
"temperament" is the psycho-biological part of the human organism from which
the Breckenridge Enneagram and Keirsey's notion of four temperaments both
emerge. See David Keirsey and Marilyn Bates, *Please Understand Me*, (Del
Mar, CA: Prometheus Nemesis Book Company, 1984), and Linda Berens,
Understanding Yourself and Others: An Introduction to the Four Temperaments,
(Huntington Beach, CA: Telos Publications, 2006).

2   This position is espoused in, Pat Wyman, *Three Keys to Self-Understanding*,
(Gainesville, FL: CAPT, 2001), pp. 4-5.

3   See Linda Berens, *A History of Psychological Type and Temperament*,
(Huntington Beach, CA: Telos Publications, 2002).

4   See Berens, *A History of Psychological Type and Temperament*, 2002.

5   For an analysis of the typologies that arose during this period see, A.A. Roback,
The Psychology of Character: With a Survey of Temperament, (New York:
Kessinger Publishing, 2007).

6   For examples of this research see, Mark Bodnarczuk, "Some Sociological
Consequences of High-Energy Physicists' Development of the Standard Model"
in Lillian Hoddeson, Laurie Brown, Michael Riordan, and Max Dresden (Eds.),
The Rise of the Standard Model: Particle Physics in the 1960s and 1970s, (New
York: Cambridge University Press, 1997), pp. 384-393, and Mark Bodnarczuk
and Lillian Hoddeson, "Megascience in Particle Physics: The Birth of an
Experiment String at Fermilab" in *Historical Studies in the Natural Sciences*,
University of California, Berkeley; Volume 38; No. 4; Fall 2008, pp. 508-534.
My development of the model of "experimental strings" was also the main
theme of "Bigger Science: Experiment Strings, 1970-1988" in Lillian Hoddeson,
Adrienne Kolb, and Catherine Westfall, *Fermilab: Physics, the Frontier, and
Megascience*, (Chicago: University of Chicago Press, 2008), pp. 262-280

7   See G.E.R. Lloyd, *Early Greek Science: Thales to Aristotle*, (New York: W.W. Norton & Company, 1970); G.E.R Lloyd, *Greek Science After Aristotle*, (New York: W.W. Norton & Company, 1973); G.E.R. Lloyd, *Scientific Folklore and Ideology: Studies in the Life Sciences in Ancient Greece*, (New York: Cambridge University Press, 1983); G.E.R. Lloyd, *Magic, Reason, and Experience: Studies in the Origins and Development of Greek Science*, (London: Cambridge University Press, 1984); David Furley, *The Greek Cosmologists*, (New York: Cambridge University Press, 1987); Arthur Berry, *A Short History of Astronomy*, (New York: Dover Publications, 1961); Lucretius, *On the Nature of the Universe*, (New York: Penguin Books, 1986); Richard Westfall, *The Construction of Modern Science*, (New York: Cambridge University Press, 1977); Allen Debus, *Man and Nature in the Renaissance*, (New York: Cambridge University Press, 1985); S. Sambursky, *The Physical World of the Greeks*, (Princeton, NJ: Princeton University Press, 1987); S. Sambursky, *The Physical World of Late Antiquity*, (Princeton, NJ: Princeton University Press, 1987); S. Sambursky, *Physics of the Stoics*, (Princeton, NJ: Princeton University Press, 1987); Richard Morris, *Time's Arrows: Scientific Attitudes Toward Time*, (New York: Simon and Schuster, 1984); Tony Rothman, "The Seven Arrows of Time" in *Discover*, February, 1987, pp. 60-77; Morris Kline, *Mathematics and the Search for Knowledge*, (New York: Oxford University Press, 1985); Morris Kline, *Mathematics and the Loss of Certainty*, (New York: Oxford University Press, 1980); Morris Kline, *Mathematics in Western Culture*, (New York: Oxford University Press, 1953); and Carl Boyer, *A History of Mathematics*, (Princeton, NJ: Princeton University Press, 1985).

8   The Breckenridge Enneagram is based on the model of the Enneagram that was developed by Claudio Naranjo. For a description of Naranjo's version of the Enneagram as a Circumplex Model, see Claudio Naranjo, *Ennea-Type Structures*, (Nevada City, CA: Gateways/IDHHB Inc. Publishers, 1991), and Claudio Naranjo, *Character and Neurosis*, (Nevada City, CA: Gateways/IDHHB Inc. Publishers, 1994). It is also based on a Circumplex Model of personality that has a 75 year history of research and analysis by psychologists, psychiatrists, and psychometricians associated with the American Psychological Association. For a description of Circumplex Models of personality see, Robert Plutchik and Hope Conte (eds.), *Circumplex Models of Personality and Emotions*, (Washington, DC: American Psychological Association, 1997).

9   See Abraham Maslow, *Motivation and Personality*, 3rd edition, (New York: Harper Collins, 1987).

10   See Abraham Maslow, *Toward a Psychology of Being*, (New York: John Wiley and Sons, 1999).

11   The substance of the content of this section is based on Maslow's descriptions
     as found in Maslow, *Toward a Psychology of Being*, p. 27 ff; and Maslow,
     Motivation and Personality, p. 15 ff.

12   The substance of the content of this section is based on Maslow's descriptions
     as found in Maslow, *Toward a Psychology of Being*, p. 27 ff; and Maslow,
     Motivation and Personality, p. 15 ff.

13   See Maslow, *Toward a Psychology of Being*, p. 55.

14   The notion of symmetric versus complementary relationships is described in,
     Paul Watzlawick, *Pragmatics of Human Communication*, (New York: W.W.
     Norton & Company, 1967), pp. 51-54 and pp. 67-71.

15   See Maslow, *Toward a Psychology of Being*, p. 60.

16   See Maslow, *Toward a Psychology of Being*, p. 60.

17   Maslow describes how understanding our fear of self-knowledge was one of the
     key discoveries and contributions that Freud made to modern psychology. See
     Maslow, *Toward a Psychology of Being*, p. 71.

18   For more information on the issue of philosophy and children, see the Institute
     for the Advancement of Philosophy for Children (IAPC) at Montclair State
     University, the Northwest Center for Philosophy for Children at the University of
     Washington, and research conducted at Stanford University on teaching philos-
     ophy to children that are as young as four or five years old. For more information
     on the Stanford Studies, see *http://plato.stanford.edu/entries/children/*.

19   I first learned the formulation of these questions and the way in which they
     "map" on to the nine types from my teachers Don Riso and Russ Hudson.

20   See Naranjo, *Character and Neurosis*, p. 36.

21   This loop is an adaptation of Peter Senge's notion of the ladder of inference in,
     Peter Senge, Art Kleiner, Charlotte Roberts, Richard Ross, and Bryan Smith,
     The Fifth Discipline Fieldbook, (New York: Currency Doubleday, 1994), p. 243.

22   The material on the left-right and top-bottom symmetries follows the work of
     Naranjo in Naranjo, *Character and Neurosis*, p. 18 ff.

23   Much of the material on left-right symmetries follows the material developed
     by Naranjo in Naranjo, *Character and Neurosis*, p. 19 ff.

24   The material on top-bottom and triadic symmetries follows the work of Naranjo
     in Naranjo, *Character and Neurosis*, p. 19 ff.

25   The material on paradoxical symmetries follows the work of Naranjo in
     Naranjo, *Character and Neurosis*, p. 20 ff.

26 See, John Gottman, *Why Marriages Succeed or Fail and How You Can Make Yours Last*, (New York: Simon & Schuster, 1994), and John Gottman, *The Marriage Clinic: A Scientifically Based Marital Therapy*, (New York: W.W. Norton & Company, 1999).

27 See Malcolm Gladwell, *Blink*, (New York: Little, Brown, & Company, 2005), pp. 18-23.

28 See Gottman, *The Marriage Clinic*, p. 35 ff. and 88 ff.

29 Theoretically, Gottman is a neo-behaviorist who does not focus on the underlying cognitive and emotional causes of the patterns-of-action and interaction in relationships. See Gottman, *The Marriage Clinic*, p. 3 ff.

30 The Breckenridge Enneagram is based on the model of the Enneagram that was developed by Claudio Naranjo. For a description of Naranjo's version of the Enneagram as a Circumplex Model, see Naranjo, *Character and Neurosis*, 1994. It is also based on a Circumplex Model of personality. For a description of Circumplex Models of personality see, Plutchik and Conte (eds.), *Circumplex Models of Personality and Emotions*, 1997.

31 The characteristics of the personality types and the clustering into Head, Heart, and Action groups shown below are an adaptation of the model developed by Claudio Naranjo and the Circumplex Theory of personality, see, Naranjo, *Character and Neurosis*, p. 14 and p. 24 ff and Plutchik and Conte (eds.), *Circumplex Models of Personality and Emotions*, 1997.

32 This metaphor about the neocortex can be found at *http://www.medterms.com/script/main/art.asp?articlekey=25283*.

33 I have purposely used the word 'somatic" here to stress the interdependent relationship between the biological aspects of the human organism, the psychological aspects of the human brain, and the environment within which people live.

34 For a more complete discussion on Maslow's Hierarchy of Needs see, Maslow, *Motivation and Personality*, p. 15 ff.

35 See Naranjo, *Character and Neurosis*, p. 9.

36 Richard Dawkins argues that when we die, the only things that we leave on earth are genes and memes, both of which are propagators of information that duplicate themselves. Genes are replicators that transmit genetic information. Memes are units of cultural information such as words, ideas, tunes, images, beliefs, values, interest-areas, and world views of individuals or groups of people that can be passed from brain-to-brain. Transmitting memes causes other people to become

carriers of these units and shapes how they view the world. See Richard Dawkins, *The Selfish Gene*, (New York: Oxford University Press, 1976), p. 203 ff.

37   See Dawkins, *The Selfish Gene*, p. 203 ff.

38   For a more complete discussion of Maslow's Hierarchy see Maslow, *Toward a Psychology of Being*, p. 25 ff., and Maslow, *Motivation and Personality*, p. 15 ff.

39   See Kurt Lewin, *Resolving Social Conflicts: Field Theory in Social Science*, (Washington, DC: American Psychological Association, 2004), p. 59 ff.

40   The material in this section echoes Maslow's work in Maslow, *Motivation and Personality*, p. 15 ff.

41   The tendency toward either-or-thinking is cultural and emerges from our Western (binary) way of viewing the world. Jim Collins and Jerry Porras refer to it as "the tyranny of the OR." For example, I can either be assertive or passive, I can be either rational or emotional, or I can either have autonomy or be controlled. Collins calls the counter point "the genius of the AND" and characterizes it as both-and-thinking. It emerges from a more Eastern approach to problem-solving and decision-making where we embrace and pursue both extremes at the same time and live in the paradox. Both-and-thinking doesn't seek to strike a balance that is mid-point between two extremes; e.g., a fifty-fifty split. Both-and-thinking is about pursuing two seemingly contradictory ideas at the same time. James Collins and Jerry Porras, *Built to Last*, (New York: Harper Business, 1994), p. 43 ff.

42   See Bruce Wexler, *Brain and Culture*, (Cambridge, MA: A Bradford Book, 2006), p. 3 ff.

43   See Clotaire Rapaille, *The Culture Code*, (New York: Broadway Books, 2006), p. 1 ff.

44   Etymologically, the word "metaphysics" comes from the Greek phrase *meta ta physika* which literally means "after the things of nature" and was used by Hellenistic commentators like the 1st Century B.C. Andronicus of Rhodes to describe the untitled body of Aristotle's writings that came after his writings on physics (*physika*). Aristotle does not use the word metaphysics in these texts but refers to this body of his writings as being about "first philosophy, theology, ontology, and wisdom." In both medieval and modern philosophy, the word "metaphysics" has come to mean the study of things that "transcend" nature and natural phenomena; e.g., things that exist apart from natural things and that have an intrinsic value and reality that is over-and-above natural things. In more recent times, the word "metaphysical" has been associated with spiritual, religious, and occult teachings and phenomena. See Paul Edward (ed.), *The*

Encyclopedia of Philosophy, Volume 5, (New York: Macmillan Publishing Company, 1972), p. 289 ff.

45   Nancey Murphy, professor at Fuller Theological Seminary, is one example of a scholar who approaches the causes of things with a largely naturalistic-attitude who still believes in God. See, Nancey Murphy, *Bodies and Souls, or Spirited Bodies*, (New York: Cambridge University Press, 2006); and Warren Brown, Nancey Murphy, and H. Newton Malony (eds.), *Whatever Happened to the Soul: Scientific and Theological Portraits of Human Nature?*, (Minneapolis, MN: Fortress Press, 1998).

46   Although some Enneagram teachers like Don Riso and Russ Hudson have tried to develop the Enneagram as a personality typing tool, the foundation of their theoretical model is still spiritual in nature, and the methods and mechanisms through which psychological growth occur are based squarely on metaphysical foundations. More specifically, Riso and Hudson argue that psychological growth and spiritual growth are not separate processes. This position is held by most traditional Enneagram teachers.

47   See Sandra Maitri, *The Spiritual Dimension of the Enneagram*, (New York: Jeremy Tarcher, Putnam, 2000), p. 3.

48   While some authors like Kripal have interpreted Maslow through the metaphysical-perspective, we believe this is a misguided view of Maslow's stated purpose, philosophy, and commitments. Rather, the writings of Maslow that we reference are based firmly on a naturalistic view of human psychology, where self-actualization is becoming who we were meant to be and transcendence is the ability to transcend the confines of our personality and the edicts and demands of our culture. See Jeffery Kripal, *Esalen*, (Chicago: University of Chicago Press, 2007), p. 135 ff.

49   See Don Richard Riso with Russ Hudson, *Personality Types*, (New York: Houghton Mifflin Company, 1996), p. 11 ff.

50   See Mark Bodnarczuk, "Some Sociological Consequences of High-Energy Physicists' Development of the Standard Model" in Lillian Hoddeson (ed.), *The Rise of the Standard Model: Particle Physics in the 1960s and 1970s*, (New York: Cambridge University Press, 1997), pp. 384-393; James Trefil, *From Atoms to Quarks*, (New York: Charles Scribner's Sons, 1980); Heinz Pagels, *The Cosmic Code: Quantum Physics as the Language of Nature*, (New York: Simon and Schuster, 1982), and Michael Riordan, *The Hunting of the Quark*, (New York: A Touchstone Book, 1987).

51   See G.E.R. Lloyd, *Early Greek Science: Thales to Aristotle*, (New York: W.W. Norton & Company, 1970); G.E.R Lloyd, *Greek Science After Aristotle*, (New

York: W.W. Norton & Company, 1973); G.E.R. Lloyd, *Scientific Folklore and Ideology: Studies in the Life Sciences in Ancient Greece*, (New York: Cambridge University Press, 1983); G.E.R. Lloyd, *Magic, Reason, and Experience: Studies in the Origins and Development of Greek Science*, (London: Cambridge University Press, 1984); David Furley, *The Greek Cosmologists*, (New York: Cambridge University Press, 1987); Arthur Berry, *A Short History of Astronomy*, (New York: Dover Publications, 1961); Lucretius, *On the Nature of the Universe*, (New York: Penguin Books, 1986); Richard Westfall, *The Construction of Modern Science*, (New York: Cambridge University Press, 1977); Allen Debus, *Man and Nature in the Renaissance*, (New York: Cambridge University Press, 1985); S. Sambursky, *The Physical World of the Greeks*, (Princeton, NJ: Princeton University Press, 1987); S. Sambursky, *The Physical World of Late Antiquity*, (Princeton, NJ: Princeton University Press, 1987); S. Sambursky, *Physics of the Stoics*, (Princeton, NJ: Princeton University Press, 1987); Richard Morris, *Time's Arrows: Scientific Attitudes Toward Time*, (New York: Simon and Schuster, 1984); Tony Rothman, "The Seven Arrows of Time" in *Discover*, February, 1987, pp. 60-77; Morris Kline, *Mathematics and the Search for Knowledge*, (New York: Oxford University Press, 1985); Morris Kline, *Mathematics and the Loss of Certainty*, (New York: Oxford University Press, 1980); Morris Kline, *Mathematics in Western Culture*, (New York: Oxford University Press, 1953); and Carl Boyer, *A History of Mathematics*, (Princeton, NJ: Princeton University Press, 1985).

52   See Plato, "The Republic" in the *Collected Dialogues of Plato*, (Princeton, NJ: Princeton University Press, 1985), p. 761, and 528 ff.

53   See Rene Descartes, *The Philosophical Writings of Descartes*, 2 Volumes, translated by John Cottingham, Robert Stoothoff, and Dugald Murdoch, (New York: Cambridge University Press, 1985).

54   See Thomas Kuhn, *The Structure of Scientific Revolutions*, 3rd Edition, (Chicago: University of Chicago Press, 1996); Thomas Kuhn, *The Copernican Revolution*, (Cambridge, MA: Harvard University Press, 1957), and Galileo Galilei, *Dialogue Concerning the Two Chief World Systems*, Translated by Stillman Drake, (Berkeley, CA: University of California Press, 1967).

55   See Arthur Berry, *A Short History of Astronomy*, (New York: Dover Publications, 1961); Galileo Galilei, *Dialogue Concerning the Two Chief World Systems – Ptolemaic and Copernican*, translated by Stillman Drake, (Berkeley, CA: University of California Press, 1967); Isaac Newton, *The Principia*, translated by I.B. Cohen and Anne Whitman, (Berkeley, CA: University of California Press, 1999); and Richard Westfall, *Never at Rest: A Biography of Isaac Newton*, (New York: Cambridge University Press, 1998).

56   See Isabel Briggs Myers, *Gifts Differing*, (Palo Alto, CA: Davies-Black Publishing, 1995), and C.G. Jung, *Memories, Dreams, Reflections*, (New York: Vintage Books, 1989).

57   See Homer, *The Iliad*, translated by Alexander Pope, (New York: Thomas Crowell & Co, 1925), and Homer, *The Odyssey*, translated by Alexander Pope, (New York: Hurst & Co Publishers, 1930).

58   See Lloyd, *Early Greek Science: Thales to Aristotle*, p. 9.

59   See Lucretius, *On the Nature of the Universe*, (New York: Penguin, 1986); W.K.C Guthrie, *The Sophists*, (New York: Cambridge University Press, 1983); Richard McKeon (ed.), *The Basic Works of Aristotle*, (New York: Random House, 1941); Edith Hamilton and Huntington Cairns (eds.), *The Collected Dialogues of Plato Including the Letters*, (Princeton, NJ: Princeton University Press, 1985); and W.K.C. Guthrie, *A History of Greek Philosophy*, Volumes I-V, (New York: Cambridge University Press, 1985).

60   See, G.I Gurdjieff, *Beelzebub's Tales to His Grandson*, (New York: Tarcher, 2006); G.I. Gurdjieff, *Meetings with Remarkable Men*, (New York: Penguin, 1991); and G.I. Gurdjieff, *Views from the Real World*, (New York: Penguin, 1991).

61   Don Riso and Russ Hudson trace the roots of the Enneagram diagram back to Greek philosophers like Pythagoras, Plato, and Neo-platonic writers (around 400-300 BC); while Richard Rohr argues that the Enneagram symbol has Christian roots that can be traced back to the Desert Fathers in the 4th Century AD. See, Don Riso and Russ Hudson, *The Wisdom of the Enneagram*, (New York: Bantam Books, 1999), p. 19 ff; Riso and Hudson, Personality Types, p. 11 ff. and Richard Rohr and Andreas Ebert, *The Enneagram: A Christian Perspective*, (New York: A Crossroad Book, 2006), pp. ix, and 8 ff.

62   See P.D. Ouspensky, *In Search of the Miraculous*, (New York: Harcourt, Brace & World, Inc. 1949); P.D. Ouspensky, *The Fourth Way*, (New York: Vintage, 1971); J.G. Bennett, *Enneagram Studies*, (York Beach, ME: Samuel Weiser, Inc., 1988); John Bennett, *Gurdjieff: Making a New World*, (New York: Bennett Publishing, 1992); and John Bennett, *Masters of Wisdom*, (New York: Bennett Books, 1995).

63   See Riso and Hudson, *The Wisdom of the Enneagram*, p. 20.

64   See Bennett, *Enneagram Studies*, p. 66 ff.

65   Sometime later Idries Shah claimed the Enneagram symbol originated from the Naqshbandi sect of Sufism. For a description of the shape of the Enneagram see, Idries Shah, *The Commanding Self*, (New York: Octagon Press, 1994);

Idries Shah, *The Way of the Sufi*, (New York: Octagon Press, 2004); and Idries Shah, *The Pleasantries of the Incredible Mulla Nasrudin*, (New York: Penguin Compass, 1968). For another description of the connection between the Enneagram shape and the Sufi see, Omar Ali-Shah, *The Sufi Tradition in the West*, (New York: Tractus, 1995).

66   Richard Rohr has stated that Ichazo believes that the nine points originate with him and were taught to him "'by an Archangel while on mescaline.'" See Richard Rohr and Andreas Ebert, *Discovering the Enneagram*, (New York: Crossroad, 1998), p. 12.

67   The connection between Ichazo and the Enneads was mentioned in, Riso and Hudson, *The Wisdom of the Enneagram*, p. 22. For more details see, Plotinus, *The Enneads*, edited by John Dillon, (New York: Penguin Classics, 1991); Pierre Hadot, *Plotinus or the Simplicity of Vision*, (Chicago: University of Chicago Press, 1998); and Brian Hines, *Return to the One: Plotinus' Guide to God-Realization*, (New York: Unlimited Publishing, LLC, 2004).

68   See Riso with Hudson, *Personality Types*, p. 19.

69   See John Lilly, *Center of the Cyclone: Looking into Inner Space*, (New York: Ronin Publishing, 2007), and John Lilly, *Dyadic Cyclone*, (New York: Pocket Books, 1977).

70   See Naranjo, *Character and Neurosis*, p. xv ff.

71   See Berens, *A History of Psychological Type and Temperament*, 2002.

72   For an analysis of the typologies that arose during this period see, Roback, *The Psychology of Character*, p. 2 ff.

73   See Carl Jung, *Psychological Types*, Volume 6, *Collected Works of C.G. Jung*, (Princeton, NJ: Princeton University Press, 1990); Marie von Franz and James Hillman, *Jung's Typology*, (New York: Spring Publications, 1975); Anne Singer Harris, *Living with Paradox*, (New York: Brooks/Cole Publishing Company, 1996); and Isabel Briggs Myers, *Gifts Differing*, (Palo-Alto, CA: Davies-Black Publishing, 1995);

74   See Ernst Kretschmer, *Physique and Character*, (New York: Humanities Press, 1951); Eduard Spranger, *Types of Men: The Psychology and Ethics of Personality*, (Berlin: Max Niemeyer Verlag, 1928); David Keirsey and Marilyn Bates, *Please Understand Me*, (Del Mar, CA: Prometheus Nemesis Book Company, 1984).

75   See William Marston, *Emotions of Normal People*, (Minneapolis, MN: Persona Press, Inc., 1979); David Merrill and Roger Reid, *Personal Styles & Effective Performance*, (New York: CRC Press, 1999); and Robert Bolton and Dorothy

Bolton, *Social Style/Management Style*, (New York: American Management Association, 1984).

76 See Plutchik and Conte, (eds.), *Circumplex Models of Personality and Emotions*, p. 1 ff.

77 Jerry Wiggins (ed.), *The Five-Factor Model*, (New York: The Guilford Press, 1996); Paul Costa and Thomas Widiger (eds.), *Personality Disorders and the Five-Factor Model of Personality*, (Washington, DC: American Psychological Association, 2002); Robert McCrae and Paul Costa, *Personality in Adulthood: A Five-Factor Theory Perspective*, 2nd Edition, (New York: Guilford Press, 2002); and Robert McCrae and Juri Allik (eds.), *The Five-Factor Model of Personality Across Cultures*, (New York: Springer, 2002).

78 See Harry Stack Sullivan, *The Interpersonal Theory of Psychiatry*, (New York: W.W. Norton, 1953).

79 L. Guttmann, "A New Approach to Factor Analysis: The Radex" in Paul Lazerfeld (ed.), *Mathematical Thinking in the Social Sciences*, (Glencoe, IL: Free Press, 1954), pp. 258-348.

80 Timothy Leary, *Interpersonal Diagnosis of Personality*, (Eugene, OR: Resource Publications, 1957), Jerry Wiggins, *Personality and Prediction*, (New York: Longman Higher Education, 1973); Jerry Wiggins, *Principles of Personality*, (New York: Longman Higher Education, 1976); Jerry Wiggins, *Psychology of Personality*, (New York: Longman Higher Education, 1971); and David Olson, Candyce Russell, Douglas Sprenke (eds.), *Circumplex Model: A Systematic Assessment and Treatment of Families*, (New York: Haworth Press, 1989).

81 Robert Plutchik, *The Emotions*, (New York: University Press of America, 1991); Robert Plutchik, *The Psychology and Biology of Emotion*, (New York: Harper Collins, 1994); Robert Plutchik, *Emotions and Life: Perspectives from Psychology, Biology, and Evolution*, (Washington, DC: American Psychological Association, 2003); Robert Plutchik, *Emotions in the Practice of Psychotherapy*, (Washington, DC: American Psychological Association, 2005); Sullivan, *The Interpersonal Theory of Psychiatry*, 1953; Lorna Smith Benjamin, *Interpersonal Diagnosis and Treatment of Personality Disorders*, (New York: Guilford Press, 1993); Richard Lazarus, *Emotion and Adaptation*, (New York: Oxford University Press, 1991; Richard Lazarus and Bernice Lazarus, *Passion and Reason: Making Sense of Our Emotions*, (New York: Oxford University Press, 1994); Keith Oatley, *Emotions: A Brief History*, (Malden, MA: Blackwell Publishing, 2004); Keith Oatley, *Best Laid Schemes: The Psychology of Emotions*, (New York: Cambridge University Press, 1992); Keith Oatley and Jennifer Jenkins, *Understanding Emotions*, (Malden, MA: Blackwell Publishing, 1996); Nico Frijda, Antony Manstead, Sacha Bem, *Emotions and*

Beliefs: How Feelings Influence Thoughts, (New York: Cambridge University Press, 2006); Nico Frijda, *The Laws of Emotion*, (Mahwah, NJ: Lawrence Erlbaum Associates Publishers, 2007); and Antony Manstead, Nico Frijda, and Agneta Fischer (eds.), *Feelings and Emotions: Studies in Emotion and Social Interaction*, (New York: Cambridge University Press, 2004).

82   For more details on the models and instruments used to empirically measure and test Circumplex theories see, Plutchik and Conte, (eds.), *Circumplex Models of Personality and Emotions*, p. 57 ff.

83   See Naranjo, *Character and Neurosis*, p. xxi-xxvii.

84   See Naranjo, *Character and Neurosis*, p. xxvi.

85   See Naranjo, *Character and Neurosis*, pp. 14-16.

86   See Naranjo, *Character and Neurosis*, p. xxii.

87   See Claudio Naranjo, *The Enneagram and Society*, (Nevada City, CA: Gateway/IDHHB Inc. Publishers, 2004), p. 31 ff.

88   See Shah, *The Way of the Sufi*, p.9 ff.

89   See Naranjo, *Character and Neurosis*, p. xviii.

90   See Naranjo, *Character and Neurosis*, p. xxix.

91   See Kripal, *Esalen*, p. 178 ff.

92   See Riso with Hudson, *Personality Types*, p. 20.

93   See A.H. Almaas, *Facets of Unity*, (Berkeley, CA: Diamond Books, 1998), p. 3.

94   See Naranjo, *Character and Neurosis*, p. 14 ff.

95   See Claudio Naranjo, *Ennea-Type Structures: Self Analysis for Seekers*, (Nevada City, CA: Gateway/IDHHB Inc. Publishers, 1990).

96   For an excellent discussion of the Freudian underpinnings of the Enneagram see Susan Rhodes, "Enneagram Type is With Us at Birth, Part II: Deconstructing the Freudian Enneagram" in *Enneagram Monthly*, December 2008, Issue 154, pp. 1 and 13-21.

97   See Almaas, *Facets of Unity*, pp. 4-5

98   See Maitri, *The Spiritual Dimension of the Enneagram: Nine Faces of the Soul*, pp. 7-8.

99   See Naranjo, *Character and Neurosis*, p. 2.

100   See Naranjo, *Character and Neurosis*, p. 38.

101 See Naranjo, *Character and Neurosis*, p. 36.

102 See Stanislav Grof, *When the Impossible Happens*, (New York: Sounds True Publishing, 2006); Stanislav Grof, *The Holotropic Mind: The Three Levels of Human Consciousness and How they Shape Our Lives*, (New York: Harper One, 1993); Stanislav Grof, *The Ultimate Journey: Consciousness and the Mystery of Death*, (San Francisco: Multidisciplinary Association for Psychedelic Studies, 2006); Stanislav Grof, *The Adventure of Self-Discovery: Dimensions of Consciousness and New Perspectives in Psychotherapy and Inner Exploration*, (New York: State University of New York Press, 1988); and Stanislav Grof, *Beyond the Brain: Birth, Death and Transcendence in Psychotherapy*, (New York: State University of New York Press, 1986).

103 At the time when I was trained by Riso and Hudson in the mid-to-late 1990s, Holotropic Breathing was one of the key elements of the Part II training program.

104 See Ken Wilber, *The Eye of the Spirit*, (New York: Shambhala, 2001).

105 See Maitri, *The Spiritual Dimension of the Enneagram*, p.35 ff.

106 See June Singer, *Boundaries of the Soul*, (New York: Anchor Books, 1994), p. 274 ff.; and C.G. Jung, "Psychological Types" Volume 6, *The Collected Works of Carl Jung*, (Princeton, NJ: Princeton University Press, 1990), paragraph 828.

107 The connection between Ichazo and the Enneads was mentioned in, Riso and Hudson, *The Wisdom of the Enneagram*, p. 22. For more details see, Plotinus, *The Enneads*, edited by John Dillon, (New York: Penguin Classics, 1991); Pierre Hadot, *Plotinus or the Simplicity of Vision*, (Chicago: University of Chicago Press, 1998); and Brian Hines, *Return to the One: Plotinus' Guide to God-Realization*, (New York: Unlimited Publishing, LLC, 2004).

108 See Almaas, *Facets of Unity*, pp 7.

109 See Plato, The Collected Dialogues Including the Letters, edited by Edith Hamilton and Huntington Cairns, (Princeton, NJ: Princeton University Press, 1985). Their ontology also has many parallels with Gnosticism. See, Birger Pearson, *Ancient Gnosticism*, (New York: Fortress Press, 2007); Karen King, *What Is Gnosticism*, (New York: Belknap Press, 2005); and Richard Smoley, *Forbidden Faith: The Secret History of Gnosticism*, (New York: Harper One, 2007).

110 This diagram is a modified version of the one Naranjo used in, Naranjo, *Character and Neurosis*, p. 11.

111 See Riso and Hudson, *The Wisdom of the Enneagram*, p. 28.

112 See Maitri, *The Spiritual Dimension of the Enneagram*, p.7 ff.

113 See Naranjo, *Character and Neurosis*, p. 9 ff.

114 See Almaas, *Facets of Unity*, p. 6 ff; Maitri, *The Spiritual Dimension of the Enneagram*, p. 2 ff; and Sandra Maitri, *The Enneagram of Passions and Virtues*, (New York: Jeremy Tarcher, Putnam, 2005).

115 As mentioned previously, I am using the word "temperament" here in the common use of the word – meaning the combination of cognitive, emotional, sensory, and motivational aspects of human beings that is their innate, inborn disposition toward being who they really are. Or put another way, our temperament is the genetic, biologically inherited foundation from which our personality emerges over time. I am not using the word "temperament" in the sense that David Keirsey used it to mean a specific typology of four temperaments. Rather, our "temperament" is the psycho-biological part of the human organism from which both the Breckenridge Enneagram and Keirsey's notion of four temperaments both emerge. See Keirsey and Bates, *Please Understand Me*; p. 2 ff; and Berens, *Understanding Yourself and Others: An Introduction to the Four Temperaments*, p. 4 ff.

116 See Naranjo, *Character and Neurosis*, p. 3 ff; and Maitri, *The Spiritual Dimension of the Enneagram*, p. 23 ff.

117 See Maitri, *The Spiritual Dimension of the Enneagram*, p. 3.

118 See Claudio Naranjo, *Transformation through Insight*, (Prescott, AZ: Hohm Press, 1997).

119 See Riso and Hudson, *The Wisdom of the Enneagram*, p. 28.

120 See Riso and Hudson, *The Wisdom of the Enneagram*, Front Matter.

121 See Maslow, *Toward a Psychology of Being*, p. 14.

122 See Martin Heidegger, *Being and Time*, (New York: Harper and Row, 1962); Karl Jaspers, *Basic Philosophical Writings*, (New York: Humanities Press, 1994); Jean-Paul Sartre, *Existentialism and Human Emotions*, (New York: Citadel, 2000); Jean-Paul Sartre, *Being and Nothingness*, (New York: Washington Square Press, 1993); Soren Kierkegaard, *Fear and Trembling*, (New York: Wilder Publications, 2008); and Soren Kierkegaard, *Either/Or: A Fragment of Life*, (New York: Penguin Classics, 1992).

123 See Maslow, *Toward a Psychology of Being*, p 13 ff. Also see Gordon Allport, *Becoming: Basic Considerations for a Psychology of Personality*, (New Haven, CT: Yale University Press, 1963); Carl Rogers, *On Becoming a Person*, (New York: Houghton Mifflin, 1995); Carl Rogers, *A Way of Being*, (New York: Houghton Mifflin, 1980); Kurt Goldstein, *The Organism*, (New York: Zone

Books, 2000); Erich Fromm, *To Have or To Be*, (New York: Bantam Books, 1981); Viktor Frankl, *Man's Search for Meaning*, (New York: Washington Square Press, 1984); Viktor Frankl, *The Unheard Cry for Meaning*, (New York: A Touchstone Book, 1978); Allen Wheelis, *The Quest for Identity*, (New York: W.W. Norton & Company, 1958); Rollo May, *Man's Search for Himself*, (New York: W.W. Norton & Company, 1953); Rollo May, *Love and Will*, (New York: A Delta Book, 1981); Rollo May, *The Cry for Myth*, (New York: W.W. Norton, 1991); Erik Erickson, *Identity and the Life Cycle*, (New York: W.W. Norton & Company, 1994); Karen Horney, *The Neurotic Personality of Our Time*, (New York: W.W. Norton & Company, 1964); and Karen Horney, *Neurosis and Human Growth: The Struggle toward Self-Realization*, (New York: W.W. Norton & Company, 1991).

124 As mentioned previously, while some authors like Kripal have interpreted Maslow through the metaphysical-perspective, we believe this is a misguided view of Maslow's stated purpose, philosophy, and commitments. Maslow's later works like Religions, Values, and Peak-Experiences try to "humanize" both science and religion, but he does not espouse a metaphysical-perspective about either science or religion. Rather, the writings of Maslow that we reference are based firmly on a naturalistic view of human psychology, where self-actualization is becoming who we were meant to be and transcendence is the ability to transcend the confines of our personality and the edits and demands of our culture. See Kripal, *Esalen*, p. 135 ff; and Abraham Maslow, *Religions, Values, and Peak-Experiences*, (New York: Penguin Compass, 1994).

125 This is the summary of key points of neo-Freudian existentialism proposed by Maslow in, Maslow, *Toward a Psychology of Being*, pp. 19-20. Also see, Richard McKeon, (ed.), *The Basic Works of Aristotle*, (New York: Random House, 1941) and G.E.R Lloyd, *Early Greek Science: Thales to Aristotle*, (New York: W.W. Norton & Company, 1970).

126 The most ancient example of this type of wisdom literature is the Egyptian "Wisdom of Ptah-hotep" which dates back to 2,500 BC. The writings of Confucius (6th Century BC) and Mencius (4th Century BC) are more sophisticated that their Egyptian counterparts, but still focus on living a good, normal life. The form of wisdom literature that had the greatest influence on Western civilization came from the Hebrew people as found in the more philo-sophical portions of the Bible (Proverbs, Psalms, Ecclesiastes, Job, and the Song of Solomon). In Greek literature, wisdom was developed by Hesiod (8th Century BC), Theognis (6th Century BC), and Pythagoras (6th Century BC).

127 Ian Hacking and Peter Galison offer philosophical rebuttals to the post-modernist, deconstructionist implications that emerged from Thomas Kuhn's model of paradigms that he proposed in *Structures of Scientific Revolutions*. In much the

same way, we adopt the power of Kuhn's model of the creation and development of human knowledge through paradigms and paradigm shifts, and hold on to a form of objective realism where the world can confirm, reject, or correct how we "see" the world by objectively intervening and not cooperating with the configuration of experimental apparatus we build, or the results that we get from our one-trip through life. See, Ian Hacking, *Representing and Intervening*, (New York: Cambridge University Press, 1983); Ian Hacking, *The Social Construction of What*, (Cambridge, MA: Harvard University Press, 1999); and Peter Galison, *How Experiments End*, (Chicago: University of Chicago Press, 1987).

128 This is discussed in Mark Bodnarczuk, *Diving In*, (Seattle, WA: Elton-Wolf Publishing, 2003), p. 80ff.

129 This is discussed in Mark Bodnarczuk, *Island of Excellence*, (Seattle, WA: Elton-Wolf Publishing, 2004), p. 135 ff. and 179 ff.

130 The notion of the Spectator Role is discussed in more detail in Bodnarczuk, *Diving In*, p. 157 ff. and Bodnarczuk, *Island of Excellence*, p. 318 ff.

131 See Rogers, *On Becoming a Person*, p. 26.

132 For more information on the issue of philosophy and children, see the Institute for the Advancement of Philosophy for Children (IAPC) at Montclair State University, the Northwest Center for Philosophy for Children at the University of Washington, and research conducted at Stanford University on teaching philosophy to children that are as young as four or five years old. For more information on the Stanford Studies, see *http://plato.stanford.edu/entries/children/*.

133 Maslow describes how understanding our fear of self-knowledge was one of the key discoveries and contributions that Freud made to modern psychology. See Maslow, *Toward a Psychology of Being*, p. 71.

134 Wilson calls this the Adaptive Unconscious, see, Timothy Wilson, *Strangers to Ourselves*, (Cambridge, MA: Belknap Press of Harvard University Press, 2002).

135 For the role of "existentialism" in psychology and a naturalistic foundation see, Maslow, *Toward a Psychology of Being*, p. 11 ff.

136 See Maslow, *Toward a Psychology of Being*, p. 27.

137 See Maslow, *Toward a Psychology of Being*, p. 55.

138 See Maslow, *Toward a Psychology of Being*, p. 27.

139 See Berens, *A History of Psychological Type and Temperament*, 2002.

140 For an analysis of the typologies that arose during this period see, Roback, *The Psychology of Character*, p. 2 ff.

141 See Wexler, *Brain and Culture*, p. 1 ff.

142 This loop is an adaptation of Peter Senge's notion of the ladder of inference in, Senge, Kleiner, Roberts, Ross, and Smith, *The Fifth Discipline Fieldbook*, p. 243.

143 See Kuhn, *The Structure of Scientific Revolutions*, p. 25 ff.

144 For a more complete discussion on the relationship between the levels on this diagram and the operations and functionality of the human brain see, Joseph LeDoux, *The Emotional Brain*, (New York: A Touchstone Book, 1996); Joseph LeDoux, *The Synaptic Self*, (New York: Viking Press, 2002); Steven Pinker, *How the Mind Works*, (New York: W.W. Norton, 1999); and Antonio Damasio, *The Feeling of What Happens*, (New York: A Harvest Book, 1999).

145 As LeDoux points out, there are many interdependent elements of functionality that are part of the frontal cortex areas that make up working-level memory. The areas of the frontal lobe that are believed to be a part of working-level memory include the lateral pre-frontal cortex and the orbital and anterior cingulated cortex. For a more complete discussion, see LeDoux, *The Emotional Brain*, p. 278 ff.

146 See Senge et all, *The Fifth Discipline Fieldbook*, p. 242 ff.

147 This metaphor about the neocortex can be found at *http://www.medterms.com /script/main/art.asp?articlekey=25283*.

148 See Keirsey and Bates, *Please Understand Me*, p. 2 ff; and Berens, *An Introduction to the Four Temperaments*, p. 4 ff.

149 See Wexler, *Brain and Culture*, p. 2 ff.

150 See Rapaille, *The Culture Code*, 1 ff.

151 For a more complete description of how the Breckenridge Equation™ and the Breckenridge Change Equation™ can be applied to culture see the forthcoming book, Mark Bodnarczuk, *Making Invisible Bureaucracy Visible: A Guide to Assessing and Changing Organizational Culture*, (Boulder, CO: Breckenridge Press, 2009).

152 This is an adaptation of a model presented in Kerry Patterson, Joseph Grenny, Ron McMillan, and Al Switzler, *Crucial Confrontations*, (New York: McGraw-Hill, 2005), p. 32 ff.

153 These six elements can be measured in organizations using the Organizational Trust Index™ developed by the Breckenridge Institute® that is part of the Breckenridge Culture indicator™ (BCI™).

154 See W. Edwards Deming, *Out of Crisis*, (Cambridge, MA: MIT Press, 1992) pp. 59-62

155 See Maslow, *Maslow on Management*, p. 20.

156 See Maslow, *Toward a Psychology of Being*, p. 72.

157   Chris Argyris, Robert Putnam, and Diana McLain Smith, *Action Science*, (San Francisco: Jossey-Bass Publishers, 1985), p. 340 ff, and Senge, Kleiner, Roberts, Ross, and Smith, *The Fifth Discipline Fieldbook*, p. 246 ff.

158   See Joseph Luft, *Group Processes*, 3rd Edition, (Mountain View, CA: Mayfield Publishing Company, 1984).

159   The model presented here is an adaptation of the notion of double-loop learning developed by Chris Argyris, Robert Putnam, and Diana McLain Smith, *Action Science*, (San Francisco: Jossey-Bass Publishers, 1985), p. 81 ff.

160   Chris Argyris, *Overcoming Organizational Defenses: Facilitating Organizational Learning*, (Needham, MA: Allyn & Bacon, 1990).

161   Chris Argyris, *Knowledge for Action*, (San Francisco: Jossey-Bass Publishers, 1993), p. 20.

162   The substance of the content of this section is based on Maslow's descriptions as described in Maslow, *Toward a Psychology of Being*, p.27 ff, and Maslow, *Motivation and Personality*, p. 15 ff.

163   This is based on a model developed by Edgar Schein see, Edgar Schein, *The Corporate Culture Survival Guide*, (San Francisco: Jossey-Bass, 1999), p. 124 ff.

164   The model of learning anxiety and survival anxiety is discussed in more detail in, Schein, *The Corporate Culture Survival Guide*, p. 121 ff.

165   Bodnarczuk, *Island of Excellence*, p. 225.

166   See James Collins and Jerry Porras, *Built to Last*, (New York: Harper Business, 1994), p. 43 ff.

167   This over emphasis on pragmatism characterizes American culture and psychology and is typified by the philosophical school of thought called Pragmatism. See William James, *Pragmatism*, (New York: Dodo Press, 2007); John Dewey, *Theory of Valuation*, (Chicago: University of Chicago Press, 1947); and Larry Hickman (ed.), *The Essential Dewey*, (Indianapolis, IN: Indiana University Press, 1998).

168   This is based on an original line by Robert Frost and subsequently popularized by Scott Peck in his best-selling book. See Scott Peck, *The Road Less Traveled*, (New York: Touchstone, 2003).

169   Maslow describes how understanding our fear of self-knowledge was one of the key discoveries and contributions that Freud made to modern psychology. See Maslow, *Toward a Psychology of Being*, p. 71.

ABOUT THE AUTHOR

Mark Bodnarczuk is the Executive Director of the Breckenridge Institute®, a research and consulting firm that focuses on organizational culture based in Boulder, Colorado. He was on the staff in the Director's Office at Fermi National Accelerator Laboratory (Fermilab) from 1980 through 1992, and the National Renewable Energy Laboratory from 1992 until 1996 when he founded the Breckenridge Institute®. While at the University of Chicago, his research focused on the sociology and culture of large high-energy physics collaborations at Fermilab.

He is an author, researcher, consultant, teacher, and facilitator with more than twenty years of experience working with companies in the area of high-tech, basic and applied research, pharmaceuticals, health care, retail as well as government and non-profit organizations. Mark has published widely in the areas of organizational culture and leadership development, and has published numerous articles on the leadership and management of science and the cultural dimensions of laboratory life. He is also the author of *Diving In: Discovering Who You Are in the Second Half of Life* which is a teaching novel about the Enneagram.

Mark was trained in the Enneagram by Don Riso and Russ Hudson, and received his training in the MBTI® assessment tool from Margaret Hartzler. He is a professional-level member of the International Society of Performance Improvement (ISPI) and the Institute of Management Consultants (IMC). Mark has a BA from Mid-America Nazarene University, an MA from Wheaton College, and an AM from the University of Chicago.

FOR MORE INFORMATION

You can find a copy of Mark Bodnarczuk's other book, *Diving In: Discovering Who You Are in the Second Half of Life* on-line at *www.amazon.com* or at your local book store.

To identify your Enneagram type, order an on-line copy of the Breckenridge Type Indicator™ (BTI™) at

https://survey.breckenridgeinstitute.com/products.bi

To have your BTI results interpreted by a teacher who has been trained and qualified by Mark Bodnarczuk, please contact the Breckenridge Institute® at the address below for a free referral to a qualified teacher.

The Breckenridge Institute® offers on-line and workshop-based training on the Breckenridge Enneagram™ for professionals who want to use the BTI in their consulting practice for coaching, teambuilding, organizational development, and organizational culture-change initiatives.

Please contact the Breckenridge Institute® *(www.breckenridgeinstitute.com)* for more information on professional-level BTI training and qualification programs.

Breckenridge Institute®
PO Box 7950
Boulder, Colorado 80306
1-800-303-2554
Fax: 1-888-745-1886

info@breckenridgeinstitute.com
www.breckenridgeinstitute.com